Also by Gene Lyons
The Higher Illiteracy

Widow's Web

The true story of a Little Rock
beauty whose deadly wiles led to two murders
and scandalized the entire state of Arkansas

Gene Lyons

Simon & Schuster

New York   London   Toronto   Sydney   Tokyo   Singapore

SIMON & SCHUSTER
Simon & Schuster Building
Rockefeller Center
1230 Avenue of the Americas
New York, New York 10020

Designed by Deirdre C. Amthor

Manufactured in the United States of America

10 9 8 7 6 5 4 3 2 1

Library of Congress Cataloging-in-Publication Data
Lyons, Gene, date.
Widow's web / Gene Lyons.
p.   cm.
1. Orsini, Mary Lee.   2. Murderers—Arkansas—Biography.   3. Women
murderers—Arkansas—Biography.   I. Title.
HV6248.068L93   1993
364.1'523'0976773—dc20   93-13026
                                                                CIP
ISBN: 0-671-64185-9

PICTURE CREDITS

Arkansas Democrat: 8, 19, 21, 27, 30; James Allison, 14, 16; Barry
Arthur, 17, 20, 23, 26; Mark Baldwin, 5, 6; Clay Carson, 15, 24, 25,
28, 29; George Fisher, 22; Gary Fountain, 4, 18; Steve Keesee, 3; Jeff
Mitchell, 13; John Rossino, 7. Jody Guenter, 10, 11. Little Rock Police
Department: 12. North Little Rock Police Department: 2. Orsini family:
1. *Springdale* (Arkansas) *News:* Mike Gauldin, 9.

For Diane

Contents

A Note to the Reader

All direct quotations have been taken either from witness statements, court transcripts, audio- and videotapes, firsthand media accounts, or personal interviews. Thoughts and motivations attributed to characters are their own. Interpretation and speculation are identified. No sources were paid or promised anything other than evenhanded treatment. The names of a few characters, none of them major figures, have been changed.

Cast of Characters

The Investigators

NORTH LITTLE ROCK POLICE DEPARTMENT

Patrolman Randy Huddleson
Patrolman Bill Mallett
Sergeant T. J. Farley
Sergeant Buddy Miles
Lieutenant Jim McFarlane
Sergeant Woody Juels
Chief Bill "Bubba" Younts

LITTLE ROCK POLICE DEPARTMENT

Patrolman Mike Willingham
Patrolman Rick Edgar
Patrolman Robert McNeely
Detective Al Dawson
Detective Forrest Parkman (retired)
Sergeant Fred Hensley
Lieutenant Bobby Thomas
Assistant Chief Jess "Doc" Hale
Chief Sonny Simpson

PULASKI COUNTY SHERIFF'S DEPARTMENT

Sheriff Tommy Robinson
Major Larry Dill
Captain Bobby Woodward

PULASKI COUNTY CORONER

Dr. L. Gordon Holt, M.D.

ARKANSAS STATE MEDICAL EXAMINER

Dr. Fahmy Malak, M.D.

BUREAU OF ALCOHOL, TOBACCO AND FIREARMS

Special Agent John Spurgeon

PRIVATE INVESTIGATORS

Fred Myers Agency (for Mary Lee Orsini)
Jim Lester (employee of Bill McArthur)
Gary Glidewell (for Mary Lee Orsini)
John Terry (for Mary Lee Orsini)

SPECIAL INVESTIGATOR FOR THE MCARTHUR GRAND JURY

Mike Mahone

The Attorneys

PROSECUTORS

Prosecutor Wilbur C. "Dub" Bentley
Deputy Prosecutor Judy Kaye Mason
Deputy Prosecutor Chris Piazza

SPECIAL PROSECUTORS

W. H. "Sonny" Dillahunty, McArthur probable cause hearing
Darrell F. Brown, McArthur grand jury

REPRESENTING MARY LEE ORSINI

William C. McArthur
Rita Gruber
Jack Lessenberry
Tom Carpenter
Tom Donovan

REPRESENTING BILL MCARTHUR

Jack Holt, Jr.
Jack Lassiter
Bill Putman
Philip Kaplan
William R. Wilson

REPRESENTING YANKEE HALL

Paul Johnson

JUDGES

Alan Dishongh, Little Rock Municipal Court
David Hale, Little Rock Municipal Court
Lee Munson, Pulaski County Chancery Court
Randall Williams, Circuit Court
John Langston, Circuit Court

Additional Characters in Alphabetical Order

Susan Anders, Bill McArthur's former lover
Art Baldwin, federal inmate
George Bentley, *Arkansas Gazette* courthouse reporter
Cary Bradburn, *Arkansas Democrat* courthouse reporter
Larry Burge, North Little Rock realtor, friend of Mary Lee
Stan Brown, McArthur grand jury foreman
Jim Bullard, McArthur grand jury witness
Joe Childers, childhood friend of Ron and Linda Orsini
Kenny Clarkson, former client of Gary Glidewell's
Vern Copeland, Ron Orsini's partner at Central Heating & Air
   Conditioning
Evelyn Daley, secretary at Central Heating & Air Conditioning
Linda Deapo, Ron Orsini's ex-wife
Howard Deapo, her husband
Suzanne Ellis, former girlfriend of Yankee Hall
"Dr." William Foote, Memphis hypnotist
Marty Freeman, alleged Malvern "hit man"
Carol Griffee, *Arkansas Gazette* reporter
Jo Growcock, Pulaski County comptroller
Eugene "Yankee" Hall, ex-convict and friend of Mary Lee
Julia Hatcher, Mary Lee's mother
Ron Hatcher, Mary Lee's brother
Joyce Holt, North Little Rock draper and friend of Mary Lee
Buddy and Linda Orsini House, Ron's sister and her husband
Michael, Diane and Cindy Kinsolving, Mary Lee's neighbors
Alice McArthur, Bill's wife
Billie and Bryan McArthur, Bill's parents

Chuck and Robyn McArthur, Bill's son and daughter
Larry Darnell McClendon, Yankee Hall's partner
Robert "Say" McIntosh, Little Rock black activist
Leonard Miller, Alice McArthur's brother
Mary Jane Murphree, North Little Rock realtor, friend of
    Mary Lee
Jerry P. Norman, client of Bill McArthur
Ron O'Neal, Little Rock tavern owner, ex-felon
Bernice and Joe Orsini, Ron and Linda's stepmother and father
Gladys Orsini, Ron and Linda's mother
Tiffany Orsini, Mary Lee's daughter
Ward Parks, relative of Donny Simmons
Sally and George Pernell, friends and neighbors of
    Alice McArthur
Phoebe Pinkston, Bill McArthur's secretary
Bob Robbins, Little Rock disc jockey and partner in BJ's
    Star-Studded Honky Tonk
Donny Simmons, alleged drug dealer
John Robert Starr, managing editor and columnist, *Arkansas
    Democrat*
Michael Swayze, alleged Malvern "hit man"
Mark Taylor, McArthur gand juror
Bob Troutt, owner of the "Kowboy Kountry Klub"
Betty Tucker, vice-president, Metropolitan National Bank
Jim Guy Tucker, ex-Congressman, Democratic gubernatorial
    candidate
Elaine Willett, McArthur grand jury witness
Herbie Wright, convicted arsonist, McArthur grand jury witness
Dr. Charles H. Wulz, North Little Rock veterinarian and friend
    of Mary Lee
Issah Zacariah, North Little Rock pawnshop owner arrested in
    "sting"
Pete Zinn, Ron Orsini's partner at Central Heating & Air
    Conditioning

Tell your Momma,
Tell your Pa,
I'm gonna send you back to Arkansas.
—*Ray Charles*

Prologue

Who indeed has ever been in it? I know New Yorkers who have been to Cochin China, Kafiristan, Paraguay, Somaliland and West Virginia, but not one who has ever penetrated the miasmatic jungles of Arkansas.
    —H. L. Mencken

Welcome to the Land of Opportunity. This book tells the story of the two most celebrated homicides in Arkansas history, a bitter private tragedy and public melodrama that intrigued, enthralled, and baffled the citizens of Little Rock and the seventy-five surrounding counties like none before or since. On an immediate human level, the story of the "McArthur case," as it was known, is one of infinite sadness: a blameless man and woman murdered, leaving the lives of their children and loved ones shattered. There were other victims, too, and terrible injustices done—injustices that have never been, and perhaps never can be, undone.

But the tale of the McArthur case cannot be told in entirely somber tones. Like many a Southern story, it is a strange, almost surreal blend of mayhem, outrage, tragedy, and farce. What began as a relatively routine homicide investigation and trial became the focus of a state-wide obsession bordering at times upon hysteria. Not only in Little Rock, but from one corner of the state to another—West Memphis to Fort Smith, Fayetteville to El Dorado, and Jonesboro to Texarkana—Arkansans gossiped and argued about the case for months, even years.

Almost every morning for months at a time, Little Rock's two bitterly competitive statewide newspapers fought to see which could run the greater number of column inches concerning the McArthur case. Reporters and editorial columnists set themselves up as the confidants of murder suspects, as amateur detectives and political touts, not to mention as prosecutor, judge, and jury. At stake in the war between the *Arkansas Gazette* and the *Arkansas Democrat* were long-standing familial grudges involving ideological hostility and mutual contempt. At risk, all too often, was anything remotely resembling the truth.

Almost every evening, Little Rock's three competing TV news teams vied with each other to present McArthur case scoops—together with footage of the photogenic principals, all of whom became celebrities at least as famous as the University of Arkansas football coach, and better known than the governor. Radio talk show hosts discussed the case with callers and guests for days at a time. Gossip ran epidemic. Reluctant participants in the drama recall bitterly the odd sensation of walking into public places—restaurants, coffee shops, bars, even religious services—and having the whole room fall silent. Others whose faces were less familiar speak of overhearing knowing and utterly fantastic accounts of their own private lives told by complete strangers.

Every bit as much as Texas or New York City, Arkansas comprises a world unto itself—"not quite a nation within a nation, but the next thing to it," as historian W. J. Cash wrote of the entire South of fifty years ago. The smallest state west of the Mississippi in land area, Arkansas comprises several distinct geographical regions—from the Ozark and Ouachita mountains, thickly forested, sparsely populated, and running with whitewater streams, to the cypress-filled bayous of the south and east, shallow, murky, and inhabited by cottonmouth moccasins and alligators.

Although it was a part of the Confederacy, only the plantation country near the Mississippi River was fully settled at the time of the Civil War. The rest was—and, some would argue, still is—a frontier. Even in the row crop country of the Delta, however, there's little talk about the wonderful antebellum days before the Civil War. The very idea of an Arkansas aristocracy is preposterous, the phrase itself unheard of. By and large, Arkansans like to think of themselves as simple country folk. If they share nothing else, it's a near-universal sympathy for the underdog—a suspicion of the rich, powerful, and sophisticated.

Arkansas leads the nation in the production of chickens and rice; most of the other numbers by which journalists and politicians purport to measure the quality of life are embarrassing. Despite marked improvement during (and before) the administration of Governor Bill Clinton, Arkansas remains at or near the bottom of the states in per capita income, literacy rate, quality of housing, teacher salaries, number of physicians, libraries, and museums. It leads the rest in the incidence of venereal disease and unwed mothers. The state motto, it has been suggested, ought to be "Thank God for Mississippi."

Even so, for decades, local schoolchildren have been taught the myth that Arkansas alone among the states has the resources—water, timber, some oil, natural gas, and vast stretches of fertile alluvial soil—to build a wall around itself and nevertheless thrive. Resentful of outside condescension yet bitterly self-critical, its people have often felt and sometimes acted as if they would love to do exactly that.

Little Rock, the state's capital, business, financial, and media center, rail and highway pivot, and only real city, sits on the Arkansas River almost exactly in the middle of the state, just where—as if it had been arranged by committee—the flatlands meet the hills. Little Rock is Paris to Arkansas' France. A leafy and disarmingly pleasant city of roughly 300,000, it often surprises visitors with its charm and sophistication. But it can also be two-faced: as brutally anonymous as any big city in America, and as intimate and small-minded as any country town.

Call it what you will: murder mystery, soap opera, morality play, political spectacle, or multi-media extravaganza. The McArthur case was all of the above and more. Gaudier than the state fair and more passionate than an Arkansas-Texas football game, it became a public entertainment having less to do with facts than with the passions and prejudices of its audience. Once aroused, that audience became a force as elemental and dangerous as the wild storms that roll across the Ozarks to the Mississippi during the spring and fall, spawning flash floods, hailstorms, and tornadoes. Indeed, years after the fact, people still speculate—with the odd blend of pride, exasperation, and bemused affection many Arkansans feel for their home —whether the events narrated in this book could have happened as they did anywhere else on earth.

Even so, for all the zeal with which Arkansans followed the story's every twist and turn for more than two years, they never really had a clue.

BOOK I

Chapter 1

1

Later on, some of the cops suspected that phoning the wrong police department had been part of the plan. Maybe somebody thought it would be easier to deal with the small town boys from Sherwood than North Little Rock detectives. Anything was possible. But most people do know where they live, and the lady was calling from home—a good half mile inside the city limits.

"I just found my husband," she said in a voice edged with panic. "He's covered with blood." She gave her address—7412 Pontiac, in the Indian Hills subdivision.

"Did he fall or . . . ?"

"I don't know! I found him. I don't know!" She began to cry.

"Settle down. Tell us your phone number so I can put 'em there." The dispatcher's voice had a graveled, soothing tone.

The caller gave her number. "It's terrible," she wept.

"I know. What is your last name?"

She gave the dispatcher her name, and spelled it: O-R-S-I-N-I. Then she waited while the dispatcher put her on hold and passed the information on to North Little Rock.

"Is there anything else you can tell me?"

"I don't know anything!" she cried. "I just got here."

· · ·

The first radio call went out at 9:42 A.M. It was Thursday, March 12, 1981, a crisp, clear morning that signaled an early spring. Overnight the temperature had dropped to 40, but by mid-morning it had already risen well into the fifties. Jonquils were up, and forsythia bloomed. Should the weather hold—always chancy in a turbulent season in Arkansas—white bass would begin their spawning runs any day now. Crappie would move into the shallows, and outdoorsmen like Ron Orsini would begin daydreaming about fishing trips with the boys at the shop.

Five minutes after the distress call went out, NLRPD Patrolman Bill Mallett pulled up in front of 7412 Pontiac. The winding streets of Indian Hills were almost empty in the lull between rush hour and the 10:00 A.M. opening of the shopping malls on nearby JFK Boulevard. The house was a brown split-level with a brick facade on an oversized lot at the corner of Pontiac and Osage. Larger than its immediate neighbors, it had a six-foot wood privacy fence enclosing the backyard and "Seventy Four Twelve" spelled out in black metal script above the middle door of a three-car garage. A white Ford service van sat in the drive.

At first Mallett wondered if he'd found the right address. An eleven-year veteran of the NLRPD, Mallett had the look of what Arkansans call "a big old country boy." In fact, he was bucking for detective, and had long ago learned the advantages to be gained by keeping his shrewd intelligence to himself. From the radio call—something about a woman finding her husband in a bloody bed—he'd anticipated chaos.

But all he saw was a woman sitting quietly, alone on the front steps. Her chin in her hand, she gazed blankly out at the street. "All she lacked was a cup of coffee and everything would have looked just normal," he said later. "So I wasn't in any great big hurry, because she didn't project any sense of urgency at all."

At first glance, the lady looked to be about in her mid-thirties. She wore a brown checked flannel shirt, blue jeans, and tennis shoes. She was an attractive, almost striking woman with a passing resemblance to the country singer Loretta Lynn. She had the same dark, nearly black hair, high cheekbones, and fair, almost translucent skin. Mary Lee Orsini was by no means a flawless beauty. Her hips were too broad, and she had a tendency to put on weight, as well as a slightly undershot jaw that she had the habit of working from side to side like a ruminant animal.

But people noticed her eyes—pale blue, luminous as a Siamese cat's, yet so light-pigmented that they appeared gray in shadow. Nearly everybody spoke of them as mesmerizing. Some saw in them promises of sexual enchantment, others an emptiness as cold and vacant as the interstellar void.

To Patrolman Mallett that morning she seemed only confused. "Visibly shaken," he wrote in his report. He asked if she had called the police. She said nothing, almost as if she hadn't heard. He asked if there were anything he could help her with. Still no answer. Recalling the radio message about a bloody bed, he asked her if the bedroom was upstairs. She nodded. He climbed the porch steps and went inside, leaving her sitting mute.

The house was still. Just inside the front door Mallett found a stairway leading to an upstairs hallway. The first bedroom was furnished, but looked unused, and there was nobody in the bathroom across the hall. A radio played softly in the second bedroom, which appeared to belong to a teen-aged girl. But it was empty too. Then Mallett noticed a metal object protruding from the last door on his right, which hung slightly ajar. A shishkabob skewer about a foot long with one pointed end and a circular handle hung precariously out of the doorknob, as if somebody had used it to push open the spring-loaded lock. Inside the room, it was quite dark. Standing in the hall-way, Mallett could barely make out the shape of a man lying face down on the bed, his face turned away from the door.

Taking care not to disturb the skewer, the policeman nudged the door open and stepped sideways into the room. Even in the half light there was no mistaking that the man was dead. His body was cool to the touch, and a huge frothy pool of blood under his head was soaking slowly into the mattress. It seemed to have come from the dead man's mouth and nose.

Mallett's first thought was suicide. He took a quick look around for a weapon. As he searched, Patrolman Randy Huddleson came into the room. Arriving soon after Mallett, he too had encountered the woman on the porch and asked her where the other officer had gone. "He's upstairs," she'd said.

Finding no gun, the officers briefly discussed the possibility of an aneurysm or a cerebral hemorrhage—some medical reason for the appalling puddle of dark arterial blood and pink froth around the dead man's head. It looked as if he had bled slowly to death while inhaling his own vital fluid, which the state medical examiner later determined to have been exactly the case. Indeed, the proximate cause of death was that he had drowned in his own blood.

Mallett went downstairs to the front porch just as the EMS crew arrived. He sent them to the master bedroom, then hunkered down next to Mrs. Orsini, who continued to stare blankly into space. He asked her if her husband had been complaining of severe headaches or anything of the kind. She turned to him with what he would later call "a look of wonder and amazement," began to speak, then seemed to catch herself and said nothing.

Patrolman Huddleson came to the door and called him inside. The ambulance attendant had produced a flashlight, and they had found something they wanted Mallett to see. "Funny," Mallett said later, "but the wound was real small. You had to hold the flashlight very close and get down and part the hair to see it. After they shaved the hair off, you could see the powder burns and it looked a whole lot different." It looked like a cerebral hemorrhage all right—of the .38 caliber, .158 grain variety.

Huddleson called downtown for help, then returned to the body. Mallett went back downstairs to tell the widow that her husband had been shot to death. Mallett asked if she had anybody she could stay with, as the police would be busy in the house for a long time. For the first time, she answered. She said she'd already called a friend. He did find it odd that in the ten minutes or so that had passed, Mary Lee Orsini had yet to shed a tear.

2

"The way it started out," Sergeant T. J. Farley said, "is I'm sitting at my desk at headquarters doing paperwork. Everybody knew that photography was my hobby, and the regular guy had the day off. . . . So the Captain walks in, and he says to me, 'Well, you wanna go take some pictures?' I said, 'What're you talking about?' He says, 'Aw, we got a cool one up in Indian Hills.' "

Farley's hobby had nothing to do with taking crime scene shots. He did nature studies mostly, and specialized in color prints of flowers. It was an odd hobby for a guy who had grown up in an Irish Catholic neighborhood in the industrial meadowlands of Secaucus, New Jersey, literally within sight of the Manhattan skyline. A stocky six-footer, who wore his gray hair combed back into a fifties tough-guy wave, Farley had ended up in North Little Rock courtesy of true love and the U.S. Air Force. After two years in the Air Police in Vietnam, he finished his hitch at Little Rock Air Force Base just north of town and married an Arkansas woman.

At first Farley found Arkansans shallow, clannish, and a bit slow on the uptake. When he joined up, the chief of the NLRPD had only an eighth-grade education, and the assistant chief had managed only the third. Even so, Farley had found his calling. By the time he made sergeant in 1976, Farley had a different Arkansas bride, and could no longer imagine going back to Jersey. Though rarely mistaken for a native, he didn't sound like a Yankee any more. Some thought he was the smartest cop in North Little Rock.

Before they left headquarters, Farley and Sergeant Buddy Miles had a quick talk. The two were not regular partners. Silver-haired and balding, Miles was six feet tall, with a barrel chest, short, powerful forearms, and an ample gut. Miles had grown up in North Little Rock and put in twenty-one years on the force. Apart from his soft-spoken demeanor, he could have won a bit part in any Hollywood concoction requiring a down-home sheriff. Yet a formidable list of killers and thieves were chopping weeds down at Cummins Prison Farm because they had underestimated him.

3

Even before they arrived, the two detectives knew that an Indian Hills address meant that their work would be carefully scrutinized. It wasn't that Indian Hills was what anybody would call an exclusive part of town. North Little Rock had very few of those. Just about all the real money in Pulaski County was across the Arkansas River in Little Rock. The state capitol was there, and the Governor's Mansion. The county, state, and federal courts were all located south of the river, along with the banks, insurance companies, and corporate law firms that controlled Arkansas' economy. Little Rock had two statewide daily newspapers, three TV and more than a dozen radio stations, the University of Arkansas Medical School and one of its two law schools, plus all the major hospitals, posh hotels, and expensive French restaurants.

Over there they called North Little Rock "Dogtown," a nickname said to date back to days when the capital's idea of animal control was to carry strays across the Broadway Bridge and dump them. Historically, it had always been a blue-collar enclave, an Army base and railroad yard town best known for its saloons and cathouses. But all that changed when Camp Robinson shut down after the Korean War, and by 1981 an outsider would have found it hard to tell one side of the river from the other, or to distinguish Indian Hills from any of a half dozen virtually identical developments in Little Rock. The name itself meant nothing in particular. The hills were modest—a series of low ridges rising a couple of hundred feet above the valley floor north of downtown. And if Native Americans had ever dwelt in the immediate vicinity, nobody knew it.

Indian Hills, in short, was Mallville, USA—a middle-class, middle-American habitat like thousands across the country. Neighborly yet anonymous, with no discernible reference to any past, individual or communal; a frontier settlement wired for cable TV. A place where so long as they avoided outward eccentricity and kept their scenarios straight, anybody could play any role, assume virtually any identity that lay within their dramatic range. Or more than one, if necessary.

4

The detectives arrived at 7412 Pontiac at a few minutes past 10:00 A.M. Pulaski County Coroner Dr. L. Gordon Holt pulled up just moments later. The ambulance crew had already gone. Corpses were not their business. At Mallett's suggestion, Mrs. Orsini was sitting outside in her friend Mary Jane Murphree's car. Summoned by phone from the real estate office where she worked, Murphree had rushed over at once. The detectives did not see either woman until that afternoon at police headquarters.

Once the uniformed officers had secured the crime scene, Patrolman Mallett managed to coax a brief statement out of Mrs. Orsini. He gave Farley and Miles the gist of it. According to his wife, Ron Orsini had gone to bed about 10:00 P.M. the night before, and she had retired not long after. Her daughter Tiffany, thirteen, had been sick for about two weeks, and she had been sleeping with the child in an adjoining bedroom. Neither she nor Tiffany heard anything during the night. When she got up at about seven, Mrs. Orsini found the bedroom door locked. As Ron often left for work without waking the rest of the family, she thought nothing of it. She called his office and left a message asking him to come home and unlock the door so she could get clean clothes. Then she woke Tiffany and treated her to breakfast at Andy's, a fast-food restaurant on McCain Boulevard.

She and Tiffany had noticed Ron's truck in the driveway, but assumed he'd been picked up by one of his partners. After taking Tiffany to school, Mrs. Orsini returned home and used the skewer to unlock the door. When she saw the blood, she ran to the phone for help.

Everything about the story suggested suicide. So where was the gun? The detectives sent Mallett outside to ask Mrs. Orsini if there were any weapons in the house.

•   •   •

Farley's first mistake, the way he saw it, wasn't his fault at all. Nobody warned him about the skewer, and as he came into the bedroom his camera bag brushed against the door and knocked it to the floor. The lock was a push-button Qwik-Set model intended for privacy rather than security. Farley had locks just like it inside his own home. It locked from the inside only. Almost any slender metal object that would slide into the round hole on the outside doorknob caused the spring-loaded mechanism inside to release and the door to open. Farley dangled the skewer from the aperture and shot a couple of pictures.

The queen-sized bed stood just to the left as one entered the master bedroom, its headboard flush against the wall. Ron Orsini lay face down almost exactly parallel with the side of the bed nearest the door, his head turned inward toward the opposite pillow and the blankets tucked in snugly around his shoulders. His left arm rested by his side under the covers, and his blood-encrusted right fist lay clenched on the pillow inches from his face—the forearm spattered with flecks of gore.

At first, Farley thought that he was looking at the "blow pattern" of an exit wound. It was a critical detail. The presence of brain matter, bone fragments, or any substance that proved the victim's arm had been lying next to his face when the shot was fired would rule out suicide. The autopsy would tell.

On the side of the bed opposite the corpse, the covers were turned down neatly at the corner and the pillow showed the clear imprint of someone's head. On the night table between the bed and the door Farley noticed a small Timex alarm clock and a Bearcat radio scanner of the kind used to monitor police and radio frequencies. The alarm was set for 4:30 A.M., but the button that activated it was in the "off" position.

There were no signs of a struggle or disturbance anywhere in the room. Expensively decorated with handsome, traditional furniture, the Orsinis' bedroom was—if anything—unusually neat. Both the full private bathroom and walk-in closet that opened off the room could have passed military inspection. Flanking the east window that looked out over the fenced backyard were a matched cherrywood "highboy" dresser and chest of drawers. An elegant rolltop desk stood against the wall opposite the foot of the bed; over it hung a framed studio photograph of the family—husband, wife, and two daughters smiling brightly.

Dr. Holt formally pronounced Ron Orsini dead at 10:15 A.M. His opinion was homicide. The coroner knew perfectly well that family members often disguise suicides—both due to shame, and for insurance purposes. But several things besides the lack of a weapon led him to conclude that Ron Orsini had been murdered.

Powder residue in the scalp made it clear that the fatal shot had been fired from a range of no more than a few inches, but the entry wound showed none of the "crater effect" of a contact wound, as suicides normally do. In his forty years as coroner, Holt had never seen a self-inflicted gunshot wound in so awkward a position. It wasn't a physical impossibility that Orsini had shot himself, but it was close.

Exactly how long ago the fatal shot had been fired, Holt couldn't say. But it was several hours at the minimum. Rigor mortis had set in fully; all the victim's extremities were stiff. The bullet tearing through the dead man's brain had very likely caused instant paralysis, but his heart must have kept pumping for a long time. Blood had seeped all the way through the mattress and box spring and begun to drip to the carpet beneath. The coroner estimated that Ron Orsini had lain unconscious and bleeding for anywhere between fifteen minutes and an hour.

Even as he worked his way around the room shooting pictures, Farley saw that things weren't adding up. If robbery had been a motive, the thieves must have known precisely what they were after and gone straight to it. So why blow the guy away? And why lock the door and shut off the alarm on the way out?

What's more, a pistol shot in that enclosed area would have made a thunderous concussion. Unless he protected them, the gunman's ears would have been ringing. How was it possible that the wife and daughter sleeping in the next room had heard nothing at all? A silencer was a remote possibility. But because their manufacture and possession is governed by strict federal law, silencers are rare, and TV melodramas to the contrary, almost never encountered by detectives investigating crimes.

While Farley and Holt attended to the body, Miles took a quick look around the house. As in the master bedroom, everything in the Orsini household was just so. In particular, Miles noticed a canopy bed in the room where Mrs. Orsini said she spent the night with her daughter, and a Queen Anne camelback sofa in the living room. Both looked brand new. There were expensive new drapes in the living room too, and a handsome oak and glass gun cabinet in the den that would have to be searched. Somebody had been spending a whole lot of money in the Orsini household recently, and wanted visitors to know it. The place was like a showroom. Every available surface was crowded with knickknacks, needlepoint, and family photographs.

. . .

Shortly after 11:00 A.M, investigators from the state Medical Examiner's Office arrived. Taking care not to disturb anything, they helped Farley pull the blankets back and lay them on the floor. Orsini wore only a pair of white jockey shorts. Near the foot of the bed lay a single, red, white, and blue footlet belonging to a woman. Farley included it in the photos he shot to illustrate the exact position of the corpse.

Something else, a seemingly trivial detail, caught the detective's attention and hit him hard. "I look down," he explained, "and see that man laying there and his legs were crossed. The thing that got me was he was asleep. Never knew what hit him."

They turned the body over, and Farley took a few last photographs while Dr. Holt sponged blood off the victim's face, searching for an exit wound. Something by the pillow caught the detective's attention. He reached down and picked up what he recognized as a spent .38 caliber slug lying in the pool of blood where the dead man's face had rested. The bullet had passed downward at a steep angle through the frontal lobes of Orsini's brain and emerged through the left nostril.

Miles dropped the bullet into a Plasticine envelope and carefully labeled it for delivery to the ballistics experts in the Arkansas state crime lab. But they both knew enough about guns to realize one thing right off: it was a soft lead slug like those used in their own .38 special revolvers, not a copper-coated round. Soft lead slugs jam automatic weapons. What the ballistics report was going to say, they were confident, was that the gun that killed Ron Orsini had been a revolver. And that, in turn, meant that they could rule out that the killer had used a silencer. They don't make silencers for revolvers.

Next the detectives watched while the medical examiner's team taped brown paper bags over Ron Orsini's hands in order to prevent accidental contamination. Later, scrapings would be made and trace metal tests run to determine if the dead man had fired a gun. Then they lifted the corpse onto a gurney, covered it with a sheet, and strapped it down for delivery to the morgue. An investigator from the Medical Examiner's Office handed Miles a signed receipt. It was dated 3-12-81, and the time was given as 11:50 A.M. Under the heading "Description of Evidence," the form listed four items:

> 1-Ron Orsini
> 1-pr. white jockey shorts
> 1-bullet slug
> 1-yellow gold wedding band

Once the body had been removed, the NLRPD detectives agreed that there were two immediate priorities: To find the murder weapon, and to search the house for any sign of an intruder.

While Farley and Holt had been busy with the body, Patrolman Huddleson had found the first of Ron Orsini's guns exactly where his wife told them to look—in the top drawer of the dresser on the opposite side of the room from where he slept. The gun was a Smith & Wesson Model 60 "Chief's Special," a five-shot, .38 caliber, stainless-steel snub-nose revolver. Holstered and unloaded, the pistol was of high quality and perfectly maintained. Next to it they found a box of fifty Federal brand .38 caliber, .158 grain shells—exactly the size Farley had found next to the body. There were fifteen bullets missing. Miles tagged and stored both items for ballistics.

Mrs. Orsini had also told the policemen that the key to the down-stairs cabinet where her husband kept the rest of his gun collection was hidden somewhere in the bedroom. After a brief search, Huddleson found it in a drawer under the bathroom sink. Besides several hunting rifles and shotguns, the cabinet also held a .357 Dan Wesson revolver, a .38 Smith & Wesson Combat Masterpiece revolver, and a .45 automatic pistol. All were expensive and in excellent condition, none were loaded, and the ammunition was locked in a separate drawer.

It was quite an arsenal, but not one that would strike an Arkansas cop as particularly unusual. As in much of the South, it is literally easier to buy a gun in Arkansas than a bottle of wine. Registered gun dealers are required to ask their customers to fill out forms provided by the federal government affirming that they are not felons or drug addicts. There are no other restrictions of any kind. It is a rare Arkansas household that has no guns at all.

Obviously, Ron Orsini was an outdoorsman and gun collector. What struck the detectives was the high quality of his guns, how well he cared for them, and how scrupulously he'd observed the rules of safe storage. Even as he tied on the evidence tags, Miles would have bet anything that the serial numbers would show that Orsini was the legal owner of each pistol, and that none had fired the fatal shot. He would have won the bet, too.

For the next two hours, the four NLRPD officers turned 7412 Pontiac Drive inside out. While Mallett and Huddleson checked the doors and windows for signs of a break-in, Farley took out his fingerprint kit. In practice, fingerprints are both harder to find and less useful to criminal investigations than the public imagines. Finding a fingerprint is like finding a penny: not bad, but almost worthless all by itself. Even when clear prints can be lifted, they're of no value unless investigators have both a suspect and the suspect's prints to compare them to. Of the scores of homicides he'd investigated, Farley couldn't remember even one in which fingerprint evidence anywhere other than on the weapon had proved conclusive.

The bedroom doorknob showed only smudges and the powder wouldn't adhere. Inside the fatal bedroom almost every surface was either fabric or wood—porous surfaces where dusting for prints would be futile. Nothing showed up on the alarm clock, or the bedside radio scanner. Farley decided he was wasting his time, and put the kit away.

Working room by room, the officers took the house apart and put it back together, double-checking each other's work. Every cabinet and drawer that might possibly conceal the murder weapon was searched, then searched again. They turned the closets inside out, looked under every bed, mattress, and pillow, and removed the cushions from every sofa and chair. They shone flashlights up and down the laundry chute. When Farley found the glass doors covering the fireplace jammed shut, he determined to break in if necessary, before leaving.

Miles pulled down the folding stairway in the hallway ceiling and climbed into the attic. He found nothing but a bed of blown insulation lying undisturbed between the joists as smoothly as new fallen snow. Miles's search of the second attic that extended out over the lower part of the house found the insulation equally untouched. The murder weapon, the investigators concluded, was not on the premises.

Nor could they find any sign of an intruder. Every window in the house was securely locked. There were no scratches or pry marks. Intact spiderwebs and films of dust on the sills between the windows and the screens told them that it had been a long time since any of the windows had been opened at all.

The front door showed no sign of forced entry. Nor did the decorative wrought-iron door that protected it. Both the sliding glass door leading from the den to the patio and the screen door covering it were locked up tight, and a length of broomstick was wedged into the track to prevent its being opened from outside. A solid wood door in the same room was secured with a deadbolt lock. Even if they imagined a killer who took time to lock up on his way out, the detectives realized, he would have needed a key.

Only in two areas did the investigators find anything worth noticing, and both bits of evidence struck them as ambiguous—almost as if they had been planted there by somebody who *wanted* them noticed. Farley came upon the first himself in the three-car garage. The two overhead garage doors farthest from the house were bolted firmly in place by a horizontal steel pole locked to the frame, while the third one behind Mrs. Orsini's black 1978 Chevrolet Caprice was secured by an automatic garage door opener. None of them was able to budge any of the three. Nobody had broken into the garage.

Then Farley discovered gouges on the wooden interior door leading from the garage to the laundry room—shallow scratches just under the doorknob, none more than a quarter inch deep, and obviously fresh. The first thing that puzzled him was the minuscule amount of sawdust and shavings on the floor. Given the damage, there should have been a lot more. But he found only a couple of slivers less than a quarter of an inch wide and a half inch long. He also noticed fresh scratches in the aluminum facing that held the weather stripping in place. Even supposing the killer had somehow spirited himself into the garage, were they supposed to think he had swept up the shavings before fleeing? Mindful of Miles's years on the burglary detail, Farley called his partner into the garage.

"This," Miles announced after studying the gouges for a few minutes, "is bullshit. No way anybody forced this door. Looks like to me somebody's been scratching on it to give us a visual aid: 'Looky here, somebody's been fuckin' with this door.' "

"You sure?" Farley asked.

"Hell, let's try it," Miles said.

After Farley shot a couple of pictures, Miles retrieved a fourteen-inch screwdriver from Ron Orsini's workbench and demonstrated that there was no way he could slide it between the frame and the door without crushing the aluminum weather stripping. "I couldn't find a way to break in," he said later, "so I went inside, closed the door, and tried to break out. I wanted to see what kind of force it would to take to move the door and the jamb to where the bolt would pass the strike plate without being unlocked."

After heaving against the door twice with all his weight and strength, Miles popped it free—leaving deep, unmistakable pry marks on the inside edges of door and frame. Anybody breaking into the house from the garage would have left an equally conspicuous scar. The "evidence" was phony.

There was something else, too: a wood chisel—just the right size to account for the gouges on the door—lay in plain view on a workbench eight to ten feet inside the garage. "That chisel," Miles said, "was the only tool out of place in the whole shop. The rest were hung up as neat as hell in a line graduated in size. Even his tool boxes had things lined up the same way—real neat. That was the way he did things. The chisel might as well have had a sign on it. That's how obvious it was."

If the tool had been used to break in, what was it doing *outside* the house? Before taking it as evidence, Farley photographed the chisel where it lay. They debated taking the door downtown, but Farley decided that his photos would do, and ordered Mallett to remove the aluminum weather stripping for delivery to the crime lab.

Miles had found something in the laundry room he wanted Farley to see. Still searching for the murder weapon, Miles had opened the washing machine. Inside he discovered a freshly laundered load of towels and two pairs of women's panties—still damp and plastered to the side of the tub. A couple of the towels, however, were pulled toward the center of the tub as if some items had been removed from the machine, yet the dryer was empty. The temperature control was set for cold water wash.

"I do most of the washing around my house," Miles explained, "and I've got sense enough to know that you wash towels in hot water. But when you want to wash blood out of something, you use cold water. Hot water will set it. So we took a photograph of the cold setting, and I went through every bit of that laundry. Every one of the towels had holes in it. One pair of panties had the crotch ripped out and the other was torn. What I figured was maybe the husband was in bed with the little girl, and maybe Mary Lee had done put a stop to that shit. Those were my thoughts."

Farley thought Miles was reaching. The cold water setting struck him as suspicious too, and certainly worth photographing. Nor did he object to taking the panties as evidence. The idea, at this point in the investigation—any investigation—was to be as inclusive as possible. But he didn't think much of the incest idea. It just didn't feel right. Men who molested their children, he felt, didn't keep spick and span tool shops—just an instinct, maybe, but a strong one.

As it happened, Miles's suspicions about the torn panties turned out to be supported by no credible evidence, neither then nor ever. He soon abandoned them entirely. But what the detectives never would be able to decide—in the wake of the maelstrom of gossip, rumor, slander, calumny, charge and countercharge the Orsini case eventually provoked—was whether Miles had accidentally provided the impetus for an alternative scenario even the killer had not foreseen.

Nor could they explain something far simpler: How on earth they could possibly have neglected to retrieve the mate to the red, white, and blue footlet they'd found lying in the bed. They both saw it sitting there, big as you please, atop a woman's nightgown on the very top layer of the clothes hamper in the same laundry room. But in all the palaver over the panties, they walked out without it.

5

How in the world had Ron Orsini, of all people, managed to shoot himself at eleven o'clock on a Thursday morning? Numbed by shock and disbelief, that was all Pete Zinn could remember thinking about when he first heard the terrible news. How could it be?

Pete had been between sales calls when Evelyn Daley's call came in over the two-way radio in his truck. She asked him to pull off the road and call the office from a pay phone, a signal that she had a message that she didn't want to broadcast over the business frequency. Zinn had been braced for bad news ever since Ron failed to show up at the shop early that morning. In all the years they'd worked together at Central Heating & Air Conditioning, Ron Orsini had been as punctual as the sunrise. For Ron to miss work for any reason was highly unusual; for him not to call in, unthinkable.

Vern Copeland, the third partner in the business, overheard Evelyn's conversation with Pete on his own truck radio. From the raw emotion in the company secretary's voice, he could tell there was something bad wrong. Only a few blocks from the company's headquarters opposite the MoPac tracks in the Mablevale section of southwest Little Rock, he drove straight to the shop. He and Ron were supposed to have met at 6:00 A.M. to switch the burners on a new furnace scheduled for installation that day. But when Orsini failed to show, Vern had been too busy getting the job done on time to give it any thought. Ron's father, Joe Orsini, had been in intensive care at Little Rock's Baptist Medical Center for several weeks now, with terminal lung cancer. Ron had never complained—as Ron never did—but his partners knew that it had been tearing at their friend to see his father suffering, and that the bedside vigil was wearing him down physically and emotionally. But no matter how hard Pete and Vern urged him, Ron had refused to cut himself any slack.

That was why Pete and Vern had both been pleased when Ron towed a brand new boat into the shop on Wednesday to show it off and do some rewiring on the trailer's brake lights. It was nothing fancy, just a fourteen-foot aluminum flat-bottom with a 10-horse Mercury outboard—pretty much a standard Arkansas country boy fishing rig—but it made them believe that maybe their partner was beginning to see his way clear to a time when the ordeal would be over. Yesterday afternoon had been the most upbeat either man had seen him in a long while. Pete reached Evelyn by phone just as Vern entered the office to find the secretary in tears. Evelyn had been with Central Heating & Air even longer than Ron, and the message she passed on to Pete and Vern had put her in a state of shock: a friend of Lee's named Joyce Holt had telephoned. Ron Orsini was dead. Shot to death in his bed. The police were at the house.

But what Pete could not figure out as he drove to Indian Hills was how the accident could have happened. Ron was the most cautious, meticulous man he had ever known. Ron's service van was so neat you could have performed open heart surgery in the back. And guns? Ron handled them as carefully as he did his tools.

Lee hadn't said anything about Ron's stopping at the hospital when she'd telephoned looking for him that morning, but Pete figured she must have reached him there. Why else would he have gone back home? She had a problem, Lee had told Pete at about 7:00 A.M. She was locked out of the bedroom, and needed Ron to open the door so she could dress for work. Would Pete ask him to call home as soon as he arrived? If she failed to answer, Lee said, Ron should keep calling. Tiffany had been out sick and Lee needed to take her by the school nurse's office before class, so there was a chance she might not be back right away.

Pete had teased Lee a bit. Why didn't she just go on to work without her clothes? Or climb in the bathroom window if she was in such a hurry? That would be quite a sight, Lee had kidded right back—her big ole butt hanging out a second-story window. They'd shared a laugh.

Zinn didn't really know his partner's wife very well. Experience had long ago taught him that it was a mistake to mix business and social life. What Zinn did know of Mary Lee Orsini, however, he liked. Maybe it was that she was in sales too—and was apparently doing pretty well at it, judging by the new house she and Ron had bought. Even over in North Little Rock, the place had to have cost close to $100,000, and no way was Ron making that kind of money out of Central Heating & Air. Pete owned a half-interest in the business, Ron and Vern 25 percent each. And while theirs was a going concern with a solid reputation, the three partners paid themselves minimal salaries and put everything they could back into the business. Some of the salaried employees took home bigger paychecks than Ron and Vern did.

Unlike Ron, moreover, Lee was talkative and vivacious—a real charmer, who dressed well and exuded self-confidence. If anything, she was a bit flashier than what you'd expect for a quiet guy like Ron. Heads turned when she entered the room. It was easy for Pete to see how she could be successful in sales. She'd been in fine spirits that morning on the telephone. Pete had assured her that he'd be sure to tell Ron to give her a call just as soon as he walked into the shop.

Copeland and Zinn arrived in front of 7412 Pontiac in their separate trucks only moments apart. They got there just in time to see their partner's corpse—shrouded in a sheet from head to toe—being lifted down the front steps and into the medical examiner's truck. Ron's service van, almost identical to their own, sat in the driveway in front of the house. Mary Lee's friend had already driven her to police headquarters.

A uniformed officer escorted Pete and Vern inside and sat them down in the den, where they watched in bewildered silence as the team of policemen searched the house. It wasn't until Sergeant Farley asked them briskly if they knew of anybody who might have wanted to kill their partner that the two men grasped what was going on.

So far as either of them knew, Ron had no enemies at all. While it was the last thing either man would have been capable of articulating that morning, both knew that the loss of Ron Orsini's expert, steady hand would badly damage the business they had worked so hard to build. Like many another small business, Central Heating & Air meant

more to the three men who owned it than a simple economic arrangement: it was what they did in the world, the focal point of their dreams.
Pete and Vern had lost more than a business associate; they had lost
their hunting and fishing buddy and their dearest friend, and in the
unspoken manner of workingmen everywhere, they had loved him like
a brother.

.   .   .

Zinn was still grappling with his feelings when the phone rang in the
house. Without thinking, he picked it up to hear the familiar voice of
Betty Tucker, who asked to speak with Lee or Ron. Tucker was a
vice-president and loan officer at Metropolitan National Bank in Little
Rock. She had believed in Pete, Vern, and Ron from the beginning
and lent them the capital to get Central Heating & Air Conditioning
off the ground. She still handled all their accounts, and had made
personal loans to each of them as well.

"Betty," Pete said, "Ron has been murdered." In a few strangled
sentences he told Tucker what little he knew. The banker had called
for Ron several times at the shop recently, but as was his custom
regarding personal matters, Ron had volunteered nothing about their
conversations, and Zinn would never have asked. Shocked speechless,
Tucker hung up quickly. Still in a daze, Zinn gave no thought to why
she might have called, and mentioned to Sergeant Farley only that the
bank had called.

.   .   .

By half past noon Farley and Miles decided they had learned all
there was to learn from the crime scene. Eventually they'd have to
return to canvass the neighborhood door to door in the hope of turning
up witnesses who may have noticed something unusual during the
night. But there was no reason to hurry. The killer's trail, if there was
a trail, was already cold, and wouldn't get much colder over the next
few hours. Until the medical examiner gave them a time of death,
there wasn't much they could ask the neighbors anyway. The likeliest
they were to get useful information was from the wife and daughter.
He hadn't yet laid eyes on her, but the longer Farley had spent at 7412
Pontiac Drive that morning, the more questions he had for Mary Lee
Orsini.

Chapter 2

1

Architecturally speaking, North Little Rock Police Department (NLRPD) headquarters fails to inspire visitors with awe for the might and majesty of the law. The 1968 structure is a flat-roofed rectangular box with a white brick, aluminum and glass exterior suitable for an insurance office or a branch bank. Located in a municipal no-man's-land near the junction of I-30 and I-40, the two interstate highways that bisect the city, the only transcendent values it calls to mind are the suburban ones of economy, centralized location, and plenty of parking. The city jail is hidden away in a basement invisible from the street.

No sooner had Mary Lee Orsini arrived at NLRPD headquarters that morning than she asked to see Lieutenant Jim McFarlane, who commanded the Service Division, responsible for all the essential clerical and bureaucratic chores of police work. Along with her husband, McFarlane had been a member of the North Little Rock Ole Main High School graduating class of 1962. Like everybody else at headquarters that morning, he'd kept one ear on the radio and telephone reports of the Indian Hills murder as they trickled in all morning.

McFarlane hadn't spoken to the detectives, but he did know that Ron had been murdered in bed. Like Farley and Miles, he also knew the statistical probabilities concerning domestic homicides. FBI numbers showed that upward of 95 percent of victims found in their bedrooms turned out to have been killed by their spouse or lover. He also had other reasons to be leery of Mary Lee Orsini, reasons that not even her husband had known. He and Ron had run in different circles during high school. But after Ron had come home from a four-year Navy hitch, his younger sister Linda had married a good friend of McFarlane's named Buddy House. While they never exactly became close friends, Jim liked Ron. Ron and Mary Lee's first date had taken place at a barbecue at the policeman's home. Ron had been so downcast after his divorce that when Linda House called to ask if she and Buddy could bring her brother and his date along, Jim and his wife were happy to oblige. It had been a pleasant evening, and Mary Lee made a good impression. Her cheerful, outgoing personality seemed to draw Ron out of his shell.

It was only after McFarlane happened to mention Mary Lee to another policeman in his command, Officer Charlie Milton, that he'd begun to learn that the woman was not, perhaps, exactly what she seemed to be. Ron had mentioned that Mary Lee had been married once before—to an officer at Little Rock Air Force Base, a much older man who had left her when Tiffany was an infant. But it seemed she had also been married again later for a time to Milton's brother in another Arkansas city. "From some of the incidents Officer Milton told me occurred during their marriage and divorce," McFarlane said later, "I knew she was just not the type of person she presented herself as being. It was as if she was hiding some of her past from Ron, especially the number of times she had been married. Seems like we'd worked it out that it was five times, counting Ron—though she'd married Tiffany's father twice."

Then there were the warrants. More than once before she took with Ron Orsini, Officer Milton had informed McFarlane, the NLRPD had taken Mary Lee into custody on hot check warrants issued by another Arkansas county—and held her briefly pending the posting of bond. Only her name wasn't Mary Lee then, it was Mary Myrtle.

McFarlane and his wife had sat up nights debating what to do. Should they tell Ron what they knew about the woman he planned to marry, or not? She seemed so good for him. And people do change for the better. Maybe Ron would be just as good for her as she seemed to be for him. "We didn't really want to be responsible for telling him," McFarlane said. "We thought that it might turn his friendship against us if we did. He might know all about her past and he might accept it, and just not be letting other people know. So we decided, 'Well, it's really none of our business.' " And while the couples never saw each

other socially—Mary Lee seemed to have grander ambitions than a
cop and his wife—the McFarlanes had long since assured themselves
that their decision had been the right one.

Until the morning of March 12, 1981, that is, when the suspicious
policeman found himself faced with the weeping widow, who responded to his question of how Ron's sister was taking his death by
confiding that she hadn't yet faced her sister-in-law with the news. She
didn't know whether Linda was strong enough to take it.

Did that mean, McFarlane asked, that Ron's family had not yet
been told? Mary Lee had telephoned *her* friends Joyce and Mary Jane
even before the police arrived—two women she'd known fewer than six
months. But she had not yet notified her husband's immediate family.
McFarlane hurried off to telephone Buddy House. He wanted to be
sure Buddy told Linda before Linda heard about it on the radio or TV.

• • •

Detectives Farley and Miles encountered Mary Lee Orsini soon
after they returned from the crime scene. "The first time I saw her,"
Farley said, "she was sitting at a detective's desk back in the Homicide
Division. She had her hands over her face and she was going 'boo-
hoo-hoo boo-hoo.' When I walked through the door she opened the
fingers, took a look at me, sized me up, went 'boo-hoo' a couple more
times, then opened the fingers to peek at me again. You know how
little kids will hide their faces and peek through their fingers? Like that
. . . I didn't size her up at that point. I just thought, 'Oh, boy what the
hell have we got here?' "

The immediate question, as Farley saw it, was whether or not to
read the widow her rights as a suspect. Eventually, they'd have to look
at her pretty hard, but he was in no hurry to inform her of that fact.
No compelling evidence said he had to. When asked, Orsini had
declined to call an attorney. Making her a formal suspect would probably change her mind—and the first thing any criminal defense lawyer
would tell her would be to say nothing. The risk they ran was that no
statement they got from the woman without reading her a Miranda
warning could be used against her. The same strictures applied to
evidence gathered as a direct result of a voluntary statement.

But suspect or no, once Mary Lee told her story she'd be stuck with
it. Should she eventually be charged with the crime and testify in her
own defense, any inconsistencies could be used to impeach her cred-

ibility. Very few murderers were cool enough to brazen it out to the end. Taking a voluntary statement from Mrs. Orsini now was a calculated risk.

The first of Mary Lee Orsini's many hours under oath began at exactly 1:12 P.M. that afternoon in an interview room off the Homicide Division—a narrow, cell-like chamber with one barred window, a bare wooden table, and folding metal chairs. Besides the two detectives, Patrolman Mallett asked to sit in, and Farley obliged him. Deputy Prosecutor Judy Kaye Mason also came in from her office down the hall. Mason brought a court reporter with her. They trusted Mason, but the quick rundown Farley gave her omitted some of the detectives' suspicions. The last time she had seen her husband alive, Mary Lee Orsini said in response to Farley's first question, was after the ten o'clock news on Channel 11. She had slept in the adjoining bedroom that night with her daughter Tiffany.

"Tiffany. Do you have more than one child?"

Mrs. Orsini did not answer, but put her face into her hands and wept loudly—long enough for Judy Kaye Mason to conceive suspicions of her own. Only thirty, Mason had taken the deputy prosecutor's job fresh out of law school. But she'd had plenty of experience inside interview rooms. A native of the town of Foreman in Little River County near the Oklahoma and Texas borders, Mason had worked her way through UA-Little Rock Law School as a court reporter.

"As soon as she raised her head up and her mascara wasn't running all over the place," Mason remembered, "we just looked at each other, my court reporter and I—and immediately we thought, 'Uh-oh.' And I thought, 'She killed him.' Right there."

Mason spoke up. "Mrs. Orsini, do you feel up to continuing? Or would you like to stop for a while?" She added firmly, "We are going to have to do this."

"I know, I know!"

"Do you have more than one child?" Farley asked. "Perhaps if you just tried to push yourself, you could get through it."

"I'm trying so hard! He has a little girl that lives in Louisiana. Our little stepdaughter, my little stepdaughter!"

"What I'm trying to establish," Farley continued, "is how many people would have been in the home last night. You, your husband and Tiffany?"

"That's right."

Tiffany, she told them, was the child of her first husband, who lived in New England and whom she hadn't seen in the five years she and Ron had been married.

"What was the reason why you two didn't sleep together?"

"Tiffany," she answered. "I'd taken her to the doctor Tuesday and she was having these blackout spells. Dr. Gosser had her stay home yesterday, and for me to watch her, because he couldn't locate the reason why she was falling downstairs and everything. The school nurse told me I needed to get her to the doctor because they thought her equilibrium was messed up. He suggested that I just monitor her—when she is awake and asleep—just try to watch and see if I could get any pattern or indication what was causing this. That's what I was doing."

Before the detectives had left the house, Orsini's friend Joyce Holt had told them that Mary Lee and Ron had been sleeping in separate rooms for two weeks.

"You two hadn't been having any problems at all but hadn't been sleeping together for the past two weeks?"

"There was a problem," she admitted. "But it wasn't anything like a husband and wife type problem."

"What type of problem would it be?"

"I don't want to go into it!" she almost shouted, and broke down weeping again.

Farley pressed ahead. "We are investigating a murder here, and we need to go into it, Ma'am. What is the problem?"

"About four months ago, I'm not sure of the exact time but it was around the deer season," she began rapidly, "Ron started having some very unusual behavior. My friends Mary Jane and Bill noticed it. He was overly nervous, and what have you, and we had a sizable amount of money in our savings account and I took care of the household things. All of a sudden, he just brings the money home. And we start getting these calls at the house where people are calling me up wanting him. Won't tell me what is going on. Nothing. . . . I overheard several unusual phone calls and it even went so far that I contacted a private investigator."

"Which investigator?" Farley asked.

"Fred Myers," she said, naming a reputable North Little Rock detective agency. "I went to Fred in January sometime—because I didn't know anything about this—to put on a telephone tap, because Ron kept getting these calls, and he was very disturbed about the calls. And

I begged him to tell me what was going on and he told me that it was best that I didn't know what was going on. . . . I tried to tell my sister-in-law and she said, 'I don't want to get involved.' Because I didn't get to explain to her fully. But Mary Jane is the one that told me about the private investigator. She's the one that has advised me all along. . . ."

"Did you hear any noises last night after you went to bed?"

"No sir."

"So it was your husband in that bedroom, you and your daughter Tiffany in the other bedroom?"

"Yes sir."

"When you got up this morning, what did you do?"

"I got up and I go to the bedroom door and I try to open it, and it's locked and I didn't think anything about it and the reason I didn't because Ron has a habit of pulling the bedroom door to, a lot of times," Mary Lee began, the words pouring out faster and faster. "And he gets up so early that like—even if I'm in there, or if he's taking a bath or whatever—he's pulled that door to. And he made the comment to Tiffany this weekend, he was going to take the lock off the door because it locked so easily. Like he would take a bath and he didn't want Tiffany to walk in on him [so] he would close the door. This is kind of embarrassing, but a lot of times he goes to the bathroom in the morning, and to keep the odor from going through the house he'll just shut the door and raise the bathroom window. . . ."

She rattled on, describing how she'd put on dirty clothes from the hamper and called Ron's office to have him sent home. Then she'd taken Tiffany out for breakfast, cashed a check, looked at some jewelry at the drugstore, window-shopped for a party dress for her daughter, taken her to school, then visited a service station on her way home— each explained in exhaustive detail. She thought she'd gotten back home around 9:30 A.M.

"What did you do then?"

"I started realizing that I was getting ready to get in the room, that Ron probably wouldn't call me back."

At exactly 7:00 A.M., Farley was thinking, she doesn't know how to open the door. She never looks out the window and sees her husband's truck sitting in the driveway. She calls him at work and leaves a message. So what does she do next? She takes off for two and a half hours, then walks back in and suddenly realizes Ron isn't going to call. How does she know that?

"Where did you park when you arrived at the house?"

"In the garage."

"Then you went through that carport door?" He meant the one with the gouges around the doorknob.

"Yes sir," Mary Lee affirmed. She had, however, noticed nothing unusual about the door.

"And you didn't see his truck still parked there when you pulled out?" Farley asked.

"Yeah, I did. When we pulled out of the driveway I saw the truck, and I mentioned it to Tiffany. I said, 'I guess something's wrong with Daddy's truck.' Because he'd made the statement about a week ago—my battery had run down on my car and—'You know, batteries do that.' And he had trouble on and off with his starter, so I didn't think anything about the truck sitting there. I figured he'd be back to pick it up."

"What happened after you got back to the house?"

"I started trying to figure out what I could get in that little hole, because I thought if I could poke something in there I could get the door open. So I went down into the kitchen. I found a thing that we use on the grill, a skewer-type thing . . . So I stuck it in the door and I was trying to jiggle the lock to get it open, and I opened the door."

"What did you do then?"

"I ran back downstairs."

"Did you see your husband laying on the bed?"

"Yes, I saw him laying on the bed!" she wailed.

Judy Kaye Mason had lapsed into total incredulity. "She had made up this too good a story—why she stopped, here, there, and everywhere. She's leaving all these tracks when nobody's after her. It's in the Bible. 'The guilty flee when no man pursueth.' "

"What did you see when you opened up the door?" Farley insisted coolly.

"I saw my husband laying with blood all over him!" Mary Lee half shouted, an edge of defiance creeping into her voice. Then, she said, she'd run downstairs and called the police.

Farley leaned back in his chair and nodded to Miles.

"Ma'am," Buddy began in a soothing drawl, "whenever you got into your car to take your daughter to school, were the garage doors closed? All three of 'em?"

Mary Lee affirmed that they were. Deliberately adopting an innocuous, half-apologetic tone, Miles took her back over her morning activities. Why, yes, she'd used the garage door opener when she got back from running errands and used her key to enter the house through the laundry room door—the very one, as Miles didn't bother to mention, that he'd popped open a couple of hours earlier. These were petty details, he seemed to imply. If she couldn't recall, why that would be just fine. The little edge gradually went out of her voice. Miles asked if she'd done any laundry that morning.

"Oh yeah, I did. I turned some towels on, a whole big load of towels . . . I just grabbed a few and stuck them in the laundry."

He changed the subject again. "We now have three guns down here," he said. "We have the small one that was in his dresser. . . . We have two from the gun cabinet which were in boxes. Does he own any more handguns?"

"I . . . I want to tell you something," she began hesitantly. "I know very little about guns, and the only one that I have really ever shot is the little one—which you probably found—the little, tiny short one. In fact, he took me out about a week or so ago and wanted me to try shooting it again. And I've got a list that I made up for him. I was telling Mr. McFarlane I've got a list of serial numbers someplace at the house, of every gun he owns. I'll be glad to try to find it. It very well could be in the gun cabinet. I don't know."

"Do you carry a gun in your purse?"

"Oh no."

"Does he keep a loaded gun around the house?" Another thing Mary Lee had told Joyce Holt was that Ron had been sleeping with a revolver under his pillow for two weeks.

"He has, yes."

"Did you know if there was one there last night?"

"No."

"We had information that maybe he had had stolen or had lost another gun," Miles said. According to NLRPD files, Ron Orsini had reported a .38 Colt revolver with a four-inch barrel stolen from under the front seat of his truck on January 14, 1981.

"That's right, he did," Mary Lee answered. Ron had discovered the theft in his driveway at 7412 Pontiac. He'd told the investigating officer that two things puzzled him: why the thief had taken his gun but left the carrying case, and how the truck had been entered to begin with. It hadn't been broken into, and because of the pistol and the expensive two-way radio built into the dash, Ron said he *never* left the vehicle unlocked.

Mary Lee professed to know nothing about it.

Farley took up the questioning again. "This may sound nit-picky," the detective asked, "but when you wash towels, what temperature setting is that washer on?"

"Usually cold," she said.

"You don't wash them hot, like the directions say?"

"No, because it takes too much energy. I wash them cold."

"Getting back to when you got out of your car," Farley asked, "did you notice any damage on the door going into the place?"

"No sir. Somebody asked me that earlier, about something to the door. I didn't notice. When you have groceries, you grab a door and stick it . . . I don't pay that much attention to it."

"This is real noticeable," Farley said. He showed her a Polaroid photograph. "You haven't noticed that there before?"

"No sir."

Farley brought the questioning back to Ron Orsini. "You say around deer season he started acting not normal. You felt like there was a problem. What would you say the problem was?"

"That has just driven me about crazy. I don't know."

"Do you think it was drugs? Or involvement with other people, other women? Anything like that?"

"No. When I went to Mr. Myers the first time, the first thing he asked me was did I think it was another woman. And I said, to be very honest, there was nothing wrong with Ron's and my marriage from a male-female standpoint. . . . He just wasn't that kind of person. Ron is as warm as anybody could be."

"Have there ever been any problems between your husband and your daughter?" Farley asked.

"No more than just telling a thirteen-year-old she can't do something, and her pouting. But I think they have a good relationship." The tears began again, and Farley let her cry herself out.

"Who would you say would have murdered your husband?" Farley asked soon as she quit. He spoke as matter-of-factly as if he were talking about the weather.

"I think my brother did," she said.

"What is your brother's name?"

"Ron Hatcher."

"Why would you think that he murdered him?"

"Because that is the only enemy Ron had," she sobbed. "The only enemy! And he's going . . ."

Ignoring her tears, Farley cut her off. "I'm going to ask you point blank, did you murder your husband?"

"Oh good God, man, no!" she shouted.

"Would you be willing to take a Voice Stress Analyzer Test on that?" he continued coolly. "Or a lie detector?"

"If I contact a lawyer and he says that's alright, yeah."

"Do you think your child could have done it?"

"Oh heavens no! Tiffany is compassionate as anybody could be. She worshipped him."

"And you didn't hear any noises at all? What time did you go to bed last night, roughly?"

She thought it was between 10:25 and 10:45. Ron had been lying in bed listening to his police scanner when she'd kissed him goodnight. The bedroom door had been open. Farley circled back to a question he'd asked before. "We've heard that you haven't slept with your husband for two weeks. What do you have to say about that? What would cause that?"

"Oh that's not true," she said. "Tiffany was sick last week—had a throat infection—and I slept with her. But as far as not *sleeping* with him—like cutting him off—that wasn't Ron's and my style."

Farley sat back and Miles took his turn. "Last night at any point," he asked, "did you lay down with him, or did you get in the bed with him?"

"He went to see his father in the hospital, who is critically ill," she said, "and I had laid down. [Tiffany] was downstairs on the phone. I had already taken my bath, and gotten in my gown and robe, and I had gotten up and went to tell her to get off the phone and get her little bottom upstairs and get in bed. And then I was downstairs waiting for him to come home."

"Okay," Miles continued. "But are you telling me that before he arrived home, you took your bath and went to bed?"

"I laid down, yeah."

"In which bed?"

"In the bed in our room."

"Where he was found this morning?"

"Yes sir. And I had a little TV set in there that's in my daughter's room now," she said. "When Tiffany went upstairs, she asked me . . . could she take the TV? And I think she did." All this, Mary Lee said, had taken place some time before 8:00 P.M.

"If you had been sleeping with Tiffany to watch her," Judy Kaye Mason asked, "why did you go to bed in your bed?"

"Because of the little TV that was in there. I just had it on. . . . She came upstairs and got in her bed. I don't totally remember it, but I

think he came home in the process of me getting her upstairs and all
this—getting her bath, and what have you."

"Why do you think Ron Hatcher would want to shoot your husband?" Farley asked.

"My brother had, and I think if you check your records has, a
background of being malicious and doing things to people that he
thinks done something to him. Back about April or May of last year he
got married and moved into a house—this old house out on Kanis
Road—and my husband had replaced my mother's air conditioner
free, because she is seventy-two and he loved her. And I feel like that's
our duty. When an air conditioner goes out for an old lady, you take
care. My brother is a junior officer at Commercial National Bank and
he expected the same thing."

As Mary Lee rambled on about her brother's feud with her husband,
Farley realized that he knew the Ron Hatcher she was talking about,
a security officer at the Little Rock bank. Farley's work on the forgery
detail took him to monthly meetings of the Metropolitan Security
Council that Mary Lee's brother also attended. According to her, Ron
Hatcher was also vindictive over a piece of property her mother had
signed over to Mary Lee and her husband—an inheritance from their
late father. Having spent his own share years ago, she claimed, her
brother had even filed a lawsuit for a share of their mother's rental
income. Over the past weekend, Ron Hatcher had infuriated her husband by circling their house in a van several times in what Ron Orsini
had taken to be a threatening gesture.

"Ron had gotten upset about it," she emphasized, "because he felt
like—the whole family felt like—that my brother was going to do
something, even to the point where my mother was afraid he would go
over and burn the house down."

"What would Ron Hatcher gain if your husband were dead?"

"Nothing." The property, she went on to say, was in both names for
that very reason. "You have to know how my brother's mind works. In
his mind, Ron and I were the cause."

"When was the last time that Ron Hatcher and your husband saw
each other? Has he ever been to your home?"

"He knew we had the house," she said. "But he was never invited
into the home."

"If I was to tell you that your husband had been dead over eight
hours when he was found," Miles said, "could you explain why you
could not have heard the shot?"

"No sir."

"Do you have normal hearing?"

"Yes sir, but I am an extremely sound sleeper," she said. "That could be verified by my mother and other people. I just go into an absolute dead sleep."

"So you're in essence telling me that Ron Hatcher could come into your home without you knowing it if you were asleep?"

"I could be picked up and thrown out a window and not know," she claimed, fixing Miles with her pale blue eyes. "I'm just one of those people that go into an absolute dead sleep."

Miles found the rapid shifts in her demeanor unsettling. Only minutes ago, Mary Lee had been weeping. Now she seemed to be daring them to doubt her story.

Judy Kaye Mason broke in. "Did you ever get a final report from Mr. Myers on what your husband was up to?" she asked.

"No," Mary Lee began. "Let me explain what all went with this. . . ." She offered a lengthy account of her dealings with the private detective, who'd told her he couldn't tap her telephone without a warrant. Just within the past week, however, she'd overheard Ron's end of some angry phone conversations about a "drop." "So I called Mr. Myers back," she concluded, "and I said, 'I think this has something to do with drugs.' "

The rush of words stopped momentarily. Then she took a deep breath and plunged ahead, adopting a confidential tone. "Okay, this is something I haven't told you. The money that he had, which was a sizeable amount—I didn't get to finish—that he never put it in a savings account, that he had it in the safe deposit box. And we were going to make an investment with the money that he had, and when I went to get the money for the investment and he said, 'I don't have it anymore.' Well, I became very upset about this with him."

The more Mary Lee talked, the faster she talked and the more animated she became. She wasn't making much sense, but nobody made any attempt to slow her down. If nothing else, it was a fascinating performance.

"You're talking about trouble?" she continued. "This is where we had some trouble. . . ." It seemed that Ron had hidden a zippered bank bag underneath a pile of dirty clothes in the bedroom closet. "We had gotten into some very, very bad arguments about the money. He had told me he would get it—he would see that it emerged again—and for me not to bug him about it, but to trust him. And I had discussed

this with Mary Jane. Mary Jane's the one that said . . . there was
something awful suspicious about it, and that I should contact a private
investigator."

"What was in the bag that you found underneath the dirty clothes?"
Miles finally asked.

The bank bag, Mary Lee said, had been stuffed with hundred-dollar
bills.

"How much money are we talking about?" Miles pressed.

"Okay, initially, Ron and I had in excess of $3,000, and there was
more than twice that much in this bag this time. And we don't have
that kind of money. He said, 'Lee, just trust me. Please, just trust
me.' "

"Earlier you said he handled the savings account and you handled
the checking. Now you're saying there was no savings account?" Mason interjected.

"That's what I didn't get to finish when we were talking earlier,"
Mary Lee responded. "That he came back to me and said this was not
in a savings account. Well, I didn't believe him. I went back and
looked over some of our previous tax things . . . and there was no large
amount of savings in the account."

"Where was your purse last night?" Mason asked.

"I don't know. I guess it was probably downstairs in the kitchen or
something."

"When did you put your make-up on? Do you keep your make-up
in your purse?"

"My daughter and I share her . . . The make-up? No, I don't. It's
up in her bathroom and she and I . . . It's kind of a thing we do in the
morning together. My make-up is up there with hers, and she uses my
eye shadow and things like that."

Orsini began another explanation, but Miles cut her off. "What size
panty would you wear?" he demanded. Farley's heart sank. Buddy was
going to try out his incest theory and there was no way to stop him.

"Beg your pardon?"

"What size panty would you wear?" the detective repeated evenly.
"Would there be a size on them?"

"Well yeah, I don't really . . . I guess 5 or 6—something like that."
Mason had to stifle a laugh. She had no idea what Miles was driving
at, but the size Mary Lee gave would fit a woman about half Orsini's
width in the beam.

"And your daughter probably wears a size what?"

"Well, she wears a children's size—because she's thin."

"If I told you there was a size 12 lady's panty in [the laundry] with a crotch torn out of it, would that surprise you?"

"Oh, you are talking about dust rags! These are cotton things that my children have outgrown and we use them for dust rags and things." She went on to explain that the maid had come in Monday and used the rags to clean with.

"In other words," Miles pressed her, "you were not having any problems with your husband towards your daughter?"

"No sir.

"Sexually?"

"No sir!" she shouted. Her eyes blazed. If she were not genuinely startled, she did an excellent job of seeming so.

"We have to look at everything, Ma'am," Miles said. "We are not trying to embarrass you."

"I know you do!" she exclaimed. "But you did not know Ron!"

"No Ma'am. We know neither one of you, and we're sorry we have to bring these things up."

"I know you do," she said, and once again began to cry.

"You have to understand," Mason said. "You tell us in one sentence that he's a wonderful man—didn't have any enemies. And then you come right back: he was really acting weird."

"That's right, that's right. But irregardless of that, he was still a good man. I don't care what he might have gotten himself involved to. But there was not a better person in this world!"

"Do you think he was taking drugs or dealing in drugs?"

"I don't know! I swear to God, I don't know! I have spent three of the most miserable months worrying about him, because I don't know what he was into." She buried her face in her hands and bawled.

Sergeant Farley had just about had his fill. If Ron Orsini had been a drug user, he'd sure done a good job of keeping the obvious kinds of evidence to himself. Their search of the house had turned up nothing of the kind. If there were any illicit substances in his system, the autopsy report would reveal them. What Farley wanted to hear more about was the missing money. Money tended to leave trace evidence too, traces he was adept at finding. He asked her where the couple did their banking, then got back to the question of the zippered bank bag full of hundred-dollar bills.

"When would you estimate," he asked, "that this $20,000 that you had at Savers was removed?" Farley plucked the figure out of thin air, just to see what would happen.

"It was more than $20,000," Mary Lee responded. "It was about

$40,000. Usually we have in excess of $40,000 and what I'm saying is what I saw—it was more than the package I originally saw—so it was in excess of, more than $40,000."

The investigators exchanged quick glances and looked away; poker faces were the order of the day. "So that would make it somewhere around $80,000 then," Farley said. "Is that what we are talking about?"

Mary Lee nodded. No longer tearful, she now claimed that Ron told her he'd never actually deposited the money in their savings account.

"I doubted this," she explained, "from the standpoint that I couldn't believe that he had that kind of money in a safe deposit box. I thought that was illegal. And again, I go back and look at our tax records and there was no huge amounts of, you know, savings interest."

"Where did this money come from?" Farley asked.

"Well, Ron did a lot of jobs on the side away from his company, and this was part of the money for that."

"So as far as you know, this $40,000 shouldn't show up on any withdrawal slips or income tax or anyplace else? It was just something he stashed away all these years?"

"That's what he indicated to me," she said flatly. She made a point of looking Farley straight in the eye.

"I have another question," Judy Kaye Mason said. "Where is the $80,000 now?" She named the higher figure deliberately.

"I don't know. The last time . . . Well, the day that I saw it was Monday. It was there in the closet, and I did not see it Tuesday and I made a point of literally tearing the house up to find it, because I told Mary Jane, I said, 'Can you give me any idea where people would stash things?' "

"So y'all were having arguments Monday and Tuesday?"

"Yeah!" she exclaimed. "They were heavy to the fact that I didn't want him to keep anything from me. I felt like he was keeping something from me. . . . Ron is not a screamer. I'm not a screamer. They were arguments. I wanted to know where it was. I was hassling him about it because I felt like I needed to know."

"When you opened that [bedroom] door . . . ," Mason said, "you didn't go over to see him, to see if he was still alive so you could help him?"

"All I saw was him in a pool of blood and I just ran to get an ambulance as fast as I could. Let me tell you something," Orsini added. "I had fainted at the sight of my own blood."

"Did you assume that he was dead?"

"I don't know that I assumed or thought anything. I just roared, and I just . . . I even think I screamed and I just ran."

"And after you called the police and an ambulance. . .," Miles asked, "did you not think of getting one of the neighbor men to try to assist your husband?"

"I didn't think," she said. "I really didn't. It was just hot and I was trying to get my head together. I just, I went out and sat on the front porch."

The investigators were running out of questions. Farley asked if Mary Lee's daughter slept as soundly as her mother. Mary Lee affirmed that she did. But neither she nor Tiffany had taken any medication that day that would make them drowsy.

"Do you have anything else you would like to say before we turn the tape off, Ma'am?" Buddy Miles asked.

"I just hope that y'all can find out whatever happened," Mary Lee said. "It's too late now as far as this other stuff goes, but I want to know who did this to Ron. Anything I can do to help you. . . . My mind is swirling and I'm having a hard time just even thinking. Anything I can do to help you, please, please call me," she begged. Then she began to cry once again as Miles reached across the table and pressed the "stop" button on the recorder. It was 2:04 P.M.

Leaving her isolated in the interview room, the investigators met briefly around Farley and Miles's desks. A technician was summoned to perform a trace metal detection test on Mrs. Orsini's hands. Given that more than twelve hours had passed since the fatal shot was fired, definitive results were unlikely. Even if she *hadn't* washed her hands or touched any metal objects in the interval, it was just too late. But she probably didn't know that, and like so many other routine aspects of any crime investigation, the job had to be done at least partly to avoid a defense lawyer's making the police look stupid. Besides, some people's skin retained evidence of firing a gun longer than others. They might get lucky.

2

Possibly alarmed by the tone of the interview, Mary Lee had decided she needed help after all. When Pete Zinn approached Sergeant Farley to ask if there was anything he could do for his partner's widow, the detective responded abruptly. "Yeah," Farley growled. "You can get her a lawyer."

Meanwhile, an oddly mixed group—all strangers to each other—
kept vigil outside the Homicide Division. Mary Lee's mother Julia
Hatcher had joined her friends Mary Jane Murphree, Joyce Holt, and
Ron's business partners. Mary Lee asked Zinn to call Judge Tom Glaze
on her behalf. She explained that Glaze had represented Ron's ex-wife
in making custody arrangements for his daughter Stacy. So impressed
had she been by his fairness that Mary Lee had worked in Glaze's
campaign for the Arkansas Court of Appeals. The two families had
developed a close friendship.

Zinn telephoned Glaze's office. Although the judge would have
been surprised to hear himself described as a friend of the family, he
was saddened to hear of Ron's death. Glaze explained to Zinn that he'd
never practiced criminal law and as a judge couldn't represent Mrs.
Orsini. But he did give him the names of three of the most respected
criminal defense lawyers in Arkansas. Pete dialed Bill McArthur's
number because he'd graduated from Little Rock Central High with
someone of that name.

•   •   •

William C. McArthur was indeed the same man Pete Zinn remembered as a boy from high school, and nobody who knew his way
around the Pulaski County Courthouse, or almost any courthouse in
the state, could have been unaware of his reputation. At forty-two, in
the fourteen years McArthur had practiced he'd probably argued and
won more jury trials, criminal and civil, than any lawyer in Arkansas.

A native of the Van Buren county seat of Clinton in the Ozark
Mountains about seventy-five miles north of the capital, McArthur
was known as a lawyer's lawyer: knowledgeable, articulate, persuasive,
and a fierce courtroom combatant. His peers considered him to be
honest, ethical, and in big cases anyway, extremely well prepared. If
McArthur had been known to dog it a bit in less complex trials, his
clients had no cause to complain. For McArthur was good on his feet
and adept at winning juries to his clients' point of view—especially,
frustrated opponents had been known to complain, women jurors.

People said things like that because whether or not McArthur was
the best trial lawyer in the state, as many thought, he was almost
certainly the best looking. Only his unassuming manner and the fact
that his nose had been broken several times in his youth prevented him
from being almost too handsome. About six feet one and 180 pounds,

McArthur had wavy blond hair, penetrating blue eyes, and aquiline features that evoked comparisons to Paul Newman—less because he actually resembled the actor than because Newman was the best-looking blond man whose name everybody knew.

"The Golden Boy," McArthur's wife Alice called him in her out-spoken, bantering way. "Get McArthur if you're guilty," she would tease. "If you're not, you don't need him." Raised along Bayou Teche in the Cajun country of Louisiana south of New Orleans, Alice McArthur was a devout Catholic who didn't much share her husband's hill-country populism and his sympathy for the underdog. The nick-name was Alice's way of flattering her husband; also of reminding him that he had a tendency to be a soft touch for any common criminal with a convincing hard luck story.

But Alice knew she couldn't change him, and never really tried. After eighteen years of marriage, the McArthurs had made it past a couple of rough spots—no secret to anyone who knew them both—and seemed to family and friends to be closer than ever, equally devoted to each other and to their two children.

Besides, Alice had a point. Practicing criminal law in a state as poor as Arkansas was no way to get rich anyway, and McArthur was noto-riously bad at squeezing payment out of his clients. McArthur made about $65,000 in 1981—a comfortable living by Little Rock standards, but a fraction of what he might have earned at one of the city's establishment law firms.

As for Bill's looks being responsible for his courtroom prowess, that was envy talking. Like everywhere else, Little Rock is full of handsome failures. Whenever McArthur showed up at the office wearing a new suit or tie, his long-time secretary Phoebe Pinkston liked to tease him by saying he looked like a Dallas lawyer. (The city, not the TV series.) In Arkansas, a compliment can't *get* a whole lot more back-handed than that.

While the press would later portray him as a debonair aristocrat, a more misleading account of McArthur's background would be hard to imagine. Until his father moved the family to Little Rock to take a job as a railroad brakeman when his son was fourteen, Bill had been an Arkansas country boy, and proud of it. He'd worked his way through college and law school both. Until marriage and law school forced him to quit, Bill had even competed for prize money as a bullrider in rodeos from Florida to Texas. He'd won some, too, though barely enough to make expenses, much less to pay for the broken bones.

· · ·

After Zinn put him in the picture, McArthur spoke briefly with Farley and Miles, who gave him the gist of what Mary Lee had told them. The detectives made no effort to hide the fact that they thought her story was bullshit. Either Mary Lee had shot Ron Orsini herself or she'd helped somebody do it. McArthur recalled Farley being very emphatic about that. But apart from something the lawyer already knew—that the police *always* looked at the husband or wife first in any domestic killing—they kept their reasons pretty much to themselves.

The detectives allowed the lawyer to meet with Mary Lee in the same room where they had taken her statement. McArthur kept things as perfunctory as he could. Mary Lee spent most of the brief interview in tears. Even so, her anger at being considered a suspect was already obvious. Assuming she hadn't done it, that was only natural.

But McArthur formed no opinion of her guilt or innocence. That wasn't his job, and he'd long ago learned the folly of jumping to conclusions. He figured the detectives must have *something* to make them sound so sure of themselves. They weren't the kind to blow smoke. But emotions ran high in every murder case; rashness and irrationality often followed. The legal question was whether the detectives thought they had enough to put her under arrest. Obviously they didn't. So McArthur asked how soon they intended to let her go home.

· · ·

The investigators never entertained the thought of arresting Mary Lee that day. Indeed, they had little choice in the matter. They had a few bits of concrete evidence—none tying her directly to the crime—plus a real fruitcake of a voluntary statement. But they didn't yet have a witness. Nobody had seen or heard anything that would put the murder weapon in Mary Lee Orsini's hand. And while the detectives couldn't be certain until they got the ballistics report, they'd have bet their gold badges that they didn't have the murder weapon either.

No witness, no weapon, no conviction; nine times out of ten, that was that.

· · ·

Only minutes after Mrs. Orsini walked out of the Homicide Division, Charlie Milton walked in. Milton was the officer under Lieutenant Jim McFarlane's command whose brother had once been married to Mary Myrtle Hatcher in another city. He'd spotted her down the hall as he was reporting for the 4:00 P.M. shift.

"What was that bitch doing here?" Milton asked Farley.

"Somebody blew her old man away last night," Farley said. "We think it was her."

"Oh yeah? Let me tell you what she did to my brother."

Under any other circumstances the story Officer Milton told would have been funny: the kind of tall tale men tell in bars to illustrate the duplicity of women. But Milton said his story was true. It seemed his brother had been married to Mary Lee—then Mary Myrtle—nine years earlier, when her daughter Tiffany was four. So far as he knew, the first year of their marriage was going just fine, and his brother was willing when she asked him to adopt the child formally.

For Mary Myrtle, giving Tiffany a "real" father instead of a stepfather seemed almost an obsession. She prodded her husband until a date was finally set for him to sign the required documents. He'd arrived at his lawyer's office on the appointed day to find that the papers weren't in order and there would be a delay. Rather than disappoint his wife, he told her a little white lie on the phone: the deal was done, formal notification would arrive by mail.

Mary Myrtle seemed elated. But when he rerturned home that afternoon he found that she and Tiffany were gone. So was every movable piece of property the couple owned, down to the knives, forks, and dishes. She'd left him cold. When the divorce papers were served a couple of days later, he found one item that amazed him almost as much as her disappearance: a petition for $1,000 a month in child support for his adopted daughter, Tiffany.

He ended up getting the furniture back. That had been his to begin with. But she got the car and he got the payments and her credit card charges, which were substantial. Thanks to his lawyer's error, however, he never did have to pay that child support.

"But I reckon he got off easy," Officer Milton told Farley.

"Yeah," Farley said. "It looks like maybe he did."

·   ·   ·

After Milton left, Farley dialed Mary Lee's brother Ron Hatcher. Hatcher seemed genuinely shocked to hear of his brother-in-law's murder, and volunteered to come to NLRPD headquarters at once to take a polygraph or Voice Stress Analyzer Test.

Hatcher arrived at 4:25 P.M. Farley read him his rights and informed him that he was a suspect in a murder. The detectives kept Mary Lee's accusations to themselves. Saying he had no need of an attorney, Hatcher denied any knowledge of the crime. Wednesday night he and his wife had left work together, spent the evening watching a rented video cassette of *2001, A Space Odyssey,* and gone to bed around midnight.

Hatcher denied that he'd ever had any serious disagreements with Ron Orsini, whom he hadn't seen for six months. He'd gone on an out-of-state camping trip the previous weekend, and had witnesses. The only family argument he knew about was between him and his sister. It concerned a piece of real estate that he believed Mary Lee had manipulated their mother into signing over to her—property that legitimately belonged to both children. Hatcher agreed to return with his wife for a formal taped interview.

It would take a few days, but Hatcher's alibi checked out in detail and Farley soon removed him from the list of suspects.

3

McArthur walked with Mrs. Orsini and her entourage as far as Vern Copeland's truck. He gave her his business card, told her to feel free to call any time she thought she needed legal advice, then drove back to his Little Rock office.

Mary Lee and Tiffany squeezed into the front seat of Vern's pickup between him and Pete Zinn. "The whole trip back to Ron's mother's was very quiet," Copeland remembers. "I didn't know what to say. Pete didn't know what to say. Tiffany was just a young teen-aged girl—just a little old kid. We was very broken up."

Gladys Orsini, Ron's mother, lived alone in a large block of garden apartments on JFK Boulevard a half mile south of Ron and Mary Lee's house on Pontiac Drive. Having been notified of Ron's death by Lieutenant Jim McFarlane, the family was gathering there to share their grief and bewilderment. Pete and Vern didn't feel it was their place to stay, and planned to return to 7412 Pontiac to fetch Pete's truck. When they arrived at Gladys's apartment, Pete walked Mary Lee to the door. She sent Tiffany inside, then turned to Pete and asked him to go back to the house and search under a pile of dirty clothes on the floor of Ron's closet for a zippered bank bag.

"What's in it?" Pete asked.

"$40,000 in cash."

Pete was flabbergasted. He knew exactly how much money Ron made. "Lee," he asked, "where did you ever get $40,000 cash?"

"We saved it," she answered with a determined set to her jaw. "And it was damned hard." She repeated her instructions, begging Pete to keep looking for the money until he found it.

And like a damn fool, he tried.

But there was no bank bag to be found.

Chapter 3

1

Americans think they understand murder. The disposition of corpses begins the evening news. TV and film melodramas either begin or end—indeed often begin *and* end—in violent death. Victims writhe in simulated agony like porn stars faking orgasm. As a plot mechanism, homicide can be a convenient way to start a tale—or end one. In reality, of course, most of us actually know less than nothing about murder. Repetition has numbed us to its elemental horror.

Nobody in the tiny, intimate circle for whom Ron Orsini was the most important person in the world had ever known a murder victim, much less a murderer. They'd known policemen, but they'd never been interviewed by a homicide detective. What they knew of the criminal justice system was confined to the generally absurd dramatizations they'd seen on TV. None had been pestered day and night by reporters, nor had their lives laid open for public scrutiny like a fish on a cutting board.

They had no way of anticipating that their sorrow would soon be transformed into suspicion, the suspicion into a fear unlike any they had known, and fear into a hatred so corrosive it would eat at their vitals like industrial acid. All they knew was that Ron had been shot to death, and that when Mary Lee Orsini walked into his mother's apartment late on the afternoon of March 12, 1981, the first words out of her mouth were: "I feel like I need to tell y'all this right now. The police think it's my brother that did this, that killed Ron. They're out looking for him."

Linda House, Mary Lee's sister-in-law, heard the news of her brother's death from her husband Buddy. After Lieutenant Jim McFarlane called him from NLRPD headquarters, Buddy left his auto mechanic's job up in Cabot and drove straight to downtown Little Rock, where Linda worked as a secretary in an investment bank. Buddy knew Linda would take it very hard and hadn't wanted to tell her on the phone. From there the couple had an awful choice to make: Should they drive to Baptist Hospital to inform her dying father, or to Gladys Orsini's North Little Rock apartment? They had chosen her mother because her mother lived alone. Joe Orsini at least would have the comfort of his wife—Ron and Linda's stepmother—Bernice.

By the time Lee made her entrance, Linda was still in a daze. Absurd hope and paralyzing grief competed in her mind. Maybe it was all a crazy misunderstanding. There were whispers of suicide, but Linda refused to hear them. Not the big brother who had been her best friend and closest confidant since early childhood. Ron was steady. Ron was gentle. Ron loved Stacy, and Lee and Tiffany, too. Ron would never do anything to hurt her or his mother or Daddy, either one. Nobody could make her doubt it.

Ron and Linda Orsini had grown up in a quiet middle-class part of North Little Rock called Park Hill. Their father Joe had been an officer at Twin City Bank. Though their name was Italian and the family worshipped at a Catholic church when they were small, their emotional ties to the "old country" had all but vanished over the generations. The family's cultural identity, later to be the subject of fantastic rumors, was Southern American—Arkansas style.

When Lee announced that the police were looking for her brother, Linda had no reason not to believe her. She'd met Ron Hatcher just once and he'd made a good impression on her and Buddy both. But for months, Lee had been telling her sister-in-law about a bitter dispute between her and Ron Hatcher—something about some property. Ron, Lee had confided, had grown increasingly upset by the situation.

But Linda never mentioned it to Ron, because that was not their style. Part of their intimacy was recognizing each other's reticence. Now it was too late. Linda's heart went out to her brother's stricken wife, whom she loved like a sister. They fell into each other's arms and cried.

The only other thing Linda specifically recalled Lee saying that night was that she meant to return to 7412 Pontiac with her nephew to spend the night. She could not leave the premises unguarded, Lee said. Ron, she believed, would have wanted her to be brave.

The thought of it terrified Linda. " 'Lee,' I said, 'you can't go back to that house. Please don't go back to that house.' But she said she was going."

And to the best of Linda House's knowledge, she did.

2

In the *Arkansas Gazette* on Friday morning, March 13, Ron Orsini's murder rated six terse, anonymous paragraphs on page 7B, stuck between a UPI account of a teachers' strike in Ohio and an announcement of the upcoming twenty-second annual convention of the Arkansas Cattlemen's Association. Its placement gave a precise indication of the victim's social status. Little Rock's second-string paper, the *Arkansas Democrat*, locked in a bitter circulation war with the older, more prestigious *Gazette*, played it almost exactly the same way.

Had the stories carried bylines, they ought to have read "by Sergeant T. J. Farley." From the moment the body was found, the NLRPD had acted to control press coverage. All of the officers had taken care to communicate by telephone rather than radio. Unlike newspaper reporters, Little Rock TV camera crews raced each other to accident sites and violent crimes like firemen to a four-alarm blaze. TV news reporters had a cynical proverb: "If it bleeds, it leads."

But what the media didn't hear on their emergency band scanners, the media didn't know. The police could manipulate the press for their own purposes. Hoping to provoke Mary Lee into doing something reckless, Farley had given the *Gazette* beat reporter what amounted to an accusation:

Ron Orsini, 38, of 7412 Pontiac Drive, North Little Rock, was found shot to death at his home in the Indian Hills addition early Thursday. The police said he had been shot once in the back of the head, apparently while he slept.

Orsini, part owner of Central Heating and Air Conditioning at 9901 Mann Road, Little Rock, was found by his wife Lee, 33, who told the police that she found his body after breaking into a locked bedroom on the second floor of the home. He had been dead several hours, the police said. His body was taken to the state medical examiner's office for an autopsy.

Detectives have not found the gun that killed Orsini nor have they found any sign of forced entry into the house. They also have not determined the motive and said nothing was missing from the house. Mrs. Orsini said she did not hear a gunshot.

If Orsini wanted to tell everybody about mysterious phone calls and vanishing bags of cash that was her business, Farley figured.

He didn't have to wait very long for her to get started. No sooner had the two detectives showed up at headquarters Friday morning than they were handed an urgent message. Mrs. Orsini had already phoned at 7:00 A.M. to report an attempted burglary. This time she'd dialed the right number on the first try.

When Farley and Miles arrived at 7412 Pontiac, Mary Lee sent them to the garage. Returning from visiting her mother, she told them, she'd activated the automatic garage door opener from her car, but the mechanism had jumped its track and the door jammed. It wouldn't open or shut all the way. The detectives had noticed the door canted sideways at an odd angle when they pulled up. Mary Lee theorized that an intruder had forced his way into the garage during the night—or the night before. It seemed to her a crucial clue.

The detectives exchanged dubious glances. Evidently Mrs. Orsini had been reading the newspapers. Not only had they checked and double-checked the garage doors during their crime scene investigation, but according to Mary Lee's statement she'd raised and lowered them twice on her way to and from taking Tiffany to school. Miles had made a point of getting her to say so for the record. Leaving Mary Lee inside, they entered the garage. As the burglary expert, Miles examined the mechanism.

"Hell," he announced. "All I see here is that somebody has loosened a couple of bolts since yesterday. They had to be inside the garage to do it."

Mary Lee seemed unimpressed by the news. She said she'd found nothing obvious missing from the house. But she hadn't managed to summon the strength to enter the bedroom where her husband had died. Now that she thought of it, the missing canvas bank bag with the $80,000 cash inside it wasn't under the dirty clothes on the floor of Ron's closet at all. Her husband must have taken those to the cleaners. No, now that she thought of it, he'd concealed the bank bag in a pile of sweaters on a shelf above his hanging clothes. She was almost certain. Would the officers please search the closet? She had every confidence they would find the $80,000.

Farley thought he knew what she was up to. "Miles and I stepped outside to talk for a minute," he remembered. "I said to Buddy, 'This is ridiculous. I'm glad we got plenty of witnesses. She's going to accuse us of stealing that damn money.' "

Even so, the detectives played the game. If the lady said there was a bank bag with $80,000 cash in the bedroom closet, then the closet was going to get searched again. And since Farley and Patrolman Huddleson had done the honors Thursday, Miles got the job Friday morning. Farley waited in the hallway with Mary Lee. If any money turned up, the detectives planned to count it and have her sign a receipt on the spot.

Somewhat to his relief, Miles found no money. But he did get a surprise. "I come back and tell her I didn't see any bank bag and she goes, 'Did you see the sweaters?' I said yes I did, and she says, 'Look in between those.' So I go back up there and I raise them up one at a time. Two or three from the bottom I find these rubbers—a package of at least a dozen condoms. I thought, 'Why does she want me to find these?' So I just acted dumb. I put them back in there and told her I found nothing."

If Mary Lee wanted Buddy to play the role of the dopey sidekick, he was happy to oblige. From that morning onward, she treated him with elaborate condescension—as if he were Barney Fife, the yokel deputy on the "Andy Griffith Show." Buddy figured he could live with it.

Meanwhile, Mary Lee had another story she had forgotten in yesterday's turmoil. It seemed that $1,300 cash had vanished from her husband's closet two months ago. She had contracted with a rug-cleaning service to steam clean her downstairs carpet in November 1980. She'd been so impressed with the young man who'd done the job that she'd asked for him by name when she called the same company three months later. Several days later he'd arrived and given her an estimate on the upstairs carpets. During his visit, the serviceman had been left alone in the master bedroom for several minutes. Apart from her and Tiffany, nobody else had been in the house all day.

When Ron Orsini got home, he discovered the $1,300 missing from his closet. He'd taken it up with the firm's manager, but gotten no satisfaction. The company claimed that the serviceman hadn't worked for them since Thanksgiving. They even denied that they'd sent anybody to 7412 Pontiac since November. Fortunately, Mary Lee had kept the young man's business card. But even after Ron Orsini had presented it to the prosecutor, he'd been refused a warrant for the serviceman's arrest. Ron had been terribly upset, and not simply because of the $1,300. Her husband, she reported, took Central Heating & Air Conditioning's reputation for trustworthiness very seriously. The carpet-cleaning firm's cavalier attitude had infuriated him.

It all struck Mary Lee as suspicious. Farley gave her his best Sergeant Joe Friday deadpan, and wrote it all down in his notebook. He didn't believe a word of it. Even an eighteen-year-old police cadet would have grasped that no evidence existed that the theft had taken place. But he and Miles would check it out all the same. Just as soon as they got around to it.

No sooner had the detectives climbed into Farley's standard issue NLRPD sedan—a 1976 Chevrolet Malibu four door, white with black-wall tires—than Miles told his partner about the condoms.

"Why the hell would she want you to find those?"

Miles was damned if he knew. During her interview the day before, Mary Lee had appeared to react with shock and anger to his suggestions about the torn panties. Next morning she practically puts a twelve-pack of pre-lubricated, reservoir tips into his hands. So what was that supposed to prove?

"That's the problem you ran into with her right from the start," Farley said. "All the time we're sitting there wondering, we're not doing our job, are we? You've got to fan all the smoke out of the way and get to the heart of the thing. We're sitting there jawing about rubbers, and we've got a dead body we found ten feet from the damn rubbers we're *not* thinking about."

And they also had a woman and a thirteen-year-old girl in the next room who had failed to hear a .38 caliber revolver blast in the middle of the night. "God dog," Farley said. "You want to talk loud? In a closed room? A .22 long rifle is loud enough to rattle your windows. It's so loud you can't hear nothing for a couple of minutes. A .38? Hell, a deaf man would feel the concussion."

·   ·   ·

Tiffany Orsini arrived at NLRPD headquarters at 2:00 P.M. Friday, accompanied by her grandmother, Julia Hatcher, and Bill McArthur. The attorney had been mildly surprised to hear from Mrs. Orsini again so soon, but agreed to sit in on the girl's interview. As far as McArthur was concerned, he was still doing Judge Tom Glaze a favor.

Like her mother's, Tiffany's was to be a "voluntary statement." She would be placed under oath, but not read her rights. McArthur's presence was largely precautionary—though if he did end up representing Mrs. Orsini, it might also give him a clue as to what kind of case the detectives thought they had.

Nobody who dealt with Tiffany Orsini during the course of the investigation ever knew exactly what to make of her. But they all came away feeling that she acted older than her thirteen years. Tiffany painted her face even more elaborately than her mother—with generous applications of lip gloss, eyeliner, and blue eye shadow. Like many of her classmates, she wore her hair in an elaborately teased mane like Farrah Fawcett on "Charlie's Angels." If she and Mary Lee resembled each other at all it was mostly around the eyes.

Bill McArthur thought Tiffany handled herself like "a very knowing little girl," but found her demeanor appropriately solemn under the circumstances. The others found it a bit spooky. "When she came in that afternoon," Judy Kaye Mason said, "I remember thinking how composed she was. It was like meeting a midget grownup. She acted like a twenty-seven-year-old woman in the seventh grade. She walks into the interview room and holds her hand out and says, 'How do you do? I'm Tiffany Orsini.' And you're thinking, 'Her Daddy's been murdered, somebody has broken into her house—allegedly—and shot her father in the next room and she's just as cool as she can be.' "

"Tiffany Rene Orsini" was how the girl identified herself in response to Farley's first question. Actually, her birth certificate read "Tiffany LaVergne," but like her mother she'd evidently found a name she liked better. She'd stayed home sick from school that Wednesday, Tiffany told the group gathered in the same cramped interview room. Her mother had stayed home to take care of her. As near as she could recall, Ron Orsini had arrived home while she was watching "Happy Days," between 5:00 and 5:30. The family had eaten an early beef stew dinner, then her stepfather left to visit his father in the hospital. Tiffany had gone up to her bedroom for a while, then come back downstairs.

"What time did you come back downstairs?" Farley asked.

"I'm really not sure. I just came down."

"What was on TV at the time?"

"I don't know. I think I went down to check on my cats, take care of them, make sure they were fed. And then I think I went back up and I asked Mom if I could have the TV, and she said it was already in my room. And so I went upstairs and I think I watched something that was on—some movie or something."

The investigators felt their pulses quicken. In her statement, Mary Lee had explained that the reason it appeared that somebody had slept on the side of the bed opposite her husband was that she'd lain there briefly in her gown and robe to watch TV before Ron had returned from the hospital. Tiffany, she'd said, had come in and asked permission to move the TV set to her bedroom.

But now the girl was saying that the TV set had been in her bedroom all along. Mason had pressed Mary Lee as to why she would lie down in the master bedroom if she'd been sleeping with her daughter. Because of the TV, she'd said.

A bit more questioning by Farley established the girl's bedtime at roughly 10:00 P.M. Her father and mother had been watching TV in the den when Tiffany came downstairs to make herself some hot chocolate. She'd talked to her stepfather for a moment about the plot of a TV movie that had confused her, then gone upstairs before the evening news.

"Did you ever see your father after that?" Farley asked.

"Yeah," she said. "He came in. Momma came in and checked on me, and then he came in and he peeked in my—he always peeks in my door—and he said: 'Goodnight, I love you.' And he closed my door, and I don't know where he went after that. I probably fell asleep ten or fifteen minutes after that, because I was real tired."

"What time did your mother come into the room?"

"I don't know . . . ." the girl hesitated. "All I remember is sleeping with her and waking up that morning."

"So after he said goodnight to you, you don't remember what time your mother came into the room?"

"No," Tiffany responded. "She probably would though."

Not until the fifth period of the schoolday, Tiffany told them— roughly 2:50 P.M.—had she been called out of class and given the terrible news. Which meant, Farley realized, that Mary Lee had spent several hours at headquarters until he and Miles finished processing the crime scene, given them an hour-long statement, met with McArthur, and only then decided to call the school.

Like her mother, Tiffany also gave rambling, digressive answers to simple questions. She rattled on about her and her mother's activities on Thursday morning. "Mom had gotten me up . . . ," she explained. "And she had got up, I guess, and she had gone downstairs and got her clothes, and fixed her hair, and put on her make-up. And she had put her make-up in my bathroom earlier that night."

Mary Lee had told them that she *always* kept her make-up in Tiffany's bathroom—that she and her thirteen-year-old shared cosmetics and enjoyed putting on their faces together every morning. Another inconsistency appeared in Mary Lee's story, one apt to impress women jurors particularly. What reason would Mary Lee have to relocate her make-up on Wednesday night? Unless, of course, she knew that the door to the master bedroom would be locked shut on Thursday morning.

Farley betrayed no sign of interest. Mary Lee, Tiffany continued, had awakened her a bit before 7:00 A.M. and told her to dress as quickly as she could. When they found the bedroom door locked, Tiffany had volunteered to open it with an ice pick as she'd done on other occasions. But Mary Lee had said no. If Tiffany scratched the finish, she remembered her mother saying, "Daddy would have a fit. I'll just let him come home and do it."

She did recall noticing her father's service van as they were pulling out of the driveway. "She said something about Daddy's truck being there," Tiffany elaborated, "and I . . . wondered why. And she said, 'Well, probably it had battery trouble.' In fact, he was going to get him a new Bronco or something. We thought nothing of it, and we thought maybe Peter [Zinn] would have to come, because sometimes they come pick him up in Pete's van."

In Mary Lee's statement, Tiffany had been the one who'd suggested battery trouble. Indeed, the girl's switch to what "we thought" made the investigators suspect that she'd been rehearsed. But whether or not she was being deliberately deceptive, they couldn't tell. Like her mother, she'd seen nothing amiss in the house that morning and couldn't remember whether they'd left the house through the front door or the laundry room exit. The harder they pushed her on details, the hazier Tiffany's memory got.

Farley decided to switch gears. "We are going to go back several months," he began. "Have you noticed anything different about your father? Has he been depressed or excitable?"

"Just a little bit upset because of his Dad being so sick," Tiffany answered. Otherwise, no. Nor had she witnessed any arguments between her parents. She knew nothing about her father getting any odd phone calls, and had seen no envelopes or bank bags filled with cash.

Judy Kaye Mason felt ambivalent. Parts of Tiffany's testimony seemed evasive to her. But others had done considerable damage to Mary Lee's story. That the girl had heard no fights and seen no money struck her as very significant. And every teen-aged girl she knew beat her parents to the phone each time it rang.

The deputy prosecutor made a few innocuous queries about what TV shows the girl had watched Wednesday night, then ventured casually: "Where was your mother whenever you asked her if you could have that television?"

"In the kitchen," Tiffany answered.

"Can you remember going in and talking to your Mom while she was in the bed?"

"No."

"Do you think you would remember," Mason asked, "if she were already dressed in her nightgown in bed in her room?"

"Yeah, I probably would remember that. Because . . . I would probably be concerned that she would either be sick, or got what I had—or gotten something."

Mason was satisfied. Like the rest of them, she'd been convinced that Mary Lee had been lying about getting in bed to watch TV in the master bedroom—indeed, that almost everything she'd said about the events of that night was a lie. But she also found it impossible to imagine how, unless Tiffany had been drugged, the child could have slept through the gunshot. Unlike her mother, Tiffany said, she wasn't a particularly heavy sleeper. An unusual noise in the night would have awakened her.

Buddy Miles asked if she thought a shot fired in the house would do the job.

"Oh yes," she responded quickly. "I know I would, because I have ear trouble, and when my Mom and I were out shooting the gun I couldn't stand the sound. It just hurt my ears, and I put my hands over my ears when she was shooting."

Her Mom, of course, had emphasized her ignorance of firearms, though she'd mentioned Ron's efforts to teach her to shoot.

Before Farley turned the tape off, Mason thought of one more area she wished to explore. "Your Mom—you said she was already dressed whenever you got up—when did she promise you to take you out to eat breakfast?"

"Well, we had been wanting to do it for such a long time—since sixth grade. And we'd done it once or twice in the sixth grade, and we wanted to do it when I was in seventh. She said, 'Well, when I get to feeling better—because she's been down a lot with this flu that's been going around—we'll probably go out to breakfast.' And she said

Wednesday night, 'We'll probably go out to breakfast in the morning.'
And I said, 'Oh, OK.' "

In Mary Lee's version, eating breakfast out had been a spontaneous
event, based upon Tiffany's having no appetite for anything her mother
had in the house that morning. Mason asked now if Tiffany was sure.
She was.

Farley too had one more small thing he wanted to know. "Would
you classify your mother a light sleeper, medium sleeper or heavy
sleeper?"

"Heavy sleeper," Tiffany answered. "She sleeps, but when she wakes
up she gets up. And by the time she gets her robe on, you know, she's
just a little bit groggy-like. But she, after that, it takes her about five
minutes and after that she's ready to go."

3

From her window across the street, Diane Kinsolving watched the
coming and going over at 7412 Pontiac all day Friday with growing
foreboding. Natives of the northwest Arkansas town of Bentonville, the
Kinsolvings were even newer to Indian Hills than the Orsinis. They
knew very little about their neighbors. Diane's ten-year-old daughter
Cindy had briefly held hands with Tiffany during a neighborhood
candlelighting ceremony on behalf of the hostages inside the U.S.
Embassy in Iran, but that was the extent of it.

Diane and her husband Michael considered themselves "Bible-
believing Christians." She'd trained as a psychiatric nurse but believed
that her most important job was to stay home and raise her children
right. Seeing Mrs. Orsini sitting outside her house in Mary Jane Murphree's car Thursday morning, she'd approached in the spirit of a
Good Samaritan—a curious Good Samaritan, admittedly, but eager to
help. Finding the woman mute and apparently overwhelmed by grief,
however, made her feel like an intruder and she'd hurried away.

Minutes later, Joyce Holt had come knocking on Diane's door asking if she had a Coke or 7-Up to settle her bereaved friend's stomach.
The two women knew each other slightly. Diane had bought her
drapes from Joyce's shop "The Window Works"—the same way that
Holt and Mary Lee had become friendly. Learning that Ron Orsini
had been shot to death frightened her badly. Things like that just didn't
happen in Indian Hills.

The brief account in Friday morning's *Gazette* had done very little
to satisfy Diane's curiosity. If anything, the story puzzled her even

more. Locked doors, no sign of an intruder? Partly to forestall their fear, she discussed the news account with her son and daughter over breakfast. To her mother's surprise, Cindy volunteered that she'd been sitting up late in her bedroom Wednesday night and had noticed a car stop briefly in front of the Orsini house, then return about five minutes later, moving very slowly.

Soon after the children had left for school, Diane received a phone call from her sister in Dallas. "She just happened to call," Kinsolving remembers. "We were talking and I told her what had happened, what little bit of evidence that was out—that there had been a murder and so far they didn't have any clues as to who had done it. My sister said, 'There will be another person that will surface. That's always the way it is down here.' "

Kinsolving hesitated to call the police about the car Cindy had seen. Probably it had no significance. But suppose it did? She decided to call Joyce Holt for advice. Minutes later she received a call from a Sergeant Farley of the NLRPD. Farley assured her that anything Cindy told them would remain confidential unless and until the murderer went to trial. Despite her misgivings, she'd allowed them to interview the child.

The two plainclothes detectives came to the door a little past four that afternoon. From Farley's point of view, the interview went smoothly. "We told the little girl who we were, and that we wanted to take a statement from her," he remembered. "She says, 'Fine.' We were in the little kitchen area. We set the recorder down, put the thing on, and wham, bam, thank you Ma'am, the little girl says it was a shiny car, real clean, and no noise. Period. That's the end of that statement."

The detectives accompanied Cindy and her mother to the girl's bedroom. The bed was high off the floor and some distance from the window. She showed them where she'd been sitting. Farley and Miles took turns imitating her, and realized that her angle of vision enabled her to see only a narrow piece of Pontiac Drive in front of the Orsini house.

Farley wanted to be sure he had it right. "From the first time you saw the car, how long after that did it return? About how many minutes would you say?"

"About five minutes."

"So in other words, Wednesday night—around 11:30 roughly—was the first time you saw it, and it stayed seven or eight seconds, the light went on inside, it took off, and then a few minutes later it came back and just cruised real slow around the house. It didn't stop?"

"Right."

Until the medical examiner gave them a firm estimate of Ron Orsini's time of death, there was no telling whether the child's statement had any relevance. One possibility, Farley realized as he sat on the girl's bed surrounded by stuffed animals and dolls, was that the dark, shiny sedan belonged to Mary Lee Orsini—the same spick and span black 1978 Chevrolet Caprice they found parked in the garage. From where Cindy sat, she couldn't see the Orsini driveway. But any car backing out of the driveway to head north on Pontiac would have come into view as it stopped to shift gears, then reappeared five minutes later before turning into the driveway from the south. Had Mary Lee taken a little late-night spin in order to ditch the murder weapon? It would bear looking into.

One more thing happened in the Kinsolving household that afternoon that did much to shape perceptions over the coming months. Or at least Diane Kinsolving later testified that it did, and at a time when she'd come to wish she didn't have to. Her neighbors certainly believed her. Buddy Miles claimed that the lady was mistaken.

Before the two detectives left the Kinsolving household, Miles asked to use the telephone. The time was nearly 5:00 P.M., and they were keen to get an official ruling before the medical examiner's switchboard closed for the weekend. Diane Kinsolving had no idea who Sergeant Miles was talking to, but what she overheard upset her terribly. She understood the detective to be betting a steak dinner not only that Ron Orsini had been murdered, but that "the bitch done it." Kinsolving found his crassness appalling, and was equally unnerved that he'd jumped to the conclusion that her poor, stricken neighbor had murdered her husband. She couldn't help wondering whether the NLRPD detectives knew what they were doing, or weren't just a pair of woman-hating rednecks eager to pin the crime on the first person who came along.

Still another consequence of what little Cindy had seen was that her mother was about to make a new friend—an Arkansas "country girl" whose strict upbringing and conservative religious values gave her much in common with the Kinsolvings. That new friend's name, of course, was Mary Lee Orsini.

·   ·   ·

At just about the time Farley and Miles were across the street interviewing Cindy Kinsolving, Mary Lee phoned her banker. Betty

Tucker was still shaken from the jolt she'd gotten Thursday morning, when her call to the Orsini household had been answered by Pete Zinn.

A farmer's daughter from Yell County, Betty took a personal interest in her accounts, and Ron Orsini had been one of her favorites. "Ron was someone that you put your faith in," she remembered. "They seemed to have a family organization down at Central Heating & Air. They worked hard together, and they all worked for the same thing. It was still a young business, still in the borrowing stage. But very successful, trustworthy—good, honest, hardworking people. I had total faith in Ron. Total. There was never a question in my mind."

But problems had developed in the repayment of a ninety-day, $30,000 note Tucker had approved to help the couple swing the deal on their new house at 7412 Pontiac—problems serious enough that when she'd phoned the Orsini home on Thursday morning, her reluctant purpose had been to tell Mary Lee Orsini that her patience had flat worn out.

The loan had started out strictly as a favor for a dependable customer with a temporary cash flow problem, not something on which the bank expected to make any money. If they wanted to buy their dream home at 7412 Pontiac, the Orsinis needed to close a couple of months before the details of a complicated "wrap-around" mortgage contract on the sale of their former home on Emerald Gardens could be worked out. The $30,000 would cover the gap. As collateral, the couple had offered the deed to Julia Hatcher's house, which Mary Lee's mother had signed over to her and her husband. As soon as the Emerald Gardens sale closed, the Orsinis would pay the bank its $30,000 back out of the $40,000 profit they expected to clear.

Since Tucker could foresee no way Metropolitan National Bank could lose money on the deal, she had never asked to see any documentation of the Orsinis' equity in the Emerald Gardens home. "Didn't need it," she emphasized. "I was working with Ron Orsini. Besides, I had collateral with her mother's house." The only oddity had been Mary Lee's insistence that both she and Ron be covered by credit life insurance for the full $30,000. Tucker had tried to persuade her that the policy was expensive and redundant. Should tragedy befall either of them, the sale of the Emerald Gardens house would cover the loan amount. But Mary Lee had insisted.

The note had come due for the first time in October 1980, but Tucker hadn't been alarmed when Mary Lee called to say that the

Emerald Gardens closing was still pending. Tucker extended the note for ninety days. Nor did it alarm the banker to hear the same response in January 1981, although she had no authority to grant a second extension without taking it to the bank's loan committee. She decided to let it lay for two weeks.

Two weeks turned into a month, and more. By early March, her conversations with Mary Lee had grown more frequent and insistent. "The money was supposed to be coming in from Kansas City, supposedly by wire transfer. She told me it was coming in through Worthen Bank rather than the Federal Reserve. How she knew all this without having worked in a bank, I don't know. There were two or three days she told me it was supposed to come in, but it never did.

"I asked the name of the people who were buying the Emerald Gardens house, because by then I really needed to get this loan closed out. She told me she couldn't remember, that it was a very unusual name. That's when I began to wonder and decided to do some checking up on her. Her stories were not adding up."

Tucker was reluctant to call Ron Orsini. As a businesswoman in a predominantly male profession, she didn't want to seem patronizing—and liked even less the implication of dishonesty. She also knew that Ron's father was dying. Mary Lee's frequent, chatty calls gave her regular reports. But she finally saw no alternative. She phoned Ron at work during the first week in March.

"I said, 'Ron, we've got a problem here. I've been told this money was being transferred. It's been two or three days. We've got to do something.' That's when he said, 'Betty, it *will* be taken care of.' I can hear Ron saying that today. It was obvious to me that he was shocked to learn that the loan was still open. I believe he thought it had been paid off."

Mary Lee called Tucker very early the next morning. Now she too had begun to suspect that there was something fishy about the wire transfer from Kansas City. She and Ron were reluctant to involve family in their private business, but they would borrow the $30,000 from her mother. Later on that same day, Ron also called. He asked whether his wife had spoken to Betty that morning about paying off the loan at once. Betty told him that she had. That was all he wanted to know. "I had no more questions," Tucker said. "When Ron said it, I believed it. As long as we had been doing business with him, his word was his word."

The next time Tucker heard from Mary Lee was on March 11. She requested the exact amount of the loan payoff to March 12—as the Emerald Gardens closing would take place late that afternoon. Tucker directed a teller to supply her with the precise figure.

Mary Lee called again at 3:30 P.M. She said she was calling from Beach Abstract, the real estate firm where the closing had been delayed by an error in the contract, which would need to be retyped. Even so, the Emerald Gardens sale would be a done deal within the hour, and she knew Betty would be relieved to have it over with.

Tucker wanted the loan off the delinquent list in time for a morning board meeting, and insisted that Mary Lee bring the money at once. She told her she'd stay at the office late to get it done. Orsini demurred. It was already late, traffic was heavy, and Ron was exhausted from sitting up at the hospital with his Daddy. After cooking him a special dinner, she'd drive over to Little Rock and put the check in the night depository. Then Tucker could debit her account to pay off the $30,000, and split the remaining proceeds into two $5,000 CDs—one for Tiffany and one for Ron's daughter Stacy.

When the check failed to turn up in the overnight depository on March 12, Tucker had begun calling Mary Lee. Mindful of his father's illness, she hadn't wanted to bother Ron at work unless she had absolutely no choice. "I was calling to say *where* is that deposit!" she said.

Pete Zinn's revelation stunned her. "I don't know what I thought when Pete told me Ron had been murdered. I have a family-like relationship with my customers. I wish I didn't. It's just not good worrying about so many people. But we went a long way back—Ron and I."

Mary Lee called a bit past 4:00 P.M. Friday to invite Betty to the funeral. She added that the newspaper accounts were mistaken, that there were definite signs of a break-in. Furthermore, the $40,000 she'd gotten from the Emerald Gardens closing had been misplaced or stolen.

Tucker told her not to worry. All she needed to do was call the abstract company and put a stop payment order on the certified check. "And she said, 'Betty, we closed that house in cash.' " Tucker said. "From right there, I was most apprehensive. I thought, 'Uh-oh!' You don't settle with an abstract company in cash. You just don't do it. Not a single thing she told me added up in my mind. Nothing. I'll tell you, it was kind of scary."

Equally disconcerting was the next turn in the conversation. Doing her best to console the bereaved widow, Tucker found their roles reversed. Betty needn't concern herself about the bank's $30,000, Mary Lee reassured her. The money would be repaid through the buy/sell clause in Central Heating & Air's partnership agreement. With Ron dead, Pete Zinn and Vern Copeland would have to buy up his share of the business.

"She already had it all figured out," said the astonished banker. " 'Don't worry, Betty, there will be plenty of money. You're going to be taken care of by the buy/sell.' She had just lost her husband. She had lost $40,000 cash. But she wasn't worried. She had dismissed it from her mind. There would be plenty of money. Money!"

A normal woman, Tucker believed, would have been close to hysteria. If anything, Mary Lee's abrupt switch from grieving widow to shrewd businesswoman struck her as more disturbing than her account of closing a $40,000 real estate deal in cash.

No sooner had Tucker hung up the phone than her Yell County grit showed through. Surely Mary Lee would soon realize—if she didn't already—that Betty had seen through her. She called her assistant into her office, and they compiled a detailed history of the entire loan transaction—including every conversation each of them had had with Ron and Mary Lee Orsini, listing dates and times. When they'd finished, they made photocopies and put them aside for safekeeping.

Tucker wasn't ready to go to the police. Despite her outrage, she was sophisticated enough to realize that what she knew didn't constitute proof of murder. Before she did anything else, she meant to attend Ron Orsini's funeral—partly to pay her respects, but partly too to see what she could see. She'd been fooled once already; she didn't intend to be fooled again.

. . .

Betty Tucker wasn't the only person to have a frightening conversation with Mary Lee that Friday. Across town in Little Rock's Baptist Medical Center, Bernice Orsini was summoned from her vigil at her husband's bedside to take a phone call at the nurses' station. Bernice had spent most of her waking hours at the hospital over the past few weeks, doing what she could to ease Joe Orsini's suffering. Chemotherapy had left him too nauseated to eat solid food and too weak to lift his head off the pillow. She'd feared the news that his only son had been murdered might literally kill him.

When Bernice told him, Joe had wept for so long it seemed that he would never stop. Later he'd asked for a telephone, and spoken privately with somebody at the NLRPD. "I know who did it," he told her. But he'd refused to elaborate and insisted that Bernice not become involved in the situation, but let the police do their job.

Bernice had a pretty good idea what Joe was thinking. He'd never revealed his feelings to Ron, but something about Mary Lee had made him leery from the start. Although they tended to see Ron and Mary Lee together only at Thanksgiving and Christmas, there had never been any discord between them. Only Mary Lee's refusal to allow Bernice—a realtor by trade—to list or even show the house on Emerald Gardens had caused a problem. The property, Mary Lee insisted, was to be sold by her friend Mary Jane Murphree and nobody else.

Joe had wanted to intervene on Bernice's behalf, but she'd asked him to let it be. There had never been anything but good feelings between her and Joe's children, and Bernice was grateful to Ron and Linda for accepting her into their lives. One lost listing wasn't worth a family feud.

Bernice also knew that during Ron's hospital visits, Joe had often been irritated by Lee's incessant calls. Every few minutes the phone would ring. Would Ron pick up a loaf of bread? When did he expect to be home? It had gotten to where every time the phone rang, Ron would get a sheepish look. "If I had a wife that checked up on me all the time," Ron's Uncle Jim had teased him one day, "I'd wonder what _she_ was up to."

On the phone that night, Lee was quick getting to the point. Although she'd never visited Joe in the hospital, she announced herself most anxious to comfort him. But the nurses had told her that her father-in-law wouldn't talk to her and didn't want to see her. How could such a thing be true?

Bernice explained that Joe's condition was graver than she understood. His doctor had ordered the phone removed and posted a "No Visitors" sign on the door. But surely, Lee insisted, the ban couldn't possibly apply to so intimate a member of the sick man's family as herself. As tactfully as she could, Bernice affirmed that it did. Only she and Linda House were permitted to enter.

"Is it the doctor, Bernice?" Lee hissed. "Or is it you?"

Fear shot through Bernice like an electric current. In effect, Lee's question was an accusation—an accusation that Bernice suspected her of murder. In the space of an instant, Bernice understood two things:

That she *did* suspect her, and that she was terrified for her husband and herself.

But she was telling the truth, and Lee eventually seemed to accept it. The threat vanished from her voice almost as abruptly as it had appeared. Indeed, so rapid was the transformation that had Lee's snarl of animosity been less frightening, she'd have wondered if she hadn't imagined it.

Chapter 4

1

Meanwhile, life in Arkansas went on as usual. Dramatic events in the overlapping realms of politics, religion, and sports overshadowed the slaying of an unknown man. In the legislature, a North Little Rock representative had introduced the "Balanced Treatment of Creation-Science and Evolution-Science Act"—a law requiring public schools and colleges to accord equal time in biology classes to Darwin and the book of Genesis. Public feeling ran very strong. Opponents argued that to pass the law would expose the state to the laughter and scorn of the outside world. Again.*

But the public event that held the vast majority in thrall that weekend was a dramatic win by the Arkansas Razorbacks in the NCAA basketball tournament at Austin, Texas. Trailing heavily favored Louisville by one point, an Arkansas guard with the unlikely name of Ulysses S. Reed had heaved a sixty-foot desperation shot that dropped through the net at the buzzer. Reed's shot—not to mention the spectacle of arch-rival Texas coach Abe Lemons "calling the Hogs" on national TV—set off a spontaneous statewide celebration. The moment would be cherished for years.

---

*The Creation-Science bill passed in the Arkansas House on March 17, 1981, by a vote of 69–18. Signed into law by Republican Governor Frank White, it was declared unconstitutional later that year by a Little Rock federal judge after a well-publicized trial. Among the plaintiffs in the lawsuit sponsored by the Arkansas ACLU were the official representatives of a dozen major religious denominations—including four bishops and a rabbi.

But the frequently televised replays of U. S. Reed's feat would always mean something different to those who loved Ron Orsini. His family and friends spent the weekend cloistered together in their pain and confusion—an isolation made more complete by the fact that their only sources of information were the newspapers and Mary Lee.

Linda House's first inkling that her sister-in-law's story might not be perfectly true came on Saturday morning. She'd been awakened from a fitful sleep by a call from a friend named Joe Childers. Joe had grown up just down the street from the Orsini house. Over the years the three of them had kept the same easy, trusting intimacy they had learned as children.

Joe had some things he wanted to get off his chest. They agreed to meet in Burns Park, a sprawling enclosure along the Arkansas River. Like lovers sharing an assignation, they sat in Joe's pickup as he tried to make Linda face the unthinkable.

"Joe, he was strong—I mean *strong*—in his mind that she had done it," Linda said later. "He was trying to make me realize that the things she had said and done just couldn't be. It just didn't make any sense that, number one, a gun of that size could go off in the house and nobody hear it. . . . I kept bringing up that maybe somebody killed Ron for the money. Joe kept saying, 'Linda, what money? Where did it come from? Who did you hear it from? It all goes back to Lee.' "

But try as he might, Childers could not overcome Linda's reluctance to face the facts. An emotionally intense woman who shared Ron's instinct for privacy, Linda's whole being was wrapped up in her family. And Lee had been more than her brother's second wife. To Linda, she'd been his very salvation after the failure of his first marriage seven years earlier had broken his heart and came close to breaking his spirit.

.   .   .

Ron Orsini had met his first wife on a blind date in Daytona Beach in the summer of 1965. He'd enlisted in the Navy directly out of high school, and had been discharged only a few days earlier. Everything about Ron made him a model sailor. A gunner's mate, he'd spent several months anchored off Vietnam without seeing active combat. But reenlistment had never been in the cards. At heart Ron was a homebody who felt he'd done his duty.

The daughter of alcoholic parents, Linda Deapo had known instability and turmoil in her life. A small woman with dark hair, hazel eyes, and a mobile, expressive face, she'd been attracted to Ron at once. "In Florida," she said, "there's a lot of transient people and they do a lot of drinking. People aren't real genuine. He was so sweet, so soft. Even after our divorce I couldn't say he wasn't a wonderful person."

They dated for two weeks. When Ron offered to pay her way to visit his family, Linda accepted at once and never returned to Florida. Her belongings got shipped by Greyhound. But even in love, Ron was never impulsive. The couple postponed marriage for two years until he found a job with a future. Linda rented an apartment and went to work in a canning factory—an unlikely job for a physician's daughter. Later she became a receptionist in a doctor's office. Ron drove a delivery truck until a family friend told him about an opening at Central Heating & Air.

Even years after his death, Ron's ex-wife could hardly speak of him without tears—as if she had never quit loving him at all. "Ron was sensitive far beyond what you'd think a man could be," she said. "Very sensitive to not hurting other people. Ron didn't have a lot of friends, but the ones he had he really loved. I don't know where it comes from. His sister Linda's the same."

Living with saints, however, can be harder than admiring them after they're gone—often notoriously so. Also, there may have been a bit more Daytona Beach in Linda's own make-up than she'd admitted. After a few years, she found her husband's self-effacement stifling. She felt that he was smarter than he let on, and went out of his way to hide his intelligence. She thought he ought to show more self-confidence and aggressiveness. Grateful for Ron's pride when she earned her nursing degree, she still wished he'd speak up more for himself. Even his neatness caused problems.

"He was a perfectionist," Linda recalled. "I never felt like I was good enough, or did anything good enough. He would send me to the grocery store sometimes so he could clean the kitchen his way. And when I would come back everything would be spotless. He would have even the cans of soup facing outward, and they would all be in order. You'd open up his medicine cabinet and all the labels would be on the outside and everything would be in order—the newer aftershave lotion would be in the back and nothing would be jammed in, like the supermarket. His clothes were always immaculate. It was just amazing.

"His fault," she believed, "was that he was extremely passive. I could run over him. And I did run over him at one point. Then he would get hurt and hold onto it." One of the most damaging fights they ever had was over her smoking. Not long before she left him, Linda had a miscarriage which drove a wedge of hurt between them. "It was like I was bad. I remember Ron crying so hard when I lost that baby, he was so disappointed." Wounded by the blame she saw in his eyes, she did and said things she wished she could take back—things Ron found it impossible to forgive.

Besides separating Ron from his daughter Stacy, Linda Deapo feels guilty about something else that happened after their divorce. Something over which, logically speaking, she had no more control than she did over her miscarriages. She recognizes that her guilt is unreasonable, even irrational. But she feels it anyway. Others who loved Ron blame her too, and think she ought to feel guilty.

The man Linda married, six weeks after her divorce from Ron, was Howard Deapo, a former neighbor. Not long before taking up with Linda, Deapo had broken off with a woman in whom he'd come to see some disturbing traits. Outwardly charming, she lied to get her way, and when doubted clung fiercely to the stories she told—no matter how improbable. Hints of disbelief brought out a vindictive streak that led him almost to fear her. Her name was Mary Myrtle Hatcher. But she called herself "Lee."

·   ·   ·

About two weeks after his divorce, Ron had gotten a phone call from a woman who wanted to meet him. "She told him that she would like to talk to him," his sister, Linda House, said. "That she knew he was married to Linda, who was dating a man named Howard Deapo—and that Lee had dated Howard Deapo. She was in the hospital, supposedly having her sinuses operated on. And Ron went up to the hospital and came home and said, 'Linda, she's a real swell girl. I really enjoyed talking with her.' She continued to call him, and they began dating."

Only days before she remarried, Linda Deapo had come to Ron begging for a second chance. But it was too late. Her ex-husband's heart had gone over to the witty, vivacious woman unfairly abandoned by the man Linda had been dating.

And so had his sister's. "Lee just had a way with her," Linda House said. "You felt comfortable around her right away. You felt like you could confide in her. You felt like she was your friend, and had been your friend forever."

Looking back, Linda realizes that there were many things she never knew about Ron's second wife. Lee almost never talked about her childhood. Neither, for that matter, did her mother Julia Hatcher. Linda and her own mother had gotten the impression that the family had been wealthy and socially prominent when Lee was a little girl, but had fallen somewhat after the untimely death of Mr. Hatcher—forcing the loss of their large cattle ranch in remote, mountainous Stone County.

Ron's new wife, the Orsinis were encouraged to believe, had been married only once before, to a much older officer at the Little Rock Air Force Base. Despite being a single mother, Lee had built a successful advertising career while earning a B.A. in marketing from the University of Arkansas–Little Rock.

Almost nothing about that version of Mary Lee's early life had anything to do with the truth. The Stone County cattle ranch was a fiction. Mary Myrtle Hatcher had grown up in poverty on a remote dirt road outside the crossroads community of Gravel Ridge, not ten miles north of the home on Pontiac Drive.

Apparently the Hatcher family kept pretty much to itself. Verifiable information about her childhood is hard to come by. Mary Lee's father had indeed died when she was a small child. Julia Hatcher had driven a county school bus and worked in a school cafeteria for a time—a job she lost after being wounded in a mysterious shooting when her daughter was about ten. To some of her women friends, Mary Lee would later blame the incident on her brother, and hint at dark family secrets including incest. To others, she stressed her purity and sexual innocence.

The older Air Force officer, however, had been an enlisted eighteen-year-old airman from Kentucky. Mary Lee was sixteen at the time of her first marriage. Far from being callously deserted, she'd married and divorced him twice. Tiffany's father would later confide to a prosecutor that he feared Mary Lee more than any individual he'd ever known.

Likewise, Mary Lee's college degree did not exist. Her formal education ended after she dropped out of Sylvan Hills High School in the tenth grade. Even her advertising career turned out under investigation to be very different from the way she represented it. But nobody in the Orsini family had any reason to be suspicious. What with Lieutenant Jim McFarlane and his wife having decided that what they knew about the woman was none of their business, and no help forthcoming from anybody on the Hatcher side, the Orsinis had taken "Lee" as they found her. And the way they found her was just about perfect.

• • •

So, the harder Joe Childers pressed his suspicions upon her that chilly morning in Burns Park, the harder Linda resisted. Joe did bring up something Ron had once told him concerning the financing of some condos his company had helped build in the resort city of Hot Springs. It was something about double payments, and Ron's suspicion that underworld types from Chicago were involved. Neither of them recalled the details, but they decided to tell the police and let them check it out.

"Joe was sure Lee had done it," Linda said. "There was no doubt in Joe's mind that she had actually pulled the trigger. But I wouldn't hear it. If anything, the reason that he talked to Farley and Miles about the Chicago story was that he wanted to make absolutely sure in his mind that it wasn't true."

But the way Childers went about doing it came very close to landing him on the detectives' suspect list himself.

• • •

When Childers met with Farley and Miles a little past 10:00 A.M. Saturday morning, the detectives had spent a couple of hours running down tips from citizens in Indian Hills who believed that they'd seen suspicious vehicles in the neighborhood. None had checked out. About the best they'd gotten was an excellent description of Ron himself backing his new boat out of the driveway on Wednesday morning.

The detectives were skeptical of Joe Childers's motives partly because of the story he told, and partly the way he told it. As they described it in their written reports, Childers spoke in secretive tones and refused to provide a tape-recorded statement. "Mr. Childers made known to me," Miles wrote,

> that back in December of 1980, he had gone deer hunting with Ron Orsini and others. During the discussions around the camp, Orsini had told him that he felt like that he and his partners in the Central Heating & Air business had been involved with Orga-

nized Crime. Mr. Childers stated that it involved an apartment
house under construction near Lake Catherine in Hot Springs,
and that some way, the company had been paid twice for the job
and that the error was not discovered for some six to nine months,
at which time Ron told him they did correct the error and send
the money that was owed to this Chicago connection back to
them and he felt like that there was going to be no problems. Mr.
Childers did not know whether the amount was $9,000 or
$18,000, but he just felt like this was a connection with some
underworld figures that could be involved in this thing. . . .
Other than that, Mr. Childers could not add anything further
that might be of help in solving this homicide.

Playing games with homicide detectives only works in private-eye
novels. Miles and Farley's instincts told them that either Childers
knew things he wasn't telling, or he was lying. They suspected that the
"Chicago connection" story came straight from Mary Lee. It had all
the earmarks of her style: vagueness, inconsistency, and implausibility.
That made Childers, in their eyes, either her dupe or her accomplice.

By the time Buddy Miles's little wager with the medical examiner
and Childers's Chicago Mob stories got run through Mary Lee's public
relations machine, many in Indian Hills seemed to believe that the
road company version of *The Godfather* had brought a more cosmo-
politan kind of mayhem to North Little Rock. Even the Italian name
fitted: Al Capone, Don Corleone, Ron Orsini. TV and movies had
wised up everybody to the Mafia except the NLRPD, which was too
dumb (or corrupt) to recognize a Mob "hit" when it was looking them
right in the face. Or so Mary Lee led many to believe.

Meanwhile, Farley and Miles had a bit of humdrum, unimaginative
police work to do. With several policemen, they drove back out to
Indian Hills on Saturday with a stopwatch. Starting at 7412 Pontiac,
they mapped every possible route through the neighborhood that could
be driven in five minutes. Then they divided up the territory and
searched every storm sewer, drainage ditch, and wooded patch acces-
sible from the street. They hunted through drainage ditches, and
scouted for tracks leading to two small artificial lakes.

They did not find the murder weapon they were looking for. Not
that afternoon, nor in the many hours Farley put in retiming various
routes, poking around in odd corners, and looking down covered-up
wells over the next few weeks.

2

Ron Orsini's funeral was scheduled for the afternoon of Monday, March 16. Early that morning, Bernice Orsini was again summoned from her husband's hospital bed to take a call. This time, Mary Lee had a plan. She'd hired a private ambulance to carry Joe Orsini to his son's funeral. Bernice's job was to make sure Joe was suitably dressed in time for the ambulance crew's arrival. The widow's demeanor was almost imperious.

"I told her I doubted she understood how sick Joe was," Bernice said. "He couldn't lift his head nor a limb of his body—hadn't been able to for months. She said, 'Nevertheless . . .' and those were her exact words, I'll never forget them. 'Nevertheless, I'm going to have him picked up and taken to Ron's funeral.' "

Bernice held her ground. Joe's doctor, she insisted, would never consent to his leaving the hospital. She couldn't help but be astonished by the younger woman's brazenness. On Friday, Mary Lee had all but accused Bernice and Joe of suspecting her of murder. Now she was handing out orders like the Queen of the Realm—almost as if that conversation had never taken place. The effect was almost as disorienting as intimidating. The ambulance, however, never did arrive.

3

Farley and Miles were sitting at their desks planning their next moves Monday morning when Linda Deapo walked in. She'd gotten the news in a phone call from Mary Lee late Thursday at her job in a Shreveport psychiatric clinic.

"I answered the phone and it was Lee," she said. "She said, 'Ron is dead. They think my brother did it.' It was so strange, so cold. I went crazy, because Ron was like an anchor for me. I got real emotional."

Linda's first instinct had been to grab up Stacy and drive to North Little Rock. But the absence of feeling in Mary Lee's voice had put her on guard, and a couple of phone calls to friends close to the Orsini family convinced her to postpone the trip until the funeral. Then, when Mary Lee called to confirm the funeral arrangements, she'd brought up the possibility of suicide. She'd asked Linda to break the news gently to Ron's daughter, but never asked to speak to the child herself.

How Stacy would deal with her father's death worried Linda terribly.

The last thing she wanted was for the girl to see anything about her father's death on TV. Among her former in-laws she felt keenly the awkwardness of her role. As Ron would have done, the Orsini family was taking it all inside—keeping their thoughts and feelings to themselves. "Nobody would say that they thought Ron had been murdered," she said. "They didn't *know* how he died. But it was suspicious. What did that lead you to believe?"

Stacy had always been a quiet, introspective child almost uncannily like her father. Knowing that the children of suicide victims often imagined themselves responsible, Linda worried that Stacy would be particularly vulnerable to feelings of guilt. Above all, Linda wanted to be able to reassure the girl that her Daddy hadn't abandoned her without a word of goodbye. So she got dressed for Ron's funeral early Monday morning and drove down to police headquarters.

The detectives handled Linda warily, but gently. So far, everything they had learned about the dead man had come from three sources: Mary Lee, Tiffany, and Joe Childers. Each had struck them as deceptive. Where Ron Orsini's ex-wife was coming from they had no idea. What could her angle be? Was it insurance money she was worried about? So, instead of answering Linda's questions directly, they put her under oath and asked some questions of their own.

The last time she had seen her ex-husband alive, Linda told them, had been just after Christmas when she'd picked up Stacy in Texarkana. She'd spoken with him often, however, by phone—most recently only a day or two before his death. In the weeks since she and Howard had split up, Ron had taken to calling Stacy almost every night to check on her well-being.

"I talked with him at length, you know, about how Stacy was doing," Linda said. "He sounded fine. I understand—I talked to Lee and—that there was a suicide thing. But I didn't pick up any sadness or upsetness." She couldn't help but wonder whether Ron had been worried over an additional $45 a month she'd asked to help cover Stacy's tuition payments.

"I assume that what you are telling me here," Miles asked brusquely, "is that you and your ex-husband ended the marriage on a friendly basis?"

"We were able to talk about Stacy," Linda said. She gave an emotional account of how she and Ron—despite her initial misgivings—had worked out one of the first joint custody agreements in Arkansas, and how her ex-husband had more than done his part. How when she needed him, Ron had always been there. How he'd driven the twelve-hour round trip to Shreveport one day just to check out the private school she'd chosen after Stacy's test scores had fallen in a mostly black public school. "The school kept remarking what an unusual relationship Stacy and her Daddy had. The fact that he wouldn't bow out. And he didn't."

"Prior to you divorcing Ron Orsini, did you or he either one know Lee Orsini—probably Lee Milton at that time?"

"I didn't know Lee. I heard of her shortly after the separation," Linda said. "She dated him for two years."

"Now this thing of Ron calling you, or calling his daughter, nightly, how long has this been going on?"

"Since separation," Linda said. "Just to check and see how Stacy was doing."

"How long were you married to Mr. Orsini?" Miles asked.

"It lacked about three months being six years."

"During that six years," the detective continued, "did you observe anything that would lead you to believe he might commit suicide?"

"Of all the people that would commit suicide—I'm a psychiatric nurse—and this is the thing that has me confused. People usually give an indication of some sort. But I never detected anything. In fact, he was a quiet person, worked hard, was always busy around the house. . . . That's the reason why I always thought he and Lee were so ideal. I'm more helter-skelter. You know, if the dishes don't get done, that's fine with me."

"During those last few conversations that you had with Ron, or overheard your daughter Stacy have with Ron," Miles asked, "did you detect any fear or any concern that alarmed you?"

"No. In fact, I was feeling more comfortable with the situation. One of my big fears," Linda admitted, "has always been that Stacy—because they had more money than what Howard and I had. . . . They have a big house, and you know, if you have ever been in it, it's like a museum full of collectors' items. One of my fears was that she would want to go live with them. Since January I have become more comfortable with my daughter. Ron was an important factor, and she loved him. But she also loved me. And I'd finally gotten to where I was no longer fearful of that."

"Now we have spoken of suicide here," Miles said in his soothing way. "But of course this has not been ruled as suicide. Now I would ask you if you know of anyone that had anything against him that would want to harm him?"

Linda could not think of anyone. Ron's relationships with his business partners had always struck her as ideal—as did his friendship with Joe Childers. She knew people were whispering about Ron Hatcher, but she'd never met the man.

"Who notified you of Ron's death?" Farley asked.

"Lee."

That was what Farley had figured. Something about Linda Deapo had irritated him from the start. Here came the ex-wife with the boo-hoo act, a pretty little thing with great big eyes all dressed up for the funeral. And what did she tell them? Just what Mary Lee Orsini told her to tell them: that Ron Hatcher did it. A guy she didn't even know.

"When did she call you?"

"Thursday afternoon. She told me, 'Linda, I'm going to have to tell you something that's probably the hardest thing I'll ever have to tell you—that Ron has been . . .' I think she said, 'Ron has been murdered,' or 'shot.' But I didn't hear that until she said, 'The medical examiner still has his body.' And then I connected."

Farley changed the subject to the dead man's insurance. Linda had knowledge of a $50,000 policy of which Stacy was the beneficiary. Their divorce decree had required that Ron keep it. Otherwise, she knew nothing about her ex-husband's finances.

"Did he make any mention about any trouble between him and Lee?" Farley asked.

"I never detected anything."

Linda couldn't bring herself to tell the detectives about her suspicions regarding Lee. Partly she felt guilty that she'd always resented the woman—even suspected her of marrying Ron out of spite. In ways most men wouldn't notice, and Ron certainly hadn't, the woman had lorded it over her—showing up to pick up Stacy in $400 dresses, implying that she was a poor mother, or insinuating that Linda's moral standards were less rigorous than her own.

"Would you say it was a good relationship between Tiffany and Ron?" Farley asked.

"Gosh, yes," she said. "He always talked favorably about Tiffany. Ron only focused on things like his work and his home. He always had time for Stacy, no matter what. . . . I can't add anything else except that knowing Ron as a father and an ex-husband and a person, I would pick him to be the last one to be a suicide victim."

Neither detective gave her the assurance she was seeking. Linda Deapo would have to await the autopsy report like everybody else.

Their faces blank as masks, they thanked her politely for coming in and showed her to the door.

4

Ron Orsini was buried on Monday afternoon following a simple graveside service at the Little Rock National Cemetery. Located east of downtown off Confederate Boulevard, the cemetery serves as the final resting place of Arkansas veterans dating back to the Civil War. He had once expressed a wish to be buried there. Had it been up to the dead man's mother and sister, there would have been a church ceremony, but Mary Lee handled all of the arrangements herself, insisting that Ron would have wanted the simplest service and the least expensive casket available.

The Reverend James Keith performed the simple burial rites of the Methodist Church over Ron's flag-draped casket. He read from John 14: "Let not your heart be troubled. If you believe in God, believe also in me." Yet even as he delivered a brief eulogy for a man whose steadfastness and humility he'd much admired over the years, the clergyman sensed that his words of comfort and hope were meeting an almost palpable resistance.

Wearing dark glasses and a well-cut brown and beige checked suit, Mary Lee played the scene down to the last poignant detail. But not everybody found her performance persuasive. Linda Deapo resented having Stacy swept away from her to be seated at her stepmother's side while she was relegated to a back row.

"Lee made too big a deal," Linda thought, "out of Stacy wearing Ron's wedding ring and Tiffany wearing hers. She made such a production out of giving Stacy the flag. And she was overly nice to me. Why would she be so nice? The woman didn't like me. She'd called me a whore and a prostitute."

Betty Tucker felt exactly the same. True to her plan since seeing through Mary Lee's story about closing a $40,000 real estate deal in cash, the banker positioned herself at the funeral to observe Mrs. Orsini's every move. After the Reverend Keith's eulogy, a member of the military honor guard which had stood at attention during the service took the flag from Ron's coffin, folded it into a triangle, and handed it to Mary Lee. The widow turned and presented it to Stacy. "It was a big production," Tucker thought. "A big to-do, just like an actress. To me, it was just as fake as it could be. It was that obvious."

After the service, the widow Orsini received callers at her handsomely appointed home at 7412 Pontiac. Mary Lee bustled about greeting family and friends at the door, seeing to it that her guests had plenty to eat and drink, and accepting the condolences of those who had seen in her demeanor at the graveside a moving display of dignity, courage, and abiding love.

After the last visitor departed, Mary Lee suggested to Linda House that they drive over to Baptist Medical Center to visit Ron's father. Linda reluctantly agreed. Like her mother, Linda had staggered through the funeral service in a state of shock. She'd spent most of the afternoon sitting alone with her prayers in the upstairs bedroom where her brother had died. She felt closer to him there. Nobody could persuade her of the terrible things people were whispering. But how Mary Lee could be so animated confused her. "I needed to be away from the crowd," she said. "I didn't want to be around anybody, truthfully. But I didn't want to be around her for sure."

Bernice Orsini had avoided Mary Lee at the funeral service. Badly shaken by her two bizarre telephone conversations with her stepson's widow, she'd returned directly to Joe Orsini's bedside.

"Linda came in to see her Daddy," Bernice said. "She didn't mention that Lee was outside in the waiting room. When we stepped outside the room, Linda said, 'Lee is here. Do you want to go see her?' Cold chills went all *over* me. I just felt something. We were walking up the hall and she was just standing there in her dark glasses that she wore to the funeral. As I walked up to her, I was just going to put my hand on her shoulder. And she drew her shoulder back, and she gritted her teeth and said, 'I'll find out who killed Ron. Even though it might be my brother.' That's what she said. She didn't say, 'Bernice, I'm sorry,' or anything about Joe being so sick. Those were her only words. Linda was standing to the side, so she couldn't see. But you've never seen such a look on a girl's face as the look she gave me."

Linda found her stepmother's behavior mystifying. "I was looking at Bernice and wondering, 'Why is Bernice being so abrupt with her? I can't believe this,' " she said. "Lee went off to use the telephone, and Bernice told me, 'I'm going to tell you right now, Lin. She killed your brother.' And I said, 'Uh-uh. There's no way.' We were in the hallway outside Daddy's room and she said, 'Linda, she killed him,' and I said, 'I will not listen to this. I can't believe you're saying this.' And Bernice said, 'I do not want her going in that room tonight. Joe does not want her. She *will not* go in there.' "

Linda felt driven to choose sides. With her brother gone, her choice lay between trust and suspicion, love and hate. Her heart made the decision. The side she chose that afternoon was Mary Lee's.

• • •

Immediately after the funeral, Ron Hatcher and his wife drove to NLRPD headquarters to make a formal statement. A small, swarthy man with acne-pitted cheeks, Hatcher's only resemblance to his sister was his jet black hair. Under oath, he gave a detailed account of his activities on the night of March 11. Interviewed separately, his wife Marilyn confirmed his story. On the night of the murder, they'd watched a rented video of *2001, A Space Odyssey*, gone to bed around midnight, and driven uneventfully to work in the morning. On the Saturday Mary Lee had accused him of threatening Ron Orsini, he'd been on a camping trip in Missouri and there were witnesses to prove it.

The lawsuit he had in arbitration, Hatcher testified, had been filed to protect his equity in a house Mary Lee had manipulated their mother into signing over to her—property that belonged to both of them according to the terms of their father's will.

"But would that make her mad enough to say something like you killed her husband?" Farley asked.

"That's her way of thinking," Hatcher said tersely. No sooner had he filed suit, he told them, than the bank he worked for received several anonymous phone calls from a woman accusing him of being involved in drug dealing. One call had been taped and played back to him. The voice on the line was Mary Lee's.

As far as Farley and Miles were concerned, they'd narrowed the suspect list to one.

Chapter 5

1

According to what she told confidants, Mary Lee first met the man who would become her lover, adviser, and most persistent defender on the weekend after her husband's death. "The night before Ron's funeral," Linda House said, "Lee told me she had gotten a call from this Dr. Wulz. She said she didn't know who he was, but that he had told her a similar situation had happened to him, and that she'd better protect herself. That, whether she knew it or not, she was in a lot of trouble. I asked her, 'Did you talk to him? What did he mean?' And she said that no, she didn't have time to talk to him. That she would wait until after the funeral. And he sent flowers. She never indicated to me that she knew who he was—never had heard of him at all."

Joyce Holt got basically the same story. So did Mary Jane Murphree. In that version, Dr. Charles H. Wulz, a veterinarian whose North Hills Animal Clinic was located on JFK a half mile from the Orsini home, was unknown to Mary Lee until he read about Ron's death in the *Gazette*—and though a total stranger, recognized in her plight a resemblance to his own.

Dr. Wulz's account of how he came to be involved with Mary Lee differs from hers in just one significant particular. Far from being a stranger, Dr. Wulz had treated the Orsini family cats. "She may have been in my office," Wulz said later, "but I don't think so. Ron always brought them. My impression of Ron Orsini was that he was a heck of a nice guy. Patriotic. Just a good guy." Wulz had hired Ron to replace the clinic's furnace in January 1981, less than two months before his murder.

But even assuming that Mary Lee hadn't known her veterinarian's name, Wulz knew her. He does not recall denying it. Wulz's daughter Tammy was a classmate of Tiffany's. They'd once visited the Orsini home on Emerald Gardens to collect Tiffany for a slumber party in honor of Tammy's twelfth birthday. The girls took ballet together. "I met Lee one time at the dance studio," Wulz recalled. "Men couldn't go backstage during the recital and I didn't have a wife, so she offered to help. So I sat next to her at this recital preparation meeting. I don't remember having contact with her other than that. I probably saw her across the room at PTA meetings."

Years later, Wulz found it credible that Mary Lee hadn't recognized him when he'd rung her doorbell the night before Ron's funeral. Until the summer of 1980, he'd worn a beard, but shaved it for his parents' fiftieth wedding anniversary. If Mary Lee told people she'd never met him, she probably believed it—especially considering the strain she'd been under.

Back in Duncan, Oklahoma, where Wulz came from—a town of roughly 20,000 in the rolling scrub oak, cattle, and oil country about 50 miles from Wichita Falls, Texas—he had awakened in his home on Country Club Road at 6:30 A.M. one morning in March 1969 to find his wife dead in bed beside him. Ann Wulz had been the veterinarian's second wife and his third marriage. Like Mary Lee, Wulz had married and divorced his first wife Earlene twice. The veterinarian had been thirty-eight years old; the dead woman was twenty-nine. Wulz was her fourth husband.

According to reports in the daily *Duncan Banner*, Wulz's ordeal began when he was charged with capital murder on April 11, 1969— roughly three and a half weeks after finding his wife's body. Before having the veterinarian arrested, Prosecutor Joseph Humphrey had been visited by Ann Wulz's mother and sister, who suspected foul play. Wulz contended that it had been the other way around, that an assistant prosecutor had—unknown to him—seen Ann shacked up in a Chickashaw motel and pressed his suspicions upon her family.

Either way, an autopsy by Oklahoma medical examiner Dr. James L. Luke concluded that "there is no question but that the deceased died of asphyxial violence by purposeful compression and obstruction of her airway." Luke deduced that Ann Wulz had been smothered— probably with a pillow.

Refused bond, Wulz spent seven months in the Duncan city jail awaiting trial. The case was heard between October 20 and November 2, 1969, by a jury of ten men and two women. Testifying for the prosecution, Dr. Luke explained that hundreds of pinpoint hemorrhages on the underside of the victim's scalp indicated death by asphyxiation—as did bruises on the interior rear surface of the trachea. "The only way these symmetrical injuries could be inflicted on the back of the airway," the medical examiner said, "is for pressure to be applied from the front."

The prosecution also introduced toxicological evidence showing that Ann Wulz's blood had a high level of phenobarbitol at the time of death—enough to render her unconscious. Both Dr. Luke and Dr. Charles S. Petty, the chief medical examiner of Dallas, Texas, agreed that the fact that the dead woman's lungs had been clear of congestion ruled out the possibility that the barbiturates alone had killed her.

Mrs. A. N. Boatman, Ann Wulz's mother, testified that the veterinarian had kept the older woman copiously supplied with tranquilizers, and had once bought 1,000 1.5 grain phenobarbitol tablets for her elderly father. She described a scene in a Duncan cafeteria after her daughter's death in which Wulz flew into a rage and "became a completely different man" after learning that she and the dead woman's sister had visited the prosecutor. According to the testimony of a woman friend, Wulz had confided that "he felt like he had been slapped in the face. He had just learned that Ann was planning to get married again."

Several witnesses portrayed Wulz as obsessively jealous and bitterly resentful that Ann was running up charge accounts and spending money faster than he could earn it. Wulz had confided to friends that Ann and her sister had been openly running around in honky-tonks with two men. "I'm just a misfit," the dead woman's father said Wulz told him. "Nothing seems to work for me. Ann was trying to get away, and if I'd let her go, she'd be with us today."

Dr. Wulz testified in his own defense for seven hours. He characterized his dead wife as "like a rebellious teenager, ready to walk out at the slightest provocation." Though he never abused her even verbally, Wulz told the jury, Ann spread false rumors about threats and beatings "whenever she wanted an excuse to leave." He claimed that their marital difficulties stemmed from constant "harassment from her mother and sister" after he'd refused to finance his mother-in-law's plan to open a dress shop.

Also testifying in Wulz's defense was a Los Angeles pathologist who believed that Ann's death was probably a suicide caused by acute barbiturate intoxication—"probably," he concluded, only because "no suicide note was left."

The jury stayed out for four days before reporting itself hopelessly deadlocked at 7 to 5. After the judge declared a mistrial, Wulz's father and three uncles were allowed to post a property bond that secured his release pending retrial.

Dr. Wulz's second trial began on April 1, 1970. This time, the prosecution produced a lawyer Ann Wulz had consulted about a divorce a week before she died. Her sister, Norma Sue Deal, testified that Ann had planned to take the children and leave on the morning her body was found. Norma Sue said Ann claimed that her husband had threatened her life and tried to choke her just four days earlier when she'd come home from a dance in the nearby town of Sulphur. Two former employees of Wulz's described him as having a short fuse and a violent temper.

Mostly, though, the issue resolved itself into a contest between dueling medical examiners. Prosecution witnesses contended that although Ann Wulz had a "massive dose" of phenobarbitol in her system, it hadn't been sufficient to kill her—merely to render her near comatose and incapable of resisting. The defense countered with two expert witnesses who testified that Ann Wulz had died of acute barbiturate poisoning, and a psychiatrist who gave his opinion that Ann Wulz's behavior in the weeks before her death indicated suicidal tendencies.

The jury of eleven men and one woman returned a verdict of not guilty after deliberating for two hours. Wulz was a free man. Broke and disgraced, but free. Defending himself had left an $80,000 debt that took him fifteen years to pay off.

Although he harbored bitter feelings against many who'd testified against him, Wulz practiced veterinary medicine in Duncan for four more years. He moved to North Little Rock only when his and Ann's daughter Tammy began school—hoping to spare the girl his notoriety. Eventually, Wulz said, he learned to forgive those whose grief made them susceptible to manipulation by ambitious and conscienceless men.

According to his version of the story—which no evidence ultimately contradicted—Wulz read the account of Ron Orsini's death in the *Gazette* over his Friday morning coffee. To his eyes, the carefully crafted account Sergeant Farley had given the newspapers communicated exactly what the detective intended.

"The clipping in the newspaper," Wulz said, "just set off all kinds of sirens and whistles in my mind . . . I felt like that they'd zeroed in on her already, and I know how they operate. They're not going to look at anything else—not really. So I wanted to warn her.

"But I didn't know her well enough to call her. I didn't feel comfortable picking up the phone and saying, 'Here's what you should do.' I assumed she was innocent, and they were going to pin this thing on her. That's sure what happened to me. So I went on over there Sunday evening and talked with her mother for an hour or two. Lee stayed off in another room most of the time. I spoke with her only a little. I guess she wondered why I was there—what my motive was. Or maybe she was upset about the funeral. I don't know."

Joyce Holt was also there that night, and remembers Mary Lee spending most of the evening in the kitchen talking on the phone. Joyce and Mrs. Hatcher sat listening for a couple of hours while Wulz recounted the saga of his wife's death and his two murder trials.

Holt found the veterinarian an odd bird, and was put off. She never did understand why Orsini took up with him. The good doctor himself, however, was fixing to embark upon yet another adventure in the murky world of crime and punishment, and to meet a lot more cops and lawyers upon whom to vent his spleen. Except that on Wulz's second go-round there would be no doubt of at least one thing: this time he volunteered. Trouble didn't find him; he went looking for it.

2

The investigators spent the week after the funeral learning more about what had not happened to Ron Orsini than what had. Ballistics confirmed what they already suspected, that none of the three weapons taken into evidence at the crime scene had fired the fatal bullet. The slug had come from a Colt .38 revolver with a four-inch barrel— exactly like the gun Ron reported stolen from his locked truck in January.

On the morning of March 18, Mary Lee returned to NLRPD headquarters. Farley and Miles wanted to run her through her basic story again. This time they informed her that she was a suspect. This time, too, Bill McArthur sat in. He hadn't agreed to represent her, but the woman needed his help. Nobody should face questioning in a homicide alone. Bill had seen cops under pressure jump to conclusions; indeed, he'd seen far worse.

Mary Lee gave a smoother performance, calmly recounting her story of an ordinary evening at home. Ron had returned from the hospital around 9:00 P.M., watched TV in the den, and turned in just after ten.

"After you kissed your husband goodnight," Farley asked, "how long before you got into bed with Tiffany after that?"

"I remember going to the restroom, and I don't think I ever went back downstairs. I just got in bed with her."

"Did you ever lay down with Ron?"

"I never laid down with Ron per se, no." Mary Lee answered. "I sat on the side of the bed, on his side of the bed there."

"Did you ever lay down on that bed any time that evening?"

"Yes sir. It was after Ron left and I had taken my shower and Tiffany was downstairs on the phone, and a little TV set that we have that usually sits in Tiffany's room was in the bedroom, and I had just laid down on the bed and was watching TV."

Tiffany had told them that the TV had been in *her* bedroom all along. The discrepancy was hardly conclusive, but the detectives wanted it on the record. Farley's crime scene photos clearly showed the covers opposite the dead man's body turned neatly back and the imprint of a head on the pillow.

Otherwise, they got nowhere. If anything, the suspect gained ground. The missing bags of cash never came up. Mary Lee had never meant to say that she didn't know how to open the bedroom door without a key, only that she'd been afraid to damage the lock. Possibly she *had* told Tiffany they'd go out for breakfast Thursday morning. She couldn't recall. How she'd gotten the Sherwood police she had no idea; she'd dialed zero.

Unable to dent Mary Lee's composure, Farley asked her bluntly: "Did you kill your husband?"

"No sir."

"Did you fire the gun that killed your husband?"

"I don't know what gun killed my husband."

"Did you ever wrap a towel around the gun that may have killed your husband?"

"I don't know," she hesitated. "Are you saying that one of his guns killed him?"

"I'm not saying that. Did you ever wrap a towel around the gun that killed your husband?"

"I don't really know how to answer that because I don't know that I ever wrapped a towel around . . . I don't . . ."

"Yes or no?"

"She can't answer that," McArthur said evenly. "Ask the question more properly and maybe she can answer it." He turned to Mary Lee. "I think what he's asking is did you wrap a towel around this gun to shoot your husband?"

"No."

"Are you part of any conspiracy to kill your husband?" Farley asked.

"No."

"Would one of your close friends be in on this conspiracy to kill your husband?"

"Don't answer that," McArthur told her. "That question is sort of like 'Do you still beat your wife?' Do you deny any conspiracy that involves you to do anything to your husband?"

She denied it. Apart from her brother, she could think of nobody who held a grudge against Ron.

Only Judy Kaye Mason got anywhere. "When did you move your make-up from your bedroom to your daughter's bedroom?" she asked.

"Okay. This is something that I have been thinking about since then, and I asked my daughter. There was my make-up in both our bedrooms, and I didn't put make-up on that morning because I occasionally will fall asleep and not wash my face. That night I went in and just put mascara on that morning. I got to thinking [and] I asked her if she remembered me putting make-up on and she said, 'No Momma, you didn't.' So what make-up I had on was what I had on, you know. I just had on my face the night before."

"You took a bath and didn't take it all off?" Mason asked.

"No. I don't wash my face in the bathtub." If Tiffany told them she'd removed her make-up, she insisted, Tiffany was mistaken.

Mason thought that was a lie. Minutes ago, Mary Lee had taken a shower. Now it was a bath. Besides, a woman like her would climb into bed with a snake before she'd sleep in her make-up. "She's the kind that'd have four pounds of grease on her face—wrinkle cream, all that stuff," Mason said later. Any woman juror would see right through her. Getting Mary Lee indicted, however, was a different matter. The investigators hadn't gotten even a step closer to that, and they all knew it.

Bill McArthur knew it too. Naturally the wife had to be a suspect. But based upon Tiffany's statement and what he'd just heard, the lawyer wondered if the NLRPD had any evidence at all. It sounded to him like they were grasping at straws.

· · ·

Interviews with Ron's business partners that morning yielded little evidence. But the man the detectives heard about hardly sounded like the victim of a criminal execution. Pete Zinn and Vern Copeland had detected none of the anxiety Mary Lee told them about. "Ron was just about the same all the time," Pete told them. "He was a quiet person, which everybody can verify, and he didn't discuss his private life with us at all. I couldn't detect any changes in the way he did his job. He was as conscientious as ever—the most conscientious person I've ever met."

Zinn explained that the financial misunderstanding Joe Childers had told the detectives about involved only $1,500, and had been settled two years ago. The owners of the Hot Springs condo were Arizona airline pilots, not Chicago gangsters. He offered to have the firm's CPA verify his memory.

Contrary to Mary Lee and Tiffany, Zinn had never picked up Ron for work. Until March 12, he'd never seen the house on Pontiac. Vern had come for Ron a time or two back on Emerald Gardens. But that had been because the house sat on a hill too steep to negotiate on snow days. Vern met him at the bottom.

Like everything else Ron did, he'd kept his truck in tip-top shape. Had it ever failed to start, he'd have repaired it at once. Nor could Pete imagine Ron taking extra jobs on the side. It would have been like stealing from his partners. Besides, he'd had no time. But suppose he had? Farley asked.

"I've been in the business twenty years now," Zinn answered." I've owned—or owned part of—Central Heating, and I don't have $40,000. There's no way." As for $80,000, that was nuts.

Strange phone calls? Nobody remembered any. Evelyn Daley answered the phones at Central Heating. "Personal calls?" she said. "No. Lee was the only one that would ever call."

· · ·

Any lingering doubts the detectives may have had were dispelled by their interviews with Mary Lee's two best friends—Mary Jane Murphree and Joyce Holt.

Murphree responded to a subpoena on the afternoon of March 18. A red-haired, full-faced woman in her early forties, she made an ideal confidante for Mary Lee. Born in Louisiana, Mary Jane had an alcoholic father who couldn't keep a job. The family stayed broke and on the lam from creditors, shifting from town to town in Louisiana, Arkansas, Oklahoma, and Missouri like Gypsies. She'd attended sixteen schools in twelve years. Often warned as a girl to hide her real name and address from strangers, she'd retained a lifelong taste for intrigue—as well as an abiding conviction that people's private lives were rarely what they seemed. Subjects like astrology, numerology, and psychic phenomena fascinated her.

Like the others in whom Mary Lee confided, Murphree knew nothing about her except what she was told. She'd barely met Ron Orsini. Almost since their friendship began just six months ago, Mary Jane told the detectives, Mary Lee had been filling her ears with tales of Ron's odd behavior. Murphree had urged her to hire a private detective. Ron's death shocked but didn't entirely surprise Mary Jane—though she'd been highly agitated ever since.

Murphree showed up at NLRPD headquarters carrying several pages of notes. She ticked items off a list one by one. At their one meeting during a small New Year's Eve party at 7412 Pontiac, Mary Jane thought Ron had seemed nervous and ill at ease. He'd hardly spoken. Mary Lee had taken her into the bedroom that night and shown her an envelope full of cash, and what she said was an expensive diamond necklace Ron had bought her. "I couldn't tell you if it was in one-dollar bills or million-dollar bills, because money is people's private business," she said. "But it was new money, new bills. I remember that."

"She never made all of it visible to you?" Miles asked.

"No, no. Just showed me the fact that it was there."

Mary Jane had lots to say about threatening phone calls. In fact, she'd received a few herself since the murder, which made her uneasy about having her statement recorded. She told the detectives about a clandestine meeting under a railway overpass between Ron and two men driving what looked to be an unmarked police car. Though Murphree had warned her not to, Mary Lee had followed her husband to the rendezvous.

Ron's health was another mystery. He'd been terribly ill in January. "He went to the doctor," Mary Jane said. "But he never gave her any of the results of what he found out. And she asked him and he told her, 'Well, it was nothing.' Well, anybody who swells up all over, that's not nothing. You have to understand that everything I'm telling you are things that she told me. So she called the doctor's office and they wouldn't tell her anything. Maybe nerves caused it. I don't know."

Mary Jane told Farley and Miles the same "Chicago connection" story they'd heard from Joe Childers. She'd gotten it from Mary Lee. Another time, Murphree said, "Lee called me at home one day just hysterical, absolutely hysterical. A man had called and his voice scared her to death and she told him Ron was not there and he started cursing her and telling her she better get him to the phone. And she called Ron at work and he told her to get out of the house and do it right now!"

More recently, Ron had become so disturbed by threatening phone calls at work that he'd left his beeper at home. One day Mary Lee had managed to scribble down the last four digits of a phone number left by an abusive caller, and the two women had searched the realtor's criss-cross phone directory for every address in Little Rock the call might have come from. Against Murphree's advice, Mary Lee had called them all, but learned nothing. "I don't remember how long ago she said that he had started sleeping with a gun," Mary Jane said. "But it scared her to death. I think it would've literally put me out the roof."

To each tale Miles responded, "Again, this is something that Lee Orsini has told you? Not Ron?"

"That's right."

"And you have no personal knowledge, then?"

"No. I saw nothing," Mary Jane admitted, although their skepticism made her furious.

They heard the same song, second verse, from Joyce Holt on March 19. Holt had also met Mary Lee through her business, "The Window Works." Having recently moved to Arkansas from Nashville, Holt had gone through a bitter divorce. She had few friends in town. An outgoing, talkative woman with a daughter Tiffany's age, she seemed to welcome the attention.

The Mary Lee whom Joyce knew was charming, witty, and did her many small kindnesses—took the kids for ice cream, brought them presents, and did more than her share of car-pooling. And told the most fascinating stories. Though she privately considered Mary Jane a bit of a kook, Holt particularly liked stories about the treachery of men. And Mary Lee Orsini was never dull. In retrospect, Joyce realized, "I was incredibly *dumb* and naive. I was a sitting duck. I was living in this little cocoon. I wasn't out socializing and didn't know anybody who knew Lee. Any name she would bring up, I wouldn't know them. I was like a blank deck of cards. She could play me any way she wanted to."

The more he listened, the more incredulous Farley got. The Holt interview was like an instant replay: phone calls, bags of cash, secret meetings—the whole nine yards. In Joyce's version, Mary Lee supposedly found $50,000 cash in Ron's dresser drawer on February 3. She remembered the exact date because she'd finished hanging the bedroom drapes that day and presented Mary Lee a bill for $4,407.

"I never gave her a bill in Ron's presence," Holt said, "because she didn't want him to know how much she was spending, which is not unusual. That happens in a lot of houses. She came by the next day and gave me $300 cash. She had to transfer money to get the rest of it, and I remember joking, well, all she had to do was get it out of the drawer."

"But you, yourself never saw this $50,000?"

"No."

"Did she ever tell you who she figures killed her husband?"

"No. Mary Jane and I both had just assumed that Ron was into something more than he could handle. We knew from conversations with Lee—which we had no reason to doubt, because Mary Jane and I have talked a lot. She has told Mary Jane some things she hasn't told me, and told me some things she hasn't told Mary Jane, but we have found no discrepancies. There's nothing that contradicts what she has told either one of us."

"Would you feel like that maybe," Miles asked, "that Lee Orsini has been using you two to build this story in case it needed to be told?"

"No," Holt said firmly. "We've thought about that—naturally talked about it between the two of us."

"Do you think Lee Orsini is capable of killing her husband?"

"Nothing I have seen leads me to believe that."

Had Farley and Miles felt free to spell out their scenario to Joyce Holt, she might have told them about the loud thump on the roof that awakened her at 11:45 P.M. the night Ron was shot—a noise so startling on a clear, windless night that she'd gone outside in her robe to see if a tree limb had fallen. None had. Joyce lived on Geronimo Circle, about a five-minute round trip from 7412 Pontiac.

· · ·

Buddy Miles won his steak dinner bet with Dr. Fahmy Malak. On March 20, the medical examiner announced officially that Ron Orsini's death was homicide. The issue had never really been in doubt. Faced with the absence of a weapon, a negative trace metal finding on the victim's hands, and Farley's crime scene photos, Malak had little choice. He estimated the time of death as a half hour to an hour after the victim had last eaten. Since Mary Lee and Tiffany were the only ones present at Ron's last meal, however, a degree of imprecision remained.

Later that day, the detectives moved a step closer to establishing the time of death. A neighbor located at 1704 Osceola—directly behind the Orsini home—told them that she and her husband had been startled by a loud noise on March 11, while they sat in their den watching the Tom Snyder show. The den was located at the end of the house opposite the Orsini home, and the windows were closed. The woman wasn't certain it was a gunshot she'd heard, nor could she specify the exact time. But her husband had checked to be sure that their doors were locked shut and none had slammed. A subsequent call to the TV station established that the segment the couple had been watching had aired between 11:36 and 11:43 P.M.—just about the time Cindy Kinsolving had seen the car from her bedroom window.

Farley and Miles spent the rest of the day talking to boat dealers. Two checks totaling $2,700 for Ron's boat and motor had bounced—and neither of the men who had sold him the equipment could believe that the amiable fellow who had written them, then returned twice to buy accessories, could have been aware that his checking account was empty. Nor could they imagine that Ron killed himself. Who pays cash for a brand new Mercury 9.8 Electric Start, then goes home to put a gun to his head? Nobody, the detectives assured them. Nobody at all.

Not everybody who knew Mary Lee, they began to learn, found her nearly so persuasive as Mary Jane and Joyce did. Several of her old neighbors on Emerald Gardens described her as a chronic liar. She'd tried to default on a student loan from a secretarial school by lying about her identity; told vivid tales of fatal auto accidents that never happened; attempted to bluff her way into the Air Base PX by posing as a war widow. More to the point, Farley and Miles compiled a list of several persons to whom Mary Lee had confided that Ron Orsini had been diagnosed with terminal bone cancer.

It was all very interesting, but practically useless. Odds were that a judge would rule even the cancer story immaterial. Many people lie and fantasize about their private lives; very few are murderers.

• • •

Linda House came to NLRPD headquarters on the afternoon of March 24. At first, the detectives got nowhere with her. Ever since her meeting with Joe Childers, Linda had known somewhere back in her mind that Mary Lee's account of her brother's death didn't add up. Joe and Bernice Orsini's suspicions affected her too. But she and her mother had been unable to make themselves face the implications. When Farley asked, she described Ron and Mary Lee as the ideal husband and wife.

Tentatively, Linda even raised the "Chicago connection."

"Have you talked this over with Pete Zinn?" Miles asked.

"Lord, no! I haven't even talked to Pete Zinn. The only thing Pete Zinn has said to me was that he was sorry . . . I don't know Pete. I don't know Vernon. I do feel like that if it *was* something like [the Chicago connection], Pete or Vernon neither one is gonna come out and say anything. Because they're probably protecting themselves and their family."

Miles told her that the audited company records showed that the matter had involved $1,500 and had been cleared up two years ago. "We've been over that thoroughly, and we're convinced that he was not killed by a Chicago connection. There's just no way that we can see it. Now we've asked you a lot of questions here. Is there anything that we have not asked you that might assist us in finding who killed your brother?"

"Everything you've said," Linda began, "it sounds like to me it's leading back to Lee. You have to know Lee. She's the happiest she's been in years. They had everything going for them. I mean Ron loved her and she loved him."

But no, she couldn't imagine how her sister-in-law could have slept through the gunshot that ended Ron's life. Nor could she picture her brother writing two hot checks for $2,700. Lee had given her an explanation—something about forgetting to transfer money from one account to another—but even as House recited it, she realized that she didn't believe it.

"Did Lee Orsini ever make the statement to you," Farley asked softly, "that your brother was dying of terminal cancer?"

"No."

"Would it surprise you that we have a list of about five people she told it to? Would that surprise you?"

"Yes, it would."

They asked her if she had any questions.

"Who do you suspect?"

"Lee Orsini," Miles said. "That's who we suspect. I know it shocks you, but everything points to her, Ma'am, everything."

"I don't understand how you can say that!"

"Ma'am, you haven't been with us these two weeks. That's the reason you don't understand. All you're hearing is what Lee Orsini wants you to hear, Ma'am."

"You know . . . I mean . . . I believe . . ." Linda stammered. "If you think it's Lee Orsini, she would have to be the best actress in the whole wide world, and she would have to be a psycho."

Once the dam was broken, Linda had scores of questions. Farley and Miles laid out their case for her in as much detail as she seemed able to stand. Some of it was unbearable. Lee had falsely told her, for example, that Ron's body was bloated with decay when she found it. But Linda couldn't rest until she'd heard it all.

Long before they finished, Linda *knew*. Everything the two policemen were telling her was the truth; everything she'd ever known about her beloved brother's wife was a lie.

Only last night Mary Lee had called. Supposedly she'd just discovered that Ron had taken out a credit life policy on the mortgage at 7412 Pontiac. Remembering Ron's thoughtfulness, the two women had cried together. Now Linda recalled a talk with her brother just before the couple bought the new house. Having worked in a mortgage department, Linda thought credit life was a ripoff. The premium stays the same for thirty years, but the payoff declines. Ron had agreed.

None of them had been able to figure out where all the money was coming from. They didn't know Ron's exact income and had no idea of Mary Lee's—but since moving into the house on Pontiac she'd been spending at a prodigious rate. "Here she was in a brand new house," Linda said later, "twice as big as the old one. She was putting new wallpaper in, new paint, new drapes. . . . You could walk into that house and feel nothing but elegance: Duncan Phyfe furniture, Ethan Allen, beautiful leather recliners. She even wanted a Cadillac.

"We felt like it was coming from her job, Mother and I. She'd be here, she'd be there. She would go to sales conventions at the big hotels. She would be off to the Governor's Ball. Ron stayed home. My brother would have been content with a simple life. Anything he bought, he wanted to pay cash for it. He would have been a nervous wreck if he'd known he had that much debt."

Later on, Linda would learn that her brother had a mild confrontation with the credit manager at Dillard's department store in December. "Do you know me?" Ron asked. The startled man admitted that he didn't. "Then why would you sell my wife $20,000 worth of furniture? I wouldn't lend *myself* $20,000."

Linda left NLRPD headquarters in a daze. On her way home to Cabot, she picked up her ten year-old daughter. "Do the police know who did it?" Kelley asked.

Before she could think, Linda blurted out the truth. "They think it was Aunt Lee."

"Do you think so too?"

"Yes, baby, I do."

Kelley curled into a ball on the back seat and cried all the way home. When they walked in the front door about 6:00 P.M. the phone was ringing off the wall. Mary Lee was on the line—highly agitated and demanding to know everything the police had asked her, and how she'd answered. Linda's knees went weak. She felt as if she might throw up.

She said she felt sick and hung up. Sergeant Farley had warned her that her family's safety depended upon treating Mary Lee as if she knew nothing and suspected less. But Linda wasn't up to faking it yet. It wasn't until she got to the office the next morning that Linda learned that Mary Lee had telephoned for her there not five minutes after she'd left to meet the police. And had kept calling and calling every ten or fifteen minutes all day long.

•   •   •

Over the next two weeks, Farley and Miles came as close to hitting the jackpot as they ever would. Two days after meeting with Linda House, the detectives walked into the Metropolitan National Bank in southwest Little Rock carrying a letter from Bill McArthur entitling them to examine Ron and Mary Lee Orsini's records. For good measure, they took along a subpoena.

Betty Tucker was relieved to see the policemen. The more she'd learned from Pete Zinn and Vern Copeland, the more certain she'd grown of Mary Lee's involvement. Even so, she'd hesitated to make the first move. Impressed with the detectives' professionalism, Tucker told them all she knew.

The banker laid out the documents and notes she'd kept in safe-keeping since her bizarre phone conversation with Mary Lee on March 13. She showed them a copy of the overdue $30,000 note covering the down payment on 7412 Pontiac, as well as the deed on Julia Hatcher's house that secured it. She explained how she'd caught Mary Lee in a flatfooted lie about receiving $40,000 cash from Beach Abstract, the real estate company. Unknown to Mary Lee, the credit life policy she'd insisted upon had expired when the note went delinquent.

And the detectives told Tucker something she hadn't known. The closing at Beach Abstract hadn't taken place on March 11. Instead, it had been three months earlier, on December 12. Every one of the elaborate tales about delayed wire transfers and mislaid documents that Mary Lee had recounted to Betty over the past three months had been a fabrication. Similarly bogus, records showed, was Orsini's distress over having supposedly written a bad check on March 11 to pay off her car loan. In fact, she'd retired the auto note back in December too—on the same day she'd deposited $7,607 in her checking account.

When Farley and Miles walked out of Metropolitan a couple of hours later, they felt a new sense of optimism. It had taken them over two weeks of spinning their wheels, but they'd finally found their motive. Ron Orsini hadn't died for love, he'd died for money—the second oldest reason in the world. Betty Tucker would make an ideal witness. Everything about the banker bespoke her credibility. Articulate, well organized, and unafraid, Tucker had no ax to grind. It was still a circumstantial case, but suddenly it looked much stronger.

Armed with subpoenas, the detectives spent the next several days rounding up and poring over the records of several accounts in three different banks on both sides of the Arkansas River. Devious as she was, Farley began to suspect that Mary Lee wasn't half as smart as she thought. She'd insisted that Ron handled the family's financial affairs. But everywhere they looked, it was Mary Lee. Compared to some of the forgers and embezzlers he had encountered, her schemes betrayed an almost childish simplicity—as if it had never occurred to her that anybody would come checking. She'd left a trail through Metropolitan Bank that stood out like a cowpath to a salt lick.

Whatever else may have incurred his wife's wrath, it became clear to the detectives that in signing the agreement to buy the house on Pontiac Drive, Ron Orsini had signed his death warrant. The evidence strongly suggested that Mary Lee had been taking active steps to profit from her husband's death since at least July of 1980, when she'd been quite adamant—a loan officer at First American remembered—about buying a $100,000 credit life policy to cover the purchase. The very policy she'd called Linda House about. The one she'd supposedly just discovered. The one they'd cried over. The one with Mary Lee's signature on the application form.

A visit to Beach Abstract yielded more damning evidence. Not only had the Emerald Gardens closing taken place on December 12, but Ron hadn't been there. Mary Lee had handled the transaction alone, using a "power-of-attorney" document signed by her husband, who'd been off at deer camp. Agent Julann Maness recalled that Mary Lee had pushed hard to close the deal that week.

Maness affirmed what the detectives already knew: that Beach Abstract *never* settled real estate closings in cash. She produced records showing that a certified check in the amount of $7,607 had been written to the Orsinis on December 12—far less than the $40,000 equity Mary Lee had claimed, and exactly the sum deposited in their checking account at Metropolitan days later. When he got his hands on the check itself, Farley's practiced eye told him that Ron Orsini's endorsement had been forged. Together with a small second mortgage, the Orsinis' equity came to $11,000—$20,000 shy of the amount needed to satisfy Metropolitan Bank.

Producing her appointment book, the agent showed them that at no time on March 11 had Mary Lee visited Beach Abstract. Maness would have remembered, she said—since Mary Lee had called her out of the blue back in January mentioning Ron's odd behavior, and asking for advice about private detectives. Mary Lee had also dropped by after the murder on March 24, ostensibly to borrow the phone. When she'd failed to complete her call, she'd kept trying and had hung around the office chatting. Linda Deapo, she'd confided to the flabbergasted woman, was trying to get her greedy little hands on Ron's life insurance—ostensibly on Stacy Orsini's behalf. But Mary Lee planned to reopen Ron's divorce settlement. Her dead husband had given his first wife too much equity in the house they'd owned, and Mary Lee meant to get her hands on it.

Farley and Miles could visualize every aspect of the crime except its central mystery: Had Mary Lee pulled the trigger alone, or did she have help? But one thing became clearer all the time: Had Ron not been murdered on the night of March 11, all hell would have broken loose on the financial front. The combined cash assets in all Orsini accounts on the morning of March 12 came to less than $15. The couple's savings account at Commonwealth Federal S&L had bottomed out at $5 in September 1980 and stayed there. Their checking account held $8.52, with Ron's two checks for $2,700 yet to be presented for payment.

The move to 7412 Pontiac Drive had more than doubled the Orsinis' mortgage payments, to $770 a month. The Dillard's furniture payment added another $903. Including life insurance premiums, the family's fixed monthly payments came to just over $2,000—this *before* they bought groceries, gasoline, clothing, or paid the phone and light bills. All this on Ron Orsini's take home pay of $568 every two weeks—or roughly $13,000 a year.

True, Mary Lee had brought home $27,000 in commissions from her own job selling advertising specialties in 1980. But that was before deducting expenses and withholding taxes. Records at Hometown Advertising showed that Mary Lee had all but quit working in 1981—telling some business associates she needed to care for her terminally ill father-in-law, others her terminally ill husband. She owed the firm $4,000 advance money.

The bottom line was that had Ron Orsini gotten out of bed that morning, Betty Tucker's call would have alerted him to the fact that he was virtually bankrupt. Within twenty-four hours, the $2,700 checks for the boat and motor would have bounced. Ron may have been a bit naive, but he was nobody's fool. Once violated, his trust would have been impossible to regain. Deliberately and systematically, Mary Lee had painted herself into a corner. The numbers told the story. Altogether, had everything gone according to plan, the widow Orsini stood to realize a profit of roughly $350,000 by her husband's death.

•   •   •

Farley now warned Bill McArthur that Mary Lee could expect to be arrested at any time during early April. Whether or not he could make good on the threat was for her to worry about. Theoretically, the detectives could bust her on their own authority if they thought they could show "probable cause"—enough evidence to convince what the law called "a prudent person." But in practice, they'd be foolish to make a move without a warrant from the prosecutor. Besides eliminating the need for a probable cause hearing under Arkansas law, a warrant guaranteed the prosecutor's full cooperation. Without it, they could end up whistling Dixie. Judy Kaye Mason was solidly in their camp. But Mason was also a rookie. The elected prosecutor for the 6th Judicial District was Wilbur C. "Dub" Bentley. As a retired military man—he'd been an Air Force lawyer for many years—Bentley was known as a stickler for details. And on a case of this magnitude, Dub would want to make his own decisions. No prosecutor appreciated having his hand forced by overzealous cops.

They were still hoping that Orsini would panic and do something dumb to strengthen what was an entirely circumstantial case. The detectives had several indications that the pressure might be getting to her.

Soon after meeting with Linda House, for example, Farley and Miles had taken statements from the attendance clerk and school nurse at Central Junior High. Both women thought that Tiffany and her mother had been acting oddly. Normally chatty, energetic, even "hyper," in their words, Tiffany hadn't been herself on the morning of March 12. Both women had been worried about her.

"She was very quiet," the nurse said. "Very unlike Tiffany, very subdued. I had talked to her mother about her blackout spells and her dizziness and I thought okay, maybe she's frightened. I don't feel like, in my professional opinion, that any drugs had been administered. Her gaze was perfectly normal, there was no slurring of speech, her pupils reacted equally. Other than being extremely, extremely quiet, she could be perfectly normal."

But "normal" wasn't a word either woman would have applied to Mary Lee. Attendance clerk Jan Agee had always found her odd. Unlike most parents who called to report children's absences, Mrs. Orsini had a habit of going into detailed, dramatic recountings of Tiffany's symptoms—as if Agee were an intimate friend. Except that they hardly knew each other.

Mary Lee had phoned the school on March 13. "I just wanted to tell you why Tiffany is not in school today."

"Lee, we're all aware of why Tiffany is not here," the clerk replied. She offered to help any way she could.

"Tiffany is very concerned about what the kids are gonna think," Mary Lee said. "We just want it known that it was definitely not suicide. It was murder. I know they're saying that there was no evidence of forced entry, but that's a lie. There's very much evidence."

But what really got the detectives' attention was a story Tiffany told when she returned to school after the funeral. She would have to miss gym class, the girl reported. "I don't have a PE suit," was how Agee remembered it. "The police think that my mother took a towel and wrapped it around the gun and shot my Daddy, and the PE suit was in the dirty clothes and they scooped it all up together and it's down at the police station."

It had been Agee's first encounter with the girl after Ron's death. So she was quite sure of the date, March 17—almost twenty-four hours *before* Mary Lee had been pressed about the towel.

Pete Zinn and Vern Copeland had also grown leery of their partner's widow. A couple of days after Ron's funeral, she'd summoned Pete to 7412 Pontiac to have a look at the furnace. He found that the unit had simply been switched off. Mary Lee asked him to climb into the attic to have a look at some new evidence that the NLRPD had overlooked. Pete found a trail of deep footprints in the blown insulation leading across the floor. Mary Lee had deduced that Ron's killer had hidden there. She insisted that Pete telephone Sergeant Miles.

Told that Miles had checked the attic March 12 but seen no footprints, Zinn grew wary. The ones he'd seen stood out like fresh tracks in the snow. Miles warned him not to visit Mary Lee alone. After talking it over, both partners decided not to visit her at all.

As an afterthought, Miles asked Pete and Vern why Ron might have kept two dozen prophylactics hidden in his bedroom. They had no idea. One of the few intimate things they knew about Ron was that he'd had a vasectomy. They knew because—perfectly in character— he'd insisted upon coming in to work that day. He'd limped around like a saddlesore cowboy, and taken a lot of kidding.

•   •   •

On Wednesday, April 1, the detectives turned the pressure up another notch. The *Gazette* had done a follow-up story. The page 3 headline read: VICTIM REPORTED THEFT OF GUN BEFORE DEATH, POLICE AT NLR REPORT. Once again Farley, identified as "a police spokesman," had told the newspaper exactly what he wanted Mary Lee to read. The stolen pistol, the *Gazette* reported, was "the same caliber and brand of gun that is believed to have killed Orsini. Police said there was no sign of forced entry to the truck." The NLRPD planned to use divers to probe nearby lakes for the murder weapon. NLRPD detectives, the *Gazette* reported, had "interviewed 20 persons, and probably will interview another seven or eight." Repeating a thumbnail version of Mary Lee's basic story, the paper noted that "there was no sign of forced entry to the house and nothing was missing." A clever sixth grader could have drawn the obvious conclusion: the wife did it.

Within days, the publicity paid off. The manager of a North Little Rock carpet-cleaning establishment told of a bad experience he'd had with the Orsinis in January. The man told the detectives exactly what he'd told a suspicious Ron Orsini. Nobody from his company had stolen $1,300 cash from the bedroom at Pontiac Drive, because nobody from his company had been inside the house since November. The young man whose business card Mary Lee had shown her husband had not only been a trustworthy employee, he hadn't worked there since Thanksgiving.

The young man himself came to NLRPD headquarters to give his version under oath. He'd prepared an estimate for Mary Lee in November, left his business card, and never heard from her again. Farley called Pete Zinn, then checked Mary Lee's bank statements. Sure enough, $1,300 had been Ron Orsini's Christmas bonus. On the same day Ron had confronted the carpet cleaners and filed a formal complaint with the prosecuting attorney, Mary Lee had deposited $1,300 in cash in her personal account. So now they knew where the dough she'd shown Mary Jane Murphree on New Year's Eve had come from too. Irrelevant and immaterial from a legal point of view, perhaps, but fascinating all the same.

A second witness, Jack Carpenter, managed the Park Hill Station Post Office. On Wednesday, March 10, he said, Mary Lee Orsini had inquired about the procedure for having her mail delivery stopped. She and her husband, she'd explained, needed to take Joe Orsini to Houston for cancer treatments.

A few days after Ron's murder, she'd dropped by the post office. "She very briefly gave me a rundown on the fact that she had taken a lie detector test," Carpenter said. "She had demanded it. Also that the two guys working on the case were ding-a-lings and weren't getting anywhere. She asked me if I'd come out Saturday and she'd fix a sandwich for me . . . I told her I'd come out, but of course I didn't." Feeling he was being offered more than lunch, Carpenter stayed away.

The ding-a-ling detectives liked the sound of the latest story. Not only hadn't Mary Lee taken a lie detector test, the NLRPD didn't own a polygraph. The machine they did use was a Voice Stress Analyzer, and she hadn't gone anywhere near it.

Poking the hornet's nest, however, also turned out to have unintended consequences. On the same day the *Gazette* story appeared,

Julann Maness of Beach Abstract was locking up for the night when she saw Mary Lee parked in front of the building in an unfamiliar silver car. A bit later, the same vehicle materialized behind her at a stoplight. Mary Lee shadowed her and her companion most of the way home. Catching the woman's eyes in the rearview mirror, Maness felt a shiver of fear. Orsini stared fixedly ahead like a cat watching a bird through a window, her pale eyes showing neither recognition nor acknowledgment. Had Maness been alone, she told the detectives later, she might have panicked.

. . .

Unknown to the detectives, something else may have gotten started that same night. Close to midnight, Mary Jane Murphree was awakened by a call from Mrs. Hatcher. She said her daughter had gone out hours ago to run errands, and had never returned.

"She wanted to know if Lee was at my house," Murphree said. "I said she wasn't. Mrs. Hatcher was just frantic. So I called Joyce. Joyce said, 'No, she's not here, but I bet I know where she's at.' So Joyce got in the car and drove down to Wulz's house. I didn't even know Wulz existed. Joyce called me. Lee's car was at Wulz's house. Joyce confronted Lee about it the next day. And that's when she told us that Wulz had seduced her, that she had been in bed with him about two weeks after Ron died."

Asked much later, Charles Wulz denied it. "She came knocking on my door," he said. "McArthur had told her that she might be arrested, and she'd decided maybe I knew what I was talking about. We had about a two-hour visit about what had happened to me and was fixing to happen to her."

From what Mary Lee told Wulz, the NLRPD had botched the investigation and decided to pin the killing on her. It seemed utterly fantastic to him that the weeping housewife he'd met at PTA meetings and ballet recitals could be capable of murder.

Apart from their mutual interest in her case, the veterinarian maintained, he never particularly liked Mary Lee. Nevertheless, they began to spend more and more time together. "I became very interested in the case," Wulz explained, "partly curious and partly defensive about how the criminal justice system operates. So one thing led to another for about a year."

Exactly when that happened, Wulz can't recall. As for that particular night, two weeks after her husband's murder, Wulz puts it this way: "I know that we talked about attorneys. I have a pretty jaundiced view of attorneys and I was saying to her, 'What do you know about this McArthur guy? You're hiring this guy you don't even know. Is he any good?' 'Well, he's got a case coming up down at the courthouse,' she said. 'Let's go watch him.' "

Chapter 6

Evidently, Wulz and Orsini liked what they saw. The trial they watched during the first week of April 1981 was a relatively straight-forward affair—an armed robbery and shooting in Little Rock's black East End. Like the vast majority of criminal cases, there wasn't a particle of glamour or intrigue: only folly, rage, and sorrow. Later on, neither McArthur nor Chris Piazza, the talented young deputy pros-ecutor who opposed him, could recall much about it. Only that the prosecution had won, as the prosecution usually does. Even so, the time was coming when McArthur would be thankful for Piazza's judg-ment, skill, and courage—when Piazza would hold McArthur's fate in his hand.

Dr. Wulz did not accompany his new friend to Bill McArthur's office in Little Rock's Quapaw Quarter, a few blocks east of the Gov-ernor's Mansion. The lawyer shared offices with his partner Jack Las-siter in a converted residential building at the corner of Broadway and 20th. Shaded by massive pin oak and pecan trees, it was a neighbor-hood of huge nineteenth-century homes currently undergoing a re-vival. The two-story brick building McArthur shared had mullioned windows and a half-timbered second floor.

McArthur's impression was that the threat of arrest had made Orsini more indignant than afraid. She informed him that she'd already hired the Fred Myers Detective Agency to perform the investigation that the NLRPD had bungled. Her impulse was to counterattack vigorously—an unlikely strategy for a guilty client, McArthur thought.

But the attorney came to no immediate conclusion. "It was," he said later, "an unusual set of circumstances, highly unusual. A fascinating case. The basic facts of her story never changed. Right away, there were two or three things I'd have had difficulty explaining to a jury, because I had trouble explaining them to myself."

Mary Lee and Tiffany's ability to sleep through the blast of a .38 caliber pistol being fired worried McArthur. What bothered him even more was Orsini's putting on dirty clothes that morning rather than simply opening the bedroom door, particularly since her husband's service van was sitting in the driveway. "The stuff she told about the money and the briefcase? Hell, that's out of some book or TV show," McArthur said. "Here's a guy that made less than $20,000 running around with hundred-dollar bills stacked in a briefcase? I doubt it. Especially when I couldn't find out anything about him that would make him do that."

Indeed, there were times when he questioned his client's emotional stability. He'd asked her pointblank if she was guilty. "Absolutely not," she'd said, and she couldn't have been more vehement. "In my office Mary Lee Orsini was always this wide-eyed—either panicky or angry—lost human being. This person who's been thrown into a set of circumstances that she can't cope with, that she doesn't understand, and she wants *out!*"

Accepting a $1,000 cash retainer, McArthur agreed to take the case. It was the kind of case no halfway ambitious defense lawyer could afford to turn down. Within a day or two, McArthur got a call from Linda House, imploring him to do all he could for her embattled sister-in-law. He promised to do his best. Unknown to him, Mary Lee was listening in on an extension in Linda's office. Ever since Linda's meeting with the NLRPD, Mary Lee wouldn't leave her alone. Sergeant Farley had urged her to keep acting as if nothing was wrong. But Linda was finding it harder and harder to do.

"While I was at work," Linda recalled, "she was just continuously calling me. Every forty-five minutes, every hour, the phone would ring. And everything was drastic. 'I've got to talk to you.' Her voice would get down real low and she would whisper. 'I've got to talk to you. Get away from work. You've got to meet me somewhere. You won't believe what's happened.' And automatically I'd just fall right into it, just like it was true. She had me running all over town. And in the back of my mind I knew that it was a big farce. She's got the ability to sway people, sway your mind."

On the same afternoon that Linda called McArthur, Mary Lee persuaded her to dial Pete Zinn too. "Every time I think about it," Linda said, "it just makes me sick. I pumped him for information. 'What do you think, Pete? Where do you think this is gonna end?' Of course he immediately got off on Lee, with her on the other line. Scared me to death. I said, 'Pete, I've got to go.' And I hung up the phone. I was just shaking. I went home that night and called him. I said, 'Pete, you're not gonna understand this. I don't understand it.' But I told him she was on the other line."

Linda never warned McArthur. In fact, the two never spoke again. Linda saw Mary Lee's attorney as a member of the enemy camp. As far as Bill knew, the Orsini family stood behind his client 100 percent.

• • •

The first thing McArthur did on Mary Lee's behalf was to pay a call on Prosecutor Dub Bentley. Since Mrs. Orsini hadn't been arrested as Sergeant Farley had warned, it figured that Bentley had some doubts about the case the NLRPD had brought him. As far as Bill knew, the NLRPD still had no witnesses and had yet to produce a murder weapon. "My intent," McArthur said, "was to convince Dub not to file charges just to be filing charges . . . I was trying to counteract the pressure I knew he was getting from the NLRPD."

A large, shambling bear of a man, with powerful shoulders and an ample paunch, Bentley was halfway through his second two-year term. He had a reputation as a cautious and methodical prosecutor—a product of both his nature and a long military career. A native of Texarkana, Bentley had enlisted in the Navy directly out of high school during World War II, gone to law school on the GI Bill, then joined the Air Force—entering as a sergeant and retiring in 1970 as a lieutenant colonel.

Those who came to judge Dub Bentley on the basis of a TV image saw a rumpled, countrified old boy—a courthouse hack, he appeared to some. But while Dub was drawling, Dub was thinking. His speech belied a keen mind with a great capacity for detail. Bentley had served as prosecutor, defense counsel, and judge in hundreds of court-martials. He'd been Chief of Civil and International Law for the Armed Forces in Japan, and Judge Advocate at Pleiku Air Force Base in Vietnam. By the time Bentley retired, he was Chief of the Torts Section in the Air Force's Litigation Division in Washington, D.C.—a formidable military bureaucrat, and nobody's fool.

· · ·

McArthur's instincts proved correct. Only weeks earlier, Dub's chief deputy had lost a highly publicized murder trial—a Manson-like slaying of an elderly Little Rock couple. The acquittal had stunned everybody on the staff, an experience none of them cared to repeat. And not simply, or even mostly for political reasons. To the prosecutor, every innocent verdict meant that somebody had gotten away with murder.

Under Arkansas law, Bentley had great discretionary power. Unlike many states and the federal system, a grand jury indictment is not needed to bring a felony case to trial. The decision rests with the prosecutor alone. And, cautious as always, Bentley was reluctant to make a hasty move. The prosecutor had read the case file carefully. He agreed that the NLRPD had sufficient probable cause to arrest Mary Lee, but not enough to convict her. He declined to issue a warrant and urged the detectives to work harder, dig deeper. Meanwhile, there could be no harm in listening to what McArthur had to offer.

Indeed, what McArthur offered Bentley was more than the prosecutor had any reason to expect. He volunteered to bring his client to the courthouse and let Dub judge for himself. "It's unusual," McArthur explained, "for a defense attorney to take his client over to the prosecutor and say, 'Here she is, talk to her.' To say, 'Hey, if you're vacillating, sit down and talk to her. Ask her whatever you want to.' "

True, there was a small tactical advantage in it for McArthur. From the questions that Bentley asked his client, he could get a better idea of where the investigation was headed. But if the prosecutor were to charge her, he'd get the entire case file on discovery anyway. And the risk to his client was grave. But Mary Lee presented herself as eager to confront the accusation head on. She had all kinds of things she wanted to say.

The meeting took place a few days later in Bentley's office at the Pulaski County Courthouse—a huge, high-ceilinged chamber on the fourth floor of the massive limestone pile on Markham Street, a block south of the Arkansas River. Immediately before talking to Orsini, Bentley met with Sergeant Farley. The detective had one significant bit of new evidence. The trace metals man at the State Crime Lab had gotten the bright idea of holding the confiscated chisel in his hand and gouging a piece of wood. Then he tested his own hand. Traces of iron showed up in the same pattern found on Orsini's hand. He'd also found traces of aluminum on the chisel, and iron on the aluminum door molding the NLRPD had removed from the laundry room door— evidence she'd faked the break-in herself.

Wary of Mary Lee, Farley had taken to hiding his case file when he left headquarters at night. "So I'm sitting there talking to Dub," he remembered, "and McArthur sticks his head in the door and asks if we're almost ready for the meeting. I said, 'What meeting?' Turns out Dub's set one up with McArthur and Orsini. 'Give me some legal advice,' I said to Dub. 'Do I have to talk to her?' 'Well, no,' he says. 'Then I'm going to be a real horse's ass,' I said. I was going to prove to her that she wasn't going to manipulate me—find out what I had and tailor her testimony to it." The meeting went on without him.

McArthur thought that his client handled her interview with the prosecutor exceptionally well. The session lasted nearly two hours. "I bet I didn't say five words," McArthur said. "She did all the talking. Very few clients would I allow to do that. But then most are not as insistent as she was."

Unlike her first interview with the NLRPD, Orsini remained composed and even witty throughout. Her basic story remained intact, and to her attorney, at least, relatively plausible. Sure, her financial situation was bad. But if carrying life insurance was evidence of murder, the police would have to investigate every death on the obit page.

Once again, McArthur saw nothing like the kind of evidence needed to make a murder charge stick. More important, neither did the prosecutor. Bentley found Mary Lee's tale of sleeping through the gunshot so hard to credit that he went home and fired a .38 out his own bedroom window. The concussion left his ears ringing. But even though Bentley avoided ticklish areas such as Betty Tucker's testimony to protect the banker's safety, he tended to agree with McArthur: the case just wouldn't make.

"I kindly felt like she did it," Bentley said. "But I wasn't real sure. Lee—and everybody who's had personal dealings with her is going to tell you—she's a very persuasive lady. She's very intelligent, extremely cunning. I felt like we needed to run it by a grand jury, hoping to further develop the case. I thought I might put her on the stand and get more information."

For the time being, Bentley kept his intentions to himself. "You gave me something to think about," he told Mary Lee as she left. Within hours, she was telling Joyce and Mary Jane that the prosecutor had told her he'd never in his life seen such a slipshod investigation, and that he and McArthur would see her through the ordeal. The women saw no reason not to believe her.

•   •   •

Meanwhile, Detectives Farley and Miles weren't exactly running out of gas, but they were getting low on new leads when the psychic showed up. Like all well-publicized murders, the Orsini case had attracted its share of crackpots. But the woman who presented herself in Homicide one morning in April came recommended by a Little Rock banker whom Farley respected. Besides, they'd scoured every ditch, drainpipe, and hole in the ground in Indian Hills without finding the Orsini murder weapon. What did they have to lose?

Anyhow, the woman was a real looker and wore skin-tight jeans and a sweater. So the three of them piled into the department's surveillance van and they drove her by 7412 Pontiac one morning. The psychic claimed that she saw a vision of Mary Lee letting a man wearing a policeman's star into the house and waiting with Tiffany while he murdered Ron. She asked to touch Farley and Miles to assure herself that they weren't the culprits.

Strictly Looney Tunes, Farley thought. Next the psychic announced that she saw the gun underwater. So they drove her to a nearby lake. As she climbed out of the van to explore the shoreline, Miles took a long, appreciative look. When she got out of earshot, he whispered to his partner.

"She's got a hell of an ass on her, hasn't she?"

"For Godsake, buddy," Farley said. "She's a mind-reader."

For the rest of the morning, the two detectives could hardly look at each other without cracking up like high school kids. All the way back to headquarters, they had to strain to keep straight faces. If the murder weapon was underwater, it stayed there.

•   •   •

On a balmy Saturday a few days later, Farley was hoeing his neglected rose bushes when he got the odd sensation that he was being watched. He turned and found himself looking into the pale blue eyes

of Mary Lee Orsini. She'd pulled her car onto the grassy strip in front
of his house and was staring at him with a look of pure hatred. How
she'd gotten his address, Farley never learned. It was supposed to be
confidential information. In his gym shorts, Farley climbed to his feet
and began walking toward her car. With a mocking smile, Mary Lee
slipped the car into gear and drove off.

Farley slammed the hoe to the ground, went inside, and strapped on
the biggest gun he owned: a .357 magnum target pistol with a six-inch
barrel. He felt like a fool, but he was damned if he'd be intimidated.

•   •   •

On April 12, a month to the day after his son's murder, Joe Orsini
died. Mary Lee stayed away from Joe's funeral. Indeed, she hardly
mentioned his death to Linda House. However, one night later, she
called Linda to say that a Sergeant Mallett of the NLRPD had called
to tell her that a black man had been arrested and confessed to the
murder. "Immediately I jumped on the phone and called Farley, after
I *knew*!" Linda said. "She was capable of telling you something to
where you're questioning, you're saying to yourself, 'Could this be?' I
knew that she was the cause of my brother's death. I *knew*! But I still
jumped on the phone and called Farley. She told so many stories, it
got to where it was 'If you don't believe this one, I'll give you something else to think about.' " For Farley, that was an easy one. Bill
Mallett had made no such call.

In early May, Linda House came home to find that an intruder had
broken into the house while she and Buddy were at work. "Whoever
it was," Linda said, "did not take one thing. Buddy had a Seiko watch
laying on the dresser, worth $300. There was money lying on Kelley's
dresser that was not taken. Every mattress, every drawer, everything
had been turned over or torn up."

Unsatisfied with a cursory investigation by the Lonoke County Sheriff's Department, Farley asked the state police to fingerprint the house.
They found nothing. Mary Lee pumped Linda for every last detail. By
then, she was no longer blaming her brother Ron Hatcher for the
murder. "She kept on throwing in the Mafia," Linda said. "Big black
cars and hit men." Mafia in Arkansas? You had to drive to St. Louis
for a good Italian meal.

Besides Mary Lee's constant phone calls, Linda House's family began to receive hang-up calls day and night. To leave the phone off the

hook would cut Linda's lifeline to her mother, Gladys Orsini. Alone among Linda's intimates, only her mother refused to accept the idea of Mary Lee's guilt. Regardless of what Buddy and Linda said, nothing could persuade the older woman to confront the facts. Once when her mother came out to Cabot to visit, they persuaded her to close herself in their bedroom while Buddy fired a .22 rifle out the back door.

"My God," Linda said. "You could have heard it two miles off—a .22! And he came back in there and tried to explain to her. That's not half the gun that was fired." But Gladys wouldn't budge. And since Mary Lee also phoned Gladys every day, as much as it pained her, Linda began keeping secrets from her mother, too.

· · ·

Toward the end of May, events were conspiring to force Linda into the open. Dub Bentley had finally notified the NLRPD that he would be putting the case before the grand jury. Exactly when remained uncertain. Mary Lee, of course, claimed that she'd insisted on a grand jury investigation all along, but Linda knew better. Sergeant Farley assured her that her testimony would be kept confidential, but she wasn't sure she believed him. Mary Lee had ways of finding things out.

Linda also expected to testify against her sister-in-law in a civil lawsuit. Ron's ex-wife Linda Deapo had retained an attorney on her daughter Stacy's behalf. In their divorce settlement, Ron had agreed to maintain a $50,000 life insurance policy naming Stacy as the beneficiary. The money was to assure the child's college education. When Ron's will went to probate, it turned out that he'd changed the beneficiary on the policy to Mary Lee, and named her as executor. As reluctant as Linda Deapo was to appear the greedy ex-wife—and still less to provoke Mary Lee—she felt compelled to act on her child's behalf. Linda House feared that if she took Stacy's side it would tip her hand.

Whatever the cause, Linda finally snapped. "I just couldn't stand it any longer," she said. "I had had the course with her. I was tired of being harassed—going outside looking under my damn truck for bombs, and looking in my rearview mirror for people following me, and coming home and my house being torn to shreds, and phone calls in the middle of the night. I was just sick of it. And I didn't care any more. I got to where I couldn't care less if she walked through the door and blew me away. If she was gonna have me done, I wanted it done right then. The scared was out of me. I was mad.

"And I never will forget that night. She'd called, and my husband was standing in the kitchen with me and I said: 'Lee, I'm gonna tell you what. If it takes everything I've got, everything I've ever lived for, I'll see that they put the person that killed my brother behind bars.' And I said: 'They know who it is.' There was dead silence. Just dead silence for a long time. Finally she came back and she said, 'I've got to hang up, Linda.' "

The daily phone calls from Mary Lee stopped for good, though hang-up and heavy-breathing calls came even more frequently.

The next time Linda visited the cemetery, her father's grave had been desecrated. Joe Orsini's tombstone had been pushed over and broken to pieces. His photograph had been mutilated and the sod ripped up. They tried to tell her it was teen-age vandalism.

Chapter 7

1

What fascinated Bill McArthur about the Orsini case would have fascinated any ambitious criminal defense lawyer. It was the same thing that fascinated the police: the difficulty of knowing exactly what had occurred inside 7412 Pontiac on the night of March 11, 1981, much less why.

Over the years, McArthur had worked out his own method of persuading his clients to deal realistically with the evidence against them. "If I don't believe their testimony," he said, "I'll do everything I can to tear it down before we ever get to trial. I say, 'You're paying me—or supposed to be paying me—for representing you. And I don't believe you. How do you expect twelve strangers to feel about it? People who aren't getting paid?' "

From the beginning, however, Mary Lee's story transcended ordinary categories of truth and falsehood. Unique in McArthur's experience, she seemed actually to thrive under the pressure of a homicide investigation. Rather than keeping still as he advised, she would begin a vigorous and noisy counterattack.

Even before she retained McArthur, Orsini had hired a private eye—the Fred Myers Agency, the same one she'd had consulted in January and again in early March. The bulk of their report consisted of rehashing her tales. Two investigators spent a week chasing them down. Like the NLRPD detectives, they came up empty.

Buried on page 31 of Myers's report, however, were two seemingly trivial bits of information that meant nothing much to her lawyer, but would have fascinated the NLRPD detectives if they'd thought of the angle themselves. The family physician who'd examined Tiffany on March 10 had found no physical cause for the dizziness she complained of, and prescribed no medication. At the Parkhill Pharmacy, just one prescription had been filled for the Orsini family during February or March, that for the lady of the house on March 3. Written for Mary Lee months earlier by a different doctor, it was for Dalmane, a sleeping pill whose side effects are dizziness and nausea.

The Myers firm was soon out of the picture, however. As long as Mary Lee was a suspect in the murder, the insurance companies holding policies on Ron Orsini's life refused to pay. Mary Lee, in turn, failed to pay the private detective, and about the time McArthur took the case, Myers dropped it.

No matter. McArthur had a man of his own, Jim Lester, a retired state cop and, the attorney believed, the most talented criminal investigator in Arkansas. The two had met when Lester was the lead prosecution witness in the case of a Black Muslim accused of slaying a retarded white boy in rural Pulaski County. McArthur won an acquittal, the only time in Lester's career as a homicide investigator that he'd ever testified on the losing side.

But the investigator ran into trouble with Mary Lee right away, and the more he saw of her, the more uneasy he got. Her basic demeanor struck him as wrong. Instinctively, he felt a hollowness about her, as if there were something missing in her soul—an emotional frequency on which she could neither send nor receive. "She was just so brazen in a quiet way, that you knew what she felt," Lester put it. "Lee Orsini's *will be done.*"

Lester's conviction grew even stronger after Mary Lee failed to pass first one, then two lie detector tests McArthur arranged for her to take. In Arkansas, polygraph results are admissible in court only by agreement of the prosecution and the defense—in practical terms, almost never. Like most defense lawyers, McArthur doubted their reliability anyway. If the test gave him something to support his client's story, so much the better. Like most cops, Lester believed lie detectors when they indicated guilt. When they didn't, he wondered how his suspect fooled the machine.

Either way, the results left plenty of room for interpretation. According to the examiner, Mary Lee answered no to every one of a series of eight questions about her husband's murder—disclaiming any knowledge of the crime. But she registered as deceptive on the very first: "Do you know who fired the shot that caused the death of Ronald Orsini on Wednesday night, March 11?"

The operator repeated the test, with the same result. But what did it mean? Even psychologists who trust lie detectors warn that such "consistently inconsistent" results can't be taken literally—only that *something* had triggered the anxiety that registered on the machine. It didn't worry McArthur much. He'd never believed that Mary Lee was telling all she knew. His job was to defend her against a murder charge, not to solve the crime.

Despite his position as a member of the defense team, Lester became determined to do exactly that. His insistence created some friction between him and McArthur—at first merely an intensification of a longstanding philosophical debate. "Jim told me from the very beginning," Bill remembered. "He said, 'She's guilty as hell. She's absolutely guilty as hell.' He and I would sit and argue about it for hours. I'd say, 'Fine. Tell me why. Where's the evidence?' He'd say, 'She's just crazy. She did it. And she's gonna get away with it. You're going to get her off. And then she's gonna do it again.' "

Late one May afternoon in McArthur's office, Lester pushed beyond what the lawyer considered legitimate bounds. "I almost got her, got inside her," Lester said later. "She almost told me the truth. We sat in Bill's office. She *haunted* that office. Everybody was gone for the day. When five o'clock came, Bill went home to Alice McArthur. I don't care who was there, or if there was more work to do, Bill would do it at home. So that particular evening, Orsini and I were left there together. I sat behind his desk and she in front, and I *almost* psyched her out.

"My strong suit was always interview and interrogation. I played the father confessor. I could almost convince you to tell me that you did what you did, through a kind, loving, understanding approach. A lot of eye contact, and right and wrong. And the Lord, always the Lord. You've heard of police brutality? I was brutal backwards."

In the face of Lester's insistent questioning, Mary Lee shook all over and broke into tears. But he didn't break her. "She calmed herself and reverted right back to the Satanic devil-murderess that she was," he said. "I wasn't just pretty sure she'd done it, I'd have bet my *life* that she'd done it. With or without help. To me it's the same."

When Lester told McArthur, Bill became furious. If Lester *had* conned Mary Lee into a confession, it would have put her lawyer into a terrible ethical bind. Because Jim was an employee of the law firm, any confession he obtained would have been bound by the attorney-client privilege. McArthur couldn't disclose it to anybody, particularly not the prosecution. To do so could mean disbarment. Yet neither could he put on perjured testimony, nor withdraw without tipping the other side that he'd learned something incriminating to his client.

McArthur made it clear that if Lester was determined to continue his career as a homicide detective, he'd have to find another employer. Not long afterward, he left the case—partly because Mary Lee made her hatred of him increasingly clear, and partly because it began to appear that he too might never get paid.

.   .   .   .

On Saturday, May 30, a star was born. The press discovered Mary Lee Orsini, and Mary Lee Orsini discovered the press. An arresting photograph of the distraught woman looking beseechingly toward McArthur appeared on the top left-hand corner of the *Arkansas Gazette* front page. The headline read: DAUGHTER OF SHOOTING VICTIM GETS STEPMOTHER REMOVED AS EXECUTRIX. It was a classic example of the picture making the story. Had Mary Lee been plain as a mud wall or the photograph less dramatic, a few paragraphs buried on the inside pages would have sufficed. The accompanying article quoted one of Stacy Orsini's attorneys to the effect that Mrs. Orsini was "a prime suspect" in Ron's death. Apart from looking dashing in profile, McArthur was not mentioned in the *Gazette* article. He had no role in the lawsuit, and showed up only because Stacy's attorneys had subpoenaed the NLRPD detectives.

A fuller account appeared on the front page of Sunday's *Gazette*— WIDOW TELLS OF PROBES IN SHOOTING DEATH; CASE MAY GO TO GRAND JURY. Both the police *and* Mrs. Orsini, it was reported, had asked the prosecutor to put the case before the grand jury. "Mrs. Orsini suggested that a 'hit man' might have killed her husband, although she didn't specify why she believes that." The newspaper recounted Mary Lee's story, including her assertion that despite what the NLRPD was saying, "big pry marks" had been found on the laundry room door.

In a same-day interview in the rival *Democrat*, Mary Lee portrayed Linda Deapo as a scheming shrew who was manipulating young Stacy to get her hands on her late husband's estate. According to the account, Linda Deapo had supposedly told Mary Lee that "unless she gets what she wants, I'll never see Stacy again. She has a lot of gall and

maybe tremendous greed." Less vividly, Deapo's lawyer denied that
she sought personal gain.

In the weeks that followed, nothing McArthur told her could keep
Mary Lee away from reporters. "Every time I turned around she was
giving an interview," he said. "I chewed her ass out so many times for
talking to the press. All of a sudden here she was exposed for public
view. People wanting to talk to her, people willing to listen to what she
had to say. My conclusion was that she had learned to love the attention. Just about the time you believed she wanted out, she would start
stirring it up again. Suddenly she was the star."

McArthur had good reasons for his warnings. Trying a murder in
the newspapers set in motion a process impossible to control. The press
had its own priorities, having nothing to do with his client's well-
being. But Mary Lee's ambitions had broadened. She wasn't going for
"not guilty." She was going for heroine and martyr, too. Once she got
started, McArthur may as well have walked two blocks north of the
courthouse and urged the Arkansas River to run uphill.

2

Early on the evening of June 8, Linda House got a disturbing phone
call from her aunt. Something was wrong with Gladys Orsini. Exactly
what, her aunt couldn't say. But her voice had sounded odd on the
phone, and she'd seemed frightened.

"I picked up the phone and called Mother," Linda said. "I could tell
something was wrong. I said, 'Mother, is there someone there?' 'Yes.'
'Who is it, Mother? Can you talk?' She said, 'No.' "

Linda jumped in her car and raced to North Little Rock. "When I
got there," she said, "the front door was open. I walked in, and Mother's sitting on the couch. And you could not see the white of her face
for blood. She was cut up at the scalp line, and it ran down. Her head
was swollen out to here, and she's just sitting there on the couch. I like
to have fell back through the door. I don't know how I stayed in
control, but I did. And I said, 'Mother, I've got to call an ambulance.' "

An NLRPD patrolman described the scene upon arrival in his report:

> I observed the victim laying in bed with a large cut and swelling
> on the right side of her forehead. The victim stated that she did
> not remember how she received the injuries. Upon further in-

vestigation I observed a large amount of blood on the rug in the living room. There was also blood spattered on the tablecloth next to the bloodstains on the rug.

While the attendants for the ambulance service was [sic] examining the victim, they found scratch marks on the victim's right arm. And the victim's fingernails were broken with blood under her fingernails. The victim, while being examined, stated that the injury occurred at approx 4:30 P.M. and that there was someone else in the apartment with her, but she refused to identify that person. There was no signs of a struggle inside the apartment. The victim refused any medical treatment and refused to go to the hospital.

At Linda's insistence, the patrolman sent for Farley and Miles. By the time the detectives arrived, Gladys Orsini was no longer sure that anybody had been in the apartment with her. But the more they looked around, the more puzzled the detectives got. There were no signs of forced entry, and Gladys Orsini's statement to Linda—that she'd walked in after work and been assaulted from behind—didn't square with the evidence. The victim was wearing a nightgown, and her dinner was in the oven, burnt to a crisp. Her refusal to be hospitalized made a rape investigation impossible.

Reassured by an NLRPD patrol car that swung by every twenty minutes, Linda stayed with her mother all night and took her to have her wound stitched in the morning. Sergeant Farley managed to keep the incident out of the papers. He figured he owed the poor woman that much.

Gladys Orsini moved up to Cabot with Linda and Buddy for a while, but continued to suffer from headaches, dizzy spells, and odd lapses of memory. Immediately before the grand jury was scheduled to take up Ron's murder during the second week in July, X-rays revealed a brain tumor that the doctors told Linda could have been present for a long time, but had swollen from the blow the woman had taken. She would require immediate surgery, with an uncertain prognosis.

• • •

Exactly one week later, on Monday, June 15, the perils of Mary Lee once again made the *Gazette* front page. She'd presented herself in the newsroom on Sunday for an exclusive interview: HIDDEN BAGS TAKEN

BY BURGLAR, WIDOW OF SLAYING VICTIM REPORTS. It seemed that Mary
Lee had surprised a burglar at 2:00 A.M. Sunday morning in her den.
Clad in a red jogging suit, the intruder was in the act of removing
mysterious contraband from a hidden compartment. She'd grappled
with him and gotten off a shot with her trusty .38 before he vanished
into the night. At first she thought she'd killed him, although police
had found no traces of blood.

> Mrs. Orsini [the newspaper reported] said she saw the man stuff
> two white bags under the sweatshirt he was wearing. The man
> took the bags from a hidden space about four inches deep un-
> derneath the bottom shelf of a bookcase in the Orsini home's
> den, she said. The space had been opened by prying up the
> bottom shelf. "I never knew it was there," she said. . . .
>   Mrs. Orsini said the bags resembled the plastic freezer bags
> used for freezing foods, and that she couldn't tell whether the
> bags themselves were white or whether they were clear and some-
> thing inside the bags was white.
>   Although plastic bags are used as containers for illegal drugs,
> Mrs. Orsini said she didn't think of drugs when trying to decide
> what could have been in the bags. "There's a large amount of
> money missing around my husband's death, and I thought of
> that," she said. . . .
>   Mrs. Orsini said her daughter was sleeping upstairs but didn't
> hear the shot.

There was more. When the investigating officers arrived, they'd
found Mary Lee standing in the front door screaming. Her nightgown
was torn and there was a red mark on her neck. Police found a bullet
hole in a den window, and the slug buried in an outside wall. The
laundry room door had a broken window, although how the deadbolt
lock had been opened remained unclear. Either the burglar alarm had
failed to work or young Tiffany had failed to turn it on.

> The police said that several items had been removed from the
> bookcase and placed around the den floor, and a pry tool had
> been used to lift the bottom shelf. The burglar "apparently was
> looking for something other than the articles in the cabinet," the
> police said.

What the police didn't tell the newspaper, however, the investigating officers told Farley and Miles. The pair had pointedly stayed away. "We decided, let's let an independent investigator have a look. Get away from our 'tunnel vision,' as she described it." Miles laughed. But what the detectives found came under the heading of "more bullshit."

The bookshelves were built-in models that had been there when the Orsinis moved in. Yet detectives found only one set of pry marks and the original paint still on the heads of the nails. Had anything been concealed underneath—white bags, pink elephants, or .38 caliber Colt revolvers—there would be *two* sets of pry marks: one to put the contraband in, another to take it out. The detectives dutifully dusted for fingerprints. But they didn't bust their butts looking for a dude in a red jogging suit.

Not for the first time, Bill McArthur found himself questioning his client's credibility. Or was it her reason? "But even though I questioned these odd events and bizarre episodes," he said, "I believed that *she* believed what she said. The basic facts of her story never changed. It was always this fringe bullshit that made you wonder. She'd be weeping, in a frenzy at times. An extremely emotional, scared, paranoid woman is what I thought."

· · ·

But McArthur had no time for speculation. The grand jury was due to take up the Orsini case in early July. In many ways, a grand jury investigation could be more dangerous than a murder trial. The original intention of the institution, created in England in 1281, was to protect the rights of individuals against unscrupulous prosecutors loyal to the Crown. Sixteen citizens would hear the evidence and deem whether or not it was sufficient to bring a suspect to trial. In contemporary American practice, however, the grand jury has evolved into a prosecutor's tool.

Besides being held in secret, grand jury trials differ from ordinary trials in several key respects. No judge presides and the prosecutor is the only attorney present. Thus the rules of evidence and criminal procedure are suspended. Hearsay, rumor, almost anything goes. A witness may leave the grand jury chamber to consult an attorney, but the lawyer can neither hear the testimony nor enter the room. Only twelve votes are needed to indict, and the jurors can pursue any line of investigation they choose and ask any question that occurs to them. In short, the prosecutor holds all the cards.

To some degree, McArthur was flying blind. He knew the NLRPD had to have more evidence than he'd seen, or Dub Bentley wouldn't be taking the case to the grand jury at all. But the big question was whether or not Mary Lee should testify. If he were going to go by the book, the answer was absolutely not.

McArthur warned Orsini that he could be accused almost of malpractice for allowing her to appear before the grand jury if she had anything to hide. "We're showing our cards and they're not showing theirs," he emphasized later. "Whatever she says is under oath and on the record, and they can use it for anything they want to. She has nobody there to determine what's relevant, not relevant, admissible, inadmissible. Nothing.

"However, I did tell her that if she was innocent, and if she was comfortable with her innocence, then I would advise her to go in there. But there was no way on God's earth that she wasn't going to testify. Outwardly, she was absolutely convinced that she was innocent, that she had nothing to fear. All she had to do was talk to those people, and they'd understand."

.   .   .

A few days before the grand jury convened, McArthur made what may have been his most fateful decision since agreeing to represent Mary Lee in the first place. Before he could permit Mary Lee to testify, McArthur thought he needed to have a talk with Tiffany—alone. He'd seen the girl infrequently since sitting in on her interview with the NLRPD, always in the company of her mother and grandmother. He'd gotten the impression that Mary Lee was very much the dominant figure among the three. But Tiffany would have to face the grand jury alone, and Bill wanted to get a better idea of what the girl would say and how she'd handle herself.

When Tiffany and her mother arrived at his office, Bill asked Mary Lee to step outside the room. At first she balked, arguing that she and her daughter had nothing to hide from each other. Eventually, McArthur had to force the issue.

The meeting itself was unremarkable. "She was a very strange little girl," the lawyer thought. "A very knowing-looking little girl, but also very enclosed, like she was in a cocoon. I had the feeling she didn't like me at all. Probably that day I got more conversation out of her than I ever did before. She was like I would expect my son or daughter to be, being interviewed by an adult—relatively quiet, relatively reticent.

She certainly was not spontaneous. But if I asked her, she'd answer.

"What I did was take the statement she had given earlier and go through it with her—just to find out what her testimony would be to the grand jury. And what she did was sit there and tell me in basically a monotone the same thing she'd told the police. Not word for word, but basically the same thing. She'd been ill, she went to bed, she woke up the next morning and she and her mother went to the drugstore. Went here, went there, and that's all she knew. She loved her step-father very much. She had no revelations or stories to tell. Not to me. As far as I know, to nobody."

And that was that. Or so it seemed at the time.

Chapter 8

The investigative file Sergeant T. J. Farley carried into the Pulaski County grand jury chambers on the morning of Wednesday, July 8, 1981, stood more than a foot high. The detective was to be the prosecutor's first witness, and he meant to leave nothing to chance. During the past week Farley had worked on nothing else, piecing together a narrative summary of the evidence that contained 162 separate entries and ran to 39 single-spaced, typed pages.

He still couldn't put the murder weapon in Mary Lee's hand, and he still had no witness who saw her use it. But Farley had always believed that if he could get the evidence away from the lawyers and into the hands of a jury, he could convince them. Page after page and hour after exhausting hour on the witness stand, the detective laid his case on the line. And when he finally got done testifying, Farley felt in his gut that he had convinced them.

But on the second day of the hearing, the detective got an unpleasant little surprise. Cindy Kinsolving, the ten-year-old neighbor who had noticed a dark, shiny late-model sedan pause in front of 7412 Pontiac between 11:30 P.M. and midnight on March 11, arrived at the courthouse arm in arm with Tiffany Orsini.

"The little girl comes up and says something like, 'Mr. Farley, I hope you don't get mad but I kind of changed my story,' " Farley said. "I looked up and there's Lee sitting there next to Mrs. Kinsolving, smiling. So now the little girl says it's a dirty car, with loud mufflers, and jacked up in the back, and I said something to the effect of, 'Well, Cindy, what you need to do is just tell the truth. You told me what it was the first time.' "

What had happened was that an investigator from the Myers Agency had driven the child to a nearby shopping center and pressed her to show him a car like the one she'd seen. Cindy had become confused, and Mary Lee had seized upon the discrepancy to persuade the child to change her testimony.

Even so, Farley figured Mary Lee's indictment was a leadpipe cinch.

•   •   •

The prosecutors saved Betty Tucker's testimony until the last. By the time the banker took the witness stand, the grand jury had reviewed virtually the entire prosecution case. Sergeant Farley had conducted a painstaking review of the physical evidence, detailed the Orsini family's shaky financial situation, and given them a day-by-day breakdown of Mary Lee's apparent effort both to hide the truth from her husband and to profit handsomely from his death. Among others, Linda House had also testified, and the jurors' sympathy with her fears did much to assure her that justice would be done.

If the object had been to indict Mary Lee as North Little Rock's Bitch of the Year, it was a done deal. But if the prosecution had a clincher, they expected it to be Betty Tucker. Until her turn came on July 13, the NLRPD and the prosecutor had kept her a secret from the defense. By testifying, she would be coming out in the open for the first time.

Tucker was uneasy, and part of it had to do with Bill McArthur. She'd known Bill since her days as a cashier in a downtown branch of Metropolitan Bank, and thought highly of him. Their hill-country origins were similar, and she could still remember his excitement the day he'd come into the bank after winning his first murder trial. To Betty, McArthur was an "intensely proud," honest man who had worked hard to make something of himself. Now she feared that he would get Orsini off.

When she saw Mary Lee outside the grand jury room for the first time since Ron's funeral, she had no idea how the woman would react. "She sat right across from me," Tucker remembered, "but she seemed to have no apprehension at all, even with the testimony that I was giving, which obviously was opposite to what she was giving. She just hugged my neck. I didn't enjoy that hug at all. It was like a rattlesnake. That was a peculiar feeling, a very peculiar feeling."

Once inside the chambers, Tucker's confidence returned. She walked the jury through the entire history of the Orsini loan transaction with Metropolitan Bank—the delays and excuses, the incomplete wire transfers, mistyped documents, Ron's surprise and anger that the loan had not been paid off, Mary Lee's promising to put the proceeds into the night deposit box on March 12, and her account of how the killer had supposedly stolen $40,000 cash that had never existed in the first place. Judging by the jury's reactions, Betty too felt sure that an indictment was imminent.

· · ·

By all accounts, Mary Lee's performance under oath on July 21 and 22 left a lot to be desired. Nobody who heard her grand jury testimony seems to have believed very much, if anything, of what she said. "She had superior control of herself," recalled Foreman E. Grainger Williams, a retired insurance executive. "There were times when she expressed indignation. Let's put it a little stronger—offended, I would say—that anybody could doubt her. And yet she never said the same thing exactly the same way twice. We'd shilly-shally around about some statement she'd made the previous day. 'Well, I meant this . . .' We never could pin her down.

"We challenged her on the veracity of her statements. The amount of money she found in his pocket changed every time she gave a report. It was $400, it was $1,000. She'd say, 'You must be mistaken.' So I'd have them read back the testimony, and she'd say, 'No. I was mistaken. It was more than that.' She was lying. She had no stalwarts on that jury. I don't remember a thing that went on where anybody was supportive of her.

"We saw the door where somebody allegedly kicked it in. I felt like she kicked it in herself, make it look like somebody had broken in. We saw the evidence where she alleged that someone broke into her house and tried to kill her. That was more imagination. I thought she did that herself. We all did."

· · ·

In the newspapers and on TV, however, a very different picture emerged. Viewers saw Mary Lee rush from the grand jury chambers in tears, overcome by the emotion, she told reporters, of having to relive the dreadful morning when she found her beloved husband's body.

Dub Bentley said little to the press, but the suspect never stopped giving interviews. In a long article in the *Democrat* illustrated by a flattering photograph, Mary Lee denounced the slipshod efforts of the NLRPD and promised startling new evidence based upon her own investigation. Not one, but two lie detector tests, she maintained, had proved her innocence.

On July 23 a front-page headline in the *Gazette* appeared to lend credence to Mary Lee's claims: SUSPECT FOUND IN ORSINI SLAYING, LR INVESTIGATOR TELLS GRAND JURY. According to Gary Glidewell, a brand new private eye working for Mary Lee, he had "new evidence" to implicate a local businessman in Ron Orsini's murder. " 'What he's got is so heavy it's unreal,' she said. 'I feel it's going to explode here within the next week.' "

In reality, Gary Glidewell's information was neither new nor evidence. A former Kansas City policeman eager to make a name for himself, Glidewell had offered his services to Bill McArthur, who turned him down. Mary Lee herself, however, jumped at the chance to hire a new champion, and had given Glidewell her husband's collection of deer rifles and shotguns as a down payment.

Glidewell had done most of his sleuthing in bars. In the course of an investigation for another client, he'd heard lots of rumors about a thug named Ron O'Neal. A Memphis native, O'Neal had done time in Tennessee and gotten sprung during the infamous pardons-for-pay scandal in the administration of Governor Ray Blanton. Having moved to Little Rock and opened a joint called the Wine Cellar, O'Neal was under investigation for crimes ranging from cocaine dealing to arson, insurance fraud to murder for hire. Although eventually convicted only of insurance fraud, barroom scuttlebutt linked him to half the unsolved crimes between Oklahoma City and Memphis.

No sooner had she heard O'Neal's name than Mary Lee became very excited. After scrutinizing a mug shot Glidewell showed her, she announced that O'Neal had been a regular visitor in Ron Orsini's garage workshop. What the two men talked about, she'd never known. It was all terribly mysterious.

Mary Lee also gave Glidewell the name of a shady character named Donny Simmons to check out—the proprietor of a North Little Rock store who turned out to have a history of drug dealing. What she'd neglected to mention, however, was that *she*—not Ron—had known Simmons since childhood. Unknown to the private detective, Simmons and Mary Myrtle Hatcher had grown up together on the same dirt roads; their photographs appeared almost side by side in the Sylvan Hills High School yearbook. Glidewell, however, never made the connection.

.   .   .

The grand jury was unimpressed with Glidewell's speculations. But before beginning their deliberations, they wanted to give Mary Lee every opportunity to confirm her testimony. Regardless of what bank records said, Mary Lee insisted, her own deposit slips would confirm that Ron had moved large sums of cash through their accounts. She promised to produce the deposit slips on Monday, July 27—along with the family's pharmacy records. The jury wanted to determine whether or not the medication Tiffany had been taking for what her mother called an inner-ear disorder had caused her to sleep more soundly than an ordinary person. Why the prosecution encouraged Orsini to fetch the records by herself remains unclear.

On their way to the courthouse Monday morning, Mary Lee and Tiffany stopped at a shopping center on JFK to run an errand. Because she would be gone only a moment, Mary Lee left her car running and her purse lying on the driver's seat. When they returned, the purse was missing—stolen in broad daylight. Inside the handbag, needless to say, she'd left her only copies of the bank deposit slips and drugstore receipts. Mary Lee's only chance to prove her innocence had been cruelly snatched away.

Who had lifted her purse from the car seat, Mary Lee could not know, of course. She suspected a conspiracy. The only pedestrian she and Tiffany had recognized in the area was a fellow named Donny Simmons—the proprietor of a shop in a nearby shopping center. He was a stranger to Mary Lee, but Tiffany had pointed him out as the father of a classmate.

.   .   .

When it came time for a decision, the grand jury found itself in a quandary. Except for Glidewell, every cop or ex-cop who looked at the evidence in the Orsini case agreed with Sergeant Farley: Mary Lee had either pulled the trigger or hired someone to do it. But except for Judy Kaye Mason—who'd helped question Mary Lee on the day of the crime—every lawyer who looked at it agreed with Bill McArthur:

Maybe Mary Lee did it, maybe not. But the evidence for a murder charge simply wasn't there.

Dub Bentley was pretty much up a tree. Experience had long ago taught him that there was a big difference between what police officers think and what a jury will do. Mary Lee might be a psychopathic liar, but that didn't make her a killer.

"I tried to be very thorough in briefing the grand jury," Dub said. "I wanted them to know that I had the prerogative of filing a charge, but that when we go to trial, *this* is the standard we must meet in order to convict. And if we go to trial today and we don't meet it, it's all over. Double jeopardy. We can't try her again. But if we don't go to trial today, there's no statute of limitations on murder."

Grand Jury Foreman E. Grainger Williams felt even more strongly about the evidence than Bentley. "I personally felt she was as guilty as she could be," he said. "I just couldn't figure out how she did it, or how we could prove it."

When it came right down to it, they never even had to take a formal vote.

• • •

To Mary Lee's friends and supporters, the grand jury's announcement on Tuesday, July 28, that it had decided to issue "no true bill" of indictment came as a cause to celebrate. But not nearly so public a celebration as Mary Lee herself had in mind.

For weeks since Ron's murder, Mary Jane Murphree and Joyce Holt had been doing everything they could to support their friend in her hour of need. More often than not, the three women sat together in the bedroom where Ron had been murdered. She felt closer to her dead husband there, Mary Lee explained. They thrashed over the "evidence" again and again.

At some point in their deliberations, Joyce remarked offhandedly that when the grand jury investigation was over, they ought to open a bottle of champagne and toast a formal end to the whole thing—time to pick up the pieces and return to normal life. Mary Lee seized upon the idea. She decided to throw herself a party.

As the time approached, however, Joyce and Mary Jane began to have second thoughts. Given all the publicity in the newspapers and TV, it just didn't seem wise. Both women had their businesses to think about. If word got out, people might take it wrong. Having a cham-

pagne party to celebrate a non-indictment for murder—that was how
it could appear.

Mary Lee, however, remained keen and could not be dissuaded.
When the day arrived, Mary Jane remembered, Joyce called her and
asked, " 'What are we going to do?' I said, 'I guess we're going to have
to do it.' Just deep down confusion, I guess. So that's what we did.
Tiffany called some people, Joyce called some people, and I called
some people. Just a few friends, that was the idea.

"But we did not call the TV people and the newspaper people. Lee
did that herself. They were already there when we got there. I couldn't
believe it. I was so tired after all of it, and I had on a sweater and a pair
of blue jeans—just really looked like hell—and didn't anticipate all of
this hoopla."

Joyce too was astonished. She'd been doing everything she could to
avoid the press, and now Mary Lee had summoned a cast of thousands
to the house on Pontiac Drive, most of them carrying cameras or
notebooks. Gary Glidewell was shocked to find himself accosted in the
front yard by reporters seeking interviews. But not too shocked to tell
the *Gazette*, "I feel very strongly that there was a conspiracy. We foiled
somebody's attempts to clear the murder by railroading. Someone
intended for her to take the rap for the crime."

Once inside, however, Glidewell was even more taken aback by the
bizarre spectacle that confronted him. There on a couch in full view
of a dozen reporters and TV cameramen, Mary Lee and Dr. Wulz
were locked in an amorous embrace like hot-blooded teen sweethearts.
Mary Jane, who'd never met the veterinarian, was stunned. "She was
sitting in his lap in the living room crawling all over him," she said.
"It was just unbelievable."

Bill McArthur arrived too late to catch Dr. Wulz and the widow
Orsini in a clinch. But he was nevertheless appalled. As soon as
Tiffany called his office with an invitation, McArthur and his law
partner had raced to Indian Hills in the hope of talking Mary Lee out
of the whole idea. He'd warned her that any public association with
Dr. Wulz was madness. Ignoring the reporters, Bill grabbed Mary
Lee's arm and pulled her into the den. "I just chewed her tail out," he
said. "I told her it looked like she was having a victory celebration. She
knew I was angry."

Mary Jane overheard the scolding, and agreed with every word.
"And that was *before* the picture," she said. On the front page of the
Gazette the next day was a photograph that seared itself into the

memories of everybody involved with the case who saw it—as well as
thousands of Arkansans: Dr. Wulz was seen uncorking a champagne
bottle as a gleeful Mary Lee peered over his shoulder. Much later,
Wulz claimed to have been "set up." He blamed the press.

On the front page of the *Democrat*, a less dramatic but equally
unsettling photograph showed Mary Lee and Tiffany sitting side by
side in front of the fireplace at 7412 Pontiac. Looking younger than her
heavily made-up daughter, Mary Lee wore the guileless smile of a
million-dollar lottery winner.

• • •

Linda House took copies of both Little Rock newspapers by her
mother's hospital room. Gladys Orsini's brain tumor had proved to be
non-malignant. She'd suffered considerable memory loss and faced a
difficult rehabilitation, but she would live. When Linda showed her
the front-page picture of Mary Lee and Dr. Wulz popping a champagne cork, she felt for the first time that her mother finally understood.

• • •

Sergeant T. J. Farley's first response was to take the grand jury
decision very badly. For a little while he entertained some hard
thoughts about Dub Bentley. "But then I got to thinking," Farley said,
" 'Wait a minute, I've put all this work in, and I've got sixteen good
people sitting in there. Maybe it's just as well.' "

Besides, as Dub kept reminding him: "There is no statute of limitations on murder."

BOOK II

Chapter 1

1

On the anniversary of her husband's death, Mary Lee gave an interview to a *Gazette* reporter. Though she'd managed to stay out of the headlines since the infamous champagne party, she'd by no means settled into a comfortable routine. The months following her non-indictment had been filled with frantic activity: lawsuits, rumors and alarms, menacing phone calls, secret wiretaps, death threats, hidden diamonds, clandestine meetings with private eyes, "hit men" dispatched from Chicago and New Orleans. She'd kept Indian Hills abuzz with gossip and speculation. Her friends and neighbors lived in a constant state of confusion and alarm.

Since her last appearance in the spotlight, many things had changed. Unknown to her friends, Mary Lee's financial fortunes had taken a sharp turn downward. Her moment of triumph after the grand jury had proved short-lived. The plan that was supposed to transform her into a poor little rich girl had failed. A credit life insurance policy had given her the home at 7412 Pontiac free and clear; she'd also realized roughly $25,000 from Ron's share in Central Heating & Air. Otherwise, however, she'd drawn a blank. A couple of policies had refused to pay as long as the NLRPD listed her as a murder suspect. Credit life insurance on the $31,000 swing loan from Metropolitan Bank had expired when it went delinquent. Betty Tucker had no choice but to foreclose on Mrs. Hatcher's home. The old woman moved into a public housing project for the elderly. Mary Lee explained to friends that without Ron's help, her poor mother couldn't keep up with the yardwork.

Nor had she calculated the cost of her defense. Besides his own fee, Bill McArthur had accumulated considerable expenses on Mary Lee's behalf. The total came to more than $15,000. McArthur was willing to be patient, but he did expect to be paid. In March 1982, he was still waiting.

So were Jim Lester and Gary Glidewell. The Fred Myers Detective Agency filed suit for its fee. Dillard's sued Ron's estate for a $16,000 furniture bill. Even the funeral home filed a claim for non-payment. The claims on Ron Orsini's estate far exceeded its assets. Bankruptcy loomed. By now far too glamorous to go back to peddling advertising trinkets, she'd quit working since two months before Ron's murder. Mary Lee was fast nearing the point where she'd have to begin selling her possessions to buy groceries.

• • •

Rita Gruber, a North Little Rock attorney, had her meter running too. Gruber was handling Mary Lee's civil suits, including defending her against one filed on behalf of Stacy Orsini by the bank serving as the child's financial guardian. By the terms of his divorce, Ron had agreed to maintain a $50,000 life insurance policy on Stacy's behalf. In 1978, however, Mary Lee had talked him into making her the sole beneficiary.

The case went to trial in September 1981 before Chancery Judge Lee Munson—the former prosecutor and Dub Bentley's boss. Legally speaking, the outcome was never really in doubt. Ron and Linda's divorce decree was an enforceable contract. Regardless of his intentions, changing the beneficiary had violated its provisions. Once Union Life refused to pay off and joined the lawsuit on Stacy's side, Mary Lee found herself facing heavy odds. Arrayed against her were a bank, an insurance company, and her nine-year-old stepdaughter. An ordinary murder suspect would have been well advised to cut her losses.

To the widow Orsini, however, an opportunity to take center stage could not be missed. Her attorney made the novel argument that if Stacy had a legitimate grievance, it was against her dead father. Gruber also filed a countersuit alleging extreme mental anguish.

In her own testimony, Mary Lee pursued a broader strategy. Inventing an entirely fictive biography for herself and the late Mr. Orsini, she portrayed herself as Lady Bountiful: more than willing to shower upon her urchin stepdaughter the benefits of her wealth and generosity.

Besides the same bogus college degree she'd always claimed, Mary Lee gave Ron three years' study at Hendrix—Arkansas' most prestigious private liberal arts college. She spoke airily of her $1,000 a week income and $260,000 trust fund, both imaginary. Turning up in a designer outfit with a plunging neckline, she positioned herself on the witness stand to afford Judge Munson an excellent view of her cleavage.

As to the niggling details of her husband's divorce decree, Mary Lee couldn't have cared less. Though she'd been actively involved in negotiating joint custody for poor Stacy—her biological mother being so sadly unfit—she hadn't troubled herself to read the two-page document.

While very little of this had anything to do with the matter at hand, the obviously fascinated judge allowed her to rattle on. Thanks to her nemesis Sergeant Farley, however, Mary Lee's performance turned sour. To the question of how often she'd been married, she answered "twice": once to Tiffany's father, once to Ron. Stacy's attorney then confronted her with a marriage license and divorce decree from Officer Milton's brother—the husband she'd abandoned on the same day she'd mistakenly believed his adoption of Tiffany became final. Mary Lee professed amazement. She'd understood that the marriage had been annulled. As such, her attorney had told her, it had no legal existence.

"Your Honor," Gruber objected, "I was not aware that this was going to be introduced into evidence in this particular action."

"Wouldn't have been if she said she'd been married three times, would it?" Judge Munson said tartly. "I assume that it's being introduced for the purpose of impeaching her credibility."

Stacy's attorney was getting ready to dig into the $260,000 trust fund and the $52,000 income when Munson waved him off.

"I tell you what," the judge said. "It's incredible. I sit here, and she has been married to him some four and a half years and knows everything about him in the world—including how much child support, pays half the clothes—and doesn't know the beneficiaries on her husband's policies. It is incredible in view of the evidence. I don't believe it."

Munson ordered the entire $50,000 put into trust for the child. Mary Lee and her attorney filed an appeal.

•   •   •

Elsewhere, there had been defections from Mary Lee's supporting cast. Certain of the bit players had grown uneasy, then frightened, and pulled away. Mary Jane Murphree was practically in hiding. Gary Glidewell was a nervous wreck, on the verge of losing his private investigator's license. But none of that, naturally, surfaced in the *Gazette*'s account on the anniversary.

"Mystery still shrouds the shooting death of Ron Orsini," the article began. Briefly recapitulating the history of the case, the account focused on the beleaguered widow's attempts—despite numerous death threats—to bring her husband's killer to justice. "I still think it was professionally done," she said. Mary Lee, the newspaper reported,

hasn't been and still isn't satisfied with the work the police have done. She said Saturday she has been investigating the case herself full time since the Grand Jury investigation ended. She's being helped by a private detective or detectives she won't name.

"I treat it just like a job," she said of her investigation. She has taken leave from her job as an advertising counselor. And she is working on a book about the case. She plans for the book to be "a tribute to my husband."

She's negotiating with a publisher, whose name she wouldn't disclose.

No book manuscript ever emerged. The publisher too was imaginary—although she'd told Joyce Holt that Bill McArthur had taken her to New York to negotiate a contract. But then she'd told Joyce an awful lot of other secrets about the handsome attorney too. She would later indignantly deny them all, and not a scrap of evidence would ever exist to confirm them.

Orsini stressed that while she continued to see friends socially, she doubted that she would ever remarry. Joyce had heard differently, and so had some of Tiffany's friends. But everybody understood the need for discretion—as both prospective bridegrooms already had wives. "She marked the anniversary of her husband's death quietly Friday," the article ended, "by placing flowers on his grave." Nobody saw her at the cemetery, and nobody saw the flowers.

2

To hear Gary Glidewell tell it, a big part of his problem was that he came from out of town. Entering the case cold out of Kansas City left him vulnerable to Mary Lee's wiles—also to every barfly, chisler, and pathological liar in Little Rock who wanted to peddle information or sing him a song. It also meant that the NLRPD and Arkansas State Police were all too willing to blame him for every scam his client pulled. But not everybody, to put it mildly, bought Glidewell's version of events.

Mary Lee's behavior at her ill-advised victory party put Glidewell on guard, but other things kept him guessing. Two days later, for example, Mary Lee's stolen purse—the one supposedly containing her deposit slips and prescription records—turned up in the dumpster behind a store run by a convicted drug dealer named Donny Simmons.

Glidewell needed help, and found it in the person of John Terry, a retired assistant chief of the Little Rock Police Department. A poker-faced six-footer with flat, watchful eyes, Terry had a reputation around town as nobody to be trifled with. Like a lot of Southern cops of his generation, he carried himself like a middle-aged James Dean.

Terry jumped at Glidewell's offer to split the fee down the middle. Through a mutual acquaintance, he'd already been supplying the Kansas City man with a *Who's Who in Arkansas Crime* as the barroom rumor mill churned up one "suspect" after another. Like most Little Rock cops, Terry had a bit of an attitude toward the NLRPD. Under pressure, could Farley and Miles have turned up the wrong suspect? He thought it was possible.

"Right at the first," Terry said, "everybody would tell me she did it. But I asked myself, 'If she's killed her husband, why does she want to hire me?' She had beat the charge. And some of those names she was throwing around were dangerous people. I thought maybe somebody might have told her she'd better shut her mouth. Some of those boys were not people to play with. They would flat kill you."

Soon enough, Terry too began to feel uneasy. It troubled him that Mary Lee had placed Tiffany strictly off limits—supposedly because it upset the girl to talk about her stepfather's death. More than that, experience had taught Terry to be wary of underworld informants. The vast majority of what they passed on turned out to be rubbish.

With Mary Lee, it was just the opposite. Not a name came up that it failed to draw a gasp of recognition. His and Glidewell's list of "suspects" began to grow almost geometrically. This hoodlum had drunk beer with Ron in the garage. Who was he? That thug resembled the man Mary Lee shot at in her den. And so it went. At one point Orsini even alleged that she'd followed her dead husband to a clandestine meeting with a man she now recognized as police chief Bill "Bubba" Younts. No wonder the NLRPD was determined to pin the crime on her.

Terry dismissed Mary Lee's allegations against Younts, but like Bill McArthur he was at first inclined to think that *she* believed them. But what really clued the former LRPD detective in were Mary Lee's tales about her phantom lover Jim Guy Tucker.

A Harvard graduate, Vietnam veteran, former Arkansas Attorney General, and U.S. congressman, the thirty-eight-year-old Tucker was one of the best-known politicians in the state. At the time Mary Lee began telling her friends about his mad passion for her, Tucker was involved in lining up supporters to run against former Governor Bill Clinton in the May 1982 gubernatorial primary. He was also married.

Unlike anybody else she knew, however, to Terry the handsome politician was more than just a face on TV. Tucker had been prosecutor during Terry's years with the LRPD. In those days the two men had been bitter enemies, but not so bitter that the ex-cop could picture Tucker in an adulterous liaison with a suspected murderess. So, when Mary Lee told him that Bill McArthur had learned that Jim Guy had a wiretap on her phone, Terry went straight to the attorney. Over the years he'd seen Bill handle some ticklish situations, and trusted him to deal off the top of the deck.

McArthur was incredulous. Not only had he told her nothing of the kind, but the set-up Orsini described would require a federal warrant. "Hell, I went and asked Jim Guy," Terry said. "That scared him to death. The word he used was 'bizarre.' He'd never even laid eyes on her. Here he was fixing to run for Governor. All he needed was Mary Lee Orsini." Using a pseudonym, Mary Lee even showed up at Tucker's campaign headquarters as a volunteer worker. Recognized by an aide, she was shown the door.

But even when confronted with evidence that her own private detectives had caught her in a barefaced lie, Mary Lee never backed completely off a story. She'd change the subject, or embroider the original tale until she could almost make them doubt themselves. Why, of course Jim Guy would deny knowing her. What else did they expect him to do, given her notoriety? Until she brought Ron's killer to justice, the shadow of suspicion would always hang over her head.

At the first sign of skepticism, Mary Lee tried alternate means of persuasion. "She always wanted to talk in the bedroom," Glidewell said. "And she has you sit down on the bed and she sits down next to you and rubs your thigh. That's a pretty strong come-on. But I never did screw her. I know I've been accused of it, but I never did. Because my instinct kept saying, 'Don't trust her.' We had discovered that her mouth was not a prayer book."

•   •   •

Exactly how Mary Lee got word to Sergeant Farley that Glidewell had put out a $50,000 contract on his life never became entirely clear. Hiring the private detective during the grand jury had suited the needs of the moment. But once he'd begun to doubt her, Glidewell posed a potential problem. Adding Terry only made things worse. The former LRPD detective, she complained, never talked— just listened. He was secretive, almost sinister. She wasn't sure she could trust him.

Indeed she couldn't. Under Arkansas law, private detectives enjoy no privilege of confidentiality. Had Glidewell and Terry uncovered evidence of Orsini's guilt, they could be arrested for obstructing justice if they failed to disclose it to the police or prosecutor.

One day, however, Glidewell made the mistake of introducing Mary Lee to a former client who soon fell under the melodramatic widow's spell. Kenny Clarkson eventually admitted to police that Orsini had persuaded him to phone Dr. Wulz for her. Impersonating Jim Guy Tucker, he'd apologized for hiring Glidewell to investigate the veterinarian's past. Even years later, Wulz could not be persuaded that the politician had never been his rival.

Soon enough Clarkson was spreading the word that Glidewell had taken out a $50,000 "hit" contract on three men: Wine Cellar owner Ron O'Neal, Orsini's brother Ron Hatcher, and Sergeant T. J. Farley. The killers were said to be a "salt and pepper team"—i.e., one white and one black man. Soon enough, the story had made its way back to Farley himself.

At first, the NLRPD detective was skeptical. Clarkson was a cocaine addict with a propensity for wearing gold neck chains, flashing stacks of hundred-dollar bills, and telling fanciful stories. But a lawyer who owed Farley a favor called to report that he'd overheard Glidewell's half of a murky phone conversation about "hit men"—one of Orsini's favorite themes at the time.

Just to be on the safe side, Farley took what he knew to state police

officials in charge of licensing private eyes. Then he passed on a warning to Ron Hatcher, packed his wife off to visit her daughter in Florida, and cautioned his neighbors. Troopers staked out his house for
ten days. The idea was to take the killers down on the spot. Everybody lost a lot of sleep, but that was all. The "hit men" never
showed.

* * *

Meanwhile, word spread that Glidewell was tainted. His business
began to dry up fast. He experienced a lot of what he considered nickel
and dime harassment from the state police, and started to feel a bit
paranoid. He began to confide in Mary Jane Murphree. Mary Jane's
own marriage had been on the rocks for a long time. Her husband
refused to understand why she'd grown so obsessed with the Orsini
murder. Partly due to her suspicious nature, Mary Jane's doubts about
Orsini had never quite been resolved, and the publicity wasn't doing
her business any good either. Extremely sensitive to gossip, the whispers she heard disturbed her. She and Glidewell found lots to talk
about.

Even so, Murphree hesitated to make a clean break. Mary Lee had
an uncanny knack of sensing her friends' discomfort almost before they
did. No sooner would they grow dubious than Mary Lee would produce "proof" of even her most unlikely tales—proof like Kenny Clarkson's phone call impersonating Jim Guy Tucker, or a tape of Terry
warning her to leave the politician alone.

Even though Joyce Holt once accompanied Mary Lee to retrieve a
tape from a recording device she'd put on Dr. Wulz's phone—drilling
a hole through his carport wall, plugging the machine into an open
jack, and hiding it in a woodpile—she never dreamed that her friend
would be capable of spying on her too. When Wulz found the tape
recorder, he assumed the culprit to be the NLRPD.

But one day Mary Lee went too far. She intimated to Glidewell that
she'd always suspected Ron and Mary Jane of having a love affair, and
hinted that the realtor knew more than she was telling. That did it. She
decided to break away from Orsini. Mary Jane tried to warn Joyce, but
her fascination with the occult made Joyce so uneasy that Mary Lee
persuaded her that Murphree had gone off the deep end.

* * *

Soon after John Terry confronted her about Jim Guy Tucker, Mary Lee fired both him and Glidewell. No longer welcome at 7412 Pontiac, the two men never saw a dime for their efforts. Indeed, the private detectives' most important contribution to the Orsini saga would turn out to be something they were completely unaware of at the time.

Roughly three weeks after the grand jury hearing, Glidewell had gotten a call from a young woman named Suzanne Ellis. Like everybody else in Little Rock, Ellis had followed the Orsini murder in the media. She'd also heard a lot of gossip and speculation at the joint where she tended bar. Rumor down at the Town Pump had it that the killing had to do with cocaine.

What she wanted to tell Glidewell was that she had a notion that an ex-boyfriend of hers might know something about the case. If drug dealing had anything to do with it, chances were that he did. Eugene "Yankee" Hall had already done time for dealing cocaine. Suzanne was sure her boyfriend hadn't actually done the killing. On March 11, he'd been visiting his folks up in Wilkes-Barre. But he'd phoned her from Pennsylvania, and Suzanne thought he'd acted funny—like he knew more about the Orsini murder than he was letting on.

Still persuaded of his client's innocence at the time, Glidewell had taken Suzanne's story straight to Mary Lee. When he told John Terry, however, the veteran cop wasn't buying. "Yankee" Hall was a familiar figure to the LRPD. Besides moving a little dope now and then, Yankee stole cars. Also boats, heavy equipment, jewelry—anything he could move for a quick buck. He'd even messed with whores a time or two. But Yankee was a con man and thief, not a killer. He might slap Suzanne around when he had a noseful of toot, but violence wasn't his style.

Unfortunately, neither Glidewell nor Terry noticed the dog that failed to bark in the night. Of all the "suspect's" names Glidewell had run by Mary Lee in 1981, only one failed to provoke a response: Eugene "Yankee" Hall. But had the private detective inadvertently given her something she could use? Or could it be that Mary Lee had known Yankee all along? Nobody ever found any solid evidence that she did, and a lot of people tried.

Because before Mary Lee got through, she had made Yankee Hall's name a household word all over Arkansas too.

Chapter 2

1

For Bill and Alice McArthur, the past year had turned out to be almost too good to be true. Their marriage was stronger than ever, and their two children were happy, healthy, and doing well in school. The couple had also begun a highly successful business together, and soon afterward came into some unexpected money. What made her happiest about the windfall, Alice told intimates, was that Bill could stop driving himself so hard and take only those cases that interested him most.

Like any couple married for eighteen years, the McArthurs had endured some hard times together—the hardest, Bill admitted, were entirely of his own making. During a crisis six years earlier they had even used the word "divorce" one traumatic evening. For a devout Catholic like Alice, this was a very serious word. But they had recommitted themselves to their vows, and gone to work on their marriage. To friends and family alike, they gave the impression of being a well-matched couple—two strong, outspoken personalities who loved and complemented each other. Through all the tumult to come, nobody close to them ever changed their minds about that. And there would be times when their constancy was the only thing that made life bearable.

At least outwardly, two white Southerners could hardly have grown up in more different worlds. They met in May 1962 at a wedding in Alice's home town of Golden Meadow, Louisiana—deep in Cajun country about seventy-five miles south of New Orleans. After their first dance, Alice told a girlfriend that the two would be married within the year.

And so they were. What Alice Marie Miller wanted, she tended to get. Bill would always recall that first long weekend as magical. There was no seduction involved; this was the Deep South in 1962. Right from the start, however, Alice exerted an almost exotic appeal upon Bill. To a native of the Arkansas Ozarks, the bayous and swamps of South Louisiana felt like a foreign country.

Everything about Alice fascinated him: her blond beauty, her bantering, outspoken manner, her deep-voiced Cajun accent and the effortless way she could shift from English to French and back. Alice's athleticism appealed to him too. She swam like a shark, and dove gracefully. Bill had all he could do to keep up with Alice at tennis and golf, more her pastimes than his. It wouldn't have occurred to Alice to let him win. Nor would McArthur have wanted her to. The rodeo cowboy in him loved her feistiness. A dual major in Phys. Ed. and English at the University of Southwest Louisiana, Alice had a quiet, contemplative side to her nature she also let him glimpse.

Neither of them had any money at all. McArthur had worked his way through college unloading trucks for Sears, Roebuck, then pulled eighteen months Army duty. Alice's people taught school, no way to get rich in Louisiana or Arkansas, either one. "Professor Miller," as Alice's father was called, was the principal of the Golden Meadow high school, and her mother taught elementary school.

During the first years of their marriage, the couple rented a small apartment in downtown Little Rock. While Bill worked days and studied law at night, Alice taught second grade at Our Lady of Good Counsel School. In 1968, McArthur earned his degree and passed the Bar on the first try. After a couple of lean years getting Bill's practice established, the McArthurs felt confident enough about the future to start a family. Their daughter Robyn was born in 1971. Soon afterward, they bought a modest home in West Little Rock and Alice gave up teaching for full-time motherhood. Their son Chuck was born in 1973.

Alice kept her priorities firmly in order. Her husband and children came first, her active religious life second, next her circle of intimate friends, then her avocations and pastimes. She believed in keeping busy. No sooner had Bill completed his law degree and Robyn gotten out of diapers than Alice began commuting to the University of Central Arkansas in Conway to earn her M.Ed. Eventually, she planned to return to teaching. But she studied mainly for her own gratification.

Besides being a voracious reader, Alice had aspirations to be a writer. She kept bound notebooks full of her own essays and poetry—very little of which she ever liked well enough to show anybody, much less to submit for publication. When she did share her work with others, it was a rare gesture of intimacy. Photography was another hobby. Over the years her framed portraits of their children began to accumulate on the walls of her friends' homes.

A fine tennis player with a stinging, left-handed serve, Alice's innate hustle helped her compete with players of much greater natural ability. On long summer days when the kids were out of school, Alice would organize tennis outings among her friends. They would make up gallons of Kool-Aid and piles of peanut butter and jelly sandwiches, and play on city park courts where the children could enjoy the nearby playgrounds and swimming pools. Even under those circumstances, Alice's will to win was so fierce that if they hadn't known better, her opponents could easily have gotten the idea that she bore them a personal grudge.

Like most good marriages, the McArthurs' had a bit of an edge to it as well. "She always called me 'The Golden Boy,' or 'Mr. Clean,' " Bill said. "I always told her, 'You know, your problem is that you're jealous. They don't say, "There's Alice McArthur, the master's in education, the famous mother; the great tennis player." ' And that'd really gripe her ass. She loved to catch me in a screw-up. Absolutely loved for me to make a mess of some little thing."

The couple also had their differences now and again over the children. Bill sometimes thought that she was too hard on the kids—too insistent that they achieve both academically and athletically, and a bit too stern a disciplinarian. As they got older, Bill often served as mediator. But the couple rarely argued over money or their social lives. Alice ran the household and served as social director. Their friends tended to be her friends. Bill had several strong friendships centered on his law practice, but he pretty much left them downtown. Strong-willed as Alice could be, she allowed her husband the same freedom he gave her. If Bill said no to a social engagement that Alice had planned, then no it would be.

For somebody who sometimes grumbled about what she called "the

Polite South"—as opposed to the rowdier world of Cajun Louisiana—
Alice always had many women friends. Whatever needed doing, Alice
jumped in—whether it was organizing a doubles league, teaching the
children to swim and dive, starting a girls' softball league, or raising
money for the St. Edward's School library. Bantering and outspoken,
she had a bawdy sense of humor. Out at the Westside Tennis Club
where she and her friends played, her close friend Sally Pernell said:
"All you had to do was walk in the front door, and wherever you heard
people laughing, she would be there. It was a phenomenon. Go where
you hear the laughter, and that's where you'd find Alice."

The most frequent arguments between Bill and Alice were more
philosophical than practical. Like many Catholics, Alice's faith was
shaken by the changes in the church after Vatican II. It upset her that
a vote taken in Rome could alter a framework of beliefs that she'd been
taught to think of as changeless and inviolable since childhood. That
Bill never did get around to converting to Catholicism also bothered
her from time to time.

Alice and Bill differed too about his profession. "Listen," Bill would
say, "I would not have Alice on any jury I ever tried a case in front of.
She thought everybody I represented was guilty as hell—everybody.
She was law and order, I mean, right-wing to the core. She'd argue
about the Fifth Amendment, Fourth and Sixth amendments—search
and seizure, all of it. Her attitude was, if you don't have anything to
hide, you don't have anything to worry about. I'd say, 'I guess it's all
right with you if the police walk right in and search your house.' She'd
say, 'Hell no, I'd shoot 'em the minute they walked in the door. This
is *my* house.' "

When the McArthurs got into it like that in front of her friends, Bill
sometimes twitted Alice about the sheltered lives they led. None of
them ever ventured east of University Avenue, he chided—a busy
north-south artery very roughly dividing the older and blacker parts of
Little Rock from the suburbs. None of them had a clue about what
went on in the less privileged parts of their own city every night of the
week. They didn't have to confront the human wreckage he dealt with
all day long—the consequences of poverty, ignorance, alcoholism and
drugs, mental illness, greed, lust and rage. Nobody in their safe little
enclave had any reason to fear the police.

Bill never gave speeches on the subject, only teased. But he knew it
galled Alice all the same—partly because she knew her husband was
right. She just hated to admit it. Alice was far too orthodox a Catholic

to imagine that tragedy and evil could never come to her door. She just prayed to God that they would stay away.

•   •   •

Bill McArthur messed up his marriage in the customary way. He jumped in bed with a woman because it was easy, only to learn that the lady had more than a casual liaison in mind. It started late in 1975. Susan Anders had met Bill five years earlier, when he represented her brother. Anders was a striking dark-haired woman with the kind of petulant sensuality that turned men's heads when she sashayed into a room. Married to a man almost thirty years her senior, she was bored and restless. She phoned Bill one day and suggested they meet for a drink. He proposed instead that she come by his office for a talk. She showed up on Saturday morning when the lawyer was alone.

From that day on, the lovers met furtively once every week or two in apartments Bill borrowed from friends—always in the daytime. Things went on that way for several months. Falling in love was out of the question, and what Alice never knew couldn't hurt her. As Anders later affirmed, he gave her no gifts, sent her no flowers, made her no promises. They never met in public. Easy come, easy go was how Bill had it figured.

But Susan had ideas of her own. When she began to make demands on his time, McArthur told her he wanted out. Anders balked. The more firmly McArthur tried to put it, the more insistent Anders became. She took to calling him at home, giving the unsuspecting Alice every excuse in the world why she needed to talk to him. Bill had told his secretary that he would no longer accept Susan Anders's phone calls. Late that day she burst weeping into his office and tore off her clothes. Rather than pity, McArthur felt anger. As coolly as he knew how, he gathered her things, handed them back to her, and told her to go home. She turned on him. Ever since Bill's first efforts to cool things, Susan had been surreptitiously recording their phone conversations. If he persisted in rejecting her, she warned now, she would call Alice and confront her with the evidence. "It had got to the point where my conscience was killing me," McArthur said. "So I finally called her bluff. I told her to go ahead and play the tapes for Alice, and I went home prepared to face the music."

At first, Alice took the shock with surprising calmness. The tape Anders played for her had been ambiguous enough that until she heard the truth from her husband, she didn't quite believe the woman's story. Bill begged for understanding and forgiveness. Alice asked her favorite priest to come over to mediate, and called her brother in Louisiana for advice. The couple spent several long, painful evenings dissecting what had gone wrong in their marriage. Tempers flared, and on one occasion, Bill walked out and spent the night at a motel. They both had such wicked tongues, he feared one of them would go too far. But he came back the next morning. To the women friends in whom Alice confided, it became clear that Bill would have done anything to keep her. Once Alice herself believed that, the crisis was over.

But not before she got a good look at the little tramp who'd tried to destroy her family. Never one to take injury lying down, she called Susan Anders and demanded a meeting. When Anders refused, Alice got her address from Bill, and with him trailing helplessly behind, forced her way into the woman's apartment. She wanted to see just what kind of slut she was dealing with, Alice announced. An angry scuffle ensued, in which Bill, trying to keep the women from attacking each other physically, ended up pushing Anders to the floor. Then he managed to haul his wife out of there before the police arrived.

After Anders moved back in with her ex-husband, she sought to swear out an assault warrant against Alice. The prosecutor's office advised her that any Arkansas jury would laugh her out of court, but not before a shamefaced McArthur was called to the courthouse to tell his side of the story. The Anderses later talked to a lawyer about filing a civil suit for "alienation of affection." By that time, however, McArthur learned that Alice had not been the first wife Anders had favored with a startling telephone call, nor the second. McArthur challenged her lawyer to file the lawsuit if he thought he had a case, and the episode ended right there. He never saw or heard from Susan Anders again.

2

During the summer of 1981, the McArthurs and several couples took up a new hobby: country and western dancing. The *Urban Cowboy* fad had made its way up from Texas, where clubs like Gilley's in Houston and Billy Bob's in Fort Worth drew large crowds to dance the Two-step and Cotton-eyed Joe. "Going redneckin', " some Arkansans called it.

Bill's first reaction was negative. Never a big dancer, he found the

steps hard to learn and the obligatory costume—boots, jeans, western
shirts, and bandannas—came close enough to the outfits he'd worn in
his rodeo days twenty years before to make him feel silly. Besides, the
"in" club in Little Rock was a dive called the Kowboy Kountry Klub.
Located in a converted warehouse in the industrial district, the joint
was run by a well-known local character named Bob Troutt. A one-
time *Democrat* reporter and press flack for Governor Orval Faubus,
Troutt had run a Hot Springs nightclub called The Vapors during the
heyday of quasilegal casinos. Later he'd operated topless joints. He
often boasted about his connections on both sides of the law.

Bill came to like the western dancing well enough, but his feelings
about the Kountry Klub never changed. "That place was just about the
nastiest joint I'd ever seen, but it was packed every night. He had
bouncers wearing these big long pistols on their legs right out in the
open. Anyhow, we got to talking about it one night, and somebody
said, 'Hell, if you can run a place as sorry as this and make money,
think what you could do if you ran it cleanly.' "

Not long afterward, Bill and an old friend named James Nelson, an
insurance agent, started thinking seriously about the idea. Neither the
Nelsons nor the McArthurs had much ambition to be nightclub owners in the long run. Bill's law practice meant too much to him. The
idea was to get the business started successfully, then sell it at a profit.

Alice was dubious at first, but she soon became an enthusiastic
participant. After working up some numbers, they approached a popular Little Rock disc jockey called Bob Robbins—then moonlighting at
Troutt's Kountry Klub. Robbins expressed an interest in a partnership.
The idea seemed like a natural, and the more they studied, the better
it looked. The same formula had worked in cities like Fort Worth,
Austin, and Oklahoma City. Why not Little Rock?

Using their home as collateral, Bill and Alice borrowed $30,000 for
their share of the start-up costs. The partners formed a corporation in
which they and the Nelsons each held a 40 percent share and Bob
Robbins the remaining 20 percent. They leased a spacious new building on the New Benton Highway in southwest Little Rock and had it
converted into a larger-than-life version of a country roadhouse. Bill
persuaded the others to hire Jim Lester to manage the place. With the
ex-state trooper in charge, security would pose no problem.

The grand opening of "BJ's Star-Studded Honky Tonk" took place
on December 28, 1981. The partners had advertised extensively on
radio, and mailed hundreds of form letters inviting friends, clients, and

business associates to the gala event. Evidently, an adult theme park was just what Little Rock needed. From the opening night, BJ's drew enthusiastic crowds. By the time Hank Williams, Jr., played BJ's first big-name show in January 1982, they knew they had a hit. Receipts averaged $100,000 a month. Expenses ran higher than expected, but it looked as if they might be able to pay off the bank and put BJ's in the black within the year.

Just one small cloud appeared on the horizon. Somewhat predictably, Bob Troutt filed a lawsuit against BJ's in January. Angered by what he considered a ripoff of his Kountry Klub—though the movie *Urban Cowboy* had popularized western dancing from coast to coast in 1981—Troutt claimed to have copyrighted the phrase "Cowboy Disco" and accused BJ's of stealing it. But phrases and ad slogans can't be copyrighted. So the lawsuit went nowhere.

Some people warned that Troutt was capable of violence, but McArthur paid them little mind. The way he saw it, Little Rock had plenty of room for both clubs. Besides, Troutt's joints had always catered to the crowd that came *looking* for a little danger on a Saturday night. "We weren't cutting his leg off or attacking him," Bill said. "Just going into competition with him."

Somebody started a fire in a Dumpster outside BJ's one night. But even that didn't cause much of a stir. The blaze did little damage. McArthur did take the precaution of showing employees a photograph of a convicted arsonist named Herbie Wright, but he didn't lose any sleep fretting about it. BJ's was fully insured, and Troutt couldn't gain much by burning it down. He might be a bully and a braggart, but Bill had never known him to do anything irrational. Getting the club running and keeping his law practice going gave McArthur plenty to think about without searching for monsters under the bed.

3

Some time before he died, Alice's father had deeded over to her and her brother Leonard about 180 acres of low-lying grass and swampland on False River Island in Pointe Coupe Parish, about thirty miles north of Baton Rouge. Almost useless from a commercial point of view, the acreage had been handed down to him by his father.

In 1979, however, an independent oil and gas company out of Midland, Texas, offered to lease the mineral rights for the modest sum of $10,000. Alice and Leonard readily agreed. It was a nice little windfall, but nobody ran out to make a down payment on a yacht. Like most folks in South Louisiana, they understood the prohibitive odds against a wildcat driller bringing in a productive oil well on their land. Alice used her share to build a swimming pool behind the McArthur home. Neighborhood kids got free swimming lessons from Alice over the next couple of summers.

But just about the time BJ's Star-Studded Honky Tonk was getting ready for its grand opening, the McArthurs learned that the improbable had become fact. An exploratory well drilled on Alice and Leonard's land by the Lantern Petroleum Corporation and Hunt Energy had struck oil and natural gas, and struck it bigtime. All of a sudden the schoolteacher's daughter from Golden Meadow looked to start collecting royalty checks in amounts she could scarcely believe. With OPEC holding a firm grip on worldwide oil production, and the price of West Texas crude standing above $34 a barrel, domestic producers couldn't pump the stuff out of the ground fast enough to keep up with demand.

Royalty checks made out to Alice M. and William C. McArthur began to arrive in late February 1982. By March 4, when the couple opened an interest-drawing checking account at Commercial National Bank, they had received three checks totaling $41,611. By the end of that month, roughly $7,000 more arrived in the mail, and in April another $7,290. Within two months, the McArthurs deposited over $56,000. What was more, there seemed no end in sight. Almost out of nowhere, it looked as if Bill and Alice were about to get rich, possibly very rich. They hardly knew how to act.

Struggling to keep his law practice going while getting BJ's on a firm footing—he and James Nelson alternated nights staying at the club until closing time—Bill hardly had time to think about what to do with Alice's money. They were both relieved to know that at the very least, Robyn and Chuck's college education would be paid for. And Alice had redecorating ideas for the house that she began to set in motion. Apart from that, McArthur couldn't think of anything much about his life that he wanted to change. He never for a minute thought about giving up his practice. Bill had set his mind on becoming a trial lawyer back when he was a kid lugging attorneys' briefcases up and down the Van Buren Country Courthouse steps for ice cream money.

Bill did make an appointment for Alice one day with a tax lawyer at the Rose Law Firm downtown to set up trust funds for Robyn and Chuck. Alice and the attorney met in early April, but what with everything else that was going on, she postponed making a decision. Nothing had to be done right away; 1982 income taxes wouldn't come due for another year. Also, under Louisiana's Napoleonic legal code, in the unlikely event that anything happened to Alice, her property there would revert directly to her children, exactly as she and Bill would want it to. The attorney in her native St. Charles Parish who deeded the land over to Alice and her brother in 1975 had made quite a point of being sure the McArthurs understood that singular oddity of Louisiana law. In any of the other forty-nine states, he'd stressed, her husband too would stand to inherit a share of her property.

So there was no need to hurry. Alice McArthur had all the time in the world.

Chapter 3

1

Precisely when Mary Lee Orsini decided to put her new plan in motion nobody knows. Neither is it possible to say with complete confidence exactly what her motives may have been at the start, nor what specific ends she hoped to achieve. Besides her manipulative skills and zeal for notoriety, the most striking thing about Mary Lee's adventures from beginning to end was her odd mixture of extreme cunning and sheer incompetence. Words like "plan," "motive," and "specific ends" may be useful for description. But they imply a kind of reasonableness and foresight of which she seems to have been incapable. A normal person with half Mary Lee's apparent intelligence ought to have seen that none of the outlandish schemes she began concocting in March or April 1982 could possibly work.

The psychopathic personality, however, never does catch on. Exactly why that is so, psychologists and psychiatrists can't really say. In fact, the word "psychopath" and its politer synonym "sociopath" cannot be found in the *DSM-III*—the *Diagnostic and Statistical Manual of Mental Disorders*, published by the American Psychiatric Association. As medical doctors, psychiatrists prefer to deal with diseases for which treatments exist. For individuals like Mary Lee Orsini, however, medical science knows neither cause nor cure.

But the *DSM-III* does offer a descriptive diagnosis that sounds eerily like Mary Lee to everybody who came to know her. Under the general heading of "Personality Disorders," it lists a cluster of three that form a close continuum: "Histrionic," "Narcissistic," and "Anti-social." Definitions overlap, and multiple diagnoses are indicated. Indeed, some have suggested that all three disorders are essentially the same entity, since most individuals labeled "Anti-social" are men, while virtually all of those classified as "Histrionic" turn out to be women.

The five criteria defining "Narcissistic Personality Disorder" appear to make it the closest fit for Mary Lee Orsini:

A. Grandiose sense of self-importance or uniqueness, e.g. exaggeration of achievements and talents, focus on the special nature of one's problems.

B. Preoccupation with fantasies of unlimited success, power, brilliance, beauty, or ideal love.

C. Exhibitionism: the person requires constant attention and admiration.

D. Cool indifference or marked feelings of rage, inferiority, shame, humiliation or emptiness in response to criticism . . . or defeat.

E. At least two of the following characteristic of disturbances in interpersonal relationships:

   (1) entitlement: expectation of special favors without assuming reciprocal responsibilities, e.g. surprise and anger that people will not do what is wanted

   (2) interpersonal exploitativeness: taking advantage of others to indulge own desires or for self-aggrandizement; disregard for the personal integrity and rights of others

   (3) relationships that characteristically alternate between the extremes of overidealization and devaluation

   (4) lack of empathy: inability to recognize how others feel, e.g. unable to appreciate the distress of someone who is seriously ill.

Elsewhere, the manual speaks of the "chronic, intense envy," displayed by such persons. Under "Histrionic Personality Disorder" (derived from the Etruscan word for "actor"), the manual notes that although "superficially charming and appealing," such persons are always drawing attention to themselves.

> They are prone to exaggeration and often act out a role, such as the "victim" or the "princess" without being aware of it. . . . Flights of romantic fantasy are common. . . .
>   Individuals with this disorder . . . [are apt to] show an initially positive response to any strong authority figure who they think can provide a magical solution for their problems. Though they adopt convictions strongly and readily, their judgment is not firmly rooted, and they often play hunches.

Criminal psychopaths live as permanent impostors. They know right from wrong; they just don't give a damn. Their world divides into user and used; morality consists of fear of getting caught. And whatever happens, somebody else is always to blame. To the question: Are psychopaths sick or are they evil? there is just one answer. They are both. Probably due to an inborn, and possibly hereditary brain defect—though no mechanism has been located—psychopaths must for now be understood as one of nature's bewildering little tricks, like ticks and water moccasins. "Moral Imbeciles" was the nineteenth-century term. The prisons are full of them.

Could it possibly be that Mary Lee had no coherent, rational motive at all? That she was playing by ear, making it up as she went along according to the needs and impulses of the moment? Inventing it all from day to day and week to week the way they make up *Dallas* and *Dynasty* and *General Hospital*? In the media-spawned frenzy of disinformation, gossip, rumor, innuendo, speculation, and downright fantasy that swept Arkansas from one border to another, that was the last thing anybody wanted to believe. To do so would have spoiled all the fun.

Yet that is almost certainly how it went down.

• • •

As she'd done a few months before her husband's murder, Mary Lee went out early in 1982 and found herself a couple of new friends. This time around, she chose men.

Like Mary Jane Murphree, Larry Burge sold real estate for a living. He met Mary Lee in February, when he made an appointment to show her house at 7412 Pontiac to a client. Whether she actually intended to sell the place or simply found making a listing a convenient way to meet strangers, there's no telling. Certainly she needed the money.

Either way, she had no difficulty attracting Burge's attention. A tall, heavyset man in his late thirties, Burge had thinning, reddish-blond hair and a round, florid face. He spoke with a rustic twang and cultivated a bristling manner. Having grown up in rural Perry County about forty miles west of Little Rock, Burge had run a John Deere dealership and owned a pawnshop before getting into real estate. He flattered himself on his country boy smarts. Nobody talked to Burge very long without his telling them what a shrewd rascal he could be.

Burge's curiosity was piqued from the start, when Mary Lee insisted that he meet her at the house in Indian Hills before showing it. She wanted to acquaint him with its finer points. Larry had no trouble with that. Selling a house where a murder has taken place can be tricky. Many buyers shy away; others sense the opportunity for a bargain.

Before Burge arrived, Mary Lee telephoned Block Realty to verify his identity. What with the death threats she'd gotten, she explained, she couldn't be too careful. The meeting went well. Burge thought the house overpriced at $110,000, but with some creative financing he figured he might turn her a nice profit. Her coy manner intrigued him. Didn't she know him from somewhere? Hadn't she seen him before? She found it hard to believe she could forget a man who made such a strong impression. Based on what happened later, some people concluded that most of the finer points Mary Lee showed Burge must have been located in the bedroom. But he insisted that he never touched her.

Larry had read about Ron Orsini's murder in the newspapers, and like everybody else in North Little Rock real estate circles, had heard all the rumors. Mary Lee didn't look like a murderess to him. So when she turned up at his office a couple of days later asking did he want to have lunch, he decided to play along. Rather than heading for a restaurant, Mary Lee drove to a scenic spot on Skyline Drive and parked. She had two loaded pistols lying openly on the seat between them. The guns didn't alarm Burge either. He owned several himself. If people had been threatening *his* life, he would damn sure go armed.

Mary Lee needed a favor—a big favor that only a strong, fearless individual like Larry Burge would be man enough to do. According to

Burge, she wanted to write a letter to the editor of the *Gazette* and have Burge sign it. The newspaper, she claimed, had already agreed to give it prominent space. What the letter would say was that Burge had overheard NLRPD Chief Bill Younts tell another man that he was so fed up with Mary Lee's investigation of her husband's murder that if he thought he could get away with it, he'd kill her himself. Supposedly a friend of hers had heard Younts say that in a bar near police head-quarters. Her friend couldn't afford to come forward himself. Because he was a parolled felon, he lacked credibility, and had no business in a bar to start with. Publishing such a letter in the newspaper, Mary Lee said, would lead to Younts being fired and new investigators assigned to probe the mystery of her husband's death.

Now Burge had drunk a beer or two with Younts and didn't doubt that the chief might have vented his frustration. But he wasn't about to sign any such letter. Orsini took him back to the realty office. Later, Burge said, she phoned to say that she appreciated his honesty and realized her request had been improper. She'd settled on another plan to deal with Chief Younts. She didn't say what it was.

A more timid man might have made up his mind to steer clear of Mary Lee. Burge, however, sensed an opportunity for adventure. "She got to where she would call down at the office. So I said, 'Shit, I'll see what I can find out around here' . . . There was just lots of questions that hadn't been answered, and I was going to see if I could run down one or two. See what was happening. You know, just doggin' off."

•   •   •

Mary Lee never told Burge the identity of the man who overheard Chief Younts's threat. But not long afterward she went out of her way to make the intimate acquaintance of a man with a criminal record. His name was Eugene "Yankee" Hall—the same man whose girlfriend had told Gary Glidewell that she suspected him of knowing something about the Orsini murder, and virtually the only name the private detective passed on to Mary Lee that had failed to provoke a response.

Small, lean, and dapper, Yankee made it a point to keep up appearances even when he was down, and when Mary Lee came looking for him, he couldn't have been much lower. Among other problems, his cocaine habit was eating him alive. Even so, he had a neatly trimmed mustache, wore his gray hair carefully styled, and kept his fingernails immaculately manicured. For a dude whose only legitimate skill was auto body work, that took some doing.

Mostly Yankee managed to avoid legitimate work. He made much of his illicit money on hot cars. He might deal some dope now and again, or fence some stolen jewelry. Whenever he could, however, it suited his ego to position himself as a middleman—a broker between thieves and buyers. The middle also tends to be the safest place in any criminal transaction: the cops want the perpetrators and the buyers want protection. As long as he takes care not to violate the unwritten underworld code, a clever dude can make deals in both directions. Yankee referred to the several Little Rock bars where he hung out— Peck's, the Whitewater, the Mason Jar—as his "offices." They took messages for him there, no questions asked.

Having come to Little Rock from Wilkes-Barre, Pennsylvania, with the Air Force twenty-five years earlier, Hall had never lost the brusque, tough-guy accent that accounted for his nickname. But as John Terry had told Glidewell, nobody ever mistook Yankee for a badass. While well known to every law enforcement agency in the area, he'd done time only once, for possession with intent to deliver cocaine.

Meeting Yankee in a bar wouldn't fit the image Mary Lee wanted to sell him, so she picked him up in a Taco Bell on Camp Robinson Road. He was sitting there with his four-year-old son one Saturday talking to friends when Mary Lee walked in. Later, as he related, he realized that their rendezvous had been no accident. "I'm a real girl-chaser anyway. Anyone that knows me can tell you that—made a profession out of it, you know. She made a point when she was walking by of just glancing at the kids talking and just blinked her eyes. She definitely got my attention, you know. Gave me a little eye. Then she went and sat down where I could see her. Every time I glanced at her, she was looking at me. She'd turn her head and give me the eye. Then when we were leaving, she just happened to walk out a little ahead of me. Her car was parked next to mine—out of the whole parking lot. It was just too convenient. And of course I said something to her, and she reciprocated.

"We talked for a few minutes and she asked me where I was going. I told her I was going to take my boy to the playground over at Burns Park, and she volunteered to go with us. We went in her car. I left the truck I was driving because it had a big refrigeration unit on the back. My boy took to her right away. She's a likable person. Got a hell of a personality—real bubbly. We stayed in Burns Park quite a while, talking. This is when I found out who she was, and about the Orsini thing. She's telling me all about it. She's innocent. She wasn't in-volved in her husband's murder. And Chief Younts hates her and he's blaming her, and he's not really looking for the killer. I mean, she run the whole thing out to me. The killer's still out there, see, and she's pissed off because Younts is trying to get her instead of looking for the real killer. Me, I'm just chasing pussy."

After a while, Mary Lee suggested they go back to her place. Yankee's son rode along in Mary Lee's black Chevrolet Caprice. She had always had a way with children. They popped some popcorn, had a few drinks and talked some more until the boy fell asleep.

"Let me tell you something," Yankee later confided. "I got me some pussy that first night. Funny thing was, she wasn't that much in bed. I've had a lot of women, though. So it'd really take something to impress me. But she wasn't that extraordinary."

In the fantasy world she drew him into, the tough-talking ex-con imagined himself the only *real* man that Mary Lee—with her sheltered childhood of church suppers and 4-H hayrides, her college degree and her trust fund—had ever known. In and out of bed, Yankee saw himself teaching the beleaguered widow all kinds of things rich girls never learn. When it came to a damsel in distress, Yankee was a pushover.

And, according to Hall, the first dragon Mary Lee wanted slain was NLRPD Chief Bubba Younts. Bill McArthur, she confided, knew an informant who could prove that Younts had been involved in her husband's murder. He and Sergeant Farley had conspired to pin the slaying on her. Mary Lee drove Yankee by Younts's house to show him the chief's unmarked Ford sedan. Her plan, Hall said, was to plant a bomb under the hood. Did Yankee know how to make a car bomb? Anybody who knew how to install a toggle switch, he told her, could make a bomb. The tricky part was getting the dynamite. But he urged her to forget it. The scheme was far too risky. Especially for a society broad.

· · ·

Right from the start, there was just one thing Yankee hadn't liked about his affair with Mary Lee. Hiding their relationship from her daughter he understood. Hall accepted that when Tiffany was home, he never got to visit. Otherwise, he saw no reason for secrecy. Indeed, for Yankee—in one of those little human foibles Mary Lee failed to take account of in making her plans—bragging about his sexual exploits gave him almost as much pleasure as having them to start with. Maybe more.

On the first night when Mary Lee had picked Yankee up at the Taco Bell, she asked him to hide the borrowed truck he drove around the corner. Then she checked to be sure the house was empty before signaling him to come in. "I could tell she was worried about somebody coming over," Yankee said. "She chain-latched the door. So when I left, I says, 'Lee, this is fine tonight, sneaking around.' But I says, 'This ain't me, parking around the corner. I'm liable to be shot sneaking through somebody's yard. They're going to think I'm a burglar.'

"She even agreed. She said, 'Yeah, you're right. That is a pain in the ass, sneaking around. I'm breaking up with this guy. He's still got the key to my house. I'll get it back.' So I knew there was another dude, but I didn't know who it was."

The dude in question was Dr. C. H. Wulz. And Mary Lee had no more intention of ending her relationship with the veterinarian than she had of introducing Yankee around as her fiancé. Whether or not Mary Lee's affair with Wulz had begun within two weeks of Ron's murder as she'd confided to Joyce Holt, the two had been dating seriously ever since the 1981 grand jury hearing. Wulz squired her everywhere: the dinner theater, the symphony, and the Repertory Theater. They took a winter ski trip to Colorado. Wulz's daughter Tammy and Tiffany Orsini became constant companions.

The affair had cooled somewhat in recent months. They remained intimate, but agreed to date others. Soon after her interview with the *Gazette* on the anniversary of Ron's death, however, the action began to pick up again, and with it the veterinarian's interest. According to Mary Lee, her promise of a reward for information leading to Ron's killer had resulted in another series of threatening phone calls from the same man. If she didn't drop the investigation, she would "get her fucking head blown off." Nobody else heard the calls, but Wulz never doubted that they were real.

On the evening of Tuesday, April 6, Mary Lee supposedly had a casual dinner date planned with a child psychiatrist whom she'd consulted about Tiffany. In fact, she used the physician's name as a decoy; they'd met at his office by appointment only. Tiffany herself was to spend the night with Wulz's daughter.

About 7:30 P.M., Mary Lee phoned Wulz at home. She claimed to be calling from St. Vincent Infirmary in Little Rock, where she'd gone to meet her date. She sounded terribly agitated. Under no circumstances, she warned, should the veterinarian allow the two girls to walk home from watching TV at a classmate's house that night. He must deliver them and pick them up. Nor could Tiffany be permitted to return home that night for any reason at all. Wulz did as he was told. After he got the girls to bed, he called Mary Lee at 11:00 P.M. to find out what was wrong. She struck him as evasive, and uncharacteristically eager to get off the phone. She claimed to be exhausted, also unusual. She'd normally talk all night. Wulz got the impression that she was not alone.

The veterinarian grew even more suspicious when he got a hang-up call at 1:30 A.M. He felt sure it was Mary Lee, checking to be sure he was home. "When somebody suspects you of doing something," he said, "frequently it's them that's doing something." Mary Lee had a right to do what she pleased, Wulz hastened to add. But he'd stuck his neck out for the woman, and it burned him up to be lied to.

"At about 1:45, I called Lee," Wulz noted in a memo he wrote himself at 3:00 A.M.

She answered in a low, whispery (sleepy?) voice—and her voice stayed low and whispery for the full 10 or 15 minutes . . . . [She spoke] as if I were her Mother or a babysitter. She would not initiate any conversation and when I suggested that I come over, she was insistent that I not leave the girls alone. . . .

She seemed awfully anxious that I not go to her house. So I put my clothes on and at about 2:15 am, I drove by her house. . . . A red coupe (Monte Carlo?) with a white top— License Tag #JBR-923 was parked in the driveway behind the garage door she uses.

Returning home, Wulz phoned Joyce Holt to ask if she knew who Mary Lee's visitor might be. Joyce thought she knew, but wasn't about to confide in Wulz.

The veterinarian got up at 5:30 A.M. and jogged past 7412 Pontiac for a second look. But the red coupe was gone. He confronted Mary Lee, and she handed him a cock and bull story about the neighbors having a party—at 3:00 A.M. on a weekday. Even Wulz doubted that. Through a friend, he got somebody at the NLRPD to run the license number. It belonged to a Little Rock woman whose name meant nothing to him. So he kept the memo he'd written a secret from Mary Lee. But he did keep it.

2

Now that Orsini had her initial cast of characters arranged, things started to happen fast. The following afternoon she showed up unannounced at Bill McArthur's office with an alarming tale. Ever since the *Gazette* article three weeks earlier, Mary Lee had complained of telephone threats. Bill had advised her to ask the phone company to put a trap on the line to record the origin and exact time of all incoming calls. But how seriously to take her, he couldn't guess. Like the Jim Guy Tucker wiretapping incident, the whole thing could be imaginary.

Mary Lee may have sensed McArthur's skepticism. The story she told that day contained more specific details. A man had called claiming to have information about her husband's murder. But he wouldn't divulge what he knew on the telephone. So Mary Lee had agreed to meet him at a remote spot in Burns Park. She described a wiry grayhaired man with a mustache, not very tall, driving a pickup. He had an odd accent—like a Cajun perhaps, or a Yankee.

Mary Lee thought the stranger had acted jumpy. He kept glancing down the road as if he expected company. She felt he was stalling. Growing uneasy, Mary Lee had said, "Look, I've got to go." As she turned to get in her car, he'd grabbed her arm.

"Don't you touch me," Mary Lee cried. Then she jumped in her car and took off. In the hubbub, she'd neglected to secure the pickup's license plate number.

Neither Bill nor his secretary Phoebe Pinkston knew what to make of that one. Could Mary Lee actually be fool enough to meet a stranger in Burns Park? In the past, Phoebe had suspected Mary Lee of overdramatizing to keep Bill's sympathy. She and the others in the office had noticed that Mary Lee's demeanor changed when McArthur returned from court or emerged from his office. Whatever they were talking about, Mary Lee would drop it and make him the center of attention. McArthur never acted as if he noticed. He treated her exactly as he did all his clients—sympathetically, but at arm's length. Obviously, nobody alienated a client who owed them $15,000.

In fact, back in the fall of 1981, just about the time he and his partners had begun to talk seriously about BJ's, Bill had a mildly unsettling episode with Mary Lee. Late one afternoon, she'd called him. Her detectives had uncovered some shocking information. He decided to humor her. He agreed to swing across the I-430 bridge on his way home and meet her in a small park next to the Arkansas River lock and dam. When he arrived, McArthur was chagrined to find that she'd laid out a picnic spread—complete with wine and cheese and a wicker hamper. He heard her out, but left as quickly as he could.

When he got home, McArthur phoned Jim Lester. The investigator minced no words. "I said, 'Bill, watch that bitch. Watch her. She is dangerous. That woman is after you, Bill.'

"He said, 'Aw, Jim, you're crazy. She ain't interested in me.'

" 'Bill, I know better. I know viper women. I picked her from day one.' "

McArthur discounted Lester's suspicions as typical cop paranoia, but he did resolve to avoid seeing Mrs. Orsini anywhere but his office, and never alone.* The time to reduce her emotional dependence upon him had come. Since Phoebe answered the office phone, Phoebe got the job.

A native of the town of Ozark, about 120 miles northwest of the state capital, Phoebe had been with Bill for eight years. Witty and opinionated, she took a generally dim view of human nature and prided herself on being hard to fool. Besides her boss's generosity, one reason she loved her job was that he often asked her what she thought about his clients' stories and listened to what she had to say. And Phoebe did love to talk.

Phoebe had formed no strong opinions about the Orsini case. She knew what Jim Lester thought, but agreed with her boss's view: unless she had an airtight alibi, Lester would suspect his own momma. Besides, she kept her distance from Bill's clients. Guilty or innocent, they tended not to be her kind of people.

Once Phoebe and Mary Lee began talking regularly on the phone, however, they turned out to have a lot in common. Phoebe loved horses. She kept a pair of Arabians at a rented stable, and was looking to buy a place of her own out in Lonoke County. Mary Lee spoke fondly of her own carefree rustic childhood and the horses she'd owned. Pinkston had recently married a man with teen-aged children, so she and Orsini had that to talk about too.

Before long, the two women had become fast friends. They chatted on the telephone every day, sometimes for hours at a time, both during

---

*McArthur would have been even more uncomfortable had he known that Sergeant T. J. Farley had gotten word of the picnic and passed it on to Linda House that very afternoon.

Phoebe's working hours and at home. There was little they *didn't* talk about. She and her husband Paul even went out to dinner with Mary Lee and Tiffany. After the grand jury, Phoebe simply *assumed* Mary Lee's innocence. She suspected her of being a bit neurotic and having a hyperactive imagination. But murder? Like most of the women Orsini manipulated, Phoebe got to where she simply couldn't imagine it. The NLRPD had blundered, for by no means the first time in Phoebe's experience.

When Mary Lee pumped her for information about Bill McArthur's home life, Phoebe figured her curiosity was only natural. "She really wouldn't ask questions," Phoebe said later. "We talked about it. The only thing she quizzed me about was what Alice was like. One time she was astounded because Alice has a very deep voice on the phone, and a lot of times you would think she was a man. She wondered what type of relationship you could build with someone like that. And I said, 'Well, Alice doesn't look like what she sounds like.' "

Soon enough, Mary Lee found a way to get a first-hand look at Alice. One Friday in October 1981, she learned that Bill and Alice and some friends were going out dancing at Bob Troutt's Kountry Klub. There hadn't been any reason not to tell her. Orsini showed up at the Kountry Klub that night with a date. She never introduced the man, but left her group to pay an uninvited visit to the McArthur table. Bill introduced her to the four couples in their party and she sat down briefly—almost as if she owned the joint, Alice remarked to Bill.

Something about Mary Lee put Alice's back up, and she cut her dead. "I can't believe that woman came by here and wanted to visit with everybody," she told Bill after Orsini walked off. "I don't like that woman." No snob, Alice believed in her instincts about people. Her husband believed in them too—or at least knew better than to argue when Alice expressed a strong antipathy.

If she noticed Alice's coolness, Mary Lee gave no indication. She presented herself at McArthur's office a few days later with a wonderful new plan. She hoped Bill didn't mind, but she'd shared what she'd learned from Phoebe about his plans for a new country and western dance club with her date—whom she identified as the son of a prominent state senator. Her date, she claimed, had become very excited. He saw it as a "can't miss" proposition, and was eager to provide start-up capital.

Nothing came of it. Next thing McArthur knew, Mary Lee was talking about mortgaging *her* home at 7412 Pontiac to raise the cash.

What with her extensive marketing background, she volunteered to handle advertising and promotions for the new club. Bill never took the mortgage idea seriously. Even if Orsini could raise the $50,000 she proposed—which given lawsuits pending against her looked impossible—she still owed him $15,000. First things first.

Just in case, McArthur did ask Alice and his partners what they thought of the notion. They didn't like it. As always, Alice was particularly vocal. It was all very well for Bill to do his bleeding heart number. But the last thing their new venture needed was a murder suspect with a habit of holding press conferences. For that matter, Bill agreed. Orsini's antics had made representing her hard enough; she'd be a nightmare as a business partner. No matter. As he'd guessed, she never came up with the money, so no formal decision ever needed to be made, nor was McArthur forced to deliver the bad news. Gradually, Mary Lee just stopped talking about it.

Some weeks later, however, Orsini did turn up with a proposal she'd persuaded a Little Rock ad agency to put together. The firm had done the work on "spec" as a favor for her, she said. In reality, she'd identified herself as the club's marketing director. They proposed to call the new club "Tumbleweeds," and had designed a logo featuring cactuses and cowboy hats. McArthur and his partners gave it a look, but found the theme too faddish and overtly Texan for Arkansas tastes. Little Rock sits half-encircled by cypress bayous on a river a half mile wide; the nearest tumbleweeds blow a thousand miles to the west.

In any event, the partners had already hired a PR man and settled on the "honky tonk" theme. They thanked her, and declined. As for her taking an active role in management, she knew better than to ask. By November of 1981 Jim Lester had been hired to manage BJ's—and he, she knew, would sooner hire Satan than Mary Lee Orsini.

By April 1982, business at BJ's was booming. So much so that Bob Troutt had shut down the Kountry Klub several weeks earlier—supposedly for renovation. The place was due to reopen in a few days. While he felt no real animus against Troutt, McArthur had permitted himself a few wry jokes about arson. The Kountry Klub's previous building had burned to the ground.

Besides his lawsuit for copyright infringement, Troutt had also sworn out a felony warrant against Bob Robbins—the disc jockey who owned a minority partnership in BJ's. Troutt alleged that Robbins had stolen hundreds of phonograph records belonging to the Kountry Klub when he switched jobs. McArthur had gotten the charges dismissed by proving that the records belonged to the radio station Robbins worked for, not Troutt.

But on April 7, a day after Mary Lee's secret tryst with Yankee, events took a more ominous turn. Shortly after 7:00 P.M., Robbins was leaving the studios of KSSN-FM after his afternoon "drive time" show when two black men confronted him in the parking lot. One mentioned something about a flat tire on Robbins's car. As the disc jockey bent over to examine the tire, the man smashed him in the face with a baseball bat. Robbins fell to the ground, his nose broken, his cheekbone and jaw shattered. By the time McArthur saw him in the Baptist Hospital emergency room, Robbins's face had turned into a ghastly, swollen mask. He required hours of reconstructive surgery. Later, Robbins would testify that his children had been unable to recognize him. His assailants escaped unrecognized. Suspicion, however, focused upon Troutt. Nobody else seemed to have a motive.

.   .   .

Almost before McArthur got over the shock, he was presented with a second life-threatening crisis. On the afternoon of April 8, Bill was interviewing a client when he saw Orsini's black Chevy Caprice skid around the corner. He heard it screech to a stop in the parking lot, then saw Mary Lee running up the walk as if somebody were chasing her. Minutes later, Phoebe beckoned him into the outer office. There stood Mary Lee with a glass of scotch Phoebe had poured to try to calm her down. She was barely coherent, and seemingly wall-eyed with terror. Her face was ashen, and she was trembling so hard that her teeth chattered. Her jet black hair and clothing were covered with tiny shards of glass. Blood trickled down her face from several superficial cuts near the hairline.

When McArthur calmed her down, Mary Lee said that she'd been driving along a remote stretch of Batesville Pike near the North Little Rock municipal airport when two gunmen had pulled alongside in a beat-up car and fired a shot, shattering the side window and narrowly missing her head. She'd seen the glint of the gun barrel just in time to throw herself down on the seat. Bill went outside to look at the car. Shattered glass covered the front seat. There was a jagged tear that looked like a bullet hole in the driver's side headrest. Had Mary Lee not dived for cover, it appeared, the shot would have been fatal.

That Orsini had raced to his office on the Little Rock side of the river didn't surprise McArthur. Her contempt for the NLRPD knew no bounds. Even so, he insisted upon calling them. As he explained, nobody else could help her. Two NLRPD detectives soon arrived at McArthur's office. One had also investigated the alleged burglary at 7412 Pontiac almost a year earlier, when Mary Lee had fired a shot at an intruder in a red jogging suit.

This time, Orsini had an even more frightening story to tell, beginning with the previous afternoon, when two stringy-haired rednecks in a beat-up green sedan had pointed a double-barreled shotgun at her as she drove up North Little Rock's JFK Boulevard on her way home from McArthur's office. She gave a vivid, detailed account. Only by taking a couple of quick turns and nailing the accelerator to the floor had she escaped. Mary Lee had told Phoebe all about it, but hadn't notified the NLRPD because she knew they'd ignore her.

After hearing her description of this latest assault, all four drove to the site of the shooting incident. The officers were polite, but privately skeptical. If she feared for her life, why had she been driving alone on a remote back road—out of sight and hearing of others? And if both cars were doing 30 to 35 mph, as Orsini claimed, the gunman had made one hell of a pistol shot to nail the headrest dead center. So how did the glass from the shattered window come to be lying in one neat little pile? The detectives did, however, dig a .38 slug out of the car seat and took it to the State Crime Lab. Alas, it matched none of the guns that had figured in the case to date.

McArthur found himself in yet another quandary. Once again, Mary Lee had turned up as the victim of a crime to which she was the only witness. Shaken by the Bob Robbins beating, at first he never doubted his client's story. On Friday, April 9—the same day accounts of the incident appeared in the newspapers—he took her to NLRPD headquarters to study mug shots. They spent several hours at it; Orsini thought she recognized several faces. But none well enough to make a positive ID.

After McArthur spoke with the detectives privately, he and Phoebe confessed their doubts to each other. Could Orsini possibly have faked the whole thing? But why? What conceivable motive would lead her to do that? When she'd come bursting in the office door, Phoebe had nearly jumped out of her skin. Besides the glass in her hair and the blood streaming down her forehead, Mary Lee looked as pale as death. Her eyes rolled back in their sockets as if she were about to faint, and she'd been shaking so hard she'd spilled most of the drink Phoebe had poured her. So unless Orsini was crazier than a Betsy-bug and the best actress in the Old Confederacy, the shooting had to be real. Maybe.

Evidently dissatisfied with the press coverage, Mary Lee summoned a *Gazette* reporter to 7412 Pontiac that same day. The resulting interview put her back on the front page for the first time since the grand jury hearing nine months earlier. There was a photograph of the car seat and a three-column headline:

MRS. ORSINI WORRIED ABOUT "HIT," SAYS
SHE'S ENDING PROBE OF HUSBAND'S DEATH

Mary Lee "was 'through pushing' an investigation into the death of her husband," the newspaper reported.

> In a brief interview Friday in her living room, Mrs. Orsini said, "I am not going to help the police investigation in any way. I had no idea they'd come after me." She wouldn't say who she thought might be "coming after her."
> She said, "Ron wouldn't want me to go on with this. . . ."

While Mary Lee also claimed that police intelligence had confirmed a "hit" on her and planned to place her in protective custody, an NLRPD spokesman was unaware of the matter.

At McArthur's urging, Mary Lee agreed to take Tiffany and leave town for a while. She would stay with friends in the town of Searcy, she said, and keep in touch by phone. The Searcy exile lasted exactly two days. By Monday, Mary Lee was back in Little Rock. Before she'd left for the weekend, she explained, the same stranger she'd met in Burns Park—the wiry one with the mustache and funny accent—had called again. This time, she'd had her tape recorder running. She'd come to believe that she'd misinterpreted the man's actions; he'd been honestly trying to warn her. She showed up in McArthur's office carrying a cassette of the conversation. She had already played it for Joyce Holt and Dr. Wulz. Now she wanted Phoebe and Bill to hear it:

"What your suggestion is," Mary Lee's voice trembled, "that I just get out of town for—not just the weekend or something—but I need to get out of town for months or weeks?"

"Yeah, I think so. And your daughter."

"Have you heard that she's in danger too?"

"No. Nobody said that. I tell you what, we've done so much talking on the telephone and there are so many people involved—you know, damn cops are involved—no telling about the phones."

Orsini assured him that her attorney had arranged to have her phone line swept for bugs.

"So how you doing?" he asked.

"I don't know. I'm numb. That's the only thing I can tell you. I'm trying to get my wits together. I want Bill to listen to me. But I tell you what's blown my mind is the fact that you knew about me being at the police station looking at those mug shots."

"I don't want to talk to you over no phone. But if you want to have a drink or something. . . ."

To Arkansas ears, the man's distinctive accent sounded like Sylvester Stallone with a mouthful of marbles. But neither Bill nor Phoebe recognized his voice. The caller warned her not to rely too heavily upon McArthur. "See, he's working for you. You don't have to do like he says. He's not some kind of a god. He has an opinion. That don't make it so. Think for yourself a little bit."

"Well, I am trying to think for myself," Mary Lee said. "And I appreciate your warning me. You don't known how much I appreciate you warning me."

"I have nothing to gain by telling you. I'm just telling you because I really care for you. . . . I tell everybody I talk to. I say, 'Look, this is a favor to me. I really care for her.' I let 'em know it's a personal favor. They started telling me things they can get their arms cut off for, you know. And I'm just telling you, boy are you—pardon my language— but you're just pissing in the wind. You are getting nowhere with this."

"How can I convince these people that I'm through with it?"

". . . Nobody seems to know. Nobody will say anything for sure. Nobody even acts like they know."

She had tried to deal with the situation like a business deal, Mary Lee told her caller. "But I can't take any more," she said. "Mentally, emotionally. I want them to leave me alone."

He sounded exasperated. "And the first thing you need to do is to eliminate that problem by eliminating you, see? You need to be gone! Not at your lawyer's office and the police station and your fucking house. Jesus Christ, who could *not* find you? . . . Two attempts have been made on your life. . . . What are you fucking doing *anywhere*? You don't need to be anywhere where you've ever fucking been. That's where you need to be. Somewhere you have never fucking been."

Mary Lee rattled on about how she'd told the newspapers she was dropping the investigation.

"I know I'm being rude, but let me interrupt you, right?" he said. "And then you spent the afternoon at the police station looking for mug shots. There's leaks everywhere. They know everything the cops are doing—everything your attorneys are fucking doing. You are in over your head, darling."

"You're right. I agree, and the goddam doorbell's ringing."

A skeptical listener *might* have caught the "darling," or seen through her ruse to hang up before the caller said anything to spoil the tape's usefulness. But nobody who heard it suspected how intimately she knew the caller—any more than Yankee Hall knew he was being taped.

. . .

Detectives Farley and Miles took no interest in the latest incident. When it came to Orsini, the NLRPD spoke with one voice. The lady was full of shit, and that was that. They had too many real crimes that needed investigating to waste their time chasing shadows.

McArthur understood, but he had a terrified client on his hands. So on April 14 he took her to see Prosecutor Dub Bentley. She arrived at the courthouse carrying the results of a lie detector test she'd taken on her own. According to the polygraph operator—unfamiliar to both McArthur and Bentley—her account of the shooting incident represented the truth.

Dub Bentley was skeptical. The prosecutor, after all, had read Farley's investigative file and heard the grand jury testimony—as her lawyer had not. "I was teetering," Bentley said. "I thought she was faking those damned phone calls, but couldn't be sure. I was concerned with one in particular—one that traced to Gyst House. [The acronym stands for "Get Your Shit Together," a drug rehab clinic for ex-cons.] I said, hell, how could Lee Orsini know somebody out at Gyst House? Even if I believed she'd killed her husband, I didn't want to pick up the paper some morning and find that Lee Orsini had been murdered."

Bentley, however, had barely enough staff investigators to keep up with the day-to-day work of the prosecutor's office. He had none to spare for wild goose chases. Particularly not if it meant antagonizing Chief Younts and the NLRPD. By then, no private investigator in town would have worked for Mrs. Orsini without seeing a stack of cash up front. So Bill really had just one option left. Despite personal misgivings amounting to near contempt for Tommy Robinson, the mercurial Sheriff, he advised Mary Lee to pick up her file at his office and carry it out to the Pulaski County Sheriff's Department (PCSD).

3

For all her notoriety, Mary Lee was far from being the biggest headline maker on the Arkansas law and order front. That honor would belong to Sheriff Tommy F. Robinson. Nobody else came remotely close. Before Robinson's arrival on the scene in 1981, the sheriff's job had been a relatively colorless one. Charged with running the county jail and patrolling far-flung rural areas outside city limits, the PCSD was chronically overworked, underpaid, and overshadowed by the LRPD and NLRPD. But where others saw drudgery, Tommy had seen opportunity. He'd left a better-paid, more prestigious job as Arkansas Director of Public Safety to campaign for sheriff like a man running for governor.

With the help of the Little Rock media, Sheriff Tommy had in the space of a year transformed himself into the best-known cop in Arkansas. But within the tight-knit world of Arkansas law enforcement, Robinson had a reputation as a big talker who'd finessed his way out of more tight spots than a hundred-dollar hooker. Among themselves, other cops spoke of him with contempt. But like cops everywhere, they also kept their opinions to themselves.

During his race against the incumbent, Robinson had portrayed himself as a reformer. The PCSD, he'd charged, was incompetent, corrupt, and wasteful. He stumped the county carrying an empty chair to dramatize his opponent's refusal to debate. Indeed, many observers agreed that the outfit needed a shake-up. Stressing his broad experience and a Criminal Justice degree from UA-Little Rock, Tommy vowed to bring professional law enforcement to the state's largest county. Instead, he brought public theater.

What Robinson's supporters saw as wide-ranging experience, some other cops saw as an inability to keep a job. Tommy had grown up in a blue-collar area of North Little Rock known as Rose City. Having joined the NLRPD in 1963 directly out of the Navy, he'd rarely stayed in one place for more than a couple of years. He and Sergeant Farley had ridden together as rookie patrolmen, and Farley had no use for him at all. Neither did Sergeant Buddy Miles.

Wherever Robinson went, it seemed, rancor and confusion followed. Yet Tommy always managed to land on his feet. In two years as an Arkansas state trooper beginning in 1966, Robinson managed to get himself into a lawsuit alleging that he'd beaten up and then sicced a police dog on a drunken black man. A jury believed Tommy, but not all of his superiors found his story persuasive. Robinson ended up back with the NLRPD in 1968.

By 1971, Robinson joined the U.S. Marshal Service, leaving in 1974 to become a campus cop at UA-Fayetteville. Transferred to the Medical School campus in Little Rock, in 1975 Tommy was appointed police chief in Jacksonville—a suburban town adjacent to Little Rock Air Force Base. Controversy began almost at once, as did Tommy's stormy love affair with the Little Rock media. "Robinson is a police rarity," ran a typical 1976 profile in the *Gazette*,

> in that he always is available to the press and opens virtually all police files for inspection. Devoutly religious, he said, "We're operating impartially. People can't call the police and get tickets torn up. We're making a definite dent in the drug traffic [according to him, thirty-five drug arrests in a month compared to not that many in ten years] . . . ."
>
> "The word's out I won't last," he said. "But they'll have to kill me to get rid of me.
>
> "I am treating the poorest man in this town the same as I would the richest one." That is some of the problem.

Something else Tommy was accused of doing, however, was spying on his enemies. In 1977, a Jacksonville detective charged that Tommy had fired him for refusing to perform "political espionage," including electronic surveillance of the mayor and sifting through the trash of public officials. Tommy insisted that they were all criminal suspects. He vowed to take a lie detector test, then backed out for fear of jeopardizing important investigations.

Casting himself as a champion of the common man, Robinson polarized the town. Several lawyers representing cops summarily fired by Robinson had angry confrontations with the irascible lawman—but none so angry as the one Bill McArthur had in August 1978, when Tommy threatened to kill him in front of several witnesses.

McArthur had already known that Tommy disliked him. Sitting in for a Jacksonville municipal judge a year earlier, McArthur had held the police chief in contempt. Angered by the dismissal of a gambling charge, Robinson had given a speech calling Judge Reed Williamson a "bastard" and hinting at a payoff. McArthur had required him to produce evidence or make a written apology. Lacking evidence of wrongdoing—his own officers had acted on an invalid search warrant—Robinson knuckled under.

Then in 1978, Bill had taken the case of a police sergeant Tommy had fired to the Civil Service Board. McArthur's client was reinstated by a unanimous vote. In the hallway of the municipal building later on, Robinson had loudly vowed revenge. Other cops told McArthur Tommy was all mouth, so Bill laughed it off.

Some others found the handsome young police chief's rhetoric more impressive. In 1979, Governor Bill Clinton chose Robinson to be director of the Arkansas Department of Public Service. Robinson hit the ground running, racing to accidents and natural disasters all over Arkansas to personally supervise—and to appear on the evening news. Soon enough, Tommy was up to his neck in controversy and the department was in turmoil. During fifteen months on the job, Robinson fired the state medical examiner and the head of Alcoholic Beverage Control Enforcement, and conducted an acrimonious public feud with the commander of the state police. The chairman of the civilian board overseeing the state police resigned, charging that Robinson was destroying the agency.

In March 1980, to Clinton's relief, Tommy resigned. He'd accumulated an unusually well-heeled group of financial backers. Closest to him personally was Robinson's boyhood friend Jerry Jones. The son of a grocer who'd later made a small fortune in the insurance business, Jones himself had made millions in natural gas. He would become famous years afterward by using part of his fortune to buy the Dallas Cowboys and naming his former teammate Jimmy Johnson—the two had been linemen on the Arkansas Razorbacks' 1964 National Championship team—as coach.

Another of Robinson's enthusiastic backers was Sheffield Nelson, president of Arkla, the state's natural gas utility. Nelson and Jones had other mutual interests besides Tommy Robinson. According to a 1983 series in *The New York Times*, the two had been involved in a highly controversial transaction between Arkla and Jones's Arkoma exploration company. Over the objections of company geologists, Arkla sold drilling rights to what turned out to be a mammoth natural gas field in western Arkansas to Jones's company for $10 million. At the time of

the sale, Jones was also on the Arkla board of directors. Long after
Nelson's departure from the utility, the company paid Jones $150
million to buy the same leases back. The state Public Utilities Commission concluded that no crime had been committed, but speculation
lingered.

Nelson and Jones not only bankrolled Tommy Robinson's campaign
for sheriff, but openly supplemented his salary by hiring him as "manager" of a duck hunting club they owned. Also prominent among
Tommy's supporters were Jerry Maulden, the chairman of Arkansas
Power & Light (the state's electric utility) and a corporate lawyer named
Larry Wallace, with major holdings in banking and commercial real
estate. Wallace was also part owner and board chairman of KARK-TV,
the Little Rock NBC outlet.

Oil, natural gas, electricity, real estate, banking, and TV. Sheriff
Tommy had the bases covered. Sheffield Nelson's friendship with
Democrat owner Walter Hussman also seemed likely to assure the
candidate a hearing at the state's second largest newspaper, which had
positioned itself as a rambunctious, right-wing populist alternative to
the patrician liberalism of the *Gazette*. Nelson also had close ties to
Stephens, Inc.—the largest investment bank in the United States outside New York.

Conservative Democrats in the state's one-party political system,
with the exception of AP&L's Maulden, these men would all soon
become Reagan supporters intent upon overturning the state's political
establishment. And Tommy was their boy.

Easily winning the nomination in the 1980 Democratic primary,
Tommy ran unopposed in the general election. Months before being
sworn in, he notified forty-seven allegedly no-account deputies that
they'd be fired come January 1. There would be no due process. When
the deputies won an injunction from Judge George Howard—the only
black federal judge in Arkansas—Tommy had an issue that kept him
in the news for weeks, as he made one defiant pronouncement after
another. Eventually, the sheriff had to back down, denouncing Howard as a "token judge."

Difficult to make credible elsewhere, Robinson's antics seemed a
throwback to a more colorful era in Arkansas politics. TV cameras
loved him. Tall, broad-shouldered, and handsome in a sharp-featured
way, the sheriff had an uncanny knack for glib one-liners that hit most
Arkansans right where they lived. It seemed that he never made a move
without notifying the press.

Sheriff Tommy hadn't been in office but about three months before starting a bitter feud with County Judge Bill Beaumont. (In Arkansas, the title "County Judge" refers to the county's chief executive—an elected, non-judicial job.) Contending that his budget was inadequate to operate the county jail, the sheriff began to overspend. Ignoring warnings, he appeared repeatedly before the county commissioners to demand more money. Without it, he predicted disaster.

All of a sudden, prisoners began to escape from the jail in carloads. On May 8, seven prisoners got away. On June 10, eight more escaped, five of whom were recaptured single-handedly by the sheriff twenty-four hours later in what he called "a stroke of luck." One of the group later charged that Tommy had orchestrated the whole thing. Five more prisoners escaped on June 25, and another four on July 12.

Two days after that, the sheriff donned riot gear, and, before an audience of TV reporters, led deputies into the jail to quell a disturbance. Later that afternoon—again accompanied by the media—Robinson stormed a house in downtown Little Rock where he'd been tipped fugitives were hiding. Hearing noises upstairs, Tommy and his boys let go a barrage of .9mm automatic fire through the ceiling, shooting one escapee in the foot and recapturing two others.

Dub Bentley and LRPD brass were furious. Not only had the sheriff violated long-standing agreements by operating inside city limits, but his behavior had been extremely reckless. Watching on TV, however, Arkansans ate it up.

Emboldened by his growing popularity, Tommy Robinson pulled his wildest stunt yet. With the state penitentiary badly overcrowded and temporarily unable (due to federal court orders) to accept new inmates, the sheriff told the media he was taking a busload of felons to Pine Bluff anyway. On July 15—only days before the grand jury declined to indict Mary Lee—Robinson and several carloads of deputies drove to the penitentiary gates accompanied by a convoy of reporters and TV trucks.

When he was refused admittance, Robinson ordered the prisoners, mostly black, shackled to the prison fence in 95-degree heat. Then he sped back to PCSD headquarters, ordered deputies to put on flak jackets and riot helmets, and blockaded the drive. If state police tried to return the prisoners, Tommy announced, they'd have to fight their way in.

The prisoners were taken to Jacksonville instead. Sheriff Robinson's stunt made others in law enforcement suspect that Tommy had gone off the deep end. To the majority of Arkansans, however, the sheriff's exploits were turning him into a folk hero. Resentful of crime and fed up with what seemed like the establishment's lily-livered behavior, they saw in Tommy a fearless man of action. The wilder he swung, the more they loved him.

And the more they loved him, the wilder Tommy swung. Soon he announced that deputies armed with shotguns would be staked out in convenience marts and liquor stores throughout the county. Armed robbers would be blown away. The sheriff appeared on the evening news aiming a 12 gauge pump directly into the camera. No robbers actually got shot, but the audience loved the melodrama.

Tensions between the PCSD and the LRPD worsened steadily. More than once, deputies in street clothes had staked out stores inside city limits, and accidental shootouts between them and LRPD officers had been narrowly averted.

Meanwhile, Robinson's feud with County Judge Beaumont had escalated into open warfare. He announced a criminal investigation of county finances. On March 18, 1982—six days after Mary Lee's press conference announcing a reward for information leading to Ron Orsini's murderer—Tommy evicted a federal court-appointed administrator from his office in the county jail at gunpoint. Two days later, he came pounding into county executive offices accompanied by TV cameras. He confronted Judge Beaumont, demanding payment on a $500 cash voucher for a clandestine drug buy. Beaumont explained that without the federal administrator's signature, the voucher was invalid. Tommy ordered him handcuffed for the crime of "restricting government operations." Then he marched downstairs and busted comptroller Jo Growcock, a middle-aged woman who wept as Tommy ordered her cuffed and taken to jail.

Fed up with the sheriff's antics, Judge Howard had him jailed for contempt. On his way into a federal prison in Memphis, Tommy bragged that he might arrest the judge. Robinson spent two nights in jail before backing down. Emerging as a triumphant victim of federal tyranny, and clutching a Bible to his chest, Sheriff Tommy announced that the experience had brought him closer to God.

In retrospect, the amazing thing is that it took Mary Lee Orsini and Sheriff Tommy as long as it did to get together.

. . .

McArthur telephoned ahead to Major Larry Dill, the head of the Criminal Investigation Division, to let him know Orsini would be arriving. Like the sheriff, Dill had less than a sparkling reputation in local law enforcement circles. Behind his back, Dill's deputies called him "Lurch"—after the dull-witted Frankenstein figure on the "Addams Family" TV show. A blond, blue-eyed man built on the lines of a professional wrestler, Dill's face seemed fixed in a permanent glare. He had been accused of brutality during his days as a Little Rock detective. In a federal lawsuit, testimony had been given that Dill administered systematic beatings to make suspects talk, black suspects in particular. Dill denied the allegations and criminal charges were never filed, but nobody shed any tears when Dill resigned to join the PCSD either.

When they wanted to find something good to say about him, other cops called Larry Dill one of the most tenacious investigators in Arkansas. Point Dill in the right direction and give him a lead, and he would work it as stubbornly as a good deerhound works a scent. Somebody would have to pull him off before he'd quit. But the boy needed leadership; pointed in the wrong direction, Dill could be dangerous. It all depended, they said, on who did the pointing. That was one of the many reasons Tommy Robinson's election as sheriff made a lot of people in law enforcement nervous. Under Robinson, Dill was less apt to act like a hound than a pit bull—fastening himself to some poor son of a bitch's throat until Tommy told him to let go.

McArthur knew all that, and so did Dub Bentley. Even so, the attorney had worked out a gruff, jocular working relationship with Dill. For occasions just like the one with Orsini, it was an occupational necessity. Anyhow, finding out who, if anybody, was threatening his client shouldn't require any brilliant detective work. Once they got the list of numbers from the phone company trap, the sheriff's deputies ought to be able either to catch the miscreant or scare him off by asking around.

Bentley, too, urged the sheriff's department to go ahead. The NLRPD wouldn't like it much, but at least he'd gotten Orsini off their backs. As for Sheriff Tommy Robinson, his publicity stunts had strained the relationship between the PCSD and the prosecuting attorney's office almost to breaking point. After the sheriff had chained the prisoners to the prison gate in July 1981, some lawyers on Bentley's staff joked that they should draw up commitment papers to have Robinson confined to the state hospital for thirty days of psychiatric observation. Chancellor Lee Munson, they speculated—the same judge who'd ruled for Stacy Orsini in the lawsuit against Mary Lee—would have had the guts to issue the order. The same staffers felt that Bentley ought to have refused to prosecute County Judge Bill Beaumont and comptroller Jo Growcock on the absurd charge of obstruction of government operations—a trial scheduled in municipal court later that same week. The prosecutor hoped that the proceedings would damage Tommy politically.

Bentley still hoped that Robinson could be cajoled into reasonable behavior. Some suspect that Bentley feared for his political career. Either way, Dub figured he was throwing the sheriff a bone. Here, after all, was a case that had *already* made the front pages. Anything the PCSD could do to solve Orsini's problems was sure to be widely publicized. Orsini herself would see to that.

Chapter 4

1

Friday, May 21, began like almost every other weekday morning at the McArthur house. As was her custom, Alice McArthur got up earlier than Bill and the kids. Particularly during the balmy Arkansas springtime, the hour around dawn was her favorite time of day. She liked to brew herself a pot of strong Louisiana-style coffee, and work her way through the *Gazette* in peace. Although she and Bill had stayed out with friends at BJ's until midnight, Alice enjoyed her morning solitude far too much to stay in bed. If she felt the need for an afternoon nap, she'd take one.

Bill got going a bit earlier than usual that morning himself. He'd been trying a civil suit all week at the federal courthouse, and wanted time to review his notes before making his closing argument. While Bill dressed and ate breakfast, Alice bustled around getting her kids out the door by 7:00 A.M. to catch the school bus. They attended St. Edward's, the Catholic grade school downtown. Eleven-year-old Robyn and eight-year-old Chuck were in the sixth and second grades, respectively.

Bill left for the twenty-minute ride to his office at about 7:40. Shortly past 8:00 several workmen arrived to continue the remodeling project Alice had under way—paid for by some of the money her Louisiana oil leases had suddenly begun producing.

At about 8:30, she put on shorts, threw her racquet in the front seat, and jumped into her car to pick up her friend Judy Harris for a

morning tennis match. She drove a tan, 1977 Olds Cutlass with an
Arkansas vanity license plate that read "CAJIN." Alice got no further
than ten feet up the driveway when a thunderous blast shook the car.
Dust and debris flew up from the floorboard, cutting and stinging her
bare legs. Her first panicky thought was that the Oldsmobile's battery
had exploded. She'd had that happen a couple of weeks earlier. But
this explosion was far more violent, and loud enough to leave her ears
ringing.

Two construction workers from a house being built nearby ran to
her aid. After determining that Alice had only minor cuts and abra-
sions on the backs of both legs, one worker spotted a six-volt battery
attached to a lead wire lying under the car. He picked it up in a gloved
hand. "Lady," he said, "you better call the police. Somebody just tried
to blow you up."

Incredible as it seemed, the man was dead right. Had the bomb
under the car detonated fully, investigators later determined, both the
Cutlass and anybody inside would have been blown to pieces.

Bill McArthur was talking on the phone with Mary Lee when Alice's
call came in on the other line. His office phone had been ringing off
the wall when he unlocked the door that morning. He put Mary Lee
on hold while he took it. McArthur hadn't talked to Mary Lee for a
couple of weeks. Ever since Bill had advised her to take her file to the
PCSD, Tommy Robinson had become her new hero. Phoebe had
warned him, however, that over the past several days his melodramatic
client had been showing signs of another first-class panic.

This time Orsini claimed that a sinister-looking stranger in a car
with Illinois plates had been following her all over North Little Rock.
When she'd given the license number to the PCSD, it came up on the
computer as a stolen car out of Chicago. Just two days ago, Tommy
Robinson's deputies had arrested the man. He turned out to have an
arrest record in Illinois for offenses involving guns, drugs, and impersonating a police officer.

Even more worrisome, the thug happened also to be a relative of
Donny Simmons—the alleged drug dealer with whom her dead husband had some kind of mysterious connection, and behind whose
business her purse stolen during the grand jury hearing had been
recovered. At the same time, Orsini had received some more threatening phone calls, one of which traced to Gyst House and another to
the Sherwood Police Department. Even Dub Bentley seemed alarmed.
Just the day before—Thursday, May 20—she'd taken her list of trapped

calls by the courthouse. This time the prosecutor had taken her seriously.

After talking to his badly shaken wife, Bill came back on the line to explain that he needed to hurry home. It appeared that somebody had planted a bomb under his wife's car. Orsini began wailing like a tornado siren. Oh my God! How many more people were going to have to die before the police got to the bottom of all this? By the time McArthur sped home to Pleasant Valley, Alice had already gotten two hang-up calls.

• • •

To federal investigators on the scene from the Bureau of Alcohol, Tobacco and Firearms (ATF), there was never any doubt of the seriousness of the attempt on Alice's life. Agent John Spurgeon's preliminary report found that

> a shampoo bottle filled with Tovex [a dynamite gel], along with a heavy duty battery and a toggle switch, all of which was taped with duct tape and placed in a King Edward cigar box was wedged under the emergency brake cable on the car. A cord was then connected to the switch and either the tire or the drive shaft, so that as the car moved forward it pulled the cord, which turned the switch and closed the circuit, setting off a #8 electrical blasting cap.

ATF's Washington, D.C., lab later concluded that the bomb had failed to detonate because the Tovex gel had lost density when it was poured into a Wella Balsam brand shampoo bottle. Either way, the bomber looked to be a semi-pro of sorts: possibly cunning enough to know that all high explosives come packaged in wrappers which allow ATF agents to trace them to their source, but not experienced enough—thank God—to know how to make them go off. That narrowed things down to about half the thugs between Nashville and Oklahoma City. Having recovered nearly 95 percent of the device, however, agents had plenty of physical evidence to go on.

As to motive, ATF agents learned little enough from Bill or Alice McArthur that they couldn't have gleaned from the local newspapers and TV. Not at all because the witnesses were uncooperative; rather, they were dumbfounded. The only person either of them could come up with who might want to kill Alice was the most obvious name in the world: Bob Troutt. Obvious because a bit more than a week after the baseball bat beating of Bob Robbins, Sheriff Tommy Robinson had made a highly publicized arrest of the Kountry Klub owner for allegedly hiring the disc jockey's attackers.

Whether or not Robinson could make the charges stick, as many doubted, he had gotten the maximum mileage out of the Troutt bust. With a primary election challenge coming up on May 25, the sheriff had busied himself during recent weeks in a wild media campaign to brand the previously obscure nightclub owner as Public Enemy Number One. To hear Sheriff Tommy tell it, full-scale mob warfare loomed in the Arkansas state capital. Only Robinson and his deputies stood between the citizens and chaos.

Alice told ATF and LRPD investigators that for the past two months she'd been concerned about the Troutt situation and made a habit of locking her car—which Bill never drove—and keeping it in the garage. On the night of May 20, she'd simply forgotten.

Bill McArthur told ATF agents that while Bob Troutt's was the only name he could come up with, he doubted the nightclub owner had the bomb planted. Maybe Troutt harbored a grudge against him; the Robbins beating had forced him to take the man's bluster more seriously. But nobody had ever called Troutt stupid. Killing Alice McArthur would gain him nothing—and constitute a serious violation of underworld code. Wives and children were off limits.

Later that afternoon, McArthur went for a ride with LRPD Assistant Chief Jess "Doc" Hale in his patrol car. Having among other achievements graduated first in his class from the FBI's Law Enforcement Academy, Hale was probably the most widely respected cop in Arkansas. A born diplomat, Hale helped keep feuding elements within the LRPD away from each other's throats—and managed the even tougher task of handling the department's dealings with Tommy Robinson and Larry Dill. He and McArthur went back many years.

To Hale, Bob Troutt's involvement in the bombing made no sense either. Bill told him that he suspected that the bomb had something to do with the Orsini case. How or why, he had no idea. But ever since he'd represented Mary Lee, one bizarre incident had followed another.

To a degree, ATF Agent Spurgeon's thinking paralleled Bill McArthur and Doc Hale's. Troutt's involvement also struck him as unlikely, and he doubted that any evidence would surface to implicate him or McArthur—whom he'd also put on his suspect list. Had Bill seen the ATF report, he would have had no complaint. As the attorney had warned Mary Lee Orsini a bit more than a year ago, the husband or wife is always the first suspect. That was the way of the world.

2

Like many episodes in the curious saga of Sheriff Tommy and Mary Lee, even the barest summary of the events that led to Bob Troutt's being listed as a suspect in the bombing of Alice McArthur's car is hard to make credible outside Arkansas. Robinson's first arrest of Troutt had taken place on April 15, five weeks before the car bombing—and a few days after Mary Lee had taken her troubles to the PCSD.

Whether or not Orsini played a role in the Troutt affair remains purely speculative, but by no means far-fetched. An anonymous call identifying Bob Robbins's assailants and fingering the Kountry Klub owner would have done the trick nicely. Put it this way: For more than a year, Mary Lee had been searching for a criminal mastermind to take the blame for Ron Orsini's murder. Within days of meeting Sheriff Tommy, she found one. Maybe it was sheer coincidence. Or maybe she helped make it happen.

Either way, the Troutt bust succeeded brilliantly in distracting attention from a potentially embarrassing pre-trial hearing in the case of County Judge Bill Beaumont for "restricting government operations" that same day. As expected, the Beaumont hearing turned into a fiasco—with the judge dismissing charges and scolding the prosecution for wasting his time.*

Two weeks later, Sheriff Tommy doubled his bet. He and Dill returned from five days in the Central American nation of Honduras to accuse Troutt of conspiring to have a Little Rock businessman slain

---

*A month later, Beaumont and Growcock filed a $2 million lawsuit against Robinson in federal court. Growcock was eventually awarded $70,000. Beaumont prevailed on some issues but was awarded no damages.

Although Troutt was eventually convicted and served time for the Robbins beating, he has continued to protest his innocence, contending that Orsini arranged the attack on the disc jockey. As we shall see, Mary Lee had both the means and—by her own strange lights—the motive. But no proof exists.

On the other hand, Troutt's vindictiveness was well known. Dub Bentley, however, never gave up his private doubts about the quality of the case. No physical evidence existed, and every bit of testimony against Troutt came from persons incarcerated in Robinson's jail. One of Bob Robbins's alleged attackers testified at the nightclubs owner's trial that Robinson and Dill had beaten a false confession out of him and ordered him to implicate Troutt. Dill and Robinson denied the claim.

there in 1980. Supposedly the killing—if, indeed, a murder had taken place—had something to do with a drug deal. The missing man's son told the press that his father had vanished two and a half years earlier in what the family believed was a boating mishap. His body had never been found.

At roughly 4:00 A.M. the following morning, two carloads of PCSD deputies—non-uniformed and armed with automatic weapons—crept through the underbrush and surrounded Troutt's home in rural Pulaski County. Awakened by the family dog, Troutt switched on all the lights and stood in plain view with his hands over his head so as to give deputies no excuse to shoot.

Alerted in advance to the arrest, newspaper photographers and TV cameramen were on hand at PCSD headquarters to get shots of the handcuffed, barefoot and bare-chested Troutt escorted from a patrol car into the county jail. Also, to Tommy's outrage, to take close-ups of the bearded suspect's bruised and swollen eye when he emerged for a court hearing. Troutt claimed that Robinson and Dill had beaten him. Both Little Rock newspapers devoted virtually their entire front pages to the daring capture. Local anchorpersons could hardly sit still for excitement.

Two days later, Tommy formally opened his campaign for reelection in the May 25 Democratic primary. Front-page photos portrayed the smiling lawman autographing a recent *National Enquirer* profile of himself for an admiring tyke. SHERIFF WARNS CROOKS: WE'LL BLOW YOU AWAY! Illustrated by a photo of Robinson squinting down a shotgun barrel, the *Enquirer* article contained a typical quote: "My basic priority is to kick butts of criminals. And if I have to use excessive force, I will."

In his opening campaign speech, Robinson compared Bob Troutt to an octopus whose tentacles extended through law enforcement statewide. Without producing a shred of proof, he named two state Supreme Court justices as Troutt's partners in crime. The sheriff claimed to have ascertained the whereabouts of the missing corpse in Honduras, and promised to deliver it to the Arkansas medical examiner. A "distinctive possibility" existed that he would bust Troutt again. He'd allow the man's attorney one hour to produce him. "If I want his client," Robinson boasted, "I'll get him at 4 A.M. If I have to, I'll pick up his lawyer too."

And that was that. Tommy never mentioned the Honduras murder in public again. No body emerged from the jungles. Maybe there had been a killing, maybe not. But the sheriff never got around to delivering his case files—assuming case files existed—to Dub Bentley's office. After eighteen months, the "speedy trial clock" quietly ran out. If Troutt had ever been in danger of a murder rap, he was home free.

3

The bombing of Alice McArthur's car spurred Sheriff Tommy into a characteristic flurry of activity. Even before ATF agents had finished picking up the pieces out at 24 Inverness Circle, Robinson summoned the press. He provided them with the details of his deputies' arrest three days earlier of one Ward Parks—the sinister figure in a stolen car out of Chicago who had supposedly been shadowing Mary Lee Orsini. Besides a history of drug offenses, two other things about Parks attracted Tommy's interest: he was related to Donny Simmons, and they'd both once worked in one of Bob Troutt's clubs.

The PCSD had gotten an anonymous call, Robinson said, warning that "the bombings were only beginning." Organized crime had moved into Little Rock. The Orsini murder, the Troutt case, and the McArthur bombing were Mob-related. "This goes beyond municipal jurisdiction in this county," Tommy declared. Dub Bentley had requested "a full-scale independent investigation." Then he and Larry Dill hustled off to take a statement from his primary source for all this startling information: Mary Lee Orsini.

The magical words "contract job" and "organized crime" once again made Tommy the center of attention. Nobody seemed to notice that the bombing probe belonged to the LRPD and the ATF, not the sheriff's department. Nor had Dub Bentley asked Robinson to investigate anything except Mary Lee's list of threatening calls. But once Tommy elbowed his way into the limelight, Bentley never publicly contradicted him. He too faced a primary challenge four days hence, and saw no harm in going along for the ride. The last thing Dub needed was another public spat with Sheriff Tommy.

• • •

Mary Lee showed up at 3:30 P.M. that same Friday afternoon in the Criminal Investigation Division at PCSD headquarters—located on a seedy stretch of the old U.S. Highway 67 & 70 near the State Fairgrounds in Little Rock. Later on, Robinson would do his best to minimize his reliance on information provided by Orsini during this period. His public would have found it hard to understand. Other cops certainly did.

From her point of view, circumstances had once again spun unexpectedly out of control. She had a new load of goods she needed to peddle—and fast. Based on the sixty-two-page, single-spaced transcript of that May 21 interview, the sheriff and his chief deputy seemed to be in a buying mood. Traces of the hard-eyed skepticism with which the two now claim to have met Orsini's stories are hard to find. Mary Lee would soon learn—if she didn't already know—that Robinson got almost as excited listening to her tales of plots and conspiracies as she did making them up. If organized crime was what Tommy wanted, organized crime was what Tommy would get.

Much of the interview Mary Lee spent embroidering oft-told tales, weaving in new material to bring things up to date. She described Ron's mysterious behavior, vanishing bank bags filled with cash, frightening phone calls, and secretive meetings in his garage workshop with the likes of Ron O'Neal and Donny Simmons.

Sheriff Tommy took her exactly where she wanted to go. Had she noticed any personality changes? Was Ron using drugs?

"If he did, I didn't know it," she said. Unlike her, Mary Lee explained, Ron was a low-key, slow-moving person.

"You're like me," Tommy said. "Real hyper."

"Yeah, I am. Like I haven't eaten in two days and it doesn't bother me." She and the sheriff were getting on famously. Besides the usual suspects, Ron Orsini had one friend in particular to whom she wished to draw their attention.

"Bill and I looked in the criss-cross [phone directory], but I cannot remember his name. He lived up there close to us. Ron and I both used to jog up—I don't know the name of the street. I could show it to you. But he was a little guy, a little thin guy. And he used to come to the house every once in a while. . . . He and Ron would sit out there and drink a beer. At the time he had a little tiny baby at his house. When I'd drive by in the afternoon, he'd have the baby out on a blanket in the yard and I'd wave at him. I never knew his name."

The man Mary Lee was describing, of course, was none other than her midnight lover Yankee Hall. Naming Yankee outright would have been too dangerous. After all, suppose they brought him in for questioning?

But establishing a connection between the cocky little ex-felon and

Ron Orsini was crucial to the trap she was setting for Yankee—which Sheriff Tommy and his sidekick were expected to spring.

She rattled on and on for hours. Detectives Farley or Miles, either one, could have recited the rest of the scenario to the sheriff from memory—assuming they could have kept straight faces. Then picked it to pieces. But Farley and Miles never got to see the transcript of the PCSD interview with Mary Lee. Nor, according to Farley and Miles, and incredible as it seems, did Robinson, or Dill *at any time* in their supposed investigation ever take a look at the NLRPD's evidence file on the Ron Orsini case. Sheriff Tommy didn't work that way. Under Robinson, the PCSD viewed law enforcement as a competitive enterprise. Once elected, the sheriff treated cops like Farley and Miles with open condescension. A bit like Orsini herself, he carried himself like a genius surrounded by fools.

Mary Lee was on a roll. She told Robinson and Dill about the time she'd followed Ron to a clandestine meeting with two strange men driving an unmarked police car. She gave detailed descriptions. One man was a liquor salesman with ties to Bob Troutt. Once when she and Joyce Holt had visited the Kountry Klub, he'd fixed her with a malevolent stare.

"Did you later identify who you think the second guy was?"

"Yes."

"Who is it?" the sheriff asked. Then he answered before she could. "Captain Dwain 'Buddy' Thompson, State Police?"

"I want to tell you something," Mary Lee said. "I went into hysterics when I saw his picture in the paper."

Robinson had publicly charged Thompson with "fingering" Bob Troutt's hypothetical murder victim in Honduras. A state police internal affairs probe had cleared him of wrongdoing. In earlier versions of the same tale, she'd identified NLRPD Chief Bubba Younts— ostensibly why she'd wanted Yankee to plant a bomb under his car. But Tommy had no way of knowing that.

He circled back to one of his favorite topics. "Did you find any drugs in the house?"

"I want to tell you something. I wouldn't know them if I saw them. Now I want to tell you something that I *have* found. This has never come out. Only Bill McArthur knows. I found filthy porno magazines downstairs. This is filth. This is lesbian black and white. I've never seen such stuff. It was in a brown paper sack."

Eventually Mary Lee worked her way back to Tommy's question

about personality changes. "Even his partners admitted," she said, "the day before he was killed—the 11th of March—Ron had a total character change. He was high. He was just absolutely euphoric."

"Did you ever notice him having a runny nose or anything?" Like most of Tommy's questions, this implied the answer he wanted.

"Yeah. He had a nosebleed about two weeks before he was killed. Real bad. Because he turned around in the bathroom and he just slung blood all over the place."

"Did you notice any change in his eyes? Did he appear to be under the influence of any drugs?"

"Tommy, I never did know."

Eventually, Dill began to show signs of restlessness. Why, with Ron dead, would somebody want to kill her?

"The only thing Bill and I can figure out is I was a scapegoat. Whoever did it set me up. And when I didn't fall in the Grand Jury— when I didn't get indicted and end up on trial—then they were gonna get me themselves. . . . [Maybe] there's somebody I saw that Ron dealt with that doesn't want me to know. Doesn't want me to divulge their name. It could have been one of the people I've already said. Maybe they're the crucial person."

Nearing the heart of her latest grand conspiracy, Mary Lee paused for effect, then plunged breathlessly ahead. Gary Glidewell, she explained, had linked her husband to drug dealers. But she and Bill McArthur had learned that the private detective was in the pay of Bob Troutt. "Gary would go to my friends. Gary would say, 'She's not telling us everything. She knows more.' Bill and I decided that he was giving us this little bit of information, but he was really trying to find out what I knew all this time. He was a plant."

In actuality, McArthur had no contact with Glidewell. But Orsini had learned that she could trust her attorney not to contradict her to the police. It was "Bill told me this," and, "Bill and I think that," all day long. If nothing else, Dill and Robinson definitely noticed that.

Reaching into her bag of tricks, she produced the cassette recording of the phone conversation between her and the unwitting Yankee which she'd already played for McArthur and Phoebe, among others. She promised to make Tommy a copy.

"Let's go back to the nosebleed," Tommy interrupted. "I'm gonna tell you something. If a person is using a good grade of cocaine, they are going to be in an elated mood and they can have nosebleeds, OK? Did [Ron's] mood change? Did he become happier?"

Never noticing that he'd been the one who suggested nosebleeds in the first place, the sheriff gave a little speech. "What he was probably doing was snorting some good coke, because it will make your nose bleed. It can cause it to bleed profusely if it's a good grade of cocaine and you're not accustomed to doing it. . . . And that's a common occurrence for someone using strong cocaine. You get nosebleeds, and you have a elated feeling like everything in the world's OK."

"Couldn't the state medical examiner determine that?" Now *she* was asking the questions. Orsini must have been almost giddy with power. At last she'd found somebody with a badge who seemed to believe what she said as readily as Joyce Holt and Dr. Wulz.

"Well no. Not necessarily." Tommy would not be deterred. "Depends on when you're using it. People use cocaine because there's no hangover. Next day you can go about your business."

Pressed by Dill for more information, Orsini tied the last knot she could think of—a digressive account of how her purse, containing the family's prescription records and the original bank deposit slips that would prove Ron had indeed deposited money that the liar Farley claimed didn't exist, had vanished from her car during the grand jury probe and materialized later in the Dumpster behind Donny Simmons's store.

To buy her story, the sheriff would have to imagine that the mysterious drug-dealing cabal had sources close enough to the grand jury to know the precise moment to steal Mary Lee's purse, thus depriving her of crucial exculpatory evidence, and to dispose of it where it could not help but be found. A cabal that had efficiently murdered Ron Orsini, but bungled everything since: taking potshots at Mary Lee in broad daylight, and planting a dud bomb under Alice McArthur's car.

"Do you know if McArthur's received any threats personally?" Dill finally asked.

"I've heard that he has."

"From who?"

"Bill let it slip back when he first took this case. To get off this case. But he won't really talk. Bill's real funny about that, you know—talking about it. Why? Have you heard that too?"

"Yeah, I heard that," he answered. "I hadn't talked to Bill about it."

She told them what she figured they wanted to hear. McArthur had gotten several threats. "The only obvious reason," she deduced, "is that if I recognize somebody that killed Ron—or that had something to do with it. They just don't want it out. Because if you really look at it, they've got a neat little package as long as they can keep me—the NLRPD—as long as I can never get anybody else to get into this, they have a neat little package."

Major Dill turned off the tape recorder. He and Tommy wanted to have a look at the scene of the crime. With the sheriff driving, they followed Orsini across the river to Indian Hills.

•   •   •

What happened next would be bitterly disputed by Robinson and Dill. According to a sworn statement Larry Burge later gave the LRPD, he showed up at 7412 Pontiac late that same afternoon to see about his car. After Mary Lee's Caprice had its window shot out back in April, Burge had lent her his 1981 Honda Prelude to drive. Six weeks later, he wondered if he'd ever get it back.

Just a couple of days earlier, an old Air Force buddy of his named Woody Juels had told him Mary Lee was sleeping with a convicted felon named Yankee Hall. A former MP, Juels was an NLRPD officer who sold and traded used cars as a sideline—which in turn put him in touch with Yankee. Juels told Burge that Yankee was nobody to fear. But Orsini was as dangerous as a cottonmouth moccasin. If Burge didn't watch his step, she'd set him up on something or get him killed.

Larry didn't know what to think. He trusted Juels, but Orsini had told him so many tales about the NLRPD he thought maybe his friend might be misinformed. So when Mary Lee whipped into her driveway followed by Robinson and Dill, he figured no harm could come from telling the sheriff what he'd heard.

According to a sworn statement Burge later gave the LRPD, he'd introduced himself to Tommy, whom he much admired at the time. "I told him," Burge said, "because I knew he was looking into the situation—that I had a name that he might ought to check out. That I had information saying that Lee Orsini and this Yankee Hall were . . . having an affair, or something to that effect. He wrote the name down and then he turned to Dill and told him they had the name Yankee Hall to check out the next day."

In less polite circumstances, Burge recalled putting it more bluntly: "I think Lee's fuckin' Yankee Hall. You need to pick him up and talk with him, because he's a convicted felon."

Tommy, however, denied that the conversation took place. At the time he also was too busy stalking larger game. In a TV interview on

Sunday, May 23, a weary Sheriff Robinson—sitting at his desk with his necktie at half-mast and the U.S. flag on display behind him—again raised the specter of organized crime. After two days of around-the-clock investigation, Tommy announced, the Orsini, Troutt, and McArthur cases were "beginning to show similarities and correlations. People involved in one case are beginning to surface in other cases. In my opinion, we're going to see a link between organized crime out of New Orleans—possibly involving people here in Little Rock that are trying to take over the turf. There's a sort of little war going on now." He invoked the name of Carlos Marcello, the reputed Mafia boss of New Orleans.

In every public statement over the next six weeks, Robinson told the same story. Just beyond his grasp lay a massive criminal conspiracy involving not only murder, drug dealing, racketeering, but high-level police and judicial corruption. The McArthur car bombing proved that the Mob was headed down I-40 from Memphis to Little Rock. Come what may, Tommy would stop them.

• • •

In the meantime, Larry Burge was not the only person who said he mentioned the Yankee Hall–Mary Lee Orsini romance to the sheriff's department. So did Sergeant T. J. Farley. Like Burge, Farley had also talked to Woody Juels. Hall had even given Mary Lee's phone number to Juels as a place he could be reached at night. The policeman had dialed the number; Orsini had answered.

In a meeting at NLRPD headquarters on May 24, Farley claims he tried to pass the news on to Larry Dill. Dill showed no interest. The PCSD was operating on a different wavelength. Eventually, Farley too testified under oath. "They were bound and determined that it was Bob Troutt that did the bombing," Farley said. Dill has flatly denied that any such conversation took place.

Sergeant Buddy Miles said he overheard the conversation between Farley and Dill. As it happened, Miles too had information that the PCSD might have found useful had they been willing to listen. Along with Bob Troutt, Sheriff Tommy had named Ward Parks as a suspect in the McArthur bombing—the man supposedly tailing Mary Lee in a hot car.

But the sheriff, Miles knew, had been duped. Several days earlier, the detective had learned, a friend of Orsini's had asked an acquaintance in the NLRPD to run an ID check on an Illinois license plate. The NCIC computer had reported the car stolen, and given the possible driver's name as one Ward Parks. So Mary Lee had known the car was hot before telling Tommy that her old high school classmate Donny Simmons's relative was following her. Miles had typed the whole story up and submitted it to Chief Younts. "If memory serves me well," Miles wrote, "[Orsini's friend] said that something 'big' would happen in the next few days."

A couple of days later, the bomb was planted under Alice McArthur's car.

• • •

On May 25, Sheriff Tommy Robinson won re-election with 58 percent of the vote in the Democratic primary. To his leading challenger, who criticized him as a publicity-seeking charlatan, Robinson gave the back of his hand. This time around he'd been too busy to campaign. Next time he promised to play "hardball" if that was what his detractors thought they wanted.

1

As early as February 1982, Mary Lee Orsini had confessed to Joyce Holt of a growing attraction between her and Bill McArthur. Working together, she claimed, had drawn them close. Sympathizing with her plight, McArthur had refused payment for the many hours he'd worked on her behalf. He'd also given her valuable advice on how to shelter her $260,000 trust fund for Tiffany's sake. When she'd offered to finance BJ's Star-Studded Honky Tonk, Bill refused to allow her to dip into her capital funds. Rather, he helped her to secure a second mortgage, and offered to make her advertising and promotions manager of the new club too.

The unhappiness of his marriage had done the rest. According to Mary Lee, McArthur hated the remodeling his wife had begun on their Pleasant Valley home, and much preferred the tasteful atmosphere at 7412 Pontiac. But he feared Alice's waspish tongue too much to object.

Orsini told Joyce that Phoebe complained bitterly about how Alice had emasculated her boss—all but destroying the poor man's self-confidence. Indeed, their romance had begun after Mary Lee had gone out of her way to pay him a public compliment. At a reception for the noted defense attorney F. Lee Bailey—who had recently visited Little Rock—Bill had introduced her as "his only innocent client." Mary Lee had countered by calling Bill "the F. Lee Bailey of the South." McArthur had beamed.

In fact, while Bailey's Little Rock trip had been covered in the press, no such reception took place. But all Joyce knew was that her friend seemed deeply infatuated, and while Mary Lee said that she and Bill felt terribly guilty, seemed destined to have a love affair.

Joyce warned her to be careful. "I even gave her a little lecture on getting involved with a married man," Holt said later, laughing. "Of all things! But she felt like they were leading up to something. In fact she called me one afternoon to tell me how wonderful everything was. She was reading *The Sensuous Woman* . . . and for her, it was just ecstasy. Just wonderful. She knew that he was not an experienced man, but he had a good body."

But Holt played dumb when Dr. Wulz had called her at 3:00 A.M. on April 6 wanting to know whose red coupe was parked in Orsini's driveway. Mary Lee had sworn her to secrecy. Not until much later would she realize that for all the trysts Mary Lee had described to her in swooning detail, Joyce had never seen McArthur's car outside. Nor the stunning string of pearls Bill purportedly bought Mary Lee, nor the touching card that came with them. As for Yankee Hall, Joyce had never heard the name until she heard it on TV.

Dr. Wulz never considered McArthur a rival. Though Mary Lee carried on as if he were the world's most brilliant attorney, and portrayed Alice as a trashy bitch, the veterinarian's suspicions still centered upon Jim Guy Tucker. He rationalized Orsini's lies as due to the politician's need for secrecy. While he no longer thought himself in love with Orsini, he did resent her making a fool of him.

·   ·   ·

On the afternoon of May 4, Orsini helped Phoebe throw a birthday party for Bill—an office tradition. They had one every year for each member of the staff. Normally, Phoebe handled the arrangements. But she was swamped with work, and Mary Lee volunteered to help. Phoebe admired Mary Lee's generosity. Most clients would have resented the action McArthur had taken in late April. With Mary Lee still owing him $15,000 and no payments forthcoming, he'd taken a second mortgage on her mother's home—the same property Betty Tucker's bank was foreclosing upon. That way, if anything *did* happen to her, McArthur would be in line to collect part of his money. Far from anger, Mary Lee had voiced satisfaction. Among her many creditors, Bill deserved payment the most.

Mary Lee arrived on May 4 carrying all the ingredients for the festivities: a birthday cake she'd had made up with a BJ's Star-Studded Honky Tonk logo, a handsome new briefcase paid for by an office collection, and two bottles of champagne. She made a big deal, Phoebe would recall later, of insisting that Bill do the honors with the champagne. Overall, the party was a great success. McArthur's partner Jack Lassiter was there, a few friends dropped by, and, of course, the women in the office.

For weeks, Mary Lee had been hinting to Phoebe that her and Bill's relationship had become a romance. Phoebe's impression was that Mary Lee was imagining the whole thing. "She couldn't figure out how he could care about her," was how Phoebe had it figured, "and not want to go to bed with her."

To test her theory, Phoebe took the occasion of the birthday party to drop a few broad hints. If Bill and Mary Lee wanted to be left alone, she said with a bawdy wink, she'd be happy to take the rest of the day off. McArthur fixed Phoebe with an incredulous stare. They'd worked together so long that he didn't need to say a word. Phoebe had her answer.

How Orsini managed to slip the empty champagne bottles out of the office, nobody ever found out. Possibly she returned that night and fished them out of the dumpster behind the building. Winos and bag ladies made the rounds in downtown Little Rock every night, so nobody would have noticed.

·   ·   ·

On Monday, May 10—six days after the birthday party—Mary Lee asked Joyce Holt to do her a small favor. While she was out running errands, would she be kind enough to rent a room in her own name for Mary Lee to use at the Best Western Motel? She and Tommy Robinson needed it to meet an informant who was frightened to be seen at the sheriff's department, and wouldn't come to 7412 Pontiac Drive. She'd pick up the key from Joyce later.

Joyce did as she was asked. Happening to drive past the motel later that night, she took a swing through the parking lot. She saw no cars parked there that she recognized, not even Mary Lee's. When she asked her friend about it, Mary Lee told her that the informant had failed to show. She, McArthur, and Robinson had listened to some tapes the sheriff had, then left early.

The contents of the tapes, Mary Lee told Joyce, had stunned Bill. During his investigation of Bob Troutt, the sheriff had learned that the corrupt nightclub owner had taken a lover: none other than Alice McArthur! Robinson had called Alice in for questioning, forced her to confess, and played the tape of her confession for Mary Lee and Bill.

Larry Burge heard a different version. Supposedly, Bill had come home unexpectedly and listened in on an extension while his wife sweet-talked Troutt on the telephone. Bill had then taken Alice to Dub Bentley's office and forced her to confess.

Either way, the implications could hardly have been more ominous. Not content to humiliate her husband with a hoodlum, Alice was conspiring with Troutt to destroy Bill's livelihood. Armed with the taped evidence, however, McArthur and Sheriff Tommy planned to turn the tables. First, Alice would be forced to tell all she knew about Troutt's criminal empire in court. As degrading as the ordeal would be for Bill, Alice's testimony would put Troutt behind bars. Then Bill could file for divorce, and also win custody of his children.

Knowing none of the characters in this fantastic melodrama first hand, Mary Lee's friends soaked it in like a sponge. And there was danger too. During the week before the bombing of Alice McArthur's car, Mary Lee confided to Larry Burge that she'd begun to have terrible nightmares. All-consuming fires and shattering explosions tormented her sleep. Mary Lee didn't know if she believed in ESP, but somehow she knew that Bill was in mortal danger.

During the second week in May she told Joyce about yet another anonymous caller—possibly the same taped voice Joyce had heard warning Mary Lee to take Tiffany and get out of town. This time, he said, word on the street had it that the heavy hitters had run out of patience. They were through fucking around. Guns hadn't worked. Next time, they would use dynamite.

2

While Tommy Robinson held press conferences, Special Agent John Spurgeon of the Bureau of Alcohol, Tobacco and Firearms did all the serious investigative work in the Alice McArthur bombing. Bombing investigations demanded a patient, systematic approach. The sophisticated lab work that led to convictions took time.

Spurgeon fully intended to run down every lead. But instinct and experience told him that despite the sheriff's televised rhetoric, looking for a Mob connection would likely be fruitless. He felt pretty much the same way about the possibility that Bill McArthur himself had planted the bomb.

"You had a bomb attached to the car that the woman always drives," Spurgeon explained. "But you never know who's going to get into the car with her. Such as the children. So initially—while I thought of Mr. McArthur—I was not leaning in that direction, because of the children. Bob Troutt might have a problem with Mr. McArthur, but he doesn't necessarily have a problem with his wife or children. Someone who will kill children is different from someone who will just kill his enemy."

On May 24, the same day Robinson and Dill met with Sergeant Farley at NLRPD headquarters, Spurgeon made modest progress. From a code on the label, he learned that the Eveready battery that sparked the blast had been sold by a supermarket located at North Hills and McCain in North Little Rock. Spurgeon also discovered that the toggle switch used to trigger the bomb was a brand carried only by wholesale electrical supply outlets.

To Sergeant Farley, those facts might have spelled O-r-s-i-n-i. The supermarket was less than a half mile from Pontiac Drive; her dead husband bought all of his electrical gear wholesale. But Spurgeon wasn't up to speed on the NLRPD case file. Anyhow, thousands of people shopped in the same supermarket.

That same afternoon, Spurgeon and two LRPD detectives drove to Hot Springs to take a statement from Troutt. The nightclub owner was more than willing to talk, but insisted upon meeting at his lawyer's office. As soon as a journalist friend tipped him that Alice McArthur had named him as a suspect in the bombing, Troutt got out of Little Rock fast. He refused to enter Pulaski County for fear of another headline-grabbing bust by the sheriff.

"I don't mind telling you," Troutt told his visitors, "I'm afraid to go back into that jail. I'll take my chances in court. But when a man looks you in the eye with your hands tied behind your back and says, 'I'm going to kill you . . .' I believe him. So I'm not going to make myself available."

Under oath, Troutt categorically denied involvement in the bombing. He offered to take a lie detector test to prove it. He insisted that McArthur was a business rival, period. They'd had no personal troubles, and he'd never threatened McArthur. He maintained that all he knew about organized crime buying into Little Rock nightclubs, he'd heard from Tommy Robinson on TV. Given his many friends in law enforcement, he doubted anybody would try to intimidate him. Sure he'd heard loose talk about cocaine dealing in town—but all from cops.

The reason Troutt had called investigators down to Hot Springs soon emerged. Never one to pass up a chance to kick a rival when he was down, he had a story to tell on Bill McArthur—an implausible tale about how the attorney and his friend Jim Lester had once solicited Troutt's help in a dispute with a woman who might, or might not, have been McArthur's wife.

On the following morning, he submitted to a state police lie detector test. As Spurgeon had expected, he passed all the questions relating to the bombing of Alice McArthur's car without a tremor. With regard to his meeting with McArthur and Lester, however, the examiner concluded that Troutt was telling something other than the truth.

Spurgeon crossed Troutt off his list. Within a few days, he'd also cleared Bill McArthur of suspicion. He could find nothing to indicate that Bill and Alice were anything other than the devoted couple they appeared to be, no evidence that McArthur had anything to gain from his wife's death, nor anybody who thought him capable of murder—not simply among the man's neighbors, associates, and friends, but among cops for whom suspicion was an ingrained habit. Had McArthur wished to be rid of his wife, he would have divorced her.

Spurgeon had never thought much of the organized crime theory. Neither McArthur nor his partners had received even an offer to buy BJ's, much less any threats. Criminals seeking to buy into legitimate businesses did all they could to avoid scrutiny. Their motive for getting into the nightclub business would be to hide illicit activities—laundering money, and peddling drugs, hookers, and stolen liquor. Not to lead the evening news broadcasts.

"If anybody had made a decent offer," Spurgeon said, "I think [McArthur and his partners] would have sold. But you don't come along and tell somebody you're interested in buying a club and when they say, 'I don't know as I'm interested in selling,' you set a bomb under the wife's car. It doesn't work like that. That just didn't make sense."

The only lead Spurgeon had left was the one McArthur had suggested to him and Doc Hale of the LRPD: That the bombing was somehow connected to the Orsini murder case. So, on June 16, he had a talk with Sergeant Farley at the NLRPD. Maybe it sounded off the wall, the AFT agent began, but the logic seemed to be leading him in the general direction of Mary Lee Orsini. Farley assured him that he didn't think that was a crazy idea at all.

Farley gave Spurgeon a half dozen new names to check out. Three were persons who might hold a grudge against McArthur for helping Mary Lee point the Orsini investigation in their direction. Gary Glidewell made the list, as did his ex-client Kenny Clarkson. Farley's suspicions against the pair dated back to the state police stakeout of his driveway, waiting for a "hit" that never came.

But the most significant name Farley passed along to ATF was that of Eugene "Yankee" Hall. Orsini had to have some motive to be banging an ex-con and certifiable lowlife like Yankee on the midnight to dawn shift. From everything Spurgeon learned that day, he tended to agree. Now Mary Lee had the Feds on her tail.

Still, why Alice McArthur? Farley knew of no relationship other than lawyer-client between Orsini and Bill McArthur. And as close a watch as they kept on her, chances were that the NLRPD would have known. So what could Orsini's motive possibly be? ATF had already checked a list of everybody in Arkansas who'd bought Tovex explosive during the past year. Spurgeon could see no obvious connection to Orsini or Yankee Hall. Nor had the lab raised any fingerprints from the bomb fragments. The ATF agent canvassed electrical supply houses trying to trace the toggle switch that triggered the blast to Ron Orsini's workshop. After a week, he came up empty.

•   •   •

This much seems clear: If ATF investigators had seen what Sheriff Tommy had—Mary Lee's itemized list of threatening calls, her little tape of Yankee's voice, and the bizarre statement she'd given Robinson and Dill on the day of the bombing—everything might have been different.

But Tommy Robinson didn't operate like other cops. In the most elementary terms, a textbook criminal investigation proceeds from broad to narrow. Like Spurgeon, a competent detective begins by considering every possible suspect, then eliminates them one by one.

Tommy turned the formula upside down. Like Clint Eastwood's "Dirty Harry"—the classic "maverick" cop of film and TV—Tommy played hunches, deciding upon the guilty party first, then ranging far and wide for evidence to support his pre-existing conclusion. He seemed to discount anything conflicting with his theories, and shared evidence with other agencies only when it helped him gain a competitive advantage. Larry Dill knew better, but Dill also did as he was told. In career terms, the next step down from the PCSD was a long drop.

Working with the sheriff on anything but humdrum cases, every other law enforcement agency in Little Rock had concluded, was a one-way street that dead ended on the TV news. LRPD detectives refused to deal with Tommy at all. Under orders, Spurgeon volunteered nothing to Robinson. He made a deal with the prosecutor to pass on anything the sheriff gathered, but nothing was forthcoming.

Exactly what sort of investigation the PCSD conducted during May and June 1982 will always remain a mystery. One useful task they could have performed—running down Mary Lee's list of threatening phone calls—apparently never got done. Two deputies with a crisscross directory could have done the job in a couple of days.

Dropped on Dub Bentley's desk by Mary Lee herself on the afternoon before the McArthur bombing, every number on it traced to one of Yankee's hangouts—mostly bars where he'd not only boasted of his affair with the famous widow, but received messages from her under the code name "Sue." Orsini's identity was an open secret to the bartenders who took her calls. But nothing in PCSD records indicated that the task was ever attempted.

Judging by PCSD files, Robinson and Dill spent the weekend after the bombing in a flurry of activity. Soon after interviewing Mary Lee on May 21, they took a statement from Ward Parks, the man deputies had picked up for allegedly shadowing her in a hot car. He categorically denied harassing Orsini. Indeed, by the time Sheriff Tommy fed his name to reporters as a suspect in the bombing, Parks had proved to a judge that he'd borrowed, not stolen, the car in which deputies busted him and was on his way back to Chicago, never to be heard from again.

Two days later, they interviewed Donny Simmons, who made no effort to hide his anger. "I've had shots fired at me about this Orsini thing till I'm about ready to smack somebody," he told Dill. "[They say] I'm right in there on top of it, and I don't know a damn thing about it." The way Simmons had it figured, somebody had put Mary Lee's purse in his Dumpster to frame him. But it wasn't going to wash.

Had he chosen to talk, Simmons knew lots of interesting things. He and Mary Myrtle Hatcher had known each other since childhood; their photographs appear almost side by side in her high school yearbook. Of more immediate interest, however, was the fact that Simmons lived with Yankee Hall's ex-wife—the mother of the same little boy who'd accompanied his father to Mary Lee's house from the Taco Bell. It was symptomatic of her recklessness to thrust Simmons into the center of her imaginary conspiracy. But if Robinson and Dill learned anything useful, they failed to document it.

Later that same day, Robinson and Dill took what would turn out to be their final documented interview with Orsini. Mary Lee spent most of the interview drawing the noose a bit tighter around Yankee's neck. Only the day before, the anonymous caller with the odd accent had phoned yet again. He'd offered a trade. If Mary Lee could tip him off to upcoming PCSD drug busts, he could tell her who'd planted the bomb under Alice McArthur's car. Furnished with a list of bogus, but plausible names, the intrepid widow supposedly spent most of Saturday driving from one pay phone to another as her caller directed. But alas, he'd gotten cold feet. So the deal never went down.

Sheriff Tommy's May 25 re-election apparently put the case on the back burner. The next activity anybody thought worth documenting took place on June 10, when Dill interviewed Kenny Clarkson—Gary Glidewell's former client who'd become infatuated with Mary Lee. The resulting file memo implies that, contrary to what Dill and Robinson later maintained, they continued to buy Mary Lee Orsini's story. Clarkson, Major Dill wrote,

> was asked about Ron Orsini. He said he had never met him, but that he did know that he was a friend of Ron O'Neal's and was associated with Donny Simmons.
>
> He said that from everything that he had heard after the death that Ron Orsini had some kind of business dealings with Donny Simmons of NLR but that he was not sure if he used cocaine or not or if he was just backing Donny in the distribution of cocaine that he was getting out of Chicago.

Any skepticism Dill may have felt about Clarkson's story, he managed to keep admirably restrained. In the three weeks since the car bombing, the PCSD had succeeded in moving the Orsini investigation backward roughly a year.

• • •

Meanwhile, Gary Glidewell had gotten cold feet. Facing a formal state police hearing to defend himself against charges brought by Sergeant Farley and the NLRPD, the private detective got a warning from Major Dill. Two brothers whose mug shots Mary Lee had identified as resembling the thugs who had threatened her with a shotgun were blaming Glidewell. He should consider them armed and extremely dangerous.

Glidewell had taken all the Arkansas he could stand. Taking Mary Jane Murphree with him, he blew off the hearing, forfeited his Arkansas private investigator's license, and beat it back to Kansas City in the middle of the night. He and Mary Jane eventually got married.

. . .

From June 10 onward no sign of activity appears in PCSD case files. Orsini visited PCSD headquarters constantly during that month, but Robinson and Dill kept her almost entirely to themselves. Officers from other police agencies noticed Tommy's own patrol car parked in her driveway at unusual hours.

Opinion in Little Rock law enforcement circles divides: Either Mary Lee had Tommy and Larry chasing their own tails until they got dizzy, or they played along with her schemes hoping to trap her in her own snare. Darker scenarios exist as well.

But apart from Mary Lee's own, the only explanation for what happened next that *nobody* buys is Sheriff Tommy's.

3

Against the advice of everybody who loved her, Alice McArthur refused to change the way she lived. For a few days after the bombing incident, the family stayed in Hot Springs at the lakeside home of friends. Phoebe Pinkston recalled their first conversation after Alice returned to Little Rock: "She called me and said, 'I decided Sunday morning I was going to go to town and go to the store. It took me two hours to get the guts up to get in the car and go. But I thought, "By God, I'm going to do it. I can't live in fear." ' That was her attitude. 'I'll go on with my life anyway.' "

The McArthurs did what they could to assure their safety. They had an expensive new burglar alarm system installed. Besides a phone company trap like the one on Mary Lee's line, they gratefully took

Larry Dill up on his offer to install a PCSD tape recorder in the event of suspicious calls. Alice quickly learned to switch it off the moment she recognized her callers. Dill also offered the services of off-duty deputies to guard the Pleasant Valley home on nights when Bill needed to be away after dark. That too they accepted two or three times.

Feeling a bit foolish, Bill even accepted a snub-nosed, nickel-plated .38 that Mary Lee offered, and stuck it under the front seat of his car. McArthur, who hadn't fired a gun since Army basic training, didn't know but that he'd be more danger to himself than his assailants. But he kept it all the same. Ever helpful, Mary Lee called Phoebe one day to pass on to Alice some tips on dodging would-be assassins. Change your schedule often, she advised. Avoid a predictable routine. "Well, you try to tell Alice McArthur something," Phoebe laughed. "Alice is going to do what she wants to do."

And so she did. Everybody truly close to Alice—Bill, his parents Bryan and Billie McArthur, Judy Harris, Sally Pernell, and her other women friends—urged her to take the children down to Golden Meadow for the summer, or at least until the investigators made some progress on finding out who planted the bomb. In Cajun country, strangers would have little chance of finding her without revealing themselves. Alice refused. She simply would not leave Bill to face danger alone. Alice was vehement about that. Unless Bill shut down his practice and came with her and the kids, she wasn't going anywhere.

Like everybody else, most of the time Alice believed that the bomb *must* have been intended for her husband. Nothing else made any sense. She kept up a brave front. "She didn't really talk to me about being afraid. She was more fearful for Bill and the kids," Sally Pernell said later. "She was afraid they would be caught in something that had nothing to do with any of them, and they'd get hurt."

Until school let out in June, the hardest part of every day for Alice was getting her children off to school. "They had to walk a half block to catch the bus," Judy Harris recalled. "We were so afraid that someone would be there. You didn't know who the bogeyman was. You just knew there was someone out there. And you wouldn't recognize him if he knocked on the front door.

"She would try to make us laugh about it. We would be at the tennis center and go out to our cars and Alice would say, "Well, come on, come on. Help me do the bomb search.' And try to lighten it up. But it never did lighten up."

For several years, Alice McArthur and a group of women had rented a condo in Fort Walton Beach, Florida, during the second week in June. Leaving their husbands to care for the kids, they would pack sandwiches and drinks, pile into a van, and drive straight through to the resort for a week of sunbathing, card playing, eating and drinking. Alice's first inclination was to cancel. She feared to leave Bill, Robyn, and Chuck at home alone.

Everybody urged her to reconsider. A week in the sunshine away from it all, they insisted, was exactly what she needed. Finally, she asked Bill's parents to come over to the house. A member of the Florida group had offered the use of her family's house on Lake Hamilton for the week. If her in-laws would agree to keep the children, leaving Bill free to make the 65-mile drive between the lake and his Little Rock office every day, Alice would go ahead to Florida and try to relax.

The elder McArthurs needed little urging to spend a week with their grandchildren. But no matter how hard she tried, Alice never succeeded in leaving her fears behind. She telephoned from Florida every night to assure herself that Bill had made it safely from Little Rock and the children were tucked in bed.

On Wednesday morning, June 9, with Alice safely in Florida, Mary Lee showed up unannounced at McArthur's office. She was all dressed up for tennis. If she was hoping to seduce her attorney, she had chosen the wrong outfit. McArthur saw her coming up the walk from his office window, and couldn't help but notice how badly shorts became her.

Phoebe found her story a bit puzzling. Mary Lee claimed to be off to Hot Springs for a tennis tournament. Afterward, she and Bill would be meeting there to go over some new evidence unearthed by the sheriff.

The McArthur family's exact whereabouts was a secret. But a few clients and colleagues who might need Bill in an emergency—Mary Lee included—knew that Phoebe could reach him in Hot Springs. What Orsini didn't know was that Bill was staying with his parents and children. With the Arkansas Bar holding its annual convention there that week, she played one of her characteristic hunches—apparently guessing that he would be in Hot Springs all day. But as so often happened, she guessed wrong.

Phoebe never understood what Mary Lee was talking about. Bill had an unusually busy day scheduled. Even as the women chatted in the outer office, McArthur had hurried out the side door on his way to a meeting at Metropolitan Bank. After lunch, Phoebe knew, he planned to drive to Pine Bluff—sixty miles in the wrong direction—to confer with his co-counsel for an upcoming trial. Later, he'd promised to visit the Pine Bluff unit of the state penitentiary to see a client from Ozark— Phoebe's home town—who faced a homicide charge. No way would he reach Hot Springs before dark.

But Bill had been known to promise more of his time than he could possibly deliver, and Mary Lee rarely failed in Phoebe's experience to translate "maybe" into "certainly." So she gave it little thought, even after Mary Lee phoned from Hot Springs a few hours later to ask her to relay a message to Larry Dill. Presumably she could have called Dill herself, but that was how Mary Lee operated. She also neglected to mention that she was phoning from the Lakeside Holiday Inn and charging the call to a room she had rented in her own name.

The content of the message Phoebe passed on to Dill was that Mary Lee would have to cancel their meeting that afternoon—at which, she confided, she'd planned to deliver some tapes implicating Jim Guy Tucker in criminal transactions.

Orsini got back to North Little Rock in late afternoon. If she'd succeeded in enticing anybody to the Holiday Inn, it was certainly not McArthur. Bill visited with his client at the penitentiary near Pine Bluff until some time after Mary Lee had returned to Pontiac Drive. Ignorant of her presence in Hot Springs, he didn't arrive in the resort city until late in the evening.

·   ·   ·

As the weeks passed, Alice McArthur's anxiety faded. She talked less about the bombing, and seemed to be making an effort to put it behind her. Friends knew that she hadn't forgotten. Toward the end of June, as she packed Chuck and Robyn's things for their annual two weeks at camp, she told everybody how much she and Bill were looking forward to spending some time together.

Only once did Sally Pernell ever know Alice's composure to falter. It happened during a phone conversation in late June, one of those rare moments when Alice put aside her bantering, bawdy manner and spoke from the heart. The two friends had been sharing confidences about their intimate lives.

All at once Alice began to cry. She'd spent night after night, she said, trying to recall anybody she'd ever wronged so badly that they might want to hurt her. "Poor thing, she had just agonized over it," Pernell said. "She told me, 'I have just pored over this in my mind.' She couldn't sleep at night for thinking about it. 'I've gone clear back to when I was a kid, trying to think of somebody that I might have hurt or made angry in some way. But for the life of me I can't think of anybody that would want to hurt me. You just can't imagine how much time I've spent just thinking, trying to remember over all the years. But I just can't come up with anyone.' It had just driven Alice crazy trying to make some sense of it. And of course there wasn't any sense to make of it. God bless her."

4

On the afternoon of Friday, June 25, Bill McArthur phoned ATF Agent John Spurgeon. Spurgeon had told McArthur that if anybody made him an offer to buy BJ's Star-Studded Honky Tonk, ATF wanted to know right away.

Spurgeon's investigation had had made scant progress since his talk with Sergeant Farley. He still regarded Mary Lee Orsini and Yankee Hall as prime suspects. But ATF had been unable to link them to the physical evidence. Nor had Spurgeon determined any motive.

McArthur informed Spurgeon that he'd received several messages over the past two days from someone called Art Baldwin, suggesting an interest in buying BJ's. He'd never spoken with Baldwin. The messages had been relayed by a third party.

Actually, the third party in question had phoned Phoebe at home and asked her to relay the messages to her boss. Mary Lee told Phoebe that she just hated to call Bill at home. According to what Orsini told the secretary, Baldwin had mistakenly deduced from the newspapers that she owned a partnership in BJ's. On the night before McArthur notified ATF, he'd dialed the number Phoebe gave him. It turned out to be Cajun's Wharf—a popular restaurant overlooking the Arkansas River. Bill had Baldwin paged, but nobody came to the phone.

On Monday, June 28, Spurgeon and another ATF agent showed up at Bill's office carrying a confidential investigative file. He felt it appropriate to warn the attorney that somebody was feeding him disinformation. "I told him it was rather peculiar," Spurgeon said. "I didn't go into much detail as to why." The agent laid two mug shots on McArthur's desk. Bill failed to recognize either man. Nor did Phoebe. Spurgeon had been sure they wouldn't.

The name "Art Baldwin" was well known to federal investigators throughout the South. Convicted in the firebombings of some topless joints in Memphis, Baldwin had turned informant for the FBI—helping to break an infamous pardon peddling ring allegedly run by Tennessee Governor Ray Blanton. He was an inmate in a federal penitentiary. Spurgeon kept the details to himself, but he did let McArthur know that something was fishy.

"It did not make me suspect Mr. McArthur," Spurgeon said. "It made me think that whoever was giving him this information was lying. But I did want him to be aware of who Art Baldwin and Danny Owens [the other man] were, in case someone came along and represented themselves to be them."

Spurgeon asked McArthur who had given him Baldwin's name. The lawyer explained that he didn't feel at liberty to say. His informant was a client, and fearful of getting involved. He would urge his client to cooperate. Spurgeon understood. Ethically speaking, both men were in a ticklish spot. Each played the meeting according to the protocols of his profession.

From McArthur's point of view, what ATF told him—while puzzling—only lent more credibility to Mary Lee's bizarre tales. Like the tape recording she'd played for him and Phoebe two months ago, here was concrete proof in the form of a federal agent, confirming information that the Mary Lee Orsini he knew—the terrified widow from Indian Hills—couldn't possibly have invented. Or so it seemed.

At the very least, somebody appeared to be playing mind games with his client. Perhaps worse. He asked Phoebe to get her into the office as soon as possible. He needed to persuade her to cooperate with ATF.

Chapter 6

1

The day after he met with Bill McArthur over the "Art Baldwin" affair, Spurgeon hit what looked like paydirt. Two weeks earlier, he'd asked an LRPD detective to approach Herbie Wright for him. A convicted arsonist, Wright was regarded as Little Rock's number one professional "torch." After the fire at BJ's Honky Tonk in January, McArthur had warned employees to be on the lookout for the man. On Tuesday, June 29, the LRPD told Spurgeon what Wright had to say.

Arsonist or not, Wright had his own code of ethics. Insurance fraud was one thing, murdering an innocent woman something else. He told the LRPD that about ten days before the McArthur car bombing, Yankee Hall had come to him looking to buy dynamite. Wright said he had none to sell. While Yankee had never revealed what he planned to do with the stuff, it seemed a good bet he wasn't using it to blow beaver dams. Orsini hadn't been with him, but Wright knew they were connected. Spurgeon had contacted Sergeant Farley. The NLRPD detective told him that the state police had an informant close to Hall in connection with an auto theft investigation. The ATF agent sought their help. On Thursday, July 1, the state police confirmed to Spurgeon that Yankee had twice attempted to buy dynamite from their informant. Like Herbie Wright, the man denied supplying the explosive. Nor had Hall disclosed why he'd wanted it. But Yankee had made himself pretty scarce around the time of the McArthur bombing.

Spurgeon figured he was about two moves from checkmate. But ATF never did get around to picking up Yankee Hall. Before confronting his suspects, Spurgeon hoped to find proof that Hall had actually bought some Tovex. At roughly 4:00 P.M. on Friday, July 2, Spurgeon got a memo from LRPD Intelligence indicating that Bob Troutt had phoned a tip to the state police that a "salt and pepper" hit team had come to Little Rock from out of state. The white half of the pair supposedly carried a .9mm automatic and drove a silver Corvette. Fearing that somebody was setting him up, Troutt had given a similar message to Sergeant Farley. Supposedly, contracts had been taken on three women: Troutt's ex-wife Holly, Mary Lee Orsini, and Alice McArthur.

Knowing what Spurgeon knew, the list of intended victims made no sense at all. The ATF agent was inclined to laugh it off. Sergeant Farley, the LRPD, and the state police reacted the same way. In fact, only one investigative agency in town turned out to be revved up and ready on that beastly hot July afternoon. And that would be the only agency in town that never got Bob Troutt's tip: the Pulaski County Sheriff's Department. To hear the sheriff tell it, Tommy's troops remained completely in the dark.

2

Bill McArthur finally got away from the office at roughly 4:40 that Friday afternoon. He'd planned to leave earlier to get a head start on the long weekend. With the kids due to remain at Camp Timberlake for another week, he and Alice planned to spend the Fourth of July weekend with friends at the same Hot Springs lake house they'd borrowed while Alice was in Florida in June. A couple of the other women had gone ahead Friday morning, but Alice told them that she'd wait for Bill. He needed to check in at BJ's, and she didn't want him to make the long drive alone after dark.

But after spending the morning in court, McArthur was running late that afternoon. Several clients needed to see him. The most insistent had been Mary Lee Orsini. Phoebe made her an appointment for 4:30, but Bill told his secretary to cancel it and ask her to drop by earlier. He'd try to work her in. Orsini had arrived a bit before 3:00 P.M., and had spent more than an hour sitting in the outer office chatting with Phoebe and Phoebe's cousin Diane Dutton, who helped out in the office part time. She'd insisted upon waiting until Bill finished with his other clients. Later, both women recalled that Mary Lee made several unsuccessful phone calls from Phoebe's desk, once remarking how foolish it was of her to forget her own mother's phone number.

Bill was mildly irritated to learn that Mary Lee seemed to have no legal business to talk about. In fact, McArthur was in the process of signing the last of her civil cases over to another attorney. But Phoebe hadn't finished typing up the releases for her signature. So they'd have to meet at least once more, he hoped for the last time. The woman had become a burden.

On the one subject *he* wanted to explore, Orsini was adamant. Under no circumstances would she allow her lawyer to inform ATF that she'd been the client Art Baldwin had called. She told McArthur that she'd decided at last that the time had come to forget the whole thing and get on with her life.

Diane Dutton finally saw Orsini out the front door, while Bill locked up for the weekend and left alone by the back.

As he pulled onto the I-430 exit ramp nearest his home, McArthur's watch showed 4:55 P.M. Allowing for heavy Friday traffic, he estimated that he arrived home between five and ten minutes later. It was a typical Arkansas July day, with blazing sunshine and stifling humidity. As he nosed down his steep driveway and parked behind Alice's Cutlass, Bill saw that the front door stood open, though the glass storm door was shut tight. Alice's miniature poodle Boo—short for "Bourgeois"—sat outside on the front steps.

Scooping the dog under one arm, McArthur walked inside. Several sacks of groceries sat by the front door ready to be loaded in the car. Hearing the TV playing in the downstairs den, he called out to Alice but got no answer.

Setting the dog on the floor, Bill walked upstairs to change. He entered a cluttered room directly across from the master bedroom that served as his closet during remodeling. He threw his jacket across a rack, then stepped across the hall into the bedroom just far enough to lay his pocket money, keys, and sunglasses on the dresser just inside the doorway. He noticed the ironing board standing at the foot of the bed, and saw that Alice had left a new pair of shorts lying out for him to try on. Back downstairs in the den, he found his wife's shoes, purse, cigarettes and lighter on the floor by the couch. But Alice herself was nowhere to be found.

Bill checked the laundry room, then the garage. He felt the first grip of fear tighten around his throat. Finding no trace of her around the backyard pool, he went back inside. With his eyes better adjusted to the dim interior light, McArthur noticed a strange mark on the wall by the bedroom door. His heart froze in place. There was a long shallow groove leading to a strip of wallpaper that stuck straight out about four inches—almost as if somebody had run a chisel along the sheetrock, peeling it back.

Suddenly panicked, McArthur hurried to the kitchen telephone to call for help. But he got no dial tone. So he ran to the den, found Alice's cordless phone off its base and shut it off. Then he raced back to the kitchen, dialed the Little Rock police, and expressed the fear that Alice had been kidnapped. LRPD records show that the call was received at 5:17 P.M. A few minutes later, McArthur phoned Larry Dill at the sheriff's department.

"I don't know what's going on here," McArthur said. "I walked in, my house is open, my dog's outside, my wife's gone, and what looks like a bullet hole's in the wall."

Dill told him to sit tight. Help would be on the way. Hoping against hope, Bill dialed Sally Pernell. None of Alice's other close friends lived within walking distance. Sally had just gotten into a tennis dress and was fixing to drive to Burger King to buy dinner for the kids. She and her husband had a doubles match scheduled at the Racquet Club at 6:00 P.M. From the tone of Bill's voice, Sally sensed his fear. He told her about finding Boo outside. Had she seen Alice? She had not.

"He said, 'I've already called the police and I'm really worried,' " Pernell remembered. "And that made me really worried. And I said, 'What else is there? Did you see anything that's making you so worried?' He said, 'Well, yes. I found a funny thing on the wall.' I said, 'What do you mean, a funny thing?' And he said, 'It's a hole.' And I said, 'A hole in the wall?' And he said, 'Yeah. It looks like it could be a bullet hole. . . .' The newspaper said that Bill had asked me to come down there, and that is absolutely not true. In fact, when we hung up the phone, the last thing I said to him was, 'Call me as soon as you know anything.' "

But Sally changed her mind. She told her husband that she wouldn't be able to enjoy tennis until she knew Alice was safe. On her way to Burger King, she stopped by the McArthur house. In her mind's eye, she envisioned Alice walking down the driveway laughing her deep, hearty laugh at her ninny of a husband. Pernell arrived just moments ahead of the first LRPD patrol car, driven by Patrolman Robert Mc-Neely. It was 5:30 P.M.

Ron Orsini: His gentle, trusting nature made him an unwitting victim.

Sergeant T. J. Farley's crime scene photo (below) of the scarred door leading from the garage to the laundry room at 7412 Pontiac Drive. Mary Lee told neighbors that a "hit man" had broken in; investigators believed she'd faked the evidence herself.

In a hallway of the Pulaski County courthouse, Mary Lee Orsini (below left) beseeches the advice of her attorney, William C. McArthur.

1

2

3

4

July 1981: Mary Lee (above) enters the grand jury chambers.

July 1981: (Below) Mary Lee and her thirteen-year-old daughter, Tiffany, enter the grand jury chambers

July 1981: (Right) Mary Lee attempts to shield Tiffany from press photographers.

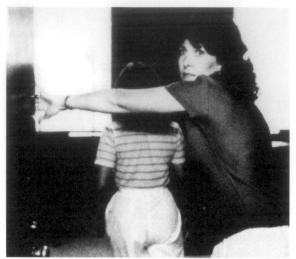

5

July 1981: On the morning after the grand jury verdict, an *Arkansas Gazette* front-page photo (right) of Mary Lee and her new friend Dr. Charles H. Wulz raised eyebrows all over the state.

7

Arkansas Gazet

COPYRIGHT, 1981, ARKANSAS GAZETTE COMPANY

162d Year—No. 252   LITTLE ROCK, WEDNESDAY, JULY 29, 1981.   96 Pa

Projected Cuts In LR Budget Are Tempered

Franchise Taxes, More Turnback Brighten Outlook

By BOB STOVER
Of the Gazette Staff

Little Rock officials are starting to temper their dismal view of the 1982 city budget with a little optimism. Cuts still will be required to balance the budget, but they won't be as extensive as was thought only a month ago.

Finance Director E. Jack Murphy said Tuesday that the cuts would be about 7 or 8 per cent, rather than the 12.5 per cent the city had been planning on.

The improvement has come from increases in a couple of revenue sources. The major one is the large increase in utility rates by the Arkansas Power and Light Company and the Arkansas Louisiana Gas Company. Their fran-

Breaking Out the Champagne

Dr. C. H. Wulz, a North Little Rock veterinarian   refused to issue indictments in the slaying of her

State May Get $30 Million For Highways

But Two Programs Might Feel the Ax, Reagan Aide Says

By JOHN BRUMMETT
Of the Gazette Staff

HOT SPRINGS — Ray Barnhart, who is President Reagan's director of the Federal Highway Administration, told Arkansas officials Tuesday that they could expect to receive about $30 million in impounded federal highway money next month.

That was good news for Governor Frank White and state Highway Director Henry C. Gray. But they weren't pleased to hear Barnhart add that he wanted to abolish two special categories of federal funding — the Great River Road Program and the "priority primary program" — that occasionally have benefited the state.

Barnhart, a former Texas high-

July 1981: (Left) Mary Lee and Tiffany strike a jubilant pose for an *Arkansas Democrat* photographer at a champagne party celebrating the grand jury's verdict.

They put him in prison! They wouldn't give him money! They were all against him because they were trash!

HE DIDN'T CARE! HE COULD BLOW THEM AWAY! HE COULD ARREST THEM ALL! HE WAS THE LAW!

TOMMY ROBINSON presents TOMMY ROBINSON in the TOMMY ROBINSON PRODUCTION of

TALKING TALL

starring TOMMY ROBINSON as TOMMY ROBINSON

"Explodes across the screen like a temper tantrum!"
—Judge George Howard

"...TR surpasses his performance in "Little Big Mouth"!"
—Judge Bill Overtonnnnt

Not since Barney Fife has the world seen a law-man like this!

Featuring Say McIntosh as an annoying Jerk

Produced by TOMMY ROBINSON   Directed by TOMMY ROBINSON
Screenplay by TOMMY ROBINSON   Music by TOMMY ROBINSON
Special Effects by TOMMY ROBINSON
Technical Advisor TOMMY ROBINSON

Now Tommy has a record! Soundtrack available from K-Tall

Because of the bizarre nature of this film, federal judges will not be seated during the last 10 minutes!

...GAULDIN... SPRINGDALE NEWS

PG PARENTAL GUIDANCE SUGGESTED
SOME MATERIAL MAY NOT BE SUITABLE FOR ADULTS

Sheriff Tommy Robinson's antics made him a hero of the common man, but the admiration was far from universal. About the same time Tommy was getting himself involved in the Orsini case, cartoonist Mike Gauldin of the *Springdale News* satirized him (left) as a character out of a popular B movie called *Walking Tall*.

Right: Alice and Bill McArthur. Their marriage would become the subject of fantastic rumors.

Below: The McArthurs and their children, Robyn and Chuck.

11

LRPD Detective Al Dawson's July 2, 1982, crime scene photo (right) of the flower arrangement found inside the fatal closet at 24 Inverness Circle. According to Sheriff Tommy, the bouquet had been thrown to the floor, scattering flower petals everywhere—evidence he deduced Bill McArthur couldn't possibly have overlooked.

ansas Gazette.

LITTLE ROCK, WEDNESDAY, JULY 7, 1982   88 Pages

Charged in McArthur Sla

McArthur and his two children are seen beyond the casket, at the cemetery.

13

14

July 7, 1982: Massive coverage in the Little Rock press helps set off a statewide orgy of speculation.

July 20, 1982: Mary Lee Orsini wearing a prisoner's uniform at a bond hearing in Little Rock Municipal Court.

15

September 1982: In response to broadcast reports that he'd hanged himself, Bill McArthur appears live on Channel 7.

16

September 1982: Equipped with his trusty chain saw, Sheriff Tommy vows to cut down community activist Robert "Say" McIntosh's cross.

Bill McArthur waiting outside the courtroom before testifying in Mary Lee Orsini's October 1982 trial.

Deputy Prosecuting Attorney Chris Piazza confidently awaits the jury's verdict at Mary Lee's first trial.

October 8, 1982: Major Larry Dill escorts Mary Lee from the courtroom. After a subsequent all-night session at the sheriff's department, she began telephoning reporters with a brand new story.

Prosecuting Attorney Wilbur C. "Dub" Bentley (left) and Sheriff Tommy (right) in one of many confrontations at the Pulaski County Courthouse.

21

22

Denouncing corruption in high places, Sheriff Tommy strikes a familiar pose.

January 1983: As Sheriff Tommy's public campaign to force Prosecutor Dub Bentley's hand heated up, *Arkansas Gazette* cartoonist George Fisher depicted the courtroom of Robinson's dreams.

23

24

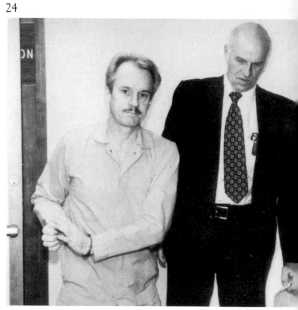

January 31, 1983: Arresting McArthur for the second time, Sheriff Tommy made a point of parading the lawyer before photographers in prisoner's garb.

February 1983: Eugene "Yankee" Hall enters the grand jury chambers.

Special Prosecutor Darrell Brown (center) and foreman Stan Brown (right) leaving the Pulaski County Courthouse after charging "improper surveillance" of the grand jury proceedings.

25

Special Prosecutor Darrell Brown (left) escorting Dr. Charles H. Wulz from the grand jury chambers.

26

McArthur hugging his mother, Billie, after hearing the grand jury verdict. Bill's father, Bryan, looks on.

27

A fashionably attired Mary Lee leaving the courtroom during her second trial.

October 1983: Attorney Phil Kaplan, NLRPD Sergeant T. J. Farley, and Larry Burge appear before a Little Rock municipal judge.

29

Mary Lee rarely missed a chance to tell her story to the press.

Meeting the two at the front door, Bill recounted all that had happened since he'd arrived home. Then he guided them both to the upstairs hallway and showed them the mysterious mark in the wallpaper. Pernell remembered convincing herself that the gouge had probably been made by a workman carrying a ladder. Officer McNeely asked McArthur whether he'd looked carefully to be sure Alice hadn't left him a note somewhere, and the two men started back down to the kitchen to check.

Exactly what took place next never became entirely clear. Police accounts—to put it mildly—differ, and neither Sally nor Bill was in any shape to make precise observations. Jittery and apprehensive, Pernell wandered alone into the master bedroom. Noticing the neatly ironed piles of clothing her friend had laid out for the weekend, she walked distractedly over to the side of the McArthurs' queen-sized bed. As she tried to imagine where Alice could be, Sally became aware of a commotion outside. Major Larry Dill and upward of a half dozen PCSD deputies—some uniformed, others in plainclothes—had arrived at the front door.

As she turned to leave the bedroom, Sally's eyes swung across the shadowy opening of Alice's large, walk-in closet. The door stood ajar about eighteen inches. Only from exactly the point in the room where she stood could the inside of the closet be seen. But something registered at the edge of her consciousness that looked wrong.

"It made me just turn back and do a double take," Pernell testified later. "The light in the room was very dim, and what I remember, when I picture it in my own mind now—there was no color in what I saw—and I saw the outline of bended knees. It took me like a second to register, because the closet had a lot of jumble in it. It was rather cluttered. And even though I couldn't identify any one object in there, I just had the feeling of it being cluttered. But sticking up were these bended knees. I just saw the outline. And as soon as it registered in my mind what it was, I ran down to where they were standing at the top of the stairs by the front door."

"Oh my God!" Pernell cried out. "Please tell me those aren't legs I see in the closet!"

. . .

In the starkly flashlit crime scene photos taken by LRPD detectives more than an hour later, only Alice McArthur's right knee and part of her left calf can be seen through the open closet door. The dead woman's body lay prone on the carpeted floor amid a clutter of cowboy boots and tennis gear—half hidden under clothing hanging down from a shelf above her head. Like Ron Orsini, Alice had been shot once through the crown of the head with a large-caliber weapon. From the position of the body and bloodstain evidence on clothing that had been pulled across her as she fell, LRPD investigators concluded that the shooting had taken place inside the closet. The body had not been moved.

Besides the bullet later recovered from the victim's skull, detectives found two matching slugs at the scene. One they dug from the hallway wall; the other had penetrated several layers of clothing and lay spent on the closet floor. All three turned out to be Federal brand hollow-nosed .38 caliber rounds of a type last manufactured in 1975; all three had been fired from the same short-barreled Smith & Wesson revolver. Detectives hypothesized that Alice had fled into the closet hoping to reach a pistol the McArthurs kept hidden in a box on a top shelf.

Both the entry angle of the wound and the way Alice had fallen caused investigators to speculate that she'd gone to her knees before the fatal shot was fired. In the opinion of Dr. L. Gordon Holt, the same country coroner who'd presided at the murder of Ron Orsini sixteen months earlier, death had been instantaneous.

Alice McArthur was barefoot. She wore a pair of blue-green terry-cloth shorts and top. Clutched tightly in her left hand—Alice was left-handed—was a black felt-tip pen. On her right shoulder, investigators noticed a small amount of white plaster dust, presumably from the bullet hole in the hallway. According to the LRPD's crime scene photos, sitting upright and undisturbed at the dead woman's feet, they found a bouquet of brightly colored flowers in a plastic florist's pot—mostly daisies, carnations, and chrysanthemums. Attached to the bouquet was a printed card reading: *"Have a Nice Day."*

Nobody doubted that the bouquet came from somewhere inside the McArthur house. Nor that Alice's murderer had used the flowers to trick the dead woman into opening her door to a stranger. Several eyewitnesses had noticed a hand-lettered florist's delivery sign stuck in the window of the beat-up old Cadillac that had pulled up in front of 24 Inverness Circle at roughly 4:00 P.M. They'd seen a thin black man in a blue baseball cap carry the flowers to the door. Moments later, a small pasty-faced white man with a mustache and sunglasses had followed him inside. Both men had emerged quickly, without the flowers. Witnesses dismissed the noises they heard as children playing with firecrackers.

Exactly how and when the bouquet came to rest at the dead woman's feet, however, would become the subject of bitter—and largely secret—controversy between LRPD detectives and the PCSD. Sally Pernell never saw them. Neither did her husband George, a physician whom officers allowed to look at Alice's body to satisfy himself that she was beyond help. More important, since the Pernells' emotional state made them shaky eyewitnesses, Patrolman McNeely failed to notice any bouquet. So did Patrolman Rick Edgar, who arrived minutes later in a second LRPD unit to provide backup.

According to sworn testimony by the two LRPD officers, chaos ensued almost from the moment Sally Pernell came running down the hallway shouting for help. McNeely told Pernell and McArthur to wait in the living room while he went upstairs. "I looked in the closet and there was the body of a white female in there," McNeely reported. "I felt of her pulse on her neck and also on her left arm. There was none. At this time I went to the phone in the bedroom and called headquarters to notify the appropriate people to come out and begin the investigation. While I was on the phone, I heard a commotion out in the living room. I walked out the door and found out there was approximately five Pulaski County deputies there, and they came into the bedroom—which Major Dill was in front of them."

According to Larry Dill's written summary, produced at an unknown interval after the fact, *he* had found Alice's body, told McNeely where to find it, and delivered the terrible news to her husband. Bill cried, "Oh, my God!" and began to weep. Sally Pernell collapsed in tears. Months afterward, McArthur thought he remembered a uniformed LRPD officer telling him of Alice's murder. Pernell was uncertain. She recalled Bill trying to struggle into the bedroom and being held back by somebody she thought was Dill. She herself began to shake all over.

By the time Patrolman Rick Edgar arrived minutes later, he found four or five PCSD patrol cars already parked in front of the McArthur house along with McNeely's LRPD unit. He knew at once that there was fixing to be trouble. The sight of sheriff's deputies at *any* call well inside city limits would infuriate LRPD headquarters. And how in the world had they beaten him there? The sheriff's department's normal response time out in the county was close to twenty-five minutes. Yet five PCSD cars had preceded him.

As Edgar walked down the McArthurs' steep driveway, he saw several deputies fanning out to canvass the neighborhood for witnesses. By the time McNeely showed him Alice McArthur's body, the corpse was already cool. The LRPD patrolmen knew that their first duty was to secure the crime scene. But with fewer than two years' experience between them, they were confused about how to deal with Major Dill and other high-ranking deputies. They knew that Tommy Robinson was racing to the scene. Once Tommy got in on the act, no telling how crazy things would get.

McNeely had already asked Dill once to pull his people out. Dill hadn't argued, but the PCSD deputies weren't budging. They roamed all over the McArthur house, poking into God knew what. Edgar phoned his patrol sergeant for advice. The sergeant was just telling him to flat *order* the PCSD to leave the premises when Edgar noticed Dill and two others heading back into the master bedroom where Alice McArthur's body lay.

Dill and two deputies were crouched inside the closet. "I said, 'We're going to have to clear the house immediately. What are you doing?' " Edgar testified later. "Their response was, 'We're looking for flowers.' I don't know which one said it. . . . Dill and this other deputy got up and turned around. Deputy Woodward was still in the closet on all fours—hands and knees. I had to grab him by the arm and pull him up."

According to Edgar, Captain Bobby Woodward came along quietly. In the excitement of the moment, the significance of the remark about the flowers was lost upon Edgar. Nor did he return to the closet to see what the three had been up to. All anybody knew was that the bouquet lay at Alice McArthur's feet when LRPD detectives arrived to process the crime scene.

And that neither McNeely, Edgar, nor Sally Pernell had seen it there before.

•   •   •

Although Woodward would later deny being at the McArthur house that day, the two LRPD officers had absolutely no doubt about the identity of the deputy whom Edgar pulled forcibly from the closet. Both had seen him around the courthouse many times. Indeed, Captain Bobby Woodward would have been hard to mistake for anybody else. Short and muscular, with a badly broken nose and an easily recognizable bush of curly reddish-blond hair, Woodward packed a huge .357 magnum hogleg in a shoulder holster. As one of several cronies from Tommy's Jacksonville days, he appeared on TV constantly at the sheriff's side.

Among other cops, Woodward had a reputation for being crooked as a snake—a shakedown artist and a con man. Any dirty tricks that needed to be pulled, Woodward figured to be the boy. Everybody knew that. LRPD detectives arriving at the crime scene also said they recognized Woodward outside the McArthur house.

•   •   •

When he'd finally escorted the deputies outside, Edgar found McArthur—whom he recognized as a fellow parishoner at Christ the King Catholic Church—sitting on the front steps crying. His hands shook so badly that he couldn't light his own cigarette. Wordlessly, Edgar took the lighter from Bill's hands and lit it for him.

3

Mary Lee Orsini arrived home at Indian Hills that afternoon at about 5:00 P.M. A few minutes past five, she received a call on Tiffany's private line from Yankee. At 5:15—just about the time Bill McArthur was making up his mind to call the police—Orsini dialed Phoebe Pinkston at her husband's pawnshop. For no particular reason, Pinkston noticed the exact time.

To Phoebe's amazement, the calm, lighthearted woman Phoebe had seen at the office two hours ago had disappeared. "She was just hysterical," Phoebe said, "saying that Bill had just told her that her phone had been bugged by the NLRPD—which we all figured all along anyway. So I couldn't understand why she was so upset.

"And she said that they were trying to implicate her and Bill— something about an incident where Bill and her went down by the river one day last fall and that she had brought some wine. And she was screaming, 'My God, how many people are going to have to be killed before they find out who's doing this?' She kept on like that and I kept going yeah, yeah, yeah, because I was wanting to leave and she was rambling on and on."

When Phoebe had just about had her fill, Mary Lee abruptly changed the subject. "She went, 'Just a minute, I hear somebody at the door.' So she puts the phone down and I hear nothing. That's when she came back and said a black man came to her door carrying a box. She didn't go to the door. She peeked out and saw him. She didn't seem upset about it, and I said, 'It's that time of year, when the blacks come around wanting to mow your lawn.' We started joking, and she said, 'Yeah, I guess my yard's in bad shape.' "

With that, Mary Lee calmed down and Phoebe made an excuse to hang up. She and her husband went out to dinner, and didn't hear about Alice's death until they returned shortly after 7:00 P.M.

• • •

Even before LRPD detectives had arrived at the crime scene, Larry Dill had ordered a statewide alert to be broadcast describing a suspicious car seen in the vicinity: an older bronze Cadillac with a black vinyl top and a hand-lettered delivery sign stuck in a side window. The vehicle was said to be driven by two black men.

Every news organization in Little Rock with a police scanner—such as the one on the night table next to the bed where Ron Orsini had been murdered—heard the broadcast. Immediately afterward, the first call to the PCSD emergency line came from Mary Lee Orsini.

"I've got something, I don't know if it's an emergency or not," she told the dispatcher, "but it's kind of scared me. I'm Lee Orsini, and two black men pulled up in front of my house a while ago. . . . And I was on the phone, and rang the doorbell. And we don't have any black people in this neighborhood. And they went away, but they keep driving by my house."

"What kind of car were they in?" the dispatcher asked.

"An old car. I don't know much about cars."

"What color is it?"

"Oh, beige-y color. Larry always told me . . ."

The dispatcher asked for her name, which he failed at first to recognize. "I live in North Little Rock," she said. "I don't want the North Little Rock cops out here . . ."

"You're inside the city, Ma'am?" he replied. "Okay, I cannot send a sheriff's car inside the city on a call, Ma'am. If you're inside the city of North Little Rock and have a suspicious vehicle around your neighborhood, you need to call them."

"I'm not going to call the North Little Rock cops."

The dispatcher repeated that he was not authorized to send a car inside city limits.

"If you happen to talk to Larry Dill or Tommy Robinson, would you tell them that I called and reported this?"

The dispatcher promised that he would.

. . .

Next Orsini phoned Diane and Michael Kinsolving, her neighbors on the opposite side of Pontiac Drive. In the same breathless voice she'd used to summon their assistance so many times, Mary Lee gave Diane an excited description of the black stranger who had knocked on her door. Since then, she claimed, two black men in a beat-up old Cadillac had twice circled the block, staring at her house. Hoping to catch a glimpse of the car, Michael Kinsolving carried a cordless phone outside. He saw nothing. He told his fifteen-year-old son to climb on his bicycle and ride around the block. The boy returned a few minutes later. He had seen no Cadillac and no black men.

When Michael phoned Mary Lee back, he had a curious experience. From none of the ordinary phones in the Kinsolving household—as Orsini knew perfectly well—was it possible to look out onto Pontiac Drive. Nor had she visited her neighbors since they'd bought a cordless. So she had no idea as she launched into yet another hysterical description of a menacing vehicle stopped right then in front of her house that Michael Kinsolving was standing outside gazing upon an empty street.

Moments later, when Diane heard the first TV bulletins of Alice McArthur's murder, she thought somebody needed to notify her neighbor. Orsini's phone was busy, so her husband ran across Pontiac and shouted to her. Raising her bedroom window, Mary Lee calmly informed him that the sheriff had already called. A deputy was coming to take her into protective custody.

That much was true. No sooner had Major Dill learned of Orsini's call than he sent a deputy to Indian Hills to fetch her to PCSD headquarters. Meanwhile, he and Robinson were burning up the Pine Bluff highway. Jefferson County authorities had stopped an aged Cadillac driven by two black men, and Sheriff Tommy was red hot to make the bust in person.

Just before taking off for Pine Bluff, Robinson had returned briefly to PCSD headquarters, where Doc Hale reached them by phone seeking the whereabouts of Sally Pernell. Like all traffic coming into the PCSD emergency line, the call was recorded.

"We've been working on a couple of deals for about the last two days," Tommy said. "And tell [LRPD Chief Sonny] Simpson to calm his little ass down. We need to work together on this deal. We've got some things going that ya'll don't know about. Ya'll do your thing. We're going to go out and see what we can find out and get back with you.

"Let me just emphasize something to you," Robinson continued. "It would be in the best interest of your department and mine . . . to work together, because ya'll have got some information. We've got a hell of a lot that we've been working our ass off on for about. . . . Around the clock for about three days."

All the way to Pine Bluff, Tommy could be heard hounding the PCSD dispatcher to put him in touch with the FBI.

· · ·

A bit past 6:30 P.M., while she and a friend were watching "Family Feud," Joyce Holt saw a TV bulletin about Alice McArthur's murder. She hurried to the phone to give Mary Lee the shocking news. Orsini acted as if she hadn't heard it yet, and to Joyce's surprise, didn't seem shocked. " 'Well, that explains why the sheriff's department is coming to pick me up,' " Joyce remembered her saying. Then she launched into her tale about two black men at her door with a package.

4

In his ten years in the Little Rock Police Department, Detective Al Dawson had never seen anything like the spectacle that greeted him when he arrived at the McArthur home shortly after 6:00 P.M. Neither had his immediate supervisors Sergeant Fred Hensley and Lieutenant Bobby Thomas. Drawn by the patrol cars parked out front, a large crowd had gathered in front of the house. With TV and radio broadcasting speculative updates, a near-circus atmosphere developed.

Dawson had been born in Piggot, a farm town in the flat, swampy northeast corner of Arkansas, and raised in the Missouri bootheel. His nickname around headquarters was "Fonzie," for his resemblance to the TV character. Gifted with a caustic intelligence, he'd joined the LRPD two years out of high school, and by 1980 was at thirty-one the youngest homicide detective on the force.

It was a little past 8:30 P.M. before Dawson allowed the medical examiner's staff to remove Alice McArthur's body. He and several others stayed on the scene taking photographs, making measurements, drawing sketches, dusting for fingerprints, and collecting evidence for several hours after that.

Regardless of what happened before they arrived, Dawson and his superiors had little practical choice but to take the physical evidence as they found it. They couldn't testify about where the bouquet of flowers at Alice McArthur's feet had been before they'd seen it.

Officially, therefore, the scuffle inside the closet never happened. Neither Patrolman McNeely nor anybody else's initial written reports mentioned it. Dawson had the bouquet photographed, then removed it from the closet and had some more pictures taken. He needed a likeness LRPD detectives could show florists in the hope of identifying the individual who had bought it. The Pulaski County deputies' intrusion was simply an inconvenient fact best ignored.

LRPD detectives never anticipated that the PCSD would make an issue out of the flowers. Nobody could possibly have guessed the bouquet's significance. After all, it was their boys who had fucked up. Were they not all on the same side? But no, they weren't all on the same side. Not hardly.

·   ·   ·

Dawson was still roughing out his crime scene sketches when John Spurgeon walked in carrying a mug shot of Yankee Hall. As soon as LRPD Intelligence had reached him at home, Spurgeon had hurried back to his office, gathered up his case file, and driven to Pleasant Valley. He'd taken LRPD Chief Sonny Simpson and Doc Hale aside and given them a rundown of what he had.

Already edgy, Dawson became even more irritated. Typical of a federal agent, Spurgeon only wanted to deal with the top brass. Dawson had played no role in the bombing investigation. "I think every police officer in the state knew the story except me," he said later. "I felt like a *big* dummy, boy. I'm out there working my ass off and they're bringing in pictures of my suspect." When they all got back to headquarters, the detective raised hell. If they intended to assign him the case, Dawson told his captain, somebody needed to tell him what was going on.

"So they came back a little later and said, 'Why don't you come have a look at this?' " Dawson said. "That's when they broke out the stuff they'd developed on the bombing of the car—the Tovex, the speculation on Yankee Hall, his connection with Lee Orsini—the whole nine yards."

Spurgeon emphasized that ATF's case against Yankee Hall was purely circumstantial. If the little creep had played a part in Alice McArthur's murder—and eyewitness descriptions of the white man seen entering the house sure sounded like him—the only way to prove it would be to do some basic police work.

Dawson sent the flower arrangement to be dusted for fingerprints. Beginning first thing Saturday, LRPD detectives carried photos of the bouquet to florist shops. Working from a computerized list, others began to search out every piece of shit brown, gold, or beige Cadillac in Pulaski County—starting in black neighborhoods and working outward. July 4th leaves were canceled across the board.

Whatever investigations they had under way, detectives put them aside. Until further notice, the LRPD had one case to solve: the murder of Alice McArthur.

5

While the LRPD was swinging into high gear, Tommy Robinson was busy organizing a game of charades. His and Dill's high-speed trip to Pine Bluff had proved fruitless. The two black men detained there had firm alibis. Returning to PCSD headquarters, the disappointed sheriff concocted a plan to test Mary Lee's veracity. He confronted her with one of the central figures in the shadowy organized crime cabal she'd been feeding him for three months. Not surprisingly, Orsini flunked.

Exactly how and why Ron O'Neal came to be dressed in civilian clothes at PCSD headquarters on the very night of Alice McArthur's murder nobody outside Robinson's inner circle ever found out. The sheriff could never be pinned down on the subject. Ever since O'Neal's 1981 insurance fraud conviction in the hit and run death of a friend, the former Wine Cellar owner had been incarcerated at the federal penitentiary in Texarkana. But Dub Bentley had been flabbergasted on a recent visit to PCSD headquarters to recognize O'Neal sitting at a desk in the CID office, wearing a lieutenant's badge. Pressed for an explanation, Robinson had said something about a drug investigation.

NLRPD detectives had eliminated O'Neal as a suspect in the Orsini murder more than a year ago. Back on May 21, however, her dead husband's clandestine meetings with O'Neal had been one of the first fairy tales Mary Lee spun for Tommy Robinson. O'Neal also had a propensity for bragging around town about his Memphis connections—specifically the "Art Baldwin" faction that Robinson had been red hot to drag into the two cases all along.

What pretext Sheriff Tommy used to spring O'Neal from Texarkana that weekend remains a mystery. According to what Mary Lee told Phoebe Pinkston in a phone call late that night, the deputy who picked her up in Indian Hills had been the first to tell her about Alice's murder—at least the third time she'd pretended to be surprised.

In Phoebe's words: "She starts telling him what this car looks like, and he says, 'Oh, my God, that's the same car that was seen at Alice McArthur's house.' He runs to the radio and comes back in, and that's when she says she found out that Alice was killed.

"She also said that they had Ron O'Neal out at the sheriff's department, and that Tommy took her into a room and Tommy said, 'Who is that?' And she said, 'I don't know who that is.' And Tommy said, 'You don't know who that is?' And she said he started screaming at her, saying, 'That's Ron O'Neal. You lied to me. You're supposed to know him.' And then they take Ron out of the room, and she's hysterical, saying, 'Tommy, what are you trying to do to me?' And he said, 'Oh, I was just doing that for O'Neal's benefit.' And she said, 'I really didn't recognize him. He had on thick, dark glasses.' "

Remarkably, Robinson's own account pretty much agrees with Orsini's. Except that in the sheriff's version, he and O'Neal had both shouted that she was a lying bitch. Years later, Tommy bragged about the incident. "We did it intentionally," he said, "and she didn't like it worth a shit. We had all the bullshit we cared to put up with from her. It shocked her. First time I'd ever seen her shocked speechless."

But Tommy remained evasive about why he had O'Neal brought to PCSD headquarters that night. The simplest explanation that fits the facts is that it was the sheriff himself who was suddenly forced to realize that he'd been conned—that the multi-state organized crime conspiracy he'd so knowingly described on TV was purely a figment of Orsini's teeming imagination.

But just how far had the sheriff been willing to go in pursuit of his ambition? That was the question that intrigued other investigators. Was it possible that Robinson had known—or thought he knew—a great deal more about the murder of Alice McArthur than he ever admitted? Robinson would vehemently deny it, but a great deal of the circumstantial evidence made it look like he did.

Besides a half dozen carloads of deputies showing up at the McArthur crime scene in no time flat, the comments Edgar claimed to have heard made it seem that they'd known in advance that there was a flower bouquet somewhere on the premises. Phone records later revealed an unexplained call to the PCSD from a pay phone very near the McArthur house—a call made minutes *before* Bill arrived home that afternoon. The following recorded exchange between the PCSD radio dispatcher and an unidentified deputy immediately after Alice's body was found also aroused suspicion:

Dispatcher: I think that they done [sighs] killed one out at
    McArthur's house.
Deputy: [laughter] We did?
Dispatcher: No. They're going out there in that area. Dill
    wanted the Sheriff to call him at that number. And I put
    out information there was a homicide.
Deputy: Well, do you think that *we* shot one or that *they* shot?
    Who shot who?
Dispatcher: I have no idea. There's a homicide in that area.
    The sheriff's called me three times on the radio trying to get
    hold of the FBI. So I don't know what we got.

Who were "they" supposed to be? The "hit" list that Bob Troutt had somehow stumbled upon—Alice McArthur, Troutt's ex-wife, and Mary Lee Orsini—appeared to have been custom-made for the sheriff. It certainly made no sense to anybody else. Given all the other "evidence" Orsini had given the PCSD that they'd kept to themselves, could Tommy and his boys have been tipped that something was about to go down, staked out the McArthur house, and simply bungled the deal? Although Tommy and Dill strenuously denied it, other investigators thought it certainly looked that way. Like the nickel and dime drugstore burglaries that Robinson and Dill would later be accused of setting up in order to make dramatic arrests, that had all the hallmarks of their style. (Both Robinson and Dill denied the charges and the allegations were never pursued.)

Could Orsini's mad scenario have included handing the sheriff Yankee Hall's head on a platter? Her subsequent actions made one thing clear: When Yankee and his accomplice got away from 24 Inverness Circle alive that afternoon, Mary Lee was faced with a problem that she would have to go to desperate lengths to resolve.

Chapter 7

1

Numb with the shock, Phoebe decided to spend Saturday with her husband at his North Little Rock pawnshop. She didn't want to stay home alone. She'd called Bill that morning and spoken to him briefly.

Minutes later, Mary Lee phoned. "Everybody thinks I'm crazy when I tell them this," Pinkston said. "But there was something she had to tell me. Right there on the phone I thought, 'She killed Alice McArthur, and she's coming over to kill me.' I saw it. I knew it. I could picture her reaching into her purse and getting out a gun to kill me. And I don't do stuff like that. I'm not that kind of person, who has visions. I just don't. But I knew. I told Paul, 'I've got to get out of here. She'll kill me if she comes over here.' And I left."

Around noon, Pinkston's husband reached her to say that Mary Lee had arrived in a highly agitated state and wasn't about to leave the shop until she saw Phoebe. Making him promise that he would not leave her alone with the woman, she reluctantly returned. "We really didn't talk that much," she said. "She'd called the LRPD and wanted me to give a statement about the black guy with the flowers at her door.

"My husband thought I was crazy. I couldn't come up with a reason for why she would kill Alice, so I just fought it. But I just couldn't fight it any more. It was just too plain that she had something to do with it.

I couldn't tell anybody *why* I knew. There was no evidence; there were no reasons. I just knew."

• • •

By 11:00 A.M. Saturday, LRPD detectives had located the florist who had sold the bouquet found at the crime scene. Both the flower arranger and the cashier at Leroy's Flower Shop on Cantrell Boulevard—not far from the McArthurs' Pleasant Valley home—had clear recollections of a white man between forty and forty-five, about five feet eight inches, with brown hair graying at the temples. He wore brown, western-style pants and a tan shirt. After seeing a photograph, both women agreed that it was definitely not Bill McArthur.

During the afternoon, a police artist working with the two women made a composite drawing of the suspect. Afterward, Al Dawson laid it on his desk next to the mug shot of Yankee Hall that Spurgeon had given him. They made a perfect match.

While the drawing was being made, they got their first look at Mary Lee. Far from the agitated demeanor she'd shown Phoebe that morning, Orsini came sweeping into the LRPD Homicide Division like a visiting celebrity. Agreeing to make a voluntary statement, she controlled the agenda from the start. Even though LRPD detectives knew more about her than she thought they did, they nevertheless found her composure unsettling.

"I've talked to a lot of people in my lifetime," Lieutenant Bobby Thomas said later. "But she is probably the only one that I ever talked to that when we got through, I thought she got more information than I did. She knew more about me than I knew about her. That's not a good thing to say, but it's probably true. She was a very shrewd individual."

With one significant exception, what Orsini told LRPD detectives on July 3 was the same account she'd given Dill and Robinson on the day of the car bombing six weeks earlier. Without mentioning her midnight lover's name, she'd once again hung Yankee out to dry. Overnight, however, the words "Ron O'Neal" had vanished from her vocabulary. "Art Baldwin" had taken their place. She rattled on for almost two hours, building a whole new organized crime conspiracy from scratch. Supposedly Baldwin had asked her to contact Bill on his behalf, then turned abusive and threatening when McArthur failed to return the call.

2

While Mary Lee was weaving her spell, Yankee was sweating bullets. When he'd finally gotten Orsini on the phone Friday afternoon to tip her that the job was done, Yankee warned her that they had a bad problem. In all the excitement, he had forgotten the flowers. The florist's sign and the clipboard with the fake delivery list that had fooled Alice McArthur into opening her door, his accomplice Larry McClendon had torn up, stuffed into a paper bag, and thrown into the Arkansas River. The gun too Yankee had wiped clean and pitched off the I-430 bridge. At least that was how he chose to tell it later. Some thought it more likely that he'd cut Dr. Wulz's revolver to pieces with a welding torch.

"She says, 'Well, don't worry about the flowers,' " Yankee testified later, " 'because Bill's going to call me,' she says. 'Before he calls the police. Soon as he gets home and makes sure everything is all right.' And she says, 'I'll tell him to dispose of the flowers.' And I said, 'Well, make sure he does now, because my fingerprints are on them.' "

No record of a call from McArthur existed. Orsini had more unexpected bad news for Yankee. There would be a problem about the $25,000 she'd promised to pay him. Mary Lee had stayed so late at Bill's office that she hadn't made it to her safe deposit box before the bank closed. First thing Monday, she'd pick up the cash. Would that be okay? Yankee reminded her that Monday was July 4; it would be Tuesday before they could put their hands on the cash.

Yankee had tried to call Orsini several times on Friday night to let her know that Larry McClendon was cool about the money. But she never answered. He'd even tried to reach her at her mother's place. Mrs. Hatcher told him that Mary Lee had left town for the weekend. So he sat in the Mason Jar all night—a dive located over a boxing gym east of downtown—getting shit-faced and listening to the know-it-alls at the bar giving their opinions about the McArthur murder.

. . .

Late Saturday morning, Officer Mike Willingham picked Yankee up downtown, where he'd crashed for the night on a friend's couch. Through his father's body shop, Willingham had known Hall for years. For months the policeman had used him as an informant, trading barroom scuttlebutt for little favors—jobs, meals, or a ten spot. Yankee had agreed to help him move that weekend. As the two drove out Cantrell, Yankee became edgy when he saw an unmarked LRPD detective's car parked in front of Leroy's Flower Shop.

"What if they got the guy that bought the flowers on that McArthur killing?" he blurted out. "They still wouldn't have enough to put a charge on him, would they?"

The policeman said he figured they would.

"Well, if they did convict him," Hall asked, "would he get the death sentence? Or could he tell what he knew and get life without parole?"

Already suspicious of Hall, Willingham tried to persuade him to talk to somebody in Homicide. He knew all about Yankee's relationship with Orsini. A couple of months ago, he'd even introduced her to the patrolman as his girlfriend "Sue." Dressed in civilian clothing, the policeman had recognized her from TV. On other occasions, Yankee had talked incessantly about Mary Lee and her problems. In fact, it had been Willingham who'd tipped Yankee off about the Art Baldwin rumors making their way around town, information he'd dutifully passed along to Mary Lee.

But Yankee refused to talk to Homicide. All he knew were rumors. Nothing more. He stayed jumpy all day. Before he'd return to the Arkansas penitentiary, Hall swore, he'd run to Mexico. Willingham became so convinced of Yankee's involvement that when the ex-con showered and changed after they were done moving, the policeman volunteered to launder his clothes—the same ones Yankee had worn Friday when he'd returned Willingham's pickup to him. He put them aside as evidence.

On Sunday, July 4, Willingham arranged a compromise. Yankee wouldn't talk to anybody from the LRPD, but he did agree to meet with a retired detective named Forrest Parkman. Then in his early fifties and working for the Justice Department's Regional Organized Crime Information Center out of Memphis, Parkman and John Terry had been partners during their careers with the LRPD. Everything Terry had learned about Mary Lee Orsini, Parkman also knew.

By the time Yankee sat down with Parkman, he'd grown even more jittery. Larry McClendon had called him at the Mason Jar to tell him that several carloads of sheriff's deputies had come barging into his mother's house on 14th Street after midnight Saturday looking for him. Luckily, he'd been gone. The deputies told Larry's mother they wanted to question her son about stolen cars, but it had to be the other thing. Nobody came looking for hot cars at 2:00 A.M. carrying sawed-off shotguns. Yankee reassured him as best he could.

Parkman met Yankee about 8:30 Sunday night. If he hoped to pick the ex-cop's brain, Yankee was out of luck. Even sober, he was no match for Parkman—a legendary investigator in his day. And Hall had been drinking all day. At first, Yankee professed to know nothing about the McArthur murder, except that a couple of dudes had been asking around about silencers and explosives. But unless Parkman had something to swap, Hall couldn't help.

Based on what he'd read in the papers, however, Yankee had a few ideas. It struck him as odd that a neighbor had found the body. Why phone a woman? A real man would have pulled his gun and searched the house himself.

"I'll tell you something else," Yankee blurted out. "Bill McArthur's old lady's fucking Troutt. Been fucking him for a long time. Looks to me like everything landed in Troutt's lap. Maybe she had enough on him that she could bury him in all that shit."

Yankee launched into a diatribe on the perfidy of women; 95 percent of the inmates in the penitentiary, he allowed, ended up there by running their mouths to women. "Don't tell women nothing you know," he advised. "Tell them lies."

"Is Mrs. Orsini in financial trouble?" Parkman interrupted. Caught by surprise, Yankee admitted that she was, then quickly added that he hardly knew her. "She's lived a sheltered life," he added. "She's a society broad. Didn't wear blue jeans until she was fucking twenty years old."

"Does she like Bill?"

"Oh yeah. They're pretty close friends," Hall said. "But there's no hanky-panky. Something a whole lot of people don't know, okay? Bill's about nine tenths gay."

"You mean he's a homo?" Parkman asked. "You got any ideas who his boyfriends are?"

"I don't think he'd know me if he passed me on the street," Yankee said. "But I know the word on the street is that he sucks dicks. But Orsini, she don't know nothing."

"I want to ask you something," Parkman said. "You don't have to answer if you don't want to. But did that come from Orsini?"

Yankee denied it, and Parkman didn't press him. Parkman asked him if he knew any blacks who might help on the case.

"I don't fuck with too many niggers," Yankee said. "I've only got one nigger [friend]—I won't even give you his name, but he's tight with me—and he can find out anything you want to know. He knows every nigger in town."

"Can you find one that's driving a seventy-something model brown Cadillac? The one that deals in flowers?"

"I imagine he got those flowers out of the cemetery," Hall said. "Cemeteries are full of fucking flowers. I don't know where they got them, of course. I mean that's what I would do."

Yankee had grown visibly pale. Despite the air conditioning, perspiration shone on his forehead. "They said at first there was two niggers. Now they're saying it was a white man and a nigger. You know, fuck. I'm not going to . . . I don't fuck with any drug dealers. I ain't done no fucking murders."

There was a lot more in the same vein. But none of it changed Parkman's mind. The white half of the salt and pepper team that murdered Alice McArthur was Yankee Hall. And the Orsini bitch had somehow or other put him up to it.

When Parkman played his tape of Yankee for his former colleagues in Homicide late Sunday night, he learned that Al Dawson was half a jump ahead of him. Not only had Dawson already made Yankee, but the black dude was going to be one Larry Darnell McClendon—a two-time loser who'd gotten tight with Hall in prison. The two had been seen drinking at several local dives recently. According to motor vehicle records, McClendon was also the proud owner of a 1975 Cadillac Sedan DeVille, with a gold body and black vinyl top, Arkansas tag JSO-853. Even as they spoke, LRPD detectives were out searching for the car.

3

Yankee she could handle. Larry Darnell McClendon, however, was a potential wild card. After eighteen months of make-believe, Mary Lee had finally succeeded in bringing her fantasies to life. Inept as they'd been—Yankee and McClendon had fucked around with a dead battery and gotten to Pleasant Valley more than an hour behind schedule—they'd managed to kill Alice McArthur and escape the scene.

Except that Mary Lee didn't have a nickel to pay them. The safe deposit box she'd told Yankee about contained nothing. Before visiting Phoebe on Saturday morning, Orsini had contacted Larry Burge shortly after dawn. "She was bawling and snuffling," he said, "and telling about the black man that came to her house—supposedly to finish her off too.

What she wanted to know was did I have a shotgun she could borrow? I didn't, still don't. She said there was two killers, and that Robinson told her there was three people on the hit list: Alice McArthur, Lee Orsini, and Holly Troutt."

The next time Burge heard from Mary Lee was on Sunday, July 4. She needed urgently to consult the criss-cross telephone directory at Block Realty. What she must have been looking for, Burge deduced later, was McClendon's address. The realtor agreed to meet her at his office. A few hours later, Mary Lee called again. The anonymous callers were at it again. She'd been given the name of the trigger man in the McArthur murder, and wanted Larry to pass it on to the sheriff for her. The tip would have more credibility coming from somebody else, she explained. Burge didn't need to get involved, merely repeat what she'd been told.

Later, Burge would maintain that he'd already grown suspicious of Orsini. "I knew she knew way too damn much," he insisted. "You just don't get these kind of plums handed to you day after day." But Burge made the call. Refusing to divulge his identity, he spoke with Dill and Robinson both. Also with Captain Bobby Woodward. Besides McClendon's name, he provided the PCSD with his mother's address and the information that one Forrest Parkman had two remaining contracts out: one for Bob Troutt's ex-wife, the other for Mary Lee Orsini. Sheriff Tommy and his boys saddled up and rode out looking for McClendon, succeeding only in putting him on guard. Otherwise, they kept the tip to themselves.

4

Unlike Ron Orsini's death, the murder of Alice McArthur began as front-page news and soon grew into a statewide obsession. For the news business in a city like Little Rock, a genuine Mob "hit" would be the next best thing to an NFL franchise. Over the weekend, Little Rock media speculation centered upon the same organized crime scenarios that Sheriff Tommy had spelled out for the TV cameras after the car bombing. The Troutt and Orsini cases were invariably linked with the crime.

On Monday morning, July 5, a front-page headline in the *Gazette* provided its readers with a new twist: "QUITE A BIT OF MONEY" INHERITED BY SLAYING VICTIM. Even more intriguing than the information contained in the article were its unmistakable innuendos. According to the newspaper, Alice McArthur had recently come into an oil fortune worth upward of $50,000 a month. "Area law enforcement officials . . ." the *Gazette* continued, "are exploring the possibility that the inheritance constituted at least part of the motive behind her slaying."

Because of the holiday weekend, investigators had been hindered in their efforts to determine who stood to gain by Alice McArthur's death—her husband, "a prominent Little Rock defense lawyer and part owner of a night club," her children, or her brother. "It is known that Mrs. McArthur talked of putting the money in a trust for her children shortly after she escaped serious injury May 21 when a bomb under her car partly detonated. Although friends said she was certain . . . that the bomb was meant for her, it could not be learned whether she carried through with the trust or even left a will."

Although it would be months before the paper got around to correcting itself, almost everything in the *Gazette* article—cleverly written by reporter Carol Griffee in such a manner as to conceal her sources—was interpreted by most readers as tantamount to an indictment of Bill McArthur. In fact, not only had Alice's murder made it impossible for her husband to share in her inheritance, but she'd died without either a will or a dime's worth of life insurance. LRPD and ATF investigators, moreover, had been in full possession of the facts since the car bombing in May. Although money was the last thing on Bill McArthur's mind that terrible weekend, Alice's death would eventually cost him almost everything he owned.*

.   .   .

Among her *Gazette* colleagues, Carol Griffee was known for her determination to get to the bottom of a story, and her fondness for conspiracies. Griffee had correctly sensed enormous tension at the crime scene, and suspected a cover-up. Quite by chance, a neighbor of hers had a cousin in Mississippi who'd been an intimate friend of Alice McArthur's since college. Did the police know, Griffee's neighbor asked her, that Alice had just inherited a pile of money? There was also something about a black notebook Alice's friend was eager to know about.

---

*Ironically, apart from the checks Alice had already cashed, there would never be any money to speak of. Hardly had the wells on Alice and her brother's land in Pointe Coupe Parish gone into production than they were capped in May 1982—never to reopen. The collapse of OPEC and the resulting worldwide petroleum glut all but shut down the oil and gas industry in Louisiana overnight. The apparent bonanza vanished as suddenly as it had appeared.

Griffee hurried to the *Gazette* newsroom. She told the city editor what she had learned. In the manner of reporters everywhere, she'd already converted the dead woman into an abstraction: the case of the bumped-off heiress. Next she got an anonymous call tipping her that Mary Lee Orsini had reported seeing the Cadillac to the sheriff. The LRPD, her source said, was trying to freeze Tommy out of the case. Griffee raced out to PCSD headquarters. Tommy had quickly verified everything she'd heard and supplied her with the $50,000 a month figure. He confided that Alice's brother had certifiable Mafia connections. Like a White House reporter concealing the identity of a "senior official," Griffee purposely crafted her account to protect her number one source. "Sheriff Tommy Robinson," she wrote, "answered a reporter's questions about the homicide itself with 'no comments' or refusals 'to confirm or deny' because he said it was the LRPD's case."

5

At 5:20 P.M. on Monday, July 5, LRPD detectives arrested Eugene "Yankee" Hall at a seedy apartment on Izard Street and brought him in for questioning. As Yankee had feared, his fingerprints had been identified both on the flowerpot and the accompanying card. Though he refused to say anything until his attorney arrived, he soon realized that the time had come to exercise his middleman's option and cut himself a deal.

The lawyer Hall called was a former partner of McArthur's named Paul Johnson. The two had severed their relationship a few years earlier on unfriendly terms. Once the lawyer arrived, Doc Hale laid the LRPD's cards on the table. And there were even more of them than Yankee had feared. Two witnesses from Leroy's Flower Shop had picked him out of a line-up of six small white men wearing mustaches. Eyewitnesses placed him at the crime scene. His fingerprints were on the flowers.

"Yankee started talking right away," Doc recalled. "He told me, 'I'll give you the top and bottom if I walk.' I said, 'Yankee, no way you're walking on this one.' "

The bargaining process began. Without some kind of a deal, Hall's lawyer informed investigators, his client would make no statement. But if he were to make a statement, what he would tell them was that Bill McArthur was the ramrod behind the whole thing: Although Yankee had never met with or spoken to McArthur about the plot, the attorney had paid Mary Lee Orsini $25,000 to be split among herself, Hall, and the triggerman. Yankee and Orsini planned to use their share to go into the cocaine business.

．　．　．

In the time elapsed, Mary Lee had persuaded Larry Burge to make another anonymous call, this one to her phone, which she'd recorded. He agreed to stage a dramatic recreation of a phone call she claimed to have received earlier Monday. To make sure Burge got it straight, Mary Lee provided him with a handwritten script, notes she had hurriedly scribbled as the *real* anonymous tipster spoke, she assured him.

After they rehearsed the script in Orsini's living room, Burge drove out to a biker bar on the old Conway highway and made the call from a pay phone. To disguise himself, Burge affected a sing-song, swishy voice. She was unhappy with the first take, and made Burge do the whole thing again. Orsini, of course, gave her customary rendition of a woman consumed with terror.

"You are one of three people on a hit list in this area," Burge read. "Mrs. McArthur was one, and Mrs. Holly Troutt is one, and Mrs. Lee Orsini is the other one. I can't stay on the phone all day with you, okay?"

"Alright, I'll hear you out."

"Mr. Larry McClendon, M-c-C-L-E-N-D-O-N, is the person who actually committed the crime last Friday afternoon."

"Who killed Alice?"

"Yes, and he intended to kill you also."

"Is this Larry McClendon a white man or a black man?"

"He is black. He is definitely black," Burge said. "Now he has a white friend who runs around with him who is even meaner than Larry himself." Burge gave a detailed description of McClendon and Yankee, and threw in Bob Troutt and Forrest Parkman's names for good measure.

"Why was Alice McArthur killed?" Orsini asked.

"Mrs. McArthur was killed because she knew too much."

"What do you mean, Mrs. McArthur knew too much?"

Burge almost wrecked the second tape as well. "Don't confuse me," he lisped. "Because the notes are very poorly written and I hoped that I wouldn't have to do this. It's been a long day already. . . . They are very, very obviously trying to set you up for something. The information is that they're going to bring in some even larger talents to take care of the sheriff himself."

"I don't think anybody's going to mess with Tommy Robinson."

"Oh, yes they will," Burge read. "They can't help theirself anymore. Things are really getting big now."

With the second run-through, Burge's doubts about Orsini's involvement vanished. "But it was sort of like working for the Mafia," he said. "You don't just go in one day and say, 'I'm fixing to retire.' "

No matter when Burge realized that Mary Lee had played him for a fool, he did have enough mother wit to protect himself. First thing next morning, he put her handwritten script in his lawyer's hands for safekeeping.

• • • •

Mary Lee took Burge's tape and ran straight to Sheriff Robinson. When Tommy fetched her to LRPD headquarters that night at Doc Hale's insistence, he brought the cassette—proof positive, he assured everybody, of her innocence. Orsini also turned out to be packing a .38 snub nose, property of the PCSD.

LRPD detectives got nothing useful out of Orsini Monday night. This time they read her her rights, and secured a consent to search the safe deposit box where she'd told Yankee that $25,000 cash was stored. The box was empty. Bank records showed it hadn't been opened in months.

Mary Lee led them all around the barn. Why she'd never even *heard* of anybody named Yankee Hall. They had no choice but to release her. Under Arkansas law, the uncorroborated testimony of an accomplice is not sufficient evidence to make an arrest. And even if Orsini hadn't already beaten one grand jury, they could all see that she was damn good—the best any of them had ever seen.

• • •

On Tuesday morning, July 6, an LRPD patrol car pulled up behind Larry Darnell McClendon on Broadway less than three blocks from police headquarters. Detectives staking out Yankee's apartment had watched the slender, bearded black man show up exactly as Hall had told them he would—ostensibly to collect his share of the $25,000.

Told that Yankee had been busted, he left on foot. After hanging back hoping he'd lead them to his car, they moved in. McClendon surrendered.

Two hours later, detectives came upon McClendon's 1975 Cadillac Sedan DeVille behind a relative's home in College Station—a poor black settlement near the Little Rock airport. After securing a warrant, they towed it to a lot behind headquarters and had it searched. They found nothing directly related to the crime, but did produce an address book listing Yankee's name and number. Witnesses identified the car and picked McClendon out of a photo line-up. He was booked for capital felony murder.

McClendon had met and mistakenly learned to trust Yankee Hall while serving a sentence for armed robbery. Alone among those involved in the case, he had apparently never laid eyes on Mary Lee. Nor, from that morning onward, did he ever make a statement to police or reporters. McClendon took the public defender's advice, hunkered down, and said not a word, then or ever.

By the time McClendon found himself occupying a windowless cell opposite Yankee in the basement of LRPD headquarters, things had begun to look much different. Whispering between the bars, they compared notes. "Even then," Yankee said, "I really wasn't convinced she was doing this to me. When I was arrested, Larry said, 'What is going on, man?' I said, 'I don't know.' And he says, 'Gotta be that fuckin' woman, man.' And I says, 'Oh, no, man. I think she's being set up by somebody. I've been trying to call her for two days and I couldn't get ahold of her.' He was thinking it was her, I was thinking it wasn't, you know. Then Doc Hale showed me that list of phone numbers."

Yankee was astonished. Not only did LRPD detectives know all about his affair with Orsini, they knew more about it than he did. The list Doc Hale put in front of him was the same one Mary Lee had taken to the prosecutor on the day before Alice's car was bombed, the one Sheriff Tommy never got around to checking out. Yankee recognized every number on it.

The Iron Horse, the Mason Jar, the Whitewater, Peck's—all beer joints Yankee called his "office." Also Gyst House, the drug rehab place. "So I says to Doc, 'What about it?' " Yankee said. "And then he tells me: [Orsini says] 'These are all Ron's killer.' "

Next Hale told Yankee about the tape recording of his voice warning Mary Lee to take Tiffany and get out of town. Did Yankee have an explanation? Entirely sober for the first time in weeks, and freed of Mary Lee's own intoxicating influence, Yankee was like a man emerging from a psychotic delusion. "When they started showing me these tape recordings they had," Yankee said, "I knew Orsini had stuck it in my butt. All this time I'm calling her—just chasing pussy, you know. As soon as I'd hang up she'd call the police and go into a crying jag, saying, 'The killer just called and threatened my life.' They, of course, wrote the numbers down. So now I'm fixing to get charged with a double murder.

"This was all part of her plot. This was all supposed to come together after Alice was dead. She's planning all this, because she's gonna say I killed Ron, I killed Alice, I tried to kill her. She planted evidence on me from the day I met her. And I was so weak, man. I never suspected a thing."

LRPD detectives placed Yankee and McClendon in adjoining cells. The more they whispered between bars, the clearer things got. "We were fixing to go to the electric chair," Yankee realized. "Me and Larry. If I didn't testify against Orsini, all the evidence she planted would have worked. I would have been convicted of a double murder, Larry would have been convicted of killing Alice McArthur, and Orsini would be sunbathing in fuckin' Acapulco."

Chapter 8

1

Alice McArthur was buried on the afternoon of Tuesday, July 6, following a funeral mass at Christ the King Catholic Church. Newspapers estimated that more than four hundred mourners crowded into the church—among them Prosecutor Dub Bentley, members of his staff, and several judges who canceled court for the day.

Photographers and TV camera crews covered the event like a Hollywood funeral. Evening news broadcasts followed the grieving family from the church doors into funeral home limousines. In a front-page photo shot at the graveside ceremony in Saline County, Wednesday's *Gazette* showed Bill and his children kneeling at Alice's casket. Just below it, the newspaper printed mug shots of Larry Darnell McClendon and Eugene "Yankee" Hall.

• • •

Immediately after the funeral, Bill and his brother-in-law drove downtown to LRPD headquarters. Doc Hale had left word that detectives had some follow-up questions they wanted to ask him. McArthur had spent the four days since his wife's murder in a daze at his parents' modest home in an older Little Rock subdivision called Cammack Village. Apart from making funeral arrangements, he had remained entirely in seclusion.

The Bill McArthur who showed up looked like anything but the handsome, self-confident attorney who had so often appeared there on behalf of his clients. Wearing blue jeans and a knit shirt, he had dark circles under both eyes, and chain-smoked. Escorting him into Lieutenant Bobby Thomas's spartan office with its tile floors, gunmetal desk, and government-issue folding chairs, all four detectives took up positions around him. As commanding officer of the Homicide Division, Thomas did the talking.

"Bill," the veteran cop said, "there isn't but one way to do this. And that's to shoot straight with you. You've been implicated as being the one that had Alice killed."

The next word out of Bill's mouth, Thomas said, was " 'Before you do anything else, get [Alice's brother] Leonard down here. I want him to hear this from ya'll.' "

They called Leonard Miller in and ran Yankee's story down to him. Alice's brother listened in silence, then turned to McArthur and asked if it was true. Shaking with emotion, Bill denied it. Yankee Hall, he said, was a complete stranger. The whole story detectives had laid out was utterly fantastic to him. After a long moment, Miller said that if Bill said he had nothing to do with Alice's death, he believed him.

Out of McArthur's presence, Thomas again asked Miller point-blank if he suspected Bill. Miller answered that he did not. Every other law enforcement officer who dealt with Miller during his stay in Little Rock got the same answer.

Except, to hear him tell it later, Major Larry Dill.

• • •

Immediately afterward, McArthur, Miller, and a close friend of Bill's named Jack Cotton took shelter at Tracks Inn, a bar located in the basement of the cavernous, nearly deserted railroad terminal near the state capitol. Huddled at a table in the almost empty bar, they proceeded to get mournfully and bitterly drunk.

Any doubts the detectives had about Yankee's story, they'd concealed from McArthur. But the longer he and the others sat drinking and talking, the clearer things got. "Was I *convinced* that Orsini was involved? No." Bill said later. "Did I believe it? Yes. The whole thing was so bizarre to me that anything in the world could have been true. But he knew too much about me. See, I knew I didn't know Yankee Hall. And he knew too much about me and Alice and our schedule and what we did in our lives. I realized, 'Well, how else could he be involved without her? How could any of this have happened without her?' "

The harrowing process of determining his own moral responsibility lay far in the future. In time, Bill would lie awake nights asking himself how Alice's "Golden Boy" could have messed up so badly. Had it been his professional ego that robbed his children of their mother? His crackerjack trial lawyer's certainty that he could keep his life in separate compartments, traffic all day with violence and evil and leave it safely downtown? Bill had teased Alice and her friends that they lived in a dream world, and didn't have a clue about life east of University Avenue. He'd spent half his career making cops look dumb. But the NLRPD had figured Orsini out in no time. And Jim Lester had warned him repeatedly. "She's guilty as hell," Lester would say. "She's just crazy. She did it. And she's gonna get away with it. You're going to get her off. And then she's gonna do it again." Typical cop paranoia, Bill had said.

The situation provided an extra little twist that the investigators all found very interesting. If Bill and his brother-in-law agreed to a plea bargain, Yankee Hall's sworn testimony would accuse him of what Arkansas law called conspiracy to commit capital felony murder. But if the prosecutor failed to come to terms with Hall, the ex-con could decide to stonewall and take his chances with a jury. In that case, the story his lawyer had told LRPD detectives about McArthur's participation in the plot would have no more legal existence than if Yankee had never spoken at all. And neither would his allegations against McClendon and Orsini. Nobody in Arkansas, they all realized, understood the alternatives more clearly than Bill McArthur.

Hung-over and haggard, McArthur and Miller walked through a phalanx of reporters at the courthouse on Wednesday morning, July 7. Meeting with Dub Bentley and two assistants in the gloomy, high-ceilinged chamber that served as the prosecutor's office, their message was succinct: "Make your deal, get your statement. But offer the murdering son of a bitch a life sentence, no less."

Which happened to be exactly what Dub intended. The hard part would be persuading Yankee that was the best he could get.

2

Not long after Bill and and his brother-in-law Leonard Miller left the courthouse Wednesday morning, Deputy Prosecutor Chris Piazza summoned Phoebe Pinkston and her cousin Diane Dutton to the courthouse.

A native of Little Rock, Piazza had begun college on a football scholarship, and was still a fitness fanatic who thrived on confrontation. Perhaps the ablest and certainly the most ambitious of Dub Bentley's assistants, he'd been eager to get his hands on the case as soon as it became apparent that Sheriff Tommy intended to turn the tragedy into a media event. Like the LRPD detectives, he could imagine only one way in which Yankee's story made sense.

No friend of McArthur's, Piazza found Orsini—with her big broad ass and exaggerated mannerisms—almost physically repellent. He couldn't help but think that Bill, who could have his pick of women who were *not* murder suspects, would too. Still, he wanted to see what Phoebe and Diane thought.

Piazza interviewed the two women one at a time. Both agreed that while Orsini's demeanor changed when Bill walked into the office, they didn't believe that McArthur had noticed, much less reciprocated.

For Phoebe, the interview confirmed what she already knew in her bones. Piazza told her, " 'You're gonna have to stay in contact with her.' " Phoebe said, " 'You can't tell her that you talked with us, nor can you tell her that you talked to Bill. You'll just have to play her along. Get as much information out of her as you can.' I knew I could only hold her off for so long. I said, 'She's gonna start not believing me. Then you're putting me in jeopardy. This ain't gonna work. You've got to do something.' "

But there wasn't a damn thing the police or prosecutor could do. Orsini denied even knowing Yankee Hall, and the LRPD had no hard evidence to prove otherwise. Until they made their case, Phoebe was going to have to tough it out.

Meanwhile, Mary Lee kept calling and calling. "She wanted to know where Bill was staying, and why wouldn't I tell her," Phoebe Pinkston said. "She wanted to know why they hadn't talked to me—the police or the prosecutor. She was pumping me for information, and I didn't have any to give her. But she had a story. She *always* had a story. It was all a big conspiracy by forces unknown."

3

Following her "scoop" about Alice's inheritance, *Arkansas Gazette* reporter Carol Griffee received a call from Mary Lee Orsini. Sensing a potential ally, Orsini volunteered to come by the newsroom for an exclusive interview. Escorted by Dr. Wulz, Orsini arrived on the evening of July 6—at the same time that McArthur and his brother-in-law were sitting down with LRPD detectives blocks away. Orsini carried the results of a lie detector test she'd hired a North Little Rock firm to administer to her.

According to the examiner—a former deputy sheriff from Texas who'd earned an Arkansas license by virtue of an eight-week extension course at the University of Houston—the polygraph showed that Orsini had no knowledge of the McArthur murder. With Wulz's help, Mary Lee spent the next few hours spinning her well-rehearsed repertoire of hair-raising tales dating back to her husband's murder.

Around the *Gazette*'s second-floor newsroom, Mary Lee's visit became legend. One possibly apocryphal anecdote encapsulated the way many at the paper came to feel about the relationship between Griffee and Orsini. The story goes that Griffee left her desk at one point to go to the bathroom. Pausing at the doorway out of sight of her visitors, the reporter put her forefinger to her head, rolled her eyes, and gave the classic screw-loose signal. Taking the same route minutes later, Orsini repeated the gesture. The punch line was that they both were right.

But none of that prevented "The Oldest Newspaper West of the Mississippi," as the *Gazette* proudly called itself, from leading the newspaper with Mary Lee's dramatics on Thursday, July 8. SHE WAS INFORMED OF HER RIGHTS, TOLD SHE IS SUSPECT, ORSINI SAYS, read the three-column front-page headline. Accompanied by a photograph of Mary Lee and shots of a grim Bill McArthur and Leonard Miller taken at the courthouse, the article gave a detailed account of Orsini's lie detector test. Griffee dropped the bombshell several paragraphs down from the lead: "Orsini spent several hours Tuesday morning at the LRPD where she said she was read her rights and was told that she was suspected of having conspired with McArthur, who is her attorney, to have his wife killed."

Allowing Orsini to incriminate McArthur in print was a controversial act. Indeed, to a journalism professor, it is obvious that *Gazette* editors had hedged their bets. Griffee's story did not state that the LRPD had *in fact* accused McArthur, only that Orsini *said* they had. The allegation was several paragraphs into a long story that implicitly questioned her credibility. Two of Little Rock's TV stations and the *Democrat* refused to use the story.

Convinced that she was being watched and followed, Carol Griffee began to carry a double-barreled 20 gauge shotgun everywhere she went. She'd check it with the guards at the *Gazette* front door each morning and pick it up at night. Fellow reporters began to wonder whether or not she had taken leave of her senses. Pressure built to pull her off the story. But for the time being, Griffee's unparalleled access to Robinson persuaded editors that she was an invaluable asset.

·   ·   ·

Within the LRPD Homicide Division, the *Gazette* article provoked amazement. Nobody had told Orsini any such thing. The police had questioned her about Yankee, but they'd given her no indication that the little creep was talking at all, much less what he was saying. Nor had anybody talked to the press. They were under strict orders to keep their mouths shut. Mary Lee had talked to the newspaper *before* LRPD detectives had finished laying their cards on the table for McArthur, so Bill couldn't have told her. Unless Tommy Robinson was running off his mouth again, there was only one way Orsini could have guessed Yankee's story: because she had fed it to him in the first place.

As for McArthur, the *Gazette* story made detectives even more skeptical. If the lawyer *had* taken part in the conspiracy, what could Orsini possibly hope to gain by saying so? Given credible evidence, the LRPD homicide detectives would have sworn out a warrant against Mother Teresa. "But even at the beginning," said Sergeant Fred Hensley, "the whole scenario was absurd. Even if McArthur wanted to kill the goose that laid the golden egg, we're talking about one of the best criminal defense lawyers in Arkansas. Know how many deaf mutes there are in prison? None. Because they don't talk. Well, McArthur knows that better than anybody. So even if he's gonna do something, no way he's gonna cut in a crazy woman and two junkies on the deal. If I'm to draw on my police experience at all, it made no sense."

Chapter 9

1

Over in North Little Rock, meanwhile, more than one of Orsini's trusted confidants had begun to grow uneasy. Larry Burge was getting real jumpy. He never really considered going to the police. Having informed Sheriff Tommy about Orsini's relationship with Yankee back in May, Larry figured he'd done his bit. He still had trouble imagining the charming, flirtatious woman to whom he'd lent his car as a murderess. But he did have to admit that it was getting easier all the time.

Orsini kept calling him to come over at odd hours, and Burge kept making excuses. "A time or two," he said, "I had the feeling I could walk up and knock on her door and get blown all the way out in the damn street. That would be a real convenient thing—if she had the idea that I knew entirely too much. She'd be scared, she wouldn't know what the deal was. And boom! My mouth's shut. Oh, she'd have been sorry. She'd have hated killing old Larry. But I'd still be dead."

• • •

One afternoon at her Window Works shop, Joyce Holt confronted Mary Lee about some things she'd been reading in the newspapers. "I asked her, 'What's this stuff about Yankee Hall? Do you really know him?'" Joyce said. "And she said well, she might. That somebody had fixed her car window by the name of Hall. A Gene Hall. That fellow had a Jacksonville phone number. But she was going to check it out. And that's when I just thought, 'Oh my God.'"

More than fear, Joyce felt shame and mortification. Bit by bit, Mary Lee's fantasy world was slipping beyond her control. But call the police? What did Joyce know? What would she say?

. . .

For safety's sake, Mary Lee had sent Tiffany to visit her father in Connecticut and moved in with Dr. Wulz. "If you're looking at Mrs. Orsini," Wulz assured Dub Bentley and Detective Al Dawson, "you're looking in the wrong direction."

The three men spoke at LRPD headquarters on July 9, a week after Alice's death. Wulz had been in Oklahoma when it happened, attending the wedding of his dead wife's son, the wife he'd been acquitted of murdering thirteen years earlier. He'd heard about the tragedy when Mary Lee phoned him from PCSD headquarters late that night.

The veterinarian couldn't say he was surprised. He'd expected the worst ever since Orsini had been shot at in April and Alice McArthur's car had been bombed in May. Infuriated by the NLRPD's refusal to protect Mary Lee, Wulz had been taking special precautions: placing strips of Scotch tape on his car doors to warn him in case somebody broke in. When he jogged through Indian Hills after dark, he packed a .38 revolver.

In part, the prosecutor had subpoenaed Wulz to compare his voice to the ones on Orsini's various tapes. To Dawson, who sat watching and listening, it appeared that Wulz's experience as a homicide defendant had taught him a lot. Angered at being called downtown, Wulz gave the briefest possible answers to most questions, and volunteered little.

Wulz insisted that he knew nothing about the McArthur case except what he'd read in the papers. He'd never heard of Yankee Hall, and knew of no man who'd been spending nights at Mary Lee Orsini's house. Though he'd never actually heard Mary Lee receive any odd phone calls, he'd never doubted they had occurred. When he was asked if he had anything to add, the veterinarian gave a short speech.

"Every time something happens," he said, "I think it through pretty carefully to see if it adds up. If she's lied to me, she has one terrific memory. I am much *less* suspicious than I was when I started with her. I feel sure that she was not involved in her husband's murder. I don't know who runs organized crime in this town, but some things have happened that she couldn't have faked. Like one day Mrs. Orsini noticed a car following her, and she made a couple of turns and it stayed with her. So she got the tag number and called it in to Bill McArthur, who called it in to Tommy Robinson—again, this is what she tells me. The car turned out to be a stolen car from Illinois, and you know the story. How in the world could she possibly have faked that? If she killed her husband, why was a hit man called into town for her? That doesn't make any sense."

2

If Al Dawson had thought there was any chance Tommy Robinson could have solved the McArthur case, the sheriff could have had the damned thing. As an intellectual challenge and a psychological puzzle, the case fascinated him. But working on it was a bureaucratic nightmare, and the trickiest part was dealing with Robinson and Dill. Dawson's superiors were anxious to keep the dispute within the law enforcement fraternity. The idea was to keep the lines of communication open without telling Tommy anything they didn't want him to read about in the newspapers.

"Tommy was bound and determined to make this case before we did," Dawson said. "But he was so tied up with Lee Orsini by then that he'd been convinced that she was not a part of it. But he'd made so much publicity, he felt that he had to come up with some type of organized crime figure to show that we do have these people in central Arkansas—and that they are, in fact, connected to Bob Troutt. That's what Orsini was offering him. They had the whole CID running down leads that she gave them. They stayed busy all the time. In essence, they never got a thing out of it."

Indeed, PCSD files for the period are almost empty. The LRPD's case against Yankee Hall, meanwhile, was getting tighter. Several witnesses had seen him and McClendon drinking together in the days before the murder. LRPD detectives found two more witnesses from whom Hall had tried to buy dynamite. Yankee's ex-wife—the same one who lived with Donny Simmons—told police about helping him out of a jam with a broken-down Corvette two days before the murder, and noticing a clipboard in the back seat. It had a florist's logo and a typed delivery list with the name "McArthur" at the bottom. The tow truck operator who hauled the car had seen it too—and remembered Yankee coming to the shop on July 2 to fetch it.

But they were still drawing a blank on Orsini. Hall had boasted about his love affair with the famous widow in half the bars in Little Rock. Hardly anybody had actually seen them together, though, and those who thought they had were lowlifes with longer rap sheets than Yankee's own. Doc Hale kept warning Yankee that if the LRPD succeeded in making their case *without* his help, he'd be out of luck. There would be no deal with the prosecutor.

Hall tried to give Orsini up, but couldn't deliver. Detectives found a Czech-made 30.06 rifle with a magnifying scope in Yankee's apartment as he'd said they would. Mary Lee, he told them, had wanted him to hide in the woods near Westside Tennis Club and shoot Alice down on the court. He'd told her he couldn't do it. He said Orsini had given him the cash to buy the rifle, but he couldn't prove it. Even when Mary Lee had gone to buy the batteries for the bomb, Yankee told them, she'd worn a blond wig and a maternity dress with a pillow stuffed inside.

Midway through the second week of the investigation, Sheriff Tommy Robinson made his first and some said only concrete contribution. Acting on a tip from a political supporter, he and Dill interviewed one of the man's employees. Carl Ray Wilson was a construction worker with a rap sheet dating back more than twenty years. A neighbor and friend of Captain Bobby Woodward's, Wilson's job gave him access to explosives. He was also an acquaintance of Yankee Hall's.

At first, Wilson, a lean, muscular man with an Oklahoma twang, denied everything—just as he had when interviewed earlier by the LRPD and ATF. Pushed hard, he'd admitted that Hall had approached him looking for dynamite, but he'd insisted that he refused. Unauthorized sale of Tovex was a federal violation—and with Wilson's record, that would send him back to prison. Even with an offer of immunity, he feared for his job.

At Tommy's urging, the owner of Danco Construction agreed not to punish Wilson for telling the truth. On the night of July 13, Dub Bentley took sworn statements from him and his girlfriend at PCSD headquarters. Robinson and Dill listened in.

In early May, Wilson admitted, Yankee and a dark-haired woman with what he later described as "big boobs and a pretty butt" had visited his home near Mayflower. They picked Orsini out of a photo line-up. Wilson said he'd taken the explosive from a construction site after it failed to explode, poured it into a plastic Wella Balsam shampoo bottle—exactly like the one identified by ATF experts—and kept it in a shed until Yankee came calling. He had suspected Yankee's involvement in the car bombing, but fear had kept him quiet.

Wilson's testimony failed to persuade Bentley to issue a warrant for Orsini's arrest. Photo line-ups are notoriously unreliable, and Mary Lee had taken no part in the transaction. With a history of prior convictions for burglary, auto theft, and armed robbery, Wilson would not make an ideal witness.

As his investigation neared the end of its second week, Al Dawson began to worry that Orsini might slip through his grasp. Under Arkansas law, the LRPD could hold accused felons in the city jail only until formal charges were filed in Circuit Court—at which time they were transferred to the county jail to await trial. During the tumultuous eighteen months of Robinson's tenure as sheriff, however, prisoners had languished in the city jail for months. Tommy's highly publicized series of battles with state and county officials—including chaining prisoners to the gates of the state penitentiary in 1981—had been waged over overcrowding at the county jail.

But when it came to Yankee and McClendon, Tommy would now find room. Dub Bentley filed charges July 14. Bright and early on July 15, the sheriff sent deputies to fetch the two accused murderers into his custody. Facing the TV cameras that had been alerted to the transfer, the sheriff assured viewers that he now had the two where he wanted them, and that dramatic results would follow.

Like everybody else at the LRPD, Dawson was furious. "See, I kept thinking I was gonna make my case off of Yankee," he said. "Now I knew I'd have to try some other way. I knew I was gonna have to get on the stick, because by the time Tommy got it screwed up I'd never make a case on her."

He went back to the tape recording Robinson and Dill had brought him—the one that was supposed to be Orsini's alibi. To him the performance was as unconvincing as a junior high drama club rehearsal. If he could find the person supposedly tipping Mary Lee off to the identity of Alice McArthur's killers, he might have something. So he began calling her known associates, and listening to their voices.

On the morning of July 16—two weeks after Alice's murder—Dawson was double-checking his list when Doc Hale stuck his head in the door and gave him Larry Burge's name and number. Orsini, Hale had learned, had been driving the North Little Rock realtor's car for weeks.

The source of Hale's information was John Terry. Ever since his stint as a private investigator for Mary Lee, Terry had kept an eye on

her. And he'd persuaded Mary Jane Murphree, back from Kansas City
for a time, to do a bit of discreet spying. She'd written down the license
number of every car she saw parked in Orsini's driveway. Despite his
own long-standing feud with Chief Sonny Simpson of the LRPD,
Terry passed the tip directly to Hale.

By coincidence, Sergeant T. J. Farley came up with even better
information later that same day. He'd played his copy of Mary Lee's
alibi tape for a friend of Linda House's, who'd identified the mystery
caller as Burge. But in all the excitement at LRPD headquarters, the
NLRPD detective's message never reached Al Dawson until long after
the fact. Farley would always assume that it had—a fateful misunderstanding, as things turned out.

At the sound of Burge's voice on the phone, Al Dawson felt the hair
stand up on the back of his neck. He asked if the realtor would come
in voluntarily to answer some questions. After hemming and hawing
a bit, Burge agreed.

Dawson was all but sure he'd found his man. Burge acted coy at
first, admitting his friendship with Orsini, but denying any knowledge
of the McArthur murder. Summoning Sergeant Fred Hensley to serve
as a witness, Dawson put a tape recorder down on the desk between
them and punched the "play" button. A voice lisping, affected but
unmistakably Burge's, filled the room. "You are one of three people on
a hit list in this area," it said. "Mrs. McArthur was one, and Mrs.
Holly Troutt is one, and Mrs. Lee Orsini is the other. . . ."

Dawson hit the "stop" button and asked Burge if he recognized the
voice. "He said no," Dawson recalled. "I said, 'Larry, you sure you
want to say this? I'll give you some time to think about it. But . . .
you're fixing to get yourself involved in a murder. You can be a
witness, or you can be a defendant.' Right then old Larry's face turned
a real bright shade of red. He said, 'Can I go talk to my attorney?' "

Dawson agreed. He gave Burge until 2:00 P.M. Burge went back to
North Little Rock and met with his attorney. Then, agreeing to ren-
dezvous with his lawyer at LRPD headquarters, he went looking for
Orsini. He found her and Wulz at lunch at a Shoney's restaurant.

As soon as she saw him coming, Mary Lee grabbed Burge's arm and
hustled him to a spot where Wulz couldn't hear them.

Burge urged her to come clean. "I said, 'Lee, I talked to these cats.
I believe they're professional, I believe they're honest. Let's tell these
boys everything we know. They're red hot on this case. They can
probably blow this case wide open.' I figured that she would think that

she was slick enough that she would walk out—and she would go with me. But she said she couldn't do that. Forrest Parkman and the Little Rock cops were going to frame her. Tommy was the only one that she could trust."

The longer and more heatedly Burge and Orsini talked, the angrier Dr. Wulz got. Finally, he picked up his check, stormed out of the restaurant, climbed into his car, and drove back to his clinic. Ever since Ron's death, as Wulz saw it, he'd been Mary Lee's confidant and supporter—sticking his neck out and taking risks friends had urged him to avoid. "I'd been a friend to her," Wulz explained later. "I'd tried to help her. And here comes somebody and she has to talk to this guy about something she can't talk about in front of me? What's going on?"

Wulz had a secret of his own. In the week since his interview with Al Dawson and Dub Bentley, he'd conceived doubts about Orsini's truthfulness. Unknown to her, he'd visited the prosecutor just the day before to give Bentley the lowdown on her odd behavior of April 6—the date he'd been convinced Orsini had spent the night with another lover. At the time, Wulz had suspected Jim Guy Tucker. Lately he'd grown more curious about this Burge character.

Like Burge, Wulz appeared to be playing cat and mouse with the authorities. Over the next few days he would recall several details he hadn't previously mentioned. Two weeks before the McArthur murder, he had discovered several items missing from a dresser drawer—among them a string of pearls belonging to his late wife, exactly like the ones Orsini had told Joyce Holt that Bill had given her.

Bentley had surprised Wulz by asking if he was also missing a pistol. Yankee had told them that Orsini had stolen the murder weapon from the veterinarian. Wulz admitted that he was, but hadn't thought the theft worth reporting. After all, it was a very old gun—one he'd bought twenty years ago from a dog catcher in Duncan, Oklahoma—a beat-up .38 revolver. Also missing were five Federal brand .158 grain, hollow-nosed cartridges exactly like the ones that ballistics experts said killed Alice McArthur.

The signed and dated note Wulz delivered to Dub Bentley on the day before he stormed out of Shoney's had given investigators a crucial bit of evidence. The description and license number of the car Wulz had seen in the driveway of 7412 Pontiac at 3:00 A.M. on April 6 were identical to one Yankee had borrowed from a body shop—the only concrete proof investigators would ever find to confirm Yankee's account of his ill-fated love affair with Mary Lee.

• • •

Exactly on time, Larry Burge walked back into Homicide with his attorney. After a brief period of negotiation with Chris Piazza, Larry was granted immunity from the class "B" felony of hindering apprehension, covering any actions he'd taken after (but not before) the murder of Alice McArthur.

They all sat down and listened to Larry and Mary Lee's dramatic production one more time—Burge, his lawyer, Dawson, Sergeant Fred Hensley, and Piazza. Then, at 4:01 P.M., Dawson slipped a blank cassette into the tape recorder, Piazza administered the oath, and Larry Burge talked.

"She told you," said Piazza, "that she needed to get this information to the police and her credibility was damaged. Did you believe her at that point?"

"Yes I did. I believed her completely and fully."

"And all the things that were said on that tape—including the fact that Larry McClendon was guilty—came from her?"

"She told me she had received this information."

"Now there were some statements in there about her being on a hit list along with Mrs. Holly Troutt and Mrs. McArthur. That came from her?"

Burge said that it did. "I did this by request of this lady because I believed . . . that it would help her and help you," he said. "I have not had any part in anything concerning Lee Orsini that I felt was morally or legally wrong."

The investigators were in no mood to quibble. Particularly not after Burge's attorney turned over Orsini's original handwritten script—containing details even more damning than the tape. Only one person on earth could have produced the document they saw before them: the person who'd planned Alice McArthur's murder.

• • •

Shortly after 6:00 P.M., LRPD officers spotted Orsini's black Chevrolet Caprice in the parking lot outside Willow House—the public housing project where her mother had moved when the bank took her house. Dawson served the warrant, read Orsini her rights, and snapped on handcuffs. "She put on a surprised act as far as 'Who, me?' " he said. "But you could tell it was an act. She had to know it was coming when she talked to Burge. It don't take a genius to figure out that when you break an alibi, somebody'll be coming after you. I think the reason she didn't run was that she thought she could pull the same flim-flam with us she had with the NLRPD."

•　•　•

The news of Orsini's arrest spread across Arkansas almost instantly. Tipped off by a source inside the LRPD who owed her a favor, a Channel 7 News reporter, Amy Oliver, had set up on the sidewalk outside police headquarters with a camera crew. The Little Rock ABC outlet broke into its nightly 6:30 broadcast of *M*A*S*H* reruns with dramatic live coverage of Orsini being escorted from a patrol car into the building by Al Dawson. The official announcement followed some minutes later.

Some more intimately involved in the case heard the news in different ways. Tipped by Doc Hale, Sergeant Farley had driven over to Little Rock and joined the handshaking, back-slapping crowd of LRPD detectives who waited for Dawson to bring her in. He telephoned Linda and Buddy House at their home in Cabot just minutes before the arrest was broadcast on TV. For Ron Orsini's sister and brother-in-law it was a bittersweet moment. Relieved as they were, they would never feel that justice had been done until Mary Lee was punished for Ron's murder as well. Linda called her mother. For the first time in months, they got no hang-up calls that night.

Assistant Chief Doc Hale also called Bill McArthur's father, who gave his son the news. Bill's emotional healing had barely begun, but for a few days at least, it appeared that the worst was over.

Phoebe Pinkston would never forget the image of Mary Lee she saw captured that night on the ten o'clock news. "She turned around and looked into the camera," Phoebe said, "and it was like she was looking right through me—just like she could see all of us. It was horrible, just horrible. They had her in the back of a car and she turned around and looked dead in those cameras as they were driving off. It was just as cold and black and evil as it could be."

What Phoebe and the rest of the TV audience never knew, however, was that the compelling scene they witnessed on late news broadcasts that night was a staged re-enactment. Set upon by newspaper photographers and TV news directors outraged by Channel 7's exclusive coverage of Orsini's arrest, the LRPD did the only fair thing. They hustled Mary Lee out the back door, loaded her into a patrol car, drove around the block, and led her dramatically past the cameras once again.

. . .

One cop who did not receive a courtesy call from Doc Hale, and who went uninvited to the impromptu celebration at LRPD headquarters, was Sheriff Tommy Robinson. Feelings still ran high among LRPD detectives over the sheriff's department's actions on July 2.

Only that afternoon the intrepid sheriff had given an exclusive interview to Channel 4 assuring viewers that months of difficult and dangerous work lay ahead. He anticipated no further arrests any time soon. When word of Orsini's arrest reached PCSD headquarters, Tommy flew into a rage. He kicked his wastebasket halfway across the room and threw the telephone against the wall. Those dumb sons of bitches in Little Rock, he screamed, had screwed up everything. Didn't they know that Orsini was just a pawn in a larger game? Didn't they realize that he, Sheriff Tommy, had been poised to make the biggest organized crime bust in Arkansas history?

BOOK III

Chapter 1

1

Life in Arkansas slows to a crawl during July and August—a time of unrelenting and enervating heat, with temperatures in the humid high 90s and only a rare afternoon thunderstorm to break the monotony. Public passions are at a low ebb. With the legislature gone from Little Rock, politics is all but suspended until after Labor Day. Razorback fans exist in suspended animation, awaiting the opening of football season. The state's only pro baseball team—the AA Arkansas Travelers —plays to small crowds. Deer season doesn't open until November, and it's too hot for all but the most dedicated all-night fishermen. Out in the Delta flatlands east of Little Rock, cotton, soybean, and rice fields lie almost unattended. Cattle huddle under trees and wallow in muddy ponds. With the woods alive with chiggers, ticks, and snakes, timber operations come to a near standstill. Poultry growers in the Ozarks set up fans to prevent thousands of chickens and turkeys in huge, tin-roofed sheds from suffocating. Only in the air-conditioned factories and offices of the bigger towns does work continue at anything like an active pace.

To local TV news producers anxious for material to fill their evening hour, the McArthur case had come along at just the right time. It dominated the media and private conversation to a degree almost unimaginable in a larger, more sophisticated place.

And everything about the Bill McArthur presented by the Little Rock media made him a focus of suspicion. Given the fortune he was supposed to be inheriting—$50,000 a month was the figure repeatedly cited—Orsini's assertion that the LRPD had accused the pair of conspiring to murder his wife was rarely questioned. In a state where forty-three out of seventy-five counties prohibit the sale of alcohol, the phrase "nightclub owner" also did him incalculable harm. What with Sheriff Tommy's televised warnings about Mob warfare in the capital city, many imagined McArthur to be a gangster in a three-piece suit. Even Bill's looks counted against him. One look at the handsome, seemingly patrician lawyer on the evening news and thousands cast him as a character out of *Dallas* or *Dynasty*.

To those who knew him personally, the earthy, blunt McArthur was about as "debonair"—to use another newspaper catch phrase—as the Grand Ole Opry. No matter. From one end of Arkansas to another, everybody knew somebody whose brother's ex-wife's cousin lived next door to a guy who worked with an old boy who said that Bill McArthur would steal the nickels off a dead man's eyes. Radio talk show hosts allowed callers to indulge their most perfervid fantasies over the air.

Pretending to be shocked and horrified, Arkansans were having the time of their lives. The titillated public waited expectantly for the other shoe to drop. "It was the popular thing to believe," said Doc Hale. "You could ask the ladies under every hair dryer in every beauty shop in Arkansas if McArthur was involved, and they'd say yes. They didn't have to know the first thing about the case. They just *knew*."

2

A bit less than a week after Mary Lee's arrest, Prosecutor Dub Bentley made a vain attempt to clear the air. With the arraignments of Orsini, Hall, and McClendon coming up during the last week in July, he and Chris Piazza had been working almost around the clock reviewing the evidence with LRPD detectives.

Mary Lee had burned Bentley twice—first during the 1981 grand jury hearing, then by the shooting incident on Batesville Pike and her bogus list of phone numbers pointing to "Ron's killer." He intended to make damned sure it didn't happen again. The woman's deviousness, Dub realized as he and Piazza assembled the fragments of evidence into a coherent picture, knew no limits.

Even before learning Yankee's story, the sheriff had insisted that Bill McArthur was the dark eminence behind the entire scheme; Orsini was merely the pigeon. Tommy had several theories about the crime, each more grandiose than the one before. Fine, Dub would say. Bring him the evidence, and he'd bust McArthur in a New York minute. If he'd told Tommy that once, Dub had told him fifty times. But he produced no proof. Dub had been down that road with Tommy before. And he sure wasn't going to charge McArthur on the basis of an uncorroborated fantasy by a crazy woman and double hearsay from Yankee Hall.

Bentley was taking nothing for granted. In his methodical way, the prosecutor personally conducted interviews with Alice's closest friends—including the women who'd been with her in Florida. They all told him the same thing: that Alice and Bill were a devoted couple whose marriage couldn't have been on firmer ground. Like Spurgeon, Dub learned that Alice had feared that Bill was the intended victim of the car bomb, and that she had been very reluctant to leave him alone. She'd phoned him every day from Florida—often twice.

Having satisfied himself, the prosecutor told reporters on July 21 that much of the information in the newspapers and most of the rumors about the McArthur murder case were false. As far as he was concerned, Bill McArthur was not a suspect. Vastly overestimating his own moral authority, he refused to elaborate, and the *Gazette* relegated his statement to the "Metro-State" page. Everybody else in the Little Rock media ignored it altogether. Bentley might as well have hollered down a well.

Intended to calm the storm, the prosecutor's announcement only stirred up Sheriff Tommy. During the week following Orsini's arrest, Robinson had vanished from public view. On July 22, however, the sheriff summoned reporters to a patrol boat anchored in the Arkansas River under the I-430 bridge. According to Carol Griffee's account in the *Gazette*, the sheriff had hired an underwater salvage expert to recover a .38 revolver from the river's navigation channel. He expected the gun to provide the missing link between the McArthur and Orsini murders. Crucial evidence that his office had shared with other agencies, the sheriff claimed, had been "misused." Any future evidence, he said defiantly, would be withheld from the prosecutor until independently evaluated by the State Crime Lab and the FBI.

The drama on the river continued for days. With a small armada of TV news crews bobbing alongside a PCSD launch shouting questions, Tommy swung wilder with every interview—taking full credit for Orsini's arrest and charging an LRPD cover-up. A furious Chief Sonny Simpson made a rare public defense of his detectives: "I don't think

Sheriff Robinson could come anywhere close to the professional job of
the officers of the LRPD. However, we can't come close to getting the
publicity that the Sheriff has. Tommy hasn't gained any publicity from
the case for two or three weeks. I guess he just couldn't stand it any
longer."

No sooner had Orsini been formally charged than deputies showed
up to escort her to the county jail. Now Tommy had his antagonists
exactly where he wanted them. To deal with Mary Lee, they had to
come through him. And with Arkansas's two most avid newsmakers
together in one place, there was no telling what follies might transpire.

The prosecutor called Tommy's bluff. He ordered the PCSD to turn
over its complete investigative files on the Orsini and McArthur cases
at once. Bentley had been seeking them since the day of Mary Lee's
arrest, but no files had been forthcoming. According to Bentley, the
deputies refused. The sheriff had instructed them to give his files to nobody, and they told the prosecutor Tommy supposedly couldn't be
reached.

On Friday, July 23, Bentley drew up a formal subpoena and decided
to deliver it personally. He commandeered a fishing boat and motored
out to where Robinson, Dill, and the team of divers were anchored in
the Arkansas River. Allegedly for safety reasons, however, a line of
buoys had been set out, preventing the prosecutor from approaching
close enough to make himself heard. Robinson made a great show of
cupping his ear and shouting that he couldn't make out what Dub
wanted. He later told reporters that Bentley had had access to his
records but that they'd been returned to his office previously. "If he
wanted the records, why didn't he get them before he filed charges?"
Robinson was quoted as asking.

                                    •   •   •

But for all his bluster, Sheriff Tommy had no real choice. Failing to
answer Bentley's subpoena could result in felony charges. He and Dill
showed up at the courthouse with their attorneys first thing Monday
and quietly surrendered a single thin file folder, which turned out to
contain almost nothing of any value. Apart from a few taped interviews
whose relevance was unclear, the sheriff's vaunted "evidence" consisted of written versions of the same dogged arguments he and Dill
had been making for weeks.

Meanwhile, Tommy quietly abandoned his search of the river. If

Yankee had indeed thrown the murder weapon off the I-430 bridge during Friday afternoon rush hour—as his lawyer had confided to Robinson—divers never found it.

Undaunted, Tommy returned to the attack. In a front-page *Democrat* interview on July 31, Tommy charged that Dub Bentley had no intention of convicting anybody in the McArthur case. Foolishly, Dub rose to the bait. Over the past few days, LRPD Detectives Al Dawson and Fred Hensley had conducted detailed interviews with Joyce Holt, Dr. Wulz, and Larry Burge—doing their level best to sort out fact from fiction. They'd pushed hard for evidence that Bill and Mary Lee had been lovers.

They came up empty. But what drove Bentley up the wall was the account Burge gave of his dealings with Tommy Robinson. Infuriated by the sheriff's taunts, the prosecutor went on the attack. "If Tommy Robinson were half the cop he claims to be," he told reporters, "Alice McArthur might be alive to-day. . . . While Tommy was visiting Lee Orsini at her home at 7412 Pontiac Drive [on the day of the bombing], he was advised of Lee's association with Yankee Hall. . . . But Tommy never bothered to talk to Yankee."

The sheriff's charges of wrongdoing, Bentley added, stemmed purely from chagrin at having been shown up by the LRPD. The prosecutor said nothing about the grave suspicions LRPD investigators harbored against the PCSD. Having dragged the fight exactly where he wanted it, Tommy lowered the tone of debate still further. Denying any knowledge of Hall before Alice McArthur's death, he revealed that he'd secretly taped phone conversations between himself and Dub, and he promised to play them at a press conference.

"Bentley has blinders on and does not want to get to the bottom of the case," Tommy charged. "I've been taping him and I've been taping other officials too. I set him up intentionally by categorically going down a list of what was wrong. I purposely set him up because I knew what was happening." The sheriff reported himself to be vigorously pursuing a fourth suspect in the McArthur murder. Nobody needed a crystal ball or a Tommy Robinson decoder ring to guess who that suspect was.

. . .

Finally, Circuit Judge Floyd Lofton had heard enough. Summoning both men before him on August 2, he issued a "gag" order requiring them to refrain from further discussing McArthur case evidence in the media. For Bentley, jumping into the mud with Tommy Robinson had proved a disastrous mistake. An editorial cartoon in the *Democrat* portrayed him as a big-bellied infant in diapers squabbling over a bottle with a pugnacious baby Tommy. The miniature sheriff appeared to be winning. Newspapers all over Arkansas chuckled over the antics of what the *Springdale News* called the "Laurel and Hardy of law enforcement."

Despite the nickname "Live at Five Dub" bestowed upon him by camera crews, Bentley came across badly on TV. In contrast to Sheriff Tommy's glib, almost manic delivery, Dub's deliberate drawl made him sound slow-witted. "Double Bubble," Robinson called him, and it stuck.

The sheriff, meanwhile, grew stronger by the day. Robinson's impudence touched a vein of social resentment that has surfaced time and again in Arkansas politics since territorial days: a deep mistrust of wealth, privilege, and cosmopolitanism in all its forms. Tommy was becoming a folk hero—a redneck Muhammad Ali.

To the vast majority of Arkansans, the case was no longer about facts, but symbols. And nobody better understood how to manipulate those symbols and the media that conveyed them than Sheriff Tommy.

3

On August 2, Major Larry Dill wrote himself another memo about the McArthur case. Mary Lee, he noted, had phoned him on the private line in his office. Having had unlimited access to TV and ample time to read and digest the newspapers over the past days—she was from the first given special privileges in the Pulaski County Jail—Orsini had been doing some heavy thinking.

"Lee indicated," Dill wrote, "she might make a statement if her attorney agreed, but she wouldn't unless Dub Bentley changed his attitude about Bill McArthur. When I asked Lee what she meant by that she stated that McArthur was the person behind the whole damn thing and nobody was looking at him."

Mary Lee had a brand new story, a real humdinger. To find it credible, it was necessary to realize that virtually every word Orsini had previously spoken under oath since NLRPD investigators had questioned her on the day of Ron Orsini's murder was a lie. She'd faked it all: the threatening phone calls, the shadowy figures following her all over North Little Rock. Each name and every story she'd fed to private detectives Gary Glidewell and John Terry had been a deliberate fraud. Ron O'Neal, Donny Simmons, Ward Parks, and the rest? Decoys. She had staged the shooting incident on Batesville Pike. Everything she'd told Robinson and Dill since the day Alice McArthur's car was bombed was disinformation. All except the calls from the Memphis gangster Art Baldwin, that is. Those, too, had been counterfeit, but they had been Bill McArthur's doing.

Now that she had the heroic sheriff's protection, Orsini was at last prepared to come clean. And Robinson and Dill seemed to be more than ready to believe her. Whatever it took to solve the case, Tommy apparently believed that his political future depended upon it.

. . .

Two days later, Bill McArthur sat down with Detective Al Dawson and Sergeant Fred Hensley to give a formal statement to the LRPD. In the month since his wife's murder, McArthur had spoken with the investigators on several occasions. But this time, Dawson told him, the detectives wanted to put the whole thing on tape for the record. He also let Bill know that there were a few points of interest that they hadn't covered before. What he didn't tell McArthur was that among them were several questions based upon Mary Lee's allegations.

McArthur agreed to tell the LRPD detectives anything they wanted to know. The three men met in Fred Hensley's office at 8:45 on the morning of August 4. They didn't bother reading McArthur his rights. Besides having no firm evidence, Dawson and Hensley felt it would be superfluous. How could Bill McArthur, of all people, ever claim that he'd been tricked by the police?

What the detectives wanted most to hear was Bill's version of his relationship with Mary Lee. The interview went on for more than two hours. McArthur recounted the whole story from day one: how he'd gone to NLRPD headquarters as a favor to Judge Tom Glaze, how Mary Lee and Wulz had come to watch him try a case, how she'd hired him to represent her. Had he ever, Dawson wanted to know, visited her home? Because Ron Orsini's body had been found there, Bill certainly had, but virtually always in the company of Jim Lester or his partner Jack Lassiter.

"How many times, Bill?" Hensley asked. "If you had to put a number, how many times would you say that you'd been to her residence?"

"Oh Lord, I would say probably—over a year and a half—ten or twelve times."

"Have all of them been during the day?"

"Oh yeah. I've never been there . . ."

"Be specific." A slight chill fell over the room.

McArthur explained that he'd visited 7412 Pontiac after working hours exactly once, and then to give Orsini hell during the famous grand jury victory party in July 1981. He'd never been there since. They discussed the $15,000 legal fee she still owed him, and the second mortgage he'd taken as a guarantee of payment. The detectives asked about the car bombing. Did Orsini have an appointment with McArthur during the week before it happened? She did not.

"Did you at any time suspect her of having anything to do with it?" Dawson asked.

"I did not," McArthur said. He'd told ATF and Doc Hale on May 21 that he thought her *case* might be connected. "But as far as suspecting her personally, I did not."

McArthur explained that he'd been more wary of Mary Lee before the grand jury hearing than after. Indeed, he'd urged her not to testify on the assumption that she might have guilty knowledge of Ron Orsini's murder. And that while Jim Lester had been absolutely convinced of her guilt, the grand jury's failure to indict had pretty much convinced him of her innocence.

Hensley asked him flatly if there had been an intimate relationship between them. "Did she or did she not come on to you," he asked, "and make it known to you that she would be available if you so desired?"

"I would say no. She didn't come on to me as such. I do believe she was available."

McArthur felt like an idiot admitting how completely Orsini had deluded him. Under the detective's prodding, he told them about the day she'd come flying into his office covered with blood and shattered glass, and about the tape she'd produced of a mystery caller with an odd accent warning her that somebody was fixing to blow her head off.

Of her dealings with Tommy Robinson, Bill had no knowledge. She'd told him little, and the sheriff had said nothing at all. After walking McArthur through an account of his actions on July 2, Dawson brought the questioning back to the week Alice spent with friends in Florida, and Bill's stay in Hot Springs.

"As far as you know, did Lee Orsini have a hotel room on June 9th in Hot Springs?"

"Nothing would surprise me."

What the detectives kept to themselves was that according to Orsini's new story, McArthur had telephoned back to his office from the motel room they shared. Phone company records showed that a call had been made from Room 417 of the Holiday Inn South to McArthur's office number at 1:32 P.M. on Wednesday, June 9. According to Mary Lee, Bill had met her there to put the finishing touches on the plot to murder his wife. McArthur had supposedly brought two bottles of champagne and a paper sack containing $25,000 in cash. She'd promised to lead Dill and Robinson to the evidence.

Appearances to the contrary, Orsini had also insisted to Larry Dill that the two had never been lovers. The lowdown on Bill, she claimed, was much worse than that; exactly what, she refused to reveal until she got some guarantees.

McArthur categorically denied ever having met with Orsini anywhere outside Little Rock. They pressed him hard, so as to leave absolutely no room for ambiguity.

"If Orsini told somebody you were gonna get a divorce, that your marriage was on the rocks," Dawson asked, "she'd be lying?"

"She would not only be lying, but lying that she had talked to me." McArthur hesitated, then plunged ahead. His two hours under oath had drained him. His voice hoarse with emotion, he fought back tears.

"Let me tell you something, gentlemen," he began. " If my wife and I were having problems that couldn't be reconciled we would have gotten a divorce, and there would have been no hesitation on either of our parts. There's no reason for us not to. Now there's been a lot said about this oil money that she had gotten from her father. That was hers. That was Alice's.

"As long as she was alive I had an interest in that if I had wanted to exercise it. Even in divorce, because I was one of the parties to that contract. Under Louisiana law—and I guess Arkansas law—if I had wanted to exercise my contractual rights I would have been entitled to half that money. But with my wife dead, I have no interest at all. Now you may believe this or may not—because you're talking about a lot of money—but money is not that important to me. If you'll check with the people that have worked for me or with me, or were my clients, or any way you want to, you're going to find that I do more free work— and I always have—than I get paid for."

"What you're basically saying," Dawson said in his best cop monotone, "is it ain't nothing?"

"I lost—my God—I lost my wife," McArthur said. "I lost the mother of my kids. I don't know how I'm going to replace that. When you're talking about money, I lost a tremendous amount of money—what could be a fantastic amount at some point. But I have no idea whether it will ever be that or not. Sure I lost. You're damned right I lost.

"Now I don't know why. If, in fact, she is guilty. I'm assuming that she is. I don't know everything that you all know, and I don't expect that I'll know right away anyway. But I had nothing to do with Lee Orsini having anything to do with my family. She had no right, no reason, to assume that."

The detectives made no comment. Hensley switched off the tape at 10:48 A.M.

• • •

Over the next several weeks LRPD detectives did everything they could to prove McArthur a liar. Not fond of defense attorneys in general, Al Dawson in particular had trouble picturing Bill as a philanthropist. Lieutenant Bobby Thomas and Sergeant Fred Hensley, on the other hand, found it hard to believe that anybody with half Bill's brains and experience would have been reckless enough to lie under oath about his relationship with Orsini. As painful and humiliating as it would have been to admit jumping in bed with Mary Lee, it would have been a walk in the park next to Cummins Prison. Moral scruples aside, the Bill McArthur they knew was nothing if not a realist.

But whatever they thought privately, the LRPD investigators took nothing for granted. Under terrific pressure, they interviewed every possible witness, some as often as two or three times. Before they finished, the McArthur case had become the most meticulously documented homicide investigation in LRPD history.

"We never so much as put McArthur in a suspicious situation," Dawson said, "that would indicate some kind of a personal relationship. Other than a controlled environment, where somebody else was around. Now Orsini—and of course this was information coming out of Tommy's office—she told of all kinds of rendezvous and meetings. We looked all of them up. We went to each one and talked to people. Hotels, motels, this place and that place."

As to the alleged June 9 meeting at the Hot Springs Holiday Inn, Orsini herself had registered at the motel early that afternoon, signing her name and giving the license number of Larry Burge's Honda. Sheriff's deputies produced the receipt—as well as the record of a lengthy phone call placed to McArthur's Little Rock office at 1:32 P.M. Mary Lee had said that Bill made the call. But Phoebe Pinkston remembered things differently. Orsini had called from Hot Springs to ask Phoebe to cancel an appointment with Larry Dill. She recalled that Orsini had stopped at the office that morning, dressed in tennis shorts, and indicating that Bill would be joining her in Hot Springs. That remark had puzzled her, Phoebe said.

LRPD detectives verified that Bill had spent most of that morning at Metropolitan Bank, stopped briefly back at his office, and then driven to Pine Bluff to meet with another lawyer about an upcoming trial—sixty miles in the opposite direction. He'd visited a client in prison late that afternoon. His parents said he'd arrived in Hot Springs before dark. He hadn't left the lakeside home any night that week.

Phone company records showed that at 12:57 P.M. that afternoon, a ten-minute call was placed from McArthur's law office to the condo in Fort Walton Beach where Alice was staying. Witnesses confirmed Mary Lee's presence at the motel, but nobody had seen Bill McArthur.

· · ·

On August 17, Tommy Robinson phoned Dub Bentley at home. "If I can give you Bill McArthur, Orsini and McClendon," Robinson asked, "if I can substantiate it and give you corroborating evidence and give you Yankee testifying . . . would you go along with letting him cop a plea on criminal attempt to commit first degree murder for 50 [years], suspend 40, let it be tried in Federal Court, and let him serve his time in the Federal pen?"

"Oh, Lord," Dub said. While publicly charging Bentley with going easy on Yankee to protect McArthur, in private Tommy was talking a different game. To protect himself, the prosecutor had begun tape-recording their conversations.

"It's not, 'Oh, Lord.' It's a very serious matter . . . fifty years is a long time, politically and in the press. Let it be tried in Federal courts on the bombing charge, let him serve in the Federal pen and let his state time run concurrent. Will you do it?"

"Tommy, ten years to be served in the Federal pen. My God!" For a deal like that, the prosecutor suspected, Yankee would say anything. Even so, Bentley told the sheriff that if he could produce corroborating evidence he was willing to listen. But nothing ever came of it.

· · · ·

Contrary to what Robinson kept telling the media, meanwhile, McArthur was getting looked at much harder than an ordinary citizen. No sooner would LRPD detectives find evidence disproving one alleged meeting than Mary Lee would come up with a new twist. As an increasingly harried Al Dawson began to see it, she and the sheriff had come to share the same goals.

" 'Lee Orsini,' Tommy would say, 'maybe she's involved and maybe she's not,' " Dawson said. " 'But if she is, she's a pawn used by Bill McArthur.' That's what he was doing. He's getting these little pieces of information, then he's throwing it back over here at us, saying, 'Hey, you missed this. You didn't do that.' And it always came back through the Chief's office and the Captain's office down to me. I was really getting fed up. Some of those times when I was taking those second and third statements from people, I was getting frustrated and angry having to go back and do this just to appease Tommy's ego."

Even so, Dawson kept plugging away. "You don't have a choice," he said. " You're not talking about jaywalking. You're talking about conspiracy to commit murder. This is not something that's just gonna be taken care of. You've got to take them as far as they go. Every question, you've got to run it down.

"But it does reach a point where it gets frustrating. Especially when the things you're coming up with—it's not something you didn't already know and it's another agency that's coming up with these questions and you're doing the footwork—*I'm* doing the footwork—and it's getting pretty damn old. It's getting to the point where it's over and over again and it turns out to be the same thing: nothing, nothing, nothing."

Chapter 2

On Monday, August 30, Sheriff Tommy Robinson made his big move. Almost two months had passed since Alice McArthur's murder. Over the weekend, Robinson had somehow talked Yankee into putting his formal statement on the record. In the deposition, Yankee agreed to accept a life sentence in exchange for a guilty plea. Later, he insisted that Sheriff Tommy had promised him clemency after he became governor. Tommy, of course, denied it. Dub Bentley said that Tommy had told him that too, but the prosecutor figured Tommy was pulling his leg. Afterward, Dub wondered. But if Yankee had been fool enough to take the deal, he'd also been too dumb to get it in writing.

The job of taking Hall's statement fell to Chris Piazza. Dill and Robinson sat in at PCSD headquarters on Sunday, August 29. To insiders, his testimony contained no surprises. As far as Yankee knew, Bill McArthur was the brains behind the whole deal. Supposedly because Alice was planning to leave him, wipe out his law practice, and take his children, McArthur had put up $15,000 for the car bombing—then raised the ante to $25,000 if the job could be done by July 4. But they hadn't seen a dime. Nor did Yankee have direct contact with McArthur—not once. Orsini had done all the negotiating. She'd provided everything for the murder but the car—the florist's sign and clipboard, Dr. Wulz's stolen .38, even the bullets.

Despite prodding from Tommy, Yankee stuck to his story. Orsini had told him all kinds of things she'd supposedly learned from McArthur, but he had no first-hand knowledge of any of it.

Yankee's plea bargain made the prosecution's case against Orsini much stronger. Wary of the sheriff's own agenda, however, Piazza had a long talk with him and Dill. Even though certain kinds of hearsay evidence were admissible to prove conspiracies, he warned them, double hearsay like Yankee's testimony against McArthur was obviously a trickier proposition. Arkansas law required independent proof of a criminal conspiracy. Otherwise, crooks could cop pleas by selling police and prosecutors any story they found convenient to buy. If and when Tommy found that proof, the prosecutor's door was open. Until then, Piazza warned, there were no legal grounds for arresting Bill McArthur. When he left PCSD headquarters late Sunday night, Piazza was under the impression that Robinson and Dill reluctantly agreed.

No sooner was the deputy prosecutor out the door than Tommy swung into action. By Monday afternoon, he was ready to act. After the media had been alerted, he dispatched Captain Bobby Woodward to haul Bill McArthur in for questioning.

·   ·   ·

If McArthur had any doubts about Tommy's intentions, they vanished the moment he pulled into the dusty gravel parking lot outside PCSD headquarters and saw TV cameramen and reporters racing toward his car. Probably contrary to Tommy's orders, Woodward had allowed Bill to drive himself while the deputy followed, the last shred of dignity the PCSD would permit him. Pushing through the swarm of shouting reporters, Bill was escorted to Dill's office.

Dill read McArthur his rights. The burly deputy waved around a sheet of paper containing a list of sixteen questions that he and Robinson demanded McArthur answer. "I told him, 'Larry, you know this is bullshit. You know this isn't right,' " McArthur said. " 'I'm not answering any questions until I have someone here who can hear my answers and record them.' I wanted someone to witness what I said. In fact, I wanted all the agencies there—LRPD, NLRPD, the prosecutor, ATF, and the FBI. Then I'd sit down and answer any questions they might have."

Instead, Dill ordered McArthur handcuffed and placed him under arrest. The charge was conspiracy to commit murder. They led the stunned attorney into the blazing lights of the TV cameras and down the hallway to be fingerprinted and booked.

Dill and Robinson told reporters that McArthur's refusal to answer questions had led to his arrest. When McArthur eventually got a look at Sheriff Tommy's vaunted list of sixteen questions, they were even more nonsensical than he'd feared. Anybody familiar with the case would have reacted the same way. Seemingly compiled with reference to Hall's confession rather than the case file, most had little to do with the existing evidence.

A few examples convey the flavor. Questions 3, 4 and 7 dealt with the bombing. "Where were your kids when the vehicle exploded?" The answer was that they'd been in school. "Did you normally take the kids to school?" No. They normally rode the bus. Then came the clincher: "How would [Orsini and Yankee] know you would be taking the kids to school the day of the bombing?" Again, they didn't, because Bill hadn't driven them. Orsini may have told Yankee that to ease his conscience. But Robyn and Chuck had ridden the bus to St. Edward's School that morning, as they'd done almost every school day for two years. Had Robinson or Dill read the LRPD or ATF case files on the car bombing, they would have known that.

To other investigators, however, the question most revealing of Tommy's focus was number 9: "Have you met Lee Orsini at the Holiday Inn in Hot Springs, the Best Western in North Little Rock, or the Holiday Inn at 6th and Broadway?" As Robinson knew, McArthur had denied this allegation under oath. A month's digging by LRPD detectives had proved that Orsini had lied about the Hot Springs meeting, and found no evidence of any others. Tommy had nothing to the contrary.

As an investigative tool, Tommy's questions were useless. As propaganda they were highly effective. Instead of releasing the list for publication, Robinson showed it to his allies in the media, leading them to believe they were on the inside track.

.   .   .

Some time after midnight Sunday night, the *Gazette*'s Carol Griffee was awakened by the ringing of her bedside phone. A male voice she did not recognize made her an offer that had her sitting bolt upright and wide awake in seconds. Yankee Hall, the voice informed her, had confessed to the murder of Alice McArthur and implicated Bill McArthur. If Griffee's newspaper wanted a big scoop, she should proceed at once to a blind drop. There she would find a tape recording of

Hall's statement. Griffee became so excited that she raced out into the pre-dawn darkness without her shotgun.

The sheriff's arrest of Bill McArthur provoked the Little Rock media to a new crescendo of excitement. In the theatrical sense, Tommy's timing couldn't have been better. Tipped off hours ahead of time, Channel 4 carried the event live on the 6:00 P.M. news. Thousands watched the grim, handcuffed attorney led down a hallway to be booked.

On the morning of Tuesday, August 31, the *Gazette* devoted almost the entire front page above the fold to Griffee's account. With the advantage of a full day in advance to digest the two-hour tape of Yankee's confession, her story delivered the gospel according to Tommy. Hall's statement, the newspaper reported without qualification, "implicated McArthur and two persons who were charged earlier." The fact that Yankee had never met nor spoken to McArthur was all but ignored.

Noting that Dub Bentley had learned of McArthur's arrest on TV, Griffee made a point of the prosecutor's surprise. She quoted Robinson's demand that Bentley dispense with a probable cause hearing and file direct on his own authority. " 'I feel our evidence against McArthur is just as strong at this point as the evidence he had against McClendon and Orsini.' If Bentley doesn't do this, Robinson said, he would ask that the prosecutor be disqualified for not doing his job." Dub had no comment.

The *Gazette* account made much of the flowers:

Hall . . . said that Mrs. McArthur dropped the flowers in the middle of the hall floor inside the front door when she realized her life was in danger and bolted up the stairs to the bedroom. Investigators saw petals from the dropped flowers in the hall when they entered the house about an hour later, it has been learned. Hall could not explain how the flowers, if Mrs. McArthur dropped them in the downstairs hall, got upstairs in her bedroom. . . .

Hall said he called Orsini later and told her things hadn't gone as planned because the flowers were left in the house and that she assured him everything would be "taken care of." The centerpiece was on the floor near Mrs. McArthur's feet when Mrs. McArthur's body was found by a neighbor and Dill.

Griffee's unacknowledged source for the flower petals in the hallway was in all probability Robinson or Dill. From the first, the sheriff had encouraged reporters to see the location of the flowers as the single most crucial bit of physical evidence in the case. According to Yankee Hall's confession itself, Griffee's stories placing the bouquet at Alice McArthur's feet had jolted the two prisoners during their first days in custody at the LRPD lockup:

> Larry would beat on the walls and I'd talk to him. And he says, "Did you read the paper?" And I says, "Yeah, I've been reading it. Why?" This was his theory. He didn't know at the time [who] was behind all this. I never did tell Larry where it was coming from. Anyway, he said, "You know what, Yankee? There was somebody else in that house." And I went, "Do what?" And he says, "There had to be. Them flowers were moved." And I said, "What do you mean, the flowers were moved?"
>
> "She dropped them flowers," he said, "long before the place where I shot her. In fact, she dropped 'em in the hall. . . ." And I says, "She did?" And he says, "Yeah. She dropped 'em and then run back into the bedroom. I chased her back there." And he said, "Them flowers weren't at her feet." He was worried how they got there. Of course it clicked on me right away. I said, "Damn, it had to be Bill. Who else could have moved them?"

In a crime scene report later produced by the PCSD and dated July 2 (although it details events occurring as late as the 6th), Dill claimed to have noticed numerous flower "pedals" in the upstairs hallway near the bedroom door. But none of the LRPD officers at the crime scene that night had seen any such thing. Nor had the coroner or the medical examiner's staff. No flower petals are visible in any of the score or more crime scene photos taken by Detective Al Dawson—several of which include the hallway and the front door area.

Griffee's follow-up story on September 2 contained generous verbatim quotes from Hall's statement that tended to support the theory Tommy had sold her. To readers avidly devouring every scrap of information about the case, it made a tidy package: McArthur had moved the flowers. Therefore, McArthur was guilty.

At LRPD headquarters, Griffee's story provoked helpless outrage. The scuffle inside the closet between LRPD Patrolman Rick Edgar and the PCSD deputies had never been placed into the written record. A deputy's supposed remark that he had been looking for the flowers had likewise been left out, since at the time no one could foresee its relevance. Since it had been Tommy's deputies who had tampered with the crime scene, LRPD detectives had simply assumed that the PCSD would never make an issue of the flowers. Even the prosecutor hadn't been informed.

Now Robinson seemed to be pursuing an agenda of his own. LRPD detectives wondered whether the PCSD had either known about the flowers beforehand or had carried them into the closet from somewhere else. Possibly both. While they had no proof, they even began to wonder if one of the PCSD deputies hadn't gotten inside the McArthur home *before* Bill got home that afternoon. That would explain how and why several carloads of deputies had arrived so fast. But if they wanted to see Orsini, Hall, and McClendon convicted, there wasn't a whole hell of a lot LRPD detectives could do about it.

When they read Yankee's account, LRPD detectives arranged a simple test. They bought an identical bouquet from the same florist who'd made the first, took it to the unoccupied McArthur home in Pleasant Valley, and dropped it on the hall carpet. Unlike the perfectly intact flower arrangement found at Alice's feet after the three deputies had been pushed out of the closet, it shattered into a hundred pieces. Flower petals were everywhere.

·   ·   ·

Dramatic as it was, Griffee's September 2 story was outshone by the sensational revelations in the *Democrat*. After managing editor John Robert Starr complained to Robinson about the favoritism shown the bigger paper, Thursday's *Democrat* carried two exclusives. One described an attempt to assassinate the sheriff. Like Orsini, Tommy had supposedly been shot at while driving along a deserted stretch of North Little Rock Highway. There were no witnesses.

And the *Democrat* had an even more exciting coup. Refusing to name its source, the newspaper printed the *entire text* of Yankee Hall's confession, filling several full pages. Despite printing thousands of extras, by mid-morning the *Democrat* sold out everywhere.

To LRPD detectives, Yankee's confession was full of absurdities—his belief that Alice McArthur had been caught in a love affair with Bob Troutt, for example—which made it clear that he'd been a man in the grips of a delusion. Lacking context, however, *Democrat* readers gobbled it up like popcorn. Even the minority capable of skepticism could hardly help but see Bill McArthur as a shadowy figure on the fringes of the underworld. TV summaries were even more damaging.

Meanwhile, the political stakes grew higher. Like prosecutors and sheriffs, all Arkansas judges—from traffic court to the State Supreme Court—are popularly elected. One after another, every judge in the 6th Circuit recused himself from trying Mary Lee. Even Dub Bentley took a walk. The prosecutor had the power simply to drop the charges against McArthur, or to submit Tommy's case to a grand jury. Instead, Dub decided that public confidence in the criminal justice system would be better served if he temporarily stepped aside. He asked a prosecutor from Pine Bluff to handle McArthur's bond hearing.

Politics even affected McArthur's actions. Instead of demanding an immediate bond hearing, Bill had spent the night of August 30 in jail so Tommy couldn't claim he'd gotten special treatment. Friends urged him to hold a press conference to answer Tommy's vaunted list of sixteen questions, exposing the sheriff's ignorance. But McArthur now expected to be tried for murder. If and when that happened, he intended to present his defense only once—without giving Mary Lee a chance to fabricate a new story in advance.

Things continued at a pitch of near hysteria for the better part of a month. At one point, Sheriff Tommy publicly challenged McArthur's attorney Jack Holt to a fistfight. A Little Rock radio station reported that McArthur had hanged himself. To quash the rumor, Bill allowed Channel 7 to film him in his office. To the media, the search for a special prosecutor acceptable to Tommy Robinson assumed the status of the quest for the Holy Grail.

• • •

In the privacy of the Pulaski County Jail, Mary Lee Orsini was busy maneuvering for position. On the morning of McArthur's August 31 bond hearing, she phoned Larry Dill on his private line at the CID. According to a report Dill wrote later, Mary Lee predicted that Dub Bentley would see to it that McArthur made bond. She expected a blow-by-blow account of the proceedings. "I told Lee that I didn't mind talking to her," Dill wrote, "but I didn't want to make Jack Lessenberry mad or get anything started that I was in any way initiating these conversations."

Lessenberry was a veteran Little Rock defense attorney who had agreed to represent Orsini. From her first days in the county lockup, the attorney had protested vigorously to the sheriff about repeated meetings between his client, Robinson, and Dill to which he was not a party. Mary Lee had an absolute right under the law to have an attorney present. On her own, Lessenberry feared that she could be tricked into damaging revelations. If the meetings continued, he could move to have the sheriff and his chief deputy cited for contempt.

If not quite so skillful a courtroom performer as McArthur, Lessenberry had a reputation as diligent, honest, and well-organized. But some things Orsini needed to keep secret from him. An ethical attorney, experience with Bill had taught her, might balk at what she had in mind.

In Larry Dill, Orsini had sensed the kind of man she could manipulate. But what she hadn't counted on was his deviousness. Dill was willing to talk all she wanted. To cover himself, he took the precaution of rigging a tape recorder to his phone. When he called Orsini back to tell her McArthur had been set free on $50,000 bond, he did not mention that he was taping her.

Dub Bentley's refusal to represent the State at McArthur's hearing had Mary Lee all excited. She and Dill mistakenly believed he'd recused himself for good—a misunderstanding shared by the press. Assured that the chief deputy was on her side, she made him an offer. "What I would like to do for you," she said, "is just to corroborate that statement. To go over it, over the statement. Yankee's statement."

Dill was wary. He didn't want to be accused of violating her rights. She assured him that her attorney had encouraged her to work with Dill to cut herself the best deal she could. "I think as much as you can check out and corroborate—and have Hall corroborate—on that statement," Mary Lee insisted, "the better off you might be. . . . I need to go over it and read it and point out to you what can be corroborated and where. Because that just makes your case that much better."

Incredibly, Dill had Orsini brought up to the CID that very night. Three days before it appeared in the *Democrat*, the two spent hours reviewing Yankee's confession. To the extent that an investigation resembles a poker game, Dill had let Mary Lee see the prosecution's hole card, and had gotten nothing in return.

Dill wrote up his report and stamped it "Confidential." Orsini had confirmed Yankee's story but refused to make a statement.

Lee also said he forgot to tell . . . about the rifle and the plan to shoot Alice at the tennis center. . . . Lee again stated Bill McArthur was behind the whole thing and was upset about him getting out on bond. . . .

[She] indicated she may give a statement when she talks to her attorney but is concerned about dealing with Dub Bentley because of his ties with Bill McArthur.

First thing Wednesday, September 1, Mary Lee phoned Dill again. Now that she'd had a chance to sleep on it, she'd come up with a new proposition. "See if y'all are willing to go for this," she offered. "I'll let Jack [Lessenberry] talk to the [special] prosecutor. . . . You kind of give me a rough draft of what it will help you to say. 'I will do thus and so, and thus and so at Bill's trial.' "

In return, Orsini wanted the charges dropped to conspiracy and to be allowed to plead innocent. "I don't want anybody to know except the prosecutor that I'm making a deal," she said. "Put me on a bond and let me get out until I can get some things. Because I can expedite things so much faster than my mother."

Among the "things" Orsini proposed to make available were champagne bottles bearing McArthur's fingerprints—supposedly from their assignation at the Hot Springs Holiday Inn. (Dill and Robinson insisted, despite the evidence assembled by LRPD detectives, that the meeting had taken place.) She'd hide the bottles inside 7412 Pontiac and tell Dill where to find them.

Dill hesitated. It troubled him that Lessenberry hadn't implicated McArthur. "That would mean, Lee," he said, "that you're either not telling him the truth or you're not telling me the truth, one."

She claimed that her lawyer knew, but was maneuvering for advantage. Orsini had Dill boxed and she knew it. As she'd learned from McArthur the first time around, Lessenberry would not—could not, ethically—contradict her to the police.

The awful truth of the matter, in the version Orsini told Dill and Robinson—the bitter truth which Mary Lee couldn't bring herself to accept, which the NLRPD had failed to investigate, which Bill McArthur had used as leverage against her, and which a sympathetic Larry Dill just didn't want to believe—went approximately as follows:

Tiffany Orsini, age thirteen, had slain her stepfather in his sleep for causes unknown. God knew what atrocities had driven the poor child to do it. But when Mary Lee had forced her way into the locked bedroom door at 7412 Pontiac on the morning of March 12, 1981, and witnessed her husband's corpse face down in a frothy sea of blood, she'd gone into shock. Everything she'd seen and done before NLRPD officers arrived had vanished from her memory.

Weeks later, Bill McArthur had driven his trusting client to Memphis to visit a hypnotist. Under a hypnotic trance, Mary Lee's amnesia had lifted—although she had no memory of the session either. Only McArthur and the hypnotist knew exactly what she'd said. Apparently, however, Mary Lee had visualized herself picking up a .38 revolver she'd found lying on the floor next to the fatal bed. Still in shock, she'd hidden it in a spot where the clumsy drones of the NLRPD had never thought to search.

"You remember on my trace metal tests when I just had it on the tip of my finger?" Mary Lee asked. "That's because I picked up the barrel of the gun. See, I just barely picked the gun up."

After they returned from Memphis, Bill had climbed into the attic crawl space. Emerging with the murder weapon in a paper sack, the unscrupulous attorney had proceeded to blackmail her into doing his unholy bidding. Unless Mary Lee served as a go-between, carrying messages and cash back and forth between him and Yankee, McArthur had threatened to turn the murder weapon—presumably bearing Tiffany's fingerprints—over to the police.

In order keep the PCSD off the track, McArthur had also forced Mary Lee to ply Sheriff Tommy with false information. The idea was to make Alice's murder appear to be the work of organized crime. Hence the fake calls from the Memphis gangster "Art Baldwin," which McArthur himself had set up.

Mary Lee was far from being the cold-blooded, manipulative murderess imagined by the NLRPD, the LRPD, and the prosecutor. Rather, she was a desperate woman struggling frantically to save her only child.

Exactly when Orsini peddled this preposterous saga to the PCSD can't be determined. Nor can the degree to which Dill and Robinson may actually have believed it. From the day of McArthur's arrest onward, they chose to *act* as if they did. Indeed, just about the only explanation that makes sense of their actions from the melee in the closet over Alice McArthur's body until the end was that Dill and Robinson *thought* they knew things nobody else knew, and that the source of that knowledge was Mary Lee.

•   •   •

"She *knew* that Tiffany did it," Tommy confided in one of his late-night phone calls to Dub Bentley. "And I'll tell you something else. That's why she wanted Tiffany to go to school that day, and she had a hard time getting her all drugged up. She didn't want the police suspecting that there was anything out of the ordinary. So she went, 'We always go to breakfast.'

"What Lee was trying to do," the sheriff explained, "was distract any attention from Tiffany. She knew that there were going to be a lot of questions asked. Lee was smart enough to know that Tiffany would be a suspect if something happened and she didn't do what she normally did. And I think that Lee doped her ass up, took her to breakfast and finally got her in a position where she could go to school."

A deliberately deceptive Mary Lee, of course, would make absolute nonsense out of the bit about being taken to Memphis and hypnotized to find the murder weapon. For that and a million other reasons, the prosecutor still wasn't buying.

•   •   •

The news that somebody had taken a potshot at Sheriff Tommy on the freeway threw Orsini into a tizzy. "Remember that anonymous call I got that I made that tape with?" she reminded Larry Dill. "What they said about TR? Told me they were going to get him? Now what does that tell you, Larry? With TR getting shot at—this is something I've believed for a long time—there's some big people that's screwed in with this thing, and I'm going to tell you something. The big people ain't Lee Orsini."

"I believe that, Lee. I believe it."

"Well, Larry, it's just like I said. We may lose some battles on and off, but in the end the war is going to be what we win."

"We're going to win the war," he agreed. "I'll guarantee you we're going to win the war."

Once again, Orsini had put her trust in a hero whom she expected to magically resolve all her problems. Unfortunately for her, Dill and Robinson's vows to defy Dub Bentley proved worthless. Under threat of contempt, Sheriff Tommy had no choice but to turn over his vaunted case files to the prosecutor. Transcripts of Dill's surreptitious tape recordings went with them. Within a week, Mary Lee's secrets had fallen into the hands of the enemy.

•   •   •

Across the river in North Little Rock, meanwhile, Sergeant T. J. Farley had no intention of putting the Ron Orsini case into mothballs. As much satisfaction as Farley had gotten from his small part in helping the LRPD put Mary Lee in jail, he'd made scant progress.

Realistically, Farley knew that his best chance to convict Mary Lee would be getting an accomplice to cave in, assuming she'd had one. He had several possibilities in mind, among them the ubiquitous Dr. Wulz. But Yankee had moved to the top of the list. According to Hall's confession, Orsini had picked him up at a Taco Bell in April 1982. But suppose they'd actually met much earlier, like March 1981? It was worth looking into.

One of Farley's purposes in showing up at PCSD headquarters on Friday, September 24, was to interview Yankee Hall. A week or so earlier, Larry Dill had phoned to offer him a favor. In phone calls Dill had secretly recorded, Orsini had admitted staging the June 1981 incident at 7412 Pontiac involving a burglar in a red jogging suit and plastic bags of white powder, as well as the April 1982 shooting on Batesville Pike. Would the NLRPD like to clear their books? He promised the transcripts within a week.

When Farley and two other NLRPD officers reached the PCSD, the place was aswarm with TV cameras and reporters. Sheriff Tommy had chosen the afternoon to stage one of his more bizarre publicity stunts. An eccentric black activist named Robert "Say" McIntosh—dressed for obscure reasons in a red sateen devil costume with horns—had erected a ten-foot wooden cross in a courtyard outside the building. He'd hang there all afternoon, Say insisted, soliciting donations for a free breakfast program for poor kids he ran at his barbecue place.

Billing himself as "The Sweet Potato Pie King," McIntosh was famous around town for the luridly illustrated advertising handbills he used as a forum for his views on the evils of racism and the sex lives of public figures. Uninhibited by fear of retribution, Say had once accused Governor Bill Clinton of an obscene lust for black women.

Sheriff Tommy had vowed to cut McIntosh's cross down with a chain saw, and the press eagerly anticipated the battle. Inside the building, it wasn't much better. While the three NLRPD cops attempted to conduct a serious meeting, Sheriff Tommy roamed up and down the hallway, hollering threats and trying to get a reluctant chain saw started. Nevertheless, all three NLRPD officers recalled the meeting exactly the same way.

According to NLRPD officers, Dill affirmed that Orsini had admitted staging the incidents, but a transcript hadn't been completed. Dill later denied telling them these things. In fact, the Dill-Orsini tapes had been typed up weeks ago. The judge in her trial had already ruled on their admissibility. Nor did they contain any such admission by Orsini.

Outside, meanwhile, the farce in the courtyard continued. Sheriff Tommy emerged before the cameras amid clouds of blue exhaust fumes, gunning the chain saw and brandishing it at the base of Say's cross. McIntosh climbed down and danced about executing karate kicks and feints. They exchanged insults like pro wrestlers.

The apparent purpose of Dill's summoning Farley emerged after Robinson returned to the office. The sheriff told the NLRPD officers that he wanted them to arrest Tiffany for the murder of Ron Orsini. He had no wish to step on the NLRPD's toes by taking over their case. The idea was to break Tiffany, forcing Mary Lee to come clean and tell everything McArthur had held over her head to force her to help him murder his wife.

Besides, the poor kid needed protection. Tiffany had twice been admitted to Memorial Hospital for botched suicide attempts. Dill said he'd secured a promise from a juvenile judge to make Tiffany a ward of the state. If they got her away from Mary Lee, Dill and Robinson were sure they could ferret out the truth.

Farley was dumbfounded. He told them they were nuts. If they'd ever bothered to read his case file, they'd realize that everything in it pointed directly to Mary Lee. Nothing to Tiffany. Maybe the kid knew more than she was telling—in fact, Farley was convinced she did—but what could anybody expect her to do under the circumstances except cling to her mother?

When he returned to North Little Rock, it took Farley just a couple of phone calls to establish that Tiffany had never been admitted to Memorial Hospital. Dill could have learned the same thing on his own. But he and Tommy were far too busy stalking larger game.

Chapter 3

1

The job of trying Mary Lee Orsini for the murder of Alice McArthur fell to Chris Piazza. Since the night of July 2, the aggressive young deputy prosecutor had been working closely with the LRPD. Detectives were quick to credit his key role in breaking the case. More swiftly than any of the other investigators, Piazza had seen through Orsini's subterfuges. In the process, he had worked up an almost theological loathing that made him determined to put her away for good.

As the best trial lawyer on Dub Bentley's staff, it was not surprising that Piazza had drawn the lead role. Dub himself would assist. Despite some speculation that Bentley doubted his own ability to handle the pressure, neither he nor Chris would lend credence to any such thing. Piazza had been on the McArthur case from the first, Bentley insisted, so it was his to handle. He wouldn't dream of upstaging a trusted assistant.

While the evidence against Orsini was powerful, the case was also a potential legal minefield. The issue of pre-trial publicity loomed. No sooner had Yankee's confession been printed in the *Democrat* than Jack Lessenberry filed for dismissal. Piazza had successfully argued that despite saturation coverage of the case, the details hadn't been so lurid as to cause unreasoning hatred of Orsini. Nor had they been conclusive enough to remove the presumption of innocence. A juror might know the gist of Yankee's statement, but conclude he was lying to save his skin.

There were other tricky procedural issues, too. But the two biggest hurdles the prosecution faced were named Tommy Robinson and Mary Lee Orsini. Chris had already had one confrontation with the sheriff that had almost come to blows. When Piazza went to fetch Yankee to LRPD headquarters for trial preparations, the sheriff had tried to stop him. "Tommy got right up in my face," Chris said, "and called me a motherfucker."

With his volatile nature, Piazza was dying for Robinson to take a swing at him. Tommy had a reputation among other cops for never backing his threats unless his opponent was either handcuffed or outnumbered. With Dill at his back, Tommy was a tough guy. But Piazza just kept walking, and Robinson stepped aside.

Before Piazza could make tactical plans, he had to decide how he would handle the sheriff's charges against McArthur. On September 13, he delivered a confidential memo to Dub Bentley evaluating the files Robinson had reluctantly surrendered. Piazza had worked through the weekend painstakingly comparing the PCSD's case to the factual record. He'd also spent hours in sometimes heated discussion with Robinson and Dill. His conclusion, Piazza wrote, was that "there is not sufficient evidence . . . to indicate that there is probable cause to hold Bill McArthur on a charge of Conspiracy to Commit Capital Murder."

Piazza's memo cut to the heart of the scenario Tommy had laid out to the press: That McArthur had moved the flowers, and that that proved his guilt. Everything about the physical evidence, he wrote, contradicted Robinson's theory. No matter what Dill said, the crime scene photos showed no flower petals anywhere but inside the closet. The hallway carpet, moreover, was matted and soiled and had not been freshly vacuumed. He'd examined it personally.

Sheriff Tommy's backup position, that McArthur had moved his wife's body into the closet to buy time, was equally absurd. Even without the medical examiner's ruling, anybody with common sense could see that the woman had been shot where she'd fallen. As she'd slumped to the floor, a pair of blue jeans had been pulled from a hanger and fallen across her shoulder. Clearly visible in the blue jeans was a bullet hole from an earlier shot that had missed. Bloodstains on the garment showed it impossible that Alice's body could have been moved. As for Orsini's allegations against McArthur, Piazza had found nothing to support them. There was no proof that the $15,000 cash Bill had supposedly paid her for the car bombing had existed. The safety deposit box where Mary Lee had purportedly stashed the loot was empty. No large withdrawals had been made from McArthur's bank accounts, nor deposits in hers.

"It is my belief," Piazza wrote, "that Lee Orsini used Bill McArthur and the possibility of money to entice Yankee Hall to commit the crime. Yankee Hall did not do such an act without being paid for it." When Orsini tried to persuade Hall to bomb Bubba Younts's car purely out of spite, Yankee had refused.

Furthermore, what rational purpose, Chris asked himself, could Orsini possibly have had for attempting to murder the NLRPD chief? Absolutely none. For Piazza, it followed that Alice McArthur's murder was hardly the crime of passion the press and general public imagined. If anything, it was a *hate* crime. Fundamentally *irrational*, Orsini's exact motives couldn't be fully comprehended. But it wouldn't have taken much to set her off.

"Lee Orsini," he wrote in his memo to Bentley,

has a history of wanting revenge. It is undetermined whether there is another person involved in this crime, but it is quite clear that Lee Orsini is capable of committing such an act on her own. . . . She would have her revenge, and she would have at least what she perceived as her chance with McArthur. . . .

There is further indication in the file that Lee was in awe of Bill. There is no indication in the file of any sexual relationship between McArthur and Orsini. Lee Orsini is the type of person who can plan these events well in advance, and if she had personal [i.e., intimate] conversations with Bill McArthur, I am quite sure they would be taped or there would be some substantive evidence of such a relationship.

Pointing to proof that McArthur couldn't possibly have been in a Hot Springs motel room with Orsini on June 9, Piazza stressed his view that the PCSD was determined to convict McArthur regardless of the facts. He charged that they had allowed Orsini to read Yankee's statement—then lied about it. Robinson flatly denied that Mary Lee had been shown Hall's confession until after it appeared in the *Democrat*. But her taped conversations with Dill proved that she had. "I find it a very questionable police tactic," Piazza added, "to allow one defendant to read a statement of another defendant and then attempt to obtain a confession or plea statement from the second defendant. I would think that it might taint any statement that Orsini would make."

The PCSD's sole purpose in leaking Yankee's statement to the media, Piazza concluded, had been to inflame public opinion against McArthur and the prosecutor in order to justify the arrest. There was simply no credible evidence against Bill McArthur.

•   •   •

Under normal circumstances, that would have been the end of it. For all the media fanfare, Dub Bentley was still the elected prosecutor and Piazza his most trusted assistant. Although Dub had declined to take part in preliminary hearings against McArthur, he had no intention of relinquishing the powers of his office.

For tactical reasons, Sheriff Tommy and his handpicked special prosecutor had managed to get McArthur's probable cause hearing postponed until *after* Orsini's trial. Intended to protect the rights of defendants, a probable cause hearing was normally a fifteen-minute affair held in municipal court within a day or two of a warrantless arrest. But regardless of how it turned out, the proceeding would be in no way binding upon Bentley. Under the Arkansas constitution, only the elected prosecutor could file criminal charges in Circuit Court. Should he decline to do so, not even the governor could force his hand.

But then, where Bill McArthur was concerned, circumstances around the Pulaski County Courthouse were anything but normal.

•   •   •

On Thursday, September 16, Eugene "Yankee" Hall stood before Judge Randall Williams and pleaded guilty to capital murder. In accordance with the deal negotiated by his lawyer, he was sentenced to life. Apparently unaware that a recent revision in the state criminal code had removed the possibility of parole, Hall expected to be out in six or eight years. Instead, Yankee walked into Cummins Prison Farm in the Delta flatlands of southeast Arkansas for the rest of his natural life.

Also on September 16, Piazza entered a motion waiving the death penalty for Mary Lee Orsini. The prevailing wisdom was that no Arkansas jury would sentence a woman to death. Certainly none ever had. Piazza also indicated, however, that the state would accept no lesser verdict than capital murder. The jury would have two options: acquittal, or life without parole.

2

The most highly anticipated criminal trial in Arkansas history got under way on Monday, October 4, 1982. For sheer public excitement, the state had seen nothing like it since President Eisenhower dispatched the 101st Airborne to Little Rock twenty-five years earlier to integrate the public schools. The local media were geared up for a gaudy show. One Little Rock TV station had requested and been denied permission to broadcast the trial statewide.

Judge Randall Williams of Pine Bluff had been appointed to hear the case by the Arkansas Supreme Court. To avoid forcing another judge to vacate his chambers, it had been agreed to hold the trial at the UA-Little Rock School of Law. Situated just across Spring Street from the courthouse, the law school was housed in a massive nineteenth-century brownstone that had once served as the city's post office and federal court building. Chris Piazza was counting upon the ornate third-floor courtroom with its dark paneling and massive oaken furniture to lend an element of dignity to the proceedings.

Jury selection had begun on the previous Thursday. To the surprise of most observers, a panel of eight men and four women had been chosen in just two days. Despite unprecedented media coverage, few would-be jurors had admitted during the voir dire to having fixed opinions about Orsini's guilt. Almost nobody owned up to reading Yankee's confession in the *Democrat*, or even hearing it talked about. Most said they either had no time to read the newspapers, or didn't trust the press anyway.

On Monday morning, eager spectators—mostly middle-aged women, including a close-knit group of Alice McArthur's friends—had begun lining up for seats before 7:00 A.M. The judge had agreed to allow TV cameras inside the courtroom only during recesses. To the delight of the cameramen, Sheriff Tommy made a great show of having a bomb-sniffing German shepherd search the premises. Both the *Gazette* and the *Democrat* had assigned several reporters to cover what they hoped would be the trial's sensational revelations.

If Chris Piazza had his way, those expectations would be dashed. He intended to try the case on the narrowest possible grounds. Given half a chance, he knew, Mary Lee would do her best to turn the trial into a full-scale dramatic production. While the press portrayed Orsini as a glamorous *femme fatale*, Piazza found her monstrous. With luck, Piazza hoped he could get Mary Lee to drop the Southern Belle act and show her fangs.

But as much as he yearned for the confrontation, Piazza also realized that putting Orsini in front of a jury could turn into a hazardous venture. The woman was a mistrial waiting to happen. He was pretty sure that Jack Lessenberry had enough sense to urge his client not to testify. But as Bill McArthur had learned, her attorney had little hope of controlling his client's actions. Despite Lessenberry's repeated warnings to the sheriff, Orsini's meetings with Robinson and Dill had continued almost daily.

When presented with the transcripts of her tape-recorded phone calls to Larry Dill in mid-September, Lessenberry had been outraged. Faced with evidence of their client's duplicity, he and co-counsel Tom Carpenter filed a sealed motion with the court asking to be relieved from representing her. The judge denied it.

In response to a defense motion, Judge Williams did agree to sequester the jury. The most significant evidentiary ruling of the case, however, had taken place at a preliminary hearing on September 21. No sooner had Piazza provided the defense with transcripts of the telephone conversations between Orsini and Larry Dill than her attorneys moved to prevent their use.

At issue was a long-settled point of criminal law. Orsini had an absolute right to have her attorney present whenever she talked to the police. But she didn't have a right to lie under oath. If she testified, Judge Williams ruled, the prosecution could use Dill's little tapes to challenge her credibility. Or if not the tapes themselves, Piazza could certainly put Dill on the stand to contradict her. The results would be devastating. Besides hinting at the Tiffany–shot–Ron scenario, she had admitted to handling a revolver she'd supposedly found lying next to Ron Orsini's body—something she'd twice denied under oath. Sheriff Tommy and his deputy had given Piazza exactly the tool to prevent Orsini from turning her trial into grand opera. No attorney could risk putting her on the witness stand. The trial was by no means over. But from then on, Piazza and Lessenberry both understood, the prosecution would fiddle and the defense would dance.

Reporters missed the whole thing. To the Little Rock media, the big issue of the day—whether or not Carol Griffee or John Robert Starr

would be jailed for refusing to identify the leaker of Yankee's statement—had already been decided. They were not.

                              .   .   .

Piazza began his opening statement shortly after 9:00 A.M. on October 4. After three months of working on the McArthur case all
around the clock, immersing himself in a thousand details, Piazza now
faced the task of reducing it all to a simple, compelling narrative. He
also faced strict legal and practical limits to his ability to tell the story
coherently. Mostly, he had to find a way to describe Mary Lee's
relationship to Bill McArthur without mentioning Ron Orsini's murder or her role as prime suspect. To do so would be prejudicial and
could result in an immediate mistrial.

Answering the question of why Alice McArthur should have been
murdered was hard enough. Without being able to explore fully all the
reasons for Mary Lee's obsession with Bill, it became twice as hard.
Piazza decided that the best he could do was to argue that Orsini's
anger over Alice's vetoing her from participating in BJ's Star-Studded
Honky Tonk had led to an act of revenge.

What Piazza needed was a way to dramatize the revenge idea for
jurors without revealing that there was very little concrete evidence to
prove it. The solution had come to him while he was jogging through
his West Little Rock neighborhood early that morning.

"Now this case," he warned the jury, "is going to appear to be
complicated. But the appearance . . . was largely brought on by the
defendant and her activities." He drew a chalk circle and wrote the
word "ORSINI" in block letters inside it.

"This case," he explained, "is one that revolves around a woman
named Orsini, Lee Orsini. And she is the hub of the activity in this
case. She is the person who is the moving force behind this death and
these activities. And it is very interesting, and very complicated."

As he introduced the name and described the testimony of each
major witness he planned to call—Yankee Hall, Joyce Holt, Carl Ray
Wilson, Phoebe Pinkston, Larry Burge, Bill McArthur, and Tommy
Robinson—Piazza walked over to the blackboard and wrote the names
one at a time in a rough circle surrounding Orsini's. Then he connected each one to the center by a series of lines resembling spokes on
a wheel.

As he was winding up his summary of the evidence, Piazza gestured
toward the figure he had drawn. "This episode," he concluded, "is

going to be a hub, where she is in the center of it. . . . And the one thing that is remarkable about this hub is that these people are not connected. She did not tell the same story to Burge that she told to Joyce Holt. She kept these people separated and isolated from each other as best she could."

With his chalk, Piazza drew a second circle around the hub containing Orsini's name, transforming the wheel into a web. His voice became charged with emotion for the first time. "What you have, ladies and gentlemen," he continued, "is a lady who spun this story, and she spun a web. And she spun a web that is very intricate. And she spun a web that is very difficult to understand. But if you will take the presentation that I have made and think of the motive, and individually look at each of these people and see how she placed them . . . this story is going to be very simple. It's not going to be hard at all. If you impartially consider the evidence, you will have an abiding proof of the charge. And you will go into that jury room and find that person, Lee Orsini, guilty of capital murder. Thank you."

.   .   .

It was a hard act to follow, and Jack Lessenberry knew it. Striding over to the blackboard, he removed his suit coat, turned it inside out, and used the lining to erase the spiderweb Piazza had drawn. Next he proceeded to attack the prosecution's case at its weakest point: Yankee Hall. Not only was Hall a con man, drug dealer, and confessed killer, but he'd made a bargain to tell the prosecution what it wanted to hear to save himself from worse punishment. When the jury heard Hall's statement, Lessenberry predicted, "It won't simply offend your common sense, your common sense will rebel. . . . The evidence will show, ladies and gentlemen, so many inconsistencies, so many irregularities, you'll want to know *who* wrote the script [and] *when*." Without saying so, he hoped to remind the jurors of things they theoretically didn't know and he didn't dare say, particularly Sheriff Tommy's charges that the prosecutor was orchestrating a cover-up to protect Bill McArthur.

.   .   .

The remainder of the morning passed relatively uneventfully. Only during Sally Pernell's testimony describing how she'd found her friend's body did sparks fly. On the grounds that it was prejudicial, the defense tried to prevent the prosecutor from questioning Alice's friend about the McArthurs' harmonious marriage. After Piazza explained that evidence would show that Orsini had described the couple as headed for a bitter divorce, Judge Williams allowed it.

But the most telling moment occurred during cross-examination. Approaching the soft-spoken Pernell with surprising aggressiveness, Lessenberry sought to make it appear that Bill had summoned her to 24 Inverness Circle that afternoon and urged her to search the premises. Having taken Sheriff Tommy's word for it, Carol Griffee had written *Gazette* stories to that effect without once interviewing her. Sally Pernell was eager to set things straight. It wasn't true, she said, that Bill had asked her to come.

"Mrs. Pernell," Lessenberry asked sarcastically, "are you telling these ladies and gentlemen that you just spontaneously went upstairs and began to look around? Or did he ask you to go?"

"He did not ask me to do that. Would you like me to explain?"

"I would like you to answer the question."

"He did not ask me to look."

•   •   •

Immediately after the lunch recess, Piazza brought Yankee Hall to the witness stand. In the glare of the TV lights from the hallway, the slight, gray-haired man made an incongruous figure. His hair and mustache neatly trimmed, Yankee wore an open-necked brown sport shirt and tan slacks. Three months in a jail cell had left him pasty-faced and somber. He looked almost frail in comparison to the elaborately coiffed defendant in her gray skirt and silky lavender blouse— and certainly no match for her overweening self-confidence. Her pale blue eyes sparkling, Mary Lee shot looks around the courtroom as if to emphasize the absurdity of the prosecution's contention that the pair could ever have been lovers.

No sooner had Hall's testimony begun, however, than Orsini's bravado faded some. Speaking rapidly in his peculiar Pennsylvania-Brooklyn accent, he made an effective witness. After asking him to describe the life sentence he'd accepted in exchange for his testimony, Piazza led Yankee through the story of his first meeting with Mary Lee at the Taco Bell and his gradual enchantment. To support Hall's contention that he had often spent the night with her, Piazza had Yankee sketch a diagram of the floor plan at 7412 Pontiac Drive. Hall was also able to describe the bedroom furniture in some detail—including the two antique cherrywood highboy dressers Sergeant Buddy Miles had admired on the morning that Ron Orsini's body had been discovered in the same bedroom. He told the jury how Mary Lee had concealed him from Tiffany on the one occasion when she'd come home unexpectedly while he was there.

"Lee said it would be alright to stay in the bedroom," Yankee said, "because the girl was going to go right to bed anyway. . . . She just locked the door, and she told me not to answer the door because she [Tiffany] might open it."

It may have meant little to the jury, but the ease with which Orsini glided in and out of the room perked up Sergeant Farley's ears. "How did she open the door?" Piazza asked.

"Well it's one of them little locks," Yankee explained, "with a little hole in the middle of it. You can stick anything in there, like an ice pick. . . . You just push it in and then turn the knob. She kept a little ice pick in her robe, you know."

Piazza had him describe the night he'd parked a red borrowed Chevy Coupe in her driveway.

"Did she offer you some money," Piazza then asked, "in order for you to do something in relation to Bill McArthur?"

Yankee described how they'd plotted to set a small fire at BJ's Honky Tonk and bomb McArthur's car for $10,000. The presence of security guards had ruled out the fire. But she told him McArthur still wanted the bombing done.

"She said he would pay $15,000," Hall explained. "And I, of course, inquired, 'Why more money to do half the job?' Then she informed me that someone was going to be in the car. . . . When I finally agreed to help her with it, she told me who it was."

"And who did she say it was?"

"Mrs. McArthur."

In a pre-trial motion, Orsini's lawyers had tried to exclude any mention of the car bombing, on the grounds that the prosecution had filed separate charges of attempted murder. Judge Williams had accepted Piazza's argument that Rule 404 of the Arkansas Rules of Procedure allowed evidence of other crimes in order to show intent, motive, or preparation.

The prosecutor led Yankee through an account of how he and Mary Lee—traveling under the pseudonym of "Sue"—had driven to Carl Ray Wilson's place to buy Tovex explosives and blasting caps. Next he described how they had put the bomb together in the den at 7412 Pontiac, scouted the McArthurs' neighborhood, and gotten together after midnight May 20 to attach it to the car. As Yankee lay on his back under the car rigging the charge, Mary Lee had kept watch on a hillside across the street.

"Did she ever say anything to you about Alice and Bob Troutt?" Piazza asked.

"Well, she indicated to me that one of the reasons that Bill was wanting her to do this was because they had been intimate."

"Have you ever had any conversations with Bill McArthur, personally or on the phone?"

"No."

"So everything you got about McArthur and Alice McArthur came through the defendant, Orsini?"

"Yes."

Within a week of the car bombing, Mary Lee had proposed shooting Alice on the tennis court. She'd given Hall $350 to buy a 30.06 deer rifle, and driven him out to Westside Tennis Club to locate a sniper position. It was only after Yankee realized he couldn't do it that Orsini raised the offer to $25,000 if he could find a triggerman. She formulated the florist's delivery gambit, made the sign for the car window, furnished a clipboard with a phony delivery list, and stole the murder weapon from Dr. Wulz. "It was a .38 Smith & Wesson," Hall said, "what they call a snub nose."

After killing Alice, he and Larry McClendon were supposed to squeeze off a couple of rounds into the front door of BJ's partner James Nelson, then drive to North Little Rock and take a few potshots at Orsini's house. Instead, he had gotten scared and dumped the clipboard, sign, and gun off the I-430 bridge.

Piazza led Yankee through a description of the times and places from which he'd phoned the McArthur home on July 2 seeking to find Alice at home. Each had been recorded by a Southwestern Bell trap. The courtroom grew very quiet when Yankee described Alice's last moments. Seated together in the spectators' seats, several of her friends wept softly.

"I sat in the car," he explained, "and Larry got out and went to the front door. I was watching out from inside the car. And what I'd told him earlier was that after I seen he got in the house . . . I would come and make sure when he was leaving that he didn't forget anything. Because he had the gun, and he had this towel, and he had the clipboard that Lee had made up. And I didn't want him to leave anything in there—especially the flowers, I told him, because my fingerprints were on them. I also was going to wipe off the doorknob, because he'd opened the door when he went in. I had a little washcloth with me to do that.

"So as he went in the house I started out just walking towards the door. And, well, she [Alice McArthur] took the flowers at the door, first of all. And she was, you know, really pretty friendly. I could tell they were smiling and talking. . . . She took the flowers and invited him in."

"What happened then?" Piazza asked.

"Well, then I eased over towards the front door, and I heard one shot, and then it was several seconds pause—I'd say not very long, just several seconds—and then there were two more shots. And then I went up. I wiped off the doorknob and I opened it up and as I stepped inside I couldn't see very well, so I took off my sunglasses. I couldn't see anybody. But as soon as I took them three steps Larry was already going out."

"What was his condition when he was coming down those steps?"

"Well, I never seen him. He was just hustling pretty fast. I heard him go by me. He was really moving quick. . . . He was saying, 'Let's get out of here!' He was pretty excited."

There was a purpose in Piazza's line of questioning. With McClendon refusing to talk, he expected Lessenberry to exploit the discrepancy in the location of the flowers to discredit Yankee. Piazza meant to suggest that McClendon had been too hopped up to know what had happened to the bouquet.

"Did he leave the flowers inside?"

"He didn't have the flowers. I thought something must have went wrong. His adrenaline was really running. He kept saying, 'Let's get out of here!' As I started to pull out, I stopped . . . and I said, 'You left them flowers in there.' He said, 'Let's go! Let's go!' So I took off."

"Did you decide to go back to get the flowers?"

"When I realized there was nothing wrong I did. . . . He indicated to me that she dropped them when he fired the first shot, which was out in the hallway going into the bedroom. He was kinda like apologizing. He said, 'She dropped them and run.' He says, 'When I fired the first shot, I missed. Then I had to chase after her. . . .' And I said, 'We'll have to go back and get them, because my fingerprints are on them.' "

In Yankee's statement, the conversation about the location of the flowers had taken place in the Little Rock city jail—only after a *Ga-*

zette story disclosing that they'd been found in the closet at Alice's feet. Possibly there had been two conversations. It was not, however, a point Piazza wished to clarify.

"Did you ever see any flowers inside the house?" he asked.

"No, I never did see any." A suspicious neighbor, Yankee added, had intimidated the killers from going back inside.

Privately, Piazza suspected that Yankee's emphasis on the flowers had been pressed upon him by the sheriff. No explanation made perfect sense. But there were loose ends in every homicide case; unless Lessenberry forced his hand, Piazza had no intention of discussing it.

"Did you ever know of your own knowledge," he asked, "where that money came from?"

"She told me she had it in the safe deposit box . . . [but that] she got tied up in traffic and couldn't get to the bank. . . . I just called Larry and told him we had a problem with the money. I told him it would be Tuesday when the banks opened up. He wasn't worried about the money because Larry trusted me, and I told him we already had the money."

"And you trusted her?"

"Yeah. I trusted Lee. I thought she actually had it. Maybe she did. I don't know."

Before he sat down, Piazza wanted to remind the jurors of the web Mary Lee had woven. He asked whether Yankee had ever met Dr. Wulz, Joyce Holt, or Larry Burge.

"I never met any of her friends," Hall said. "She made it a point that she didn't want us to be seen together . . . until this was over with and kinda died down."

"Did she ever indicate what type person she thought Alice McArthur was?"

"Well, just really sorry. She just had a list of things. First of all she indicated that [Alice] had been going out with Bob Troutt for quite a while, and this Bob and Bill McArthur evidently are pretty serious enemies. In fact she referred to him as the enemy, you know. And she said also that [Alice] was fixing to leave Bill and take his two children and move to Louisiana. . . . She said that [Alice] knew something about Bill and was going to wipe out his law practice. And she was going to try and take over the interest in the club. She really made her sound like, you know, just a cold-blooded person."

Piazza knew a perfect exit line when he heard one. He turned abruptly to Lessenberry at the defense table. "You may ask," he said, and quickly sat down.

It had been a masterful performance, holding observers spellbound for more than an hour. In his opening argument, Piazza had warned jurors that they would find Yankee "a hard and cold individual." In the end, however, the pasty-faced junkie seemed merely pathetic.

•   •   •

Jack Lessenberry began his cross-examination after a ten-minute recess. Having promised to expose numerous "inconsistencies and irregularities" in the prosecution's case, he labored without much success to pick holes in Yankee's story, implying that Hall's testimony was the result of police coaching.

On several occasions, the defense attorney repeated the same questions in slightly different form after Hall had already said that he didn't know or couldn't remember the answer. Intended to suggest that some of Yankee's memory lapses were too convenient to be credible, Lessenberry's sarcasm succeeded only in making the witness angry. But the lawyer had his reasons. Courtesy of Dr. Wulz, Orsini had come up with a brand new alibi for the night of the car bombing. The veterinarian claimed to have discovered only days before the trial that he and Mary Lee had attended a production of *Oh What a Lovely War* at the Arkansas Repertory Theater on May 20. Wulz had produced the ticket stubs. The play had ended after 10:00 P.M. As a result of this last-minute revelation, Wulz would be testifying for the defense rather than the prosecution.

Claiming a poor memory for dates and times, Yankee testified that he and Orsini had met around midnight. On previous nights, they'd made test runs by the McArthur home to reconnoiter. Once they'd even masqueraded as joggers, giving Mary Lee a chance to slip down the steep driveway in front of 24 Inverness Circle to identify Alice's car. On May 20, however, they'd dallied by the river before making their move.

Lessenberry hammered away, but Yankee never budged. Challenged, he grew more belligerent by the moment. As Hall saw it, he had no choice but to testify against McClendon to save himself from the electric chair. The cops had already known Larry's name when they busted him. But testifying against Orsini was an act of revenge. From where Yankee sat, her lawyer was the personification of everything in "straight" society he despised. And the harder Lessenberry pushed him, the more openly he let it show.

"Why did you ask [around] for a silencer for a .38?"

"Lee was wanting one."

"I'll bet I could have guessed that answer, Mr. Hall."

"Amazing, isn't it?"

Piazza objected, and Lessenberry apologized and changed directions. If the original plan had been for Mary Lee herself to plant the bomb on Alice's car, he wondered, why had Yankee volunteered to do it?

"I was just afraid that she might make a mistake."

"You were afraid that she might get hurt?"

"Yes."

"But you weren't afraid that someone might get killed?"

"I just said I agreed to do it," Yankee answered.

"You weren't afraid that somebody would get killed?"

"No."

After a brief recess, an exasperated Lessenberry ran himself into a final corner. Apparently hoping to suggest the absurdity of doing a murder without seeing the money, he asked Yankee if he'd ever sold cocaine on credit. Hall witheringly answered that he had. How deep a hole the defense had dug for itself became evident on re-direct. Piazza asked Yankee why he'd refused to bomb Chief Younts's car. Essentially, Hall answered, because it was a screwy idea and he had nothing to gain.

"You were asked if you sold cocaine ever on credit, and you said you did," Piazza continued. "Why would you do that?"

"It's called 'fronting' people," Yankee explained. "You fronted them until they got rid of it."

"Would you front people that you didn't trust?"

"Oh no. Very few people."

"You trusted her, didn't you?"

"Yes, sir."

The prosecutor's re-direct had taken fewer than three minutes. Eugene "Yankee" Hall's time in the spotlight was done. Orsini's attorney had never mentioned the flowers.

•   •   •

In what remained of Monday afternoon, Piazza managed to present five more prosecution witnesses. The medical examiner testified that Alice's death had been instantaneous and the body had not been moved. A ballistics expert established that the bullets recovered at the crime scene had been fired from a Smith & Wesson snub-nose .38 exactly like Dr. Wulz's missing gun. An ATF agent described the mechanism of the bomb found under Alice's car on May 21, and introduced into evidence the shampoo bottle filled with Tovex explosive found lying in the driveway.

In terms of corroborating Hall's testimony, the two most important witnesses were Tammy Oaks and Carl Ray Williams. Oaks described how Yankee and Mary Lee had showed up at their place in Faulkner County to pick up the explosive from her boyfriend. She identified Mary Lee without hesitation. What had stuck in her mind, she said, were the defendant's "real pretty blue eyes."

The swarthy, bearded Williams, who admitted under cross-examination that he'd realized that Yankee had planted the bomb from the moment he'd read about the shampoo bottle in the newspaper, also remembered Orsini vividly. "She had a pretty butt," he told the jury, "and some nice boobs."

•   •   •

Press and broadcast accounts of the trial's first day were unanimous in giving the most prominent possible play to Bill McArthur's supposed involvement in the plot. Ignoring the crime scene photos and the testimony of several witnesses, the *Gazette* courtroom reporter described how Sally Pernell had discovered Alice McArthur's legs "sticking out of a closet." The same account made much of Piazza's spiderweb metaphor, but took more than twenty paragraphs to get around to mentioning that Yankee had never met the victim's husband. The latter point proved altogether too subtle for TV. To the casual viewer, the effect was as damning as a grand jury indictment. McArthur himself, announcers promised, was expected to take the witness stand some time Tuesday.

Piazza's first witness on Tuesday morning, however, was Joyce Holt. He quickly drew from Holt a description of the fantasy world in which Orsini had enmeshed her—her supposed partnership in BJ's Honky Tonk, the McArthurs' marital problems, Orsini's torrid affair with Bill, and Sheriff Tommy's revelation of Alice's affair with the nefarious Bob Troutt.

Joyce told the jury about an anonymous call Orsini had supposedly gotten in May warning that Troutt was planning a bombing. Based upon Mary Lee's almost daily meetings with Tommy Robinson, Holt said, she'd simply assumed that her friend had informed the sheriff. Her cheeks reddened with embarrassment as Piazza asked repeatedly whether or not she had personal knowledge that any of the stories Mary Lee told her were true. Over and over again, Holt answered that she had none.

On cross-examination, Lessenberry did his best to suggest that Holt herself had originated much of the gossip. Getting nowhere, he tried another tack. "Now you yourself knew," he began, "that Bill McArthur had been sued for alienation of affection for somebody's wife he was seeing . . ."

Piazza jumped to his feet to object—as Lessenberry had known he would—but not fast enough to prevent the press from snapping to attention. A brief but acrimonious hearing followed out of the jury's hearing, with the prosecution arguing that Bill's love affair six years ago was irrelevant and prejudicial, and reporters happily scribbling every word. In fact, no lawsuit had ever been filed, but that wasn't the point. Nor was Judge Williams's ruling that Lessenberry could ask witnesses only about their direct personal knowledge of the McArthur marriage. Until now, the public had only its imagination to go on. Tomorrow's newspapers would be avidly consumed.

•   •   •

A pair of expert witnesses followed Holt, each helping Piazza to corroborate Yankee's confession. Anticipating Larry Burge's testimony, he presented a state police handwriting expert who verified Orsini's handwriting on the script she'd written out for Burge. Next the Southwestern Bell security director traced the documented trail which Mary Lee, with her odd mix of cunning and stupidity, had left on her phone bill. On May 8, a third-party long-distance charge from the Bates Bait Shop in Mayflower to Carl Ray Wilson confirmed Yankee's memory that they'd phoned ahead for directions en route to buying the dynamite.

Phone company traps on both the Orsini and McArthur telephones outlined the rest of the story. Orsini had called the McArthur residence four times between noon and 2:00 P.M. on the fatal afternoon of July 2. The trap on her own phone documented each call Yankee said he'd made that day too. Interestingly enough, Orsini, while supposedly afraid for her life, had ordered the trap removed four days *after* the McArthur murder. But not before the device had recorded the two calls Larry Burge had made from coin phones on July 5 to read Mary Lee's handwritten script.

. . .

Phoebe Pinkston took the stand in the late morning. The secretary hadn't laid eyes on Orsini since their meeting at her husband's pawn shop on July 3, when she'd come away convinced of the woman's involvement. She'd already made up her mind that she would refuse to look at Mary Lee.

Phoebe was a nervous wreck. Already consumed with guilt for blurting out to Orsini information about her boss's life that she had no business telling, she was also afraid that she would say the wrong thing and provoke a mistrial. Whatever she did, Piazza had warned her forcefully in a pre-trial interview, she mustn't refer to the Ron Orsini murder case. Aware of what a good criminal defense lawyer could do to a witness, she dreaded facing Lessenberry on cross-examination. What if he tricked her into it?

Had it not been for her obsession with Bill McArthur, Piazza believed, a social climber like Orsini wouldn't have given the secretary a moment's notice. He thought the jury would sense that. Besides demonstrating how Mary Lee had used the unsuspecting woman to pry into Bill and Alice's private lives, Piazza drew from Phoebe a history of Orsini's fascination with BJ's Honky Tonk. Phoebe also told the jury about the peculiar conversation she'd had with Orsini at 5:15 P.M. on July 2—interrupted by Orsini's melodramatic announcement of a mysterious black man at her front door carrying flowers.

The confrontation with Jack Lessenberry that Phoebe had been dreading never really happened. The defense attorney contented himself with establishing that there was nothing unusual about clients developing an emotional dependency upon their lawyers.

"Did she ever express any concern about the safety of Alice McArthur to you?" Lessenberry asked.

"Yes she did. The best that I can remember, one time she called me and she said, 'Phoebe, tell Alice not to set up any particular pattern of what she does every day.' This was after the bombing incident. She said she had made the same mistake herself, and if somebody is following you and you do the same thing every day, they know what you are doing all the time."

"Did that seem like good advice?"

"At the time, it seemed like good advice."

Excusing Phoebe for a few minutes on re-direct, Piazza then brought Detective Al Dawson to the stand just long enough to introduce the cassette tape LRPD detectives had removed on July 2 from the tape recorder attached to the McArthurs' home phone. Bringing Phoebe back to the stand, Piazza asked Dawson to punch the "play" button. The jury heard Alice answer the phone and a woman's voice asking for her mother, then apologizing for a wrong number. The second voice, Phoebe affirmed, was Mary Lee Orsini's.

"Have you, over a year, talked to her almost daily on the telephone?"

"Yes, sir."

"And the person who responded," Piazza asked, "who is that?" Choking back tears, Phoebe identified Alice McArthur.

"Did she have somewhat of a deep voice?"

"Yes, sir."

The witness was excused. Phoebe's cousin Diane Dutton then described Orsini's making the calls from McArthur's office that afternoon, and also identified her voice on the tape.

• • •

After the lunch recess, florist Lillian Garnette described the bouquet she'd made up for Yankee, and identified it in a photograph. From their undamaged condition, she concluded that the flowers couldn't possibly have been dropped.

• • •

Having set the stage for what he hoped would be the trial's most dramatic testimony, Piazza stepped aside. By prior agreement, Dub Bentley took on the job of questioning Larry Burge.

Taking his sweet old time as usual, the rumpled prosecutor led Burge through an account of how he'd met Orsini by listing her home with Block Realty, and had swapped cars with her after the April 8 shooting incident. When she'd finally returned his maroon Honda on June 28, the car looked as if it had run half the gravel roads in the Ozarks, and had a cracked windshield.

"Did she ever mention that she knew Yankee Hall?"

"No," Burge said. "She told me repeatedly that she did not know Yankee Hall."

Dub established that Burge had never met Bill McArthur, but had heard Orsini's story about Alice's supposed affair with Bob Troutt. Then the prosecutor turned to the weekend after the murder. Burge said he'd made three anonymous calls to the PCSD on July 4 identifying Larry Darnell McClendon as the killer. "The first call, I believe, went to Bobby Woodward. I also talked to Larry Dill, and later . . . I talked with Tommy Robinson himself."

"You didn't know whether it was true or not, did you?"

"I did not know. She had told me that she got this call and I didn't have any reason not to believe it."

Bentley moved ahead to Monday, July 5. "She showed me some notes," Burge said, "that she had taken down from the telephone call that she had received and had the information jotted down on these yellow pages of paper."

Burge explained that she'd convinced him that the sheriff would give her story more credibility if she could produce physical proof. He sheepishly described how he drove out to a pay phone on the Old Conway Highway and read the script, then did it a second time after she told him the recorder had malfunctioned.

"What was it she told you to tell her?"

"Well, the information that she said the Sheriff's Department needed was to reiterate the accusation against Mr. McClendon and to name Mrs. Alice McArthur, Mrs. Holly Troutt and Mrs. Lee Orsini as three persons who were supposedly on a hit list. . . . She'd mentioned that McClendon had a white, male running buddy who was even meaner than him."

On the handwritten script Bentley subsequently introduced, McClendon's running buddy is described in considerable detail as "a small man—about 5'7"—talks funny—mustache—thinning hair—early 40's—long, but thin scar on left side of face—this is an ex-con, friend of Mike Willingham and Forrest Parkman. This man has stalked and asked lots of questions about Lee Orsini & Holly Troutt." There could be no mistake: it was Yankee Hall.

The most dramatic moment of the trial arrived exactly as Piazza had planned it. Dub brought in Detective Al Dawson with his tape recorder. The courtroom grew quiet as the tape began to roll. Burge's poorly disguised, lisping voice was unmistakable.

"These cases are all related now by the news," they heard him tell

Mary Lee. "You know, you can't mention Troutt without thinking of
Orsini. . . . Some people are very unhappy with you, Mrs. Orsini.
You were on the news again today. What do you need to be on the
news for? You're not doing this purposefully, are you?"

"I don't have anything to do with [what] . . . the media picks up
every time they pick up something about Troutt and McArthur."

"Well, it seems like the three of you have become household words,
and I can see where that could be very detrimental to you. . . . In fact,
I think you probably escaped narrowly Friday—from the information
in the paper—and since you were on the list. Your picture has been
circulated around a little bit. Also the picture of Mrs. Troutt and Mrs.
McArthur. The same man had all three pictures. . . . You need somebody to help you out, lady. You are going to be as dead as a thousand-
year-old mummy."

"Well, the Sheriff is helping. I'm very confident in Tommy Robinson and Larry Dill," Orsini maintained stoutly. "I'll assure you that
Tommy Robinson is not going to let anything happen to me. . . . I
didn't kill my husband. Somebody wouldn't be trying to kill me if I
killed my husband. . . . I don't even know Bob Troutt. I don't like
being associated with that person."

When the tape had ended, Dub approached the witness.

"Mr. Burge, does that tape accurately reflect the conversation that
you and Lee Orsini had on . . . Monday, July 5?"

"Yes it does."

"And the information contained there is information that you were
given by her to record at her request?"

"That's true."

On cross-examination, Lessenberry had an easy time making Burge
look like a fool, a harder time making him look like a liar.

"The thing I'm having trouble with," he asked, "is *why* was this
arrangement made on July 5?"

"She had these notes," Burge explained, "and she wanted to put this
on tape because I had asked her earlier if she could tape this person that
was calling."

Lessenberry grasped the only available straw. "And *you* then," he
suggested, "asked Lee if there was some means by which some sort of
re-enactment might be put together?"

"She asked me if I would help her in making this tape to give to the
Sheriff's Department, and I said, 'Yes, I will.' "

"Were you motivated in doing this to hide anything?"

"Me? I didn't want to be in the paper."

A less experienced trial lawyer might have savaged Burge. But his humiliation was so clear that attacking him might only make things worse, and Lessenberry cut his losses.

Judge Williams called for a brief recess. To all the lawyers involved —if not to the reporters on hand—the most compelling evidence against Mary Lee had just been presented. The conclusion was inescapable. Only the person responsible for sending McClendon and Yankee on their mission could have written the script for Burge to read.

Privately, Orsini's lawyers believed that Burge's testimony would have a devastating impact on the jury. During the recess, Tom Carpenter noticed, his client remained unusually subdued. For once, Orsini had no opinions or suggestions, but sat quietly staring out the window into downtown Little Rock. He got the feeling that the gravity of her situation had at last begun to sink in.

●   ●   ●

Piazza had just two more witnesses, and he'd deliberately waited to present them back to back. "It was a calculated decision," he said later, "to prove that the dragon lady was a liar."

Before he called Tommy Robinson to the witness stand, Piazza had pointedly reminded the sheriff that they were on the same side. Neither he nor the judge would tolerate any monkey business in a capital murder trial. Piazza needn't have worried. For all his bluster in front of a TV camera, Robinson almost always behaved himself before a judge. The prosecutor gave him little choice. His part of the questioning took about two minutes.

"In your investigation of this case, and in your dealings with Bill McArthur relative to the bombing incident of May 21st, did you ever have an occasion to interview Alice McArthur and take a tape of her confessing to a relationship with Bob Troutt?"

"No."

"It didn't happen?"

"No."

Lessenberry took a bit longer with the sheriff, with mixed success. He asked Tommy about meeting Burge in Orsini's driveway on the day of the car bombing. Burge had testified that he'd advised Robinson and Dill to check out Yankee Hall. Tommy recalled speaking with the realtor, but denied that they'd discussed anything about the case. Arkansas juries could normally be relied upon to take the word of a police officer over a civilian. If Burge had invented that story, Lessenberry wanted them to think, maybe he'd invented other things too.

"After the bombing of Mrs. McArthur's car," Lessenberry continued, "had you—as Sheriff of Pulaski County—begun to hear different theories about the people that might be involved in the bombing that would make reference to the Troutt incident?"

"Yes."

"Did you hear virtually every conceivable relationship with the different people that were involved here—that is the McArthurs—at one time or another?"

"Twenty-four hours a day, seven days a week."

"Was one of the things you heard the fact or the existence of a relationship between Alice McArthur and Bob Troutt?"

"Objection to what he heard," Piazza said. "That is hearsay, Your Honor." Lessenberry countered that his intent wasn't to show the truth of the statement, merely that others besides Orsini had spread rumors. But Judge Williams sustained the objection. To the dismay of reporters, Sheriff Tommy's testimony came to a quick and uneventful end.

•   •   •

The witness whose testimony all Arkansas had been waiting to hear finally appeared a bit past 4:00 P.M. Tuesday. Immaculately turned out in a three-piece gray suit, Bill McArthur had dressed for his role as a prosecution witness as he always did for a trial. A stranger would have found it impossible to distinguish the handsome attorney from any of the other lawyers in the courtroom. To sympathetic onlookers, Bill's composure reflected a courageous refusal to be broken by tragedy or shamed by Tommy Robinson's accusations. To the majority of Arkansans catching a glimpse on the evening news, however, it seemed to confirm his image as cold, manipulative, and above it all.

Once again, Chris Piazza hoped to confound those who anticipated melodrama. He had two quite limited purposes in calling McArthur as a witness: To underline Orsini's resentment at failing to become a partner at BJ's, and to show that she'd deceived her attorney as thoroughly as she'd fooled everybody else.

Above all, McArthur was a *prosecution* witness. If anybody was going to turn his appearance into an inquiry into Sheriff Tommy's

allegations, it would have to be Lessenberry, and Piazza would do all
he could to prevent that. Not because he intended to try to exonerate
McArthur. Though he'd satisfied himself as to Bill's innocence, the
prosecutor intended to try one case at a time. His job was to put Orsini
away. Period.

"When did you first meet the defendant Lee Orsini?" Piazza asked
after a few preliminary questions.

"In March, 1981."

"And did you represent her from that point forward?"

"Yes, I did." McArthur had not needed to be reminded how important it was not to discuss what he'd represented her about.

Piazza moved quickly to the establishment of BJ's Honky Tonk in
the fall of 1981. "Did you," he asked, "discuss the possibility of the
defendant becoming involved in that organization?"

"At first," McArthur explained, "she mentioned to me that she
might have some friends that might be interested in investing some
money or loaning some money for such a venture." The only name he
recalled, Bill said, was that of a state senator's son Orsini said she'd
been dating. "Later on that passed out of existence and she then talked
about the possibility of her borrowing some money on some land that
she owned, or some property that she had, and investing or loaning the
money to the corporation."

"Did you present the proposition to the members of this organization—including your wife—of the possibility Lee Orsini would become involved?"

"Yes, I did."

"After you made the proposal to your partners, was Mrs. Lee Orsini
accepted in the organization?"

"No."

Piazza next elicited from McArthur a description of how Orsini had
brought him a proposal from an advertising agency that the new club
be named "Tumbleweed." "I did not get the idea," McArthur said,
"that she had actually worked on it—[but] that someone else had. That
she had arranged for it or talked with someone."

"And were these ideas ever incorporated into your organization?"

"No. As a matter of fact, we hired a separate advertising agency to
assist us."

"So she did not become involved in your club?"

"No, not in any way."

Piazza elicited from McArthur a description of Bob Troutt's filing a lawsuit against BJ's, and the surrounding publicity. "During the time that your problems began at the club," he asked, "did you start having more visits from the defendant Orsini?"

McArthur said that he had, starting about the time his partner Bob Robbins was beaten with a baseball bat. "She seemed to be having more and more problems, such as . . . threatening phone calls, an instance where someone shot into her car, and other things."

Not surprisingly, McArthur made an ideal witness. He answered only the questions the prosecutor asked him, without elaborating or adding his opinions.

"And as her attorney, I think you took steps—suggested a trap on the phone?"

"Well, that and got her with law enforcement agencies."

"Sheriff Robinson?"

"Eventually, Sheriff Robinson."

"Were you ever aware that she got another [telephone] upon which there was not a trap?"

"No."

After brief testimony basically reiterating what Phoebe and her cousin Diane had already told the jury about the May 5 birthday party in Bill's honor, Piazza got around to the car bombing. "Mr. McArthur," he asked, "if you had been involved in the bombing incident, is there some particular part of her car—or identifying feature of her car—that you could have told someone who was planning to bomb it?"

McArthur described Alice's beige Cutlass Supreme, with its T-Top and C-A-J-I-N vanity plate.

"It wouldn't take a close inspection of that car to figure out it was Alice's?"

"No. I've never seen one exactly like it."

Yankee had told of jogging past the McArthur home as a pretext for Orsini's looking for a telltale bumper strip.

Only during an account of his last conversation with Alice—a call from his office at 12:37 P.M. on the day of the murder—did McArthur become visibly emotional. Relating how the couple had planned to drive down to Hot Springs that night to spend the Fourth of July weekend with friends, Bill's voice caught and he stopped talking for a moment to brush away a tear. Pausing while he regained his composure, Piazza then asked McArthur what it was Orsini had been so eager to talk about on the afternoon of July 2.

"It really was not terribly important," McArthur said. He described her call from "Art Baldwin" and his notifying ATF agents and the PCSD. "But because of the instructions that she'd given to Phoebe— that she didn't want her name involved—I hadn't told them who the information had come from."

"Why were you concerned with someone who was interested in purchasing your club? Did that create a problem, or suspicion?"

"Yes. I felt that the bombing incident that occurred in May was coming from this club."

"The information that you had regarding harassing calls, shooting out the window of Mrs. Orsini's car—everything you knew about Mrs. Orsini—did it not come through her?"

"If you are talking about those incidents, yes." The only evidence he'd seen, McArthur added, was the day Orsini came running into his office covered with shattered glass.

"Had you ever," Piazza asked, "been present to observe a tape that Sheriff Robinson had where Alice confessed to having a relationship with Bob Troutt?"

"No," McArthur said sharply. "That's absurd."

Piazza led McArthur through a detailed account of his actions on the afternoon of July 2. Using a schematic drawing of the McArthur home and the crime scene photos, he took care to demonstrate to the jury that from the bedroom doorway where McArthur had emptied his pockets upon the dresser, it was a physical impossibility to see into the closet at all—much less into the rear of the large, walk-in closet where Alice's body lay.

"And you did not see your wife in the closet?"

"I did not."

Piazza handed McArthur an 8½ by 11 copy of a photograph taken from the vantage of the dresser. "*Can* you see her in the closet from that particular picture?"

"No sir," McArthur said. "I can't."

Piazza had just a couple of loose ends he wanted to tie up. "Now defendant Lee Orsini," he asked, "had she ever discussed with you the possibility of having a book published?"

"Yes. As a matter of fact, she told me one time that she was supposed to go to New York to visit with the publisher and they were supposed to pay her way up there."

"Was there any reason for her to be calling your home?"

"Unless it would be on business, no."

"In that line," Piazza asked, "had you ever had a relationship—a physical relationship—with Lee Orsini?"

"No," McArthur said firmly, "I did not."

When Piazza turned McArthur over to the defense, Lessenberry seemed at a loss. Anticipating that Orsini's defense counsel would rough him up, McArthur was surprised at how cautiously Lessenberry dealt with him.

From the defense attorney's point of view, however, he had little choice. Very little of what Bill had testified about was in dispute. Unlike the press and general public, Lessenberry had read the sworn statements McArthur had made to the LRPD. He had no evidence to disprove any of it, nor any reason to believe in the existence of a police conspiracy to protect McArthur.

Lessenberry also had an ethical problem. Back before the Dill tapes had materialized, Orsini had authorized him to tell McArthur's own lawyer that Bill had nothing to do with the crime. If Sheriff Tommy ever succeeded in bringing McArthur to trial, Lessenberry might end up being called as a defense witness.

Suppose that Lessenberry *did* succeed in answering the prayers of half the reporters and all the soap opera fans in Arkansas by insinuating a love affair? (Which his client now denied.) Might the jury not conclude that he'd simply done a better job of uncovering Mary Lee's motive than the prosecutor?

About the best that Lessenberry thought he could do was to counter Piazza's theory that Mary Lee had become vengeful over her failure to become involved in BJ's. Given that McArthur was representing Orsini in civil suits, he asked, "would it be unusual . . . that as a client's case was about to come to trial that you began to hear more from them to finalize preparation?"

"No, that would not be unusual, Mr. Lessenberry," Bill said coolly. "But the activity that was being talked about did not relate to the civil matters."

"Oh, it didn't?"

"It related to things like threatening and harassing phone calls. That's what the visits were about."

After venturing down two or three blind alleys apparently suggested by his client, Lessenberry threw in the towel. "Mr. McArthur," he said, "I don't want the prosecutor to think there's anything personal that is about to be asked you, but after your wife's death, do you remember if I wrote you a letter?"

"Yes, you did. A very nice one."

"We have never had any problems, have we?"

"No, sir."

On that apologetic note, Lessenberry took his seat. His entire cross-examination had lasted ten minutes.

Immediately after McArthur stepped down at 5:10 P.M., Piazza rested his case. In two days, the prosecution had presented twenty-five witnesses. Judge Williams recessed the court until 9:00 A.M. Wednesday.

3

Inside Judge Randall Williams's courtroom anyway, Mary Lee was down to her last hero. Sheriff Tommy having meekly done as the prosecutor told him, her entire defense strategy now hinged upon the testimony of Dr. Charles H. Wulz.

Wulz took the stand at mid-morning, Wednesday. An experienced hand at testifying in murder trials, the veterinarian had taken a circuitous route to the witness stand. Until the day before jury selection had begun, Piazza had Wulz penciled in as a prosecution witness. From the moment he'd stomped out of Shoney's on the day of Mary Lee's arrest, Wulz had willingly provided investigators with several pieces of telling evidence.

In the meantime Wulz had been caught in the media spotlight. After several radio and TV stations had publicized the fact of the veterinarian's 1970 acquittal on charges of murdering his wife, Carol Griffee had driven out to Duncan, Oklahoma, to research newspaper files. Besides writing an article stressing Wulz's unhappiness at having his past dragged up again, Griffee had also compiled a more detailed account of the veterinarian's two trials for Sheriff Tommy—highly unusual behavior for a reporter.

During pre-trial witness interviews, Chris Piazza had been amazed to learn that Wulz had switched sides. Once again Wulz had persuaded himself that Mary Lee was the victim of a police conspiracy. When he'd read Yankee Hall's confession in the *Democrat*, he claimed, he'd recognized it as a tissue of lies.

Wulz showed up at the courthouse the day before jury selection claiming that Mary Lee couldn't possibly be guilty. On the night of the car bombing, Orsini had attended the theater with him, he now remembered, then spent the night at his place. He had produced the two ticket stubs, and seemed to expect that the charges would be dropped.

Piazza and Bentley were disbelieving and angry. Taking a calculated risk, Piazza decided not to call him as a prosecution witness. The Rules of Procedure would allow him far more latitude to attack Wulz's credibility on cross-examination. For the defense, on the other hand, Wulz was their only hope. Next to a lowlife like Yankee Hall, the veterinarian's professional standing made him practically royalty, and Lessenberry played it for all it was worth. Midway through Wulz's description of the tasteful, upscale activities he and Lee Orsini enjoyed—theater, ballet, the symphony, and the opera—Piazza objected.

"Your Honor, I don't think *The Barber of Seville* is relevant to the murder of Alice McArthur."

Lessenberry responded sharply. "Mr. Piazza has basically described Mrs. Orsini as a tramp that goes to the Bates Bait Shop to make a telephone call and see Carl Wilson and stay out all hours of the night and plant bombs in places and go around to the Mason Jar. We think this information is pertinent."

Judge Williams asked him to go easy on the details. A few minutes later, Lessenberry got to the heart of the matter.

"Doctor, eventually I'm going to have to ask this question, and I ask that you understand the necessity of it. Have you become sexually intimate with Mary Lee Orsini?"

"Of course," Wulz announced impatiently, as if his manliness had been questioned. There were titters in the gallery.

Wulz began to explain how Tiffany and his daughter stayed together when their parents attended the theater, and how Mary Lee—who hated to sleep at home alone—would spend the night at his house. Piazza objected again. What the couple normally did, he said, was of no relevance.

"I can give you lots of dates," Wulz snapped. Sensing the witness's combativeness, Piazza was deliberately provoking him.

Judge Williams permitted Lessenberry to continue. Wulz began to describe the couple's family-like relationship and Orsini's loving concern for his own daughter. Again Piazza objected. This time the judge sustained him. Wulz was visibly seething.

Lessenberry turned to the night of May 20. Wulz testified that he and Mary Lee had eaten at a wonderful new French restaurant, then proceeded to the performance of *Oh What A Lovely War*. Lessenberry introduced the ticket stubs that the veterinarian had dug from his scrapbook when he'd read Yankee's statement in the *Democrat*. The ticket did not specify a particular date, but Wulz was certain he and Mary Lee had attended the Thursday night performance, as he normally took the afternoon off. After the play, they'd returned to Wulz's condo around 11:30 P.M., where Mary Lee, he believed, had spent the night on his couch.

"I'm not positive," he said, "but I'm pretty sure, because I think I would remember deviations from the normal. The reason for her to spend the night would not be sexual—or not necessarily sexual. . . . If her daughter's at my house, she's going to be at my house most of the time. I would wonder, you know, why is this night different?"

Though hardly ironclad, Wulz offered the alibi with great conviction. A skeptic might have noted that it would be virtually impossible to disprove. Wulz then corrected what he claimed had been his erroneous statements regarding his missing .38 revolver. When he'd spoken to Dub Bentley in July, he had forgotten that he'd last seen the gun several days *after* Yankee had supposedly gotten the murder weapon from Mary Lee. On Friday, June 26, he and Orsini had attended a concert and the veterinarian had been packing heat— made him feel like an idiot, carrying a pistol among respectable people.

Since Wulz's testimony had opened the door, Piazza decided to walk right through it. "You've got notes, extensive notes," he said, indicating a sheaf of paper Wulz held. "Do you recall the date that you came to Mr. Bentley's office to visit with him?"

"July 18th."

"And on that date, did you not tell Mr. Bentley that you weren't sure if Mrs. Lee Orsini spent the night on May 20th?"

"I was not sure of a lot of things the first time I talked with him," Wulz said. "I really hadn't dug into anything like this. I hadn't gone to look for tickets. I hadn't gone through wastebaskets looking for things."

"So really what you are testifying to is what usually happens, is that correct? . . . So she *usually* spent the night with you. What time did she *usually* go home?" With each repetition Piazza grew more sarcastic.

Most of the time, Wulz said, she'd be asleep on the couch when he went off to work.

"And since I talked with you in my office, have you come up with an explanation as to why you called her May 21st at 6:47 in the morning?" Once again, Mary Lee appeared to have shot herself in the foot. The trap on her phone had recorded the call. Wulz wasn't certain, but she'd worn a jogging outfit to bed and had probably gotten up early to exercise.

From Piazza's point of view, things were getting better and better. Yankee had testified, he felt sure the jury would recall, that Mary Lee had worn the same jogging suit to slip around the McArthurs' Pleasant Valley neighborhood undetected. For good measure, he decided to have another go at the theater tickets.

"Isn't it strange," he began, "the Repertory Theater—as I understand—they don't have assigned seating, do they?"

"No, they do not."

"So when you go to Repertory Theater, you give them your ticket and, generally, they just take it, don't they?"

"That's not right," Wulz objected. "I didn't tear that ticket, if that's what you are saying."

"I didn't say that," Piazza said coolly. "Dr. Wulz, you've mentioned that you have this relationship with Mrs. Orsini. You mentioned that you and she like to participate in Repertory Theater, etc. Now the truth of the matter is that you remained friends because she kept you on the edge of your seat, did she not?"

"That's true." Wulz couldn't deny it. He'd used those exact words in an interview with Detective Al Dawson—confiding that while he'd fallen in and out of love with Mary Lee, her adventures held him in thrall "like a good detective novel."

"And the reason you were on the edge of your seat is because things seemed to happen to her, did they not?"

"That's true. That's not the only reason, but what you're saying is true." Wulz admitted he'd had no personal experience of threatening calls, "hit men," or any of the other thrilling events Orsini described to him. But he'd indeed feared for his life.

"In fact, it got to the point where you carried your gun while you jogged, didn't you doctor?"

"I did."

"And which gun did you carry, the .38 or the .22?"

"Sometimes one and sometimes the other."

Spectators, who had begun to titter a few minutes earlier, burst into guffaws. His lips compressed into a thin line, Wulz flushed with anger and embarrassment. Piazza played to the crowd.

"Where do you carry a .38 when you jog?"

"In my hand."

"And do you recall that when you determined that the pistol was missing, that you made a report to the police?"

Until Dub Bentley asked him on the phone, Wulz had not reported the theft. " 'How in the world do you know that?' " he'd asked the prosecutor. "He said, 'Oh, just a wild guess.' It really sent chills up my spine because I couldn't imagine how he would know that."

"And you probably couldn't imagine how you had lost it?"

"Well, I really couldn't," Wulz said.

Piazza moved in for the kill. "You'd become somewhat jealous in this relationship, hadn't you?"

Wulz denied it, but Piazza drew from him a description of the night of April 6, when he'd written down the license number of a car parked in Orsini's driveway at 3:00 A.M., then jogged by at 5:00 A.M. and seen that it was gone. (The young woman who'd given the car to Yankee for repair had previously testified.)

"Did Lee tell you Yankee Hall had been there that night?"

"No."

"Did she admit that anybody had been there that night?"

"No."

Piazza pilloried Wulz a bit longer. "And is your relationship," he asked, "more than just Arkansas Repertory Theater, but is it based upon rather bizarre circumstances such as, did she not inform you that Jim Guy Tucker had you followed?"

That brought Carpenter and Lessenberry to their feet. In chambers, Orsini's attorneys moved for a mistrial on the grounds of intentional misconduct. A heated argument ensued. Piazza had the ex-congressman waiting in the wings, prepared to testify that he'd never knowingly laid eyes on Mary Lee Orsini. The defense argued that Piazza's only purpose was to prejudice the jury. The fact that Orsini might be a liar didn't make her a murderer.

The prosecutor countered that he meant to prove the good doctor just another bit player in the fantasy melodrama that had led to Alice McArthur's death. If Wulz were permitted to answer the Jim Guy Tucker question, Piazza would seek to draw him out on a statement he'd made to Sergeant Al Dawson to the effect that Orsini was obsessed with marrying a person of wealth or position. Rule 404 *did* permit evidence that spoke to the planning and preparation for the crime.

Legally speaking, it was a close call. Judge Williams recessed for lunch to give everybody a chance to think it over. Over a sandwich, Piazza decided that he'd already discredited Mary Lee's alibi for the

night of the bombing. There was no point winning the argument at the
risk of reversible error. He agreed to drop the Jim Guy Tucker question, and the judge admonished jurors to disregard it.

Wulz's time on the witness stand came to an indecisive end—
leaving him perhaps even more embittered about lawyers and judges
than his own two trials had done.

· · ·

What remained of Orsini's defense went downhill fast. Lessenberry
called an expert witness, a telephone installer, for an explanation as to
how Mary Lee had come to phone Alice McArthur several times on
the day of her murder. Supposedly she'd somehow misprogrammed
the automatic dialer on her telephone. The man testified that in examining the device in October—three months after the fact—he'd
pushed a button marked "Mom," only to have the fool thing ring the
McArthur residence.

Before Lessenberry called Tiffany Orsini, he requested a meeting in
chambers with the judge. He wished to have his client state for the
record that she wanted to testify.

"Do you think that you are prepared to take the witness stand at this
time?" Lessenberry asked.

"No," Mary Lee said. "We have not had time to make arrangements
for you and I to get together with all the other things you have had to
do in preparing for this case in order for me to testify."

Lessenberry and Carpenter had convinced themselves that if Orsini
were convicted, an appeal would win her a new trial on either of two
issues: inadequate discovery, or pre-trial publicity. With some difficulty they had persuaded Orsini that it would be in her best interest not
to take the witness stand and face cross-examination.

Whether or not Tiffany Orsini was aware, as she took the witness
stand in her mother's defense, that Mary Lee had accused her of
murdering her stepfather is impossible to say. Her testimony was limited to the domestic arrangements in the Orsini household. Indeed,
Lessenberry himself seemed uncertain exactly what it was that the
fifteen-year-old was expected to contribute to the defense.

"I want to ask you if there is an ice pick in the house?"

"No, sir. Not to my knowledge."

Yankee, of course, had testified that Mary Lee would lock him into
the bedroom lest Tiffany come blundering in and discover him. Upon

returning, she would adroitly balance two coffee cups in one hand and unlock the bedroom door with an ice pick. Instead, the girl said, she used barbecue skewers.

Tiffany recognized Yankee, whom she said had replaced the glass in the window of her mother's Caprice when it was shot out. She'd personally admitted him to the house and shown him to her own bathroom.

Tiffany affirmed that she had never known her mother to date anybody other than Dr. Wulz, that Bill McArthur had called Mary Lee on Tiffany's private line, and that she herself had gotten hang-up calls on her mother's line—although no threats or anything that upset her.

Piazza approached the cross-examination gingerly. None of Tiffany's testimony touched directly upon his case. The defense had put her on, he figured, mainly to generate sympathy. He could only alienate the jury by appearing to pick on a child.

"Tiffany," he said, "your relationship with Dr. Wulz is one where you probably trust him pretty much, don't you?"

"No, sir."

"You don't trust him?"

"I don't trust anybody," Tiffany said sullenly.

"You don't trust anybody?"

"Well, except for my mother."

For a long moment, the courtroom went dead silent. Even the law students in a glassed-in enclosure overlooking the courtroom who had been hooting during the testimony about the misprogrammed telephone went quiet. Piazza felt his neck prickle. "My God," he remembered thinking, "it's *Rosemary's Baby, Part II*—sequel to Mary Lee."

"Except for your mother," he repeated. He turned to the judge. "That's all I have, Your Honor."

The defense rested. An audible groan went up from spectators who had filled every seat and jammed the aisles of the courtroom as it dawned upon them that the glamorous defendant herself would not be testifying. Giving both sides overnight to prepare their closing arguments, Judge Williams recessed the court until 9:00 A.M. the following morning.

After the judge left the courtroom, Tiffany flung herself into her mother's arms. PCSD deputies serving as bailiffs made no attempt to interfere as Julia Hatcher joined them, and the three women cried long and hard in full view of the jury. Afterward, Mary Lee was led away in handcuffs.

The Little Rock media made no effort to hide its disappointment over Mary Lee's failure to testify. Faithful throughout to its own preoccupations, the press had continued to play the sex and money angle for all it was worth. An out-of-town reader trying to make sense of the proceedings in the *Gazette* might easily have gotten confused about who was on trial. MCARTHUR TESTIFIES IN WIFE'S SLAYING, DENIES CHARGE HE HAD AFFAIR WITH ORSINI, read the headline on Wednesday's front page.

In ordinary newspaper usage, of course, the word "charge" indicates an accusation made by the police—almost the exact opposite of what had actually taken place. Nowhere in veteran courthouse reporter George Bentley's voluminous but confusing account of the day's testimony could the reader learn *who* had asked McArthur the fateful question, much less *why*.

Preoccupied with the sexual angle, the *Gazette* also focused on the Did they or didn't they? angle in Phoebe Pinkston's testimony. The newspaper neglected to mention that Sheriff Tommy had testified, and all but ignored Joyce Holt's appearance. Larry Burge's crucial testimony was relegated to a brief summary forty-odd paragraphs into the story. Orsini's handwritten script, regarded by every lawyer involved as the single most crucial piece of evidence in the case, was barely mentioned in the *Gazette*'s story. But the dispute in chambers between Piazza and Lessenberry concerning McArthur's ill-fated six-year-old love affair drew coverage in both Little Rock newspapers.

The rival *Democrat* did a far better job of describing the prosecution's case and assessing the relative importance of its witnesses. But the smaller newspaper had roughly half the *Gazette*'s circulation and a fraction of its influence among that portion of the Arkansas populace capable of making critical judgments about anything more complicated than a Razorback game. TV and radio reports, as always, followed the *Gazette*'s lead.

By far the most hurtful aspect of the *Gazette*'s coverage, however, had come in a front-page "sidebar" by Carol Griffee. Ostensibly sent to the trial to file "color" pieces about the spectators, Griffee weighed in with a thinly disguised editorial:

IN BEDROOM, BUT DIDN'T SEE
BODY, MCARTHUR TESTIFIES

William C. McArthur testified Tuesday that he walked into the bedroom where his wife, Alice, lay dead and emptied his pockets on a dresser without seeing her body. . . .

Investigators have long wondered why McArthur didn't see his wife's legs in the doorway of a closet of the bedroom even though he had hung his coat on a rack at the bedroom door and had gone into the bedroom and emptied his pockets on the dresser.

Actually, McArthur had hung his jacket in a room across the hall. But like the "investigator" who was feeding her information, Griffee had evidently neglected to examine the crime scene photos and paid scant attention to McArthur's testimony. The *Democrat* weighed in with an unsigned "Analysis" listing all the information—Alice's $50,000 a month inheritance, for example—that the prosecution had supposedly withheld from the jury. The accusation couldn't have been clearer had the articles been written by Sheriff Tommy himself.

· · ·

Chris Piazza was entirely too combative not to notice the press criticism, but the only audience that concerned him on Thursday, October 7, was the twelve jurors. The prosecutor's passionate closing argument lasted nearly an hour. Utilizing the same drawing of a spiderweb he'd used to open the trial, he left nothing to chance, pounding away relentlessly at every piece of evidence corroborating Yankee's confession, and lampooning Dr. Wulz.

A bitter conflict broke out in the midst of Jack Lessenberry's closing argument. "This jury cannot, this jury should not, this jury must not find Mary Lee Orsini guilty," he contended, "because she is, one, not guilty. Two, because she hasn't been proven guilty. And three, if you find her guilty the investigation of the murder of Alice McArthur will be closed."

Piazza jumped to his feet with an objection, and Judge Williams sustained him. Lessenberry turned to the judge. "I think it is appropriate, Your Honor. I want those who are responsible for the death of Alice McArthur to come to trial and to be baked. But what you do here to this lady is going to affect that."

Piazza approached the bench. The prosecutor's problem was twofold: That the jury had heard no evidence to support Lessenberry's argument, and that the investigation had, in fact, not been closed. Williams again sustained him.

Picking up where he left off, Lessenberry tried to argue that the car bombing and the murder were separate crimes. "You have heard evidence about a bombing," he said, "but you are not to use that in reaching guilt on the entire case. . . . Another jury at another time . . . will consider that bombing."

"I hate to interrupt Mr. Lessenberry," Piazza said, "but that is not the law."

"That is a fact," the judge agreed. "That is not the law. Jack, that is not the law and the jury is to consider the evidence that was submitted in this case."

Piazza objected several more times to aspects of Lessenberry's arguments, and the judge sustained him every time. Obviously flustered, Lessenberry confessed to the jury that they'd just heard the worst closing argument of his career.

•   •   •

Toward the end of his rebuttal, Piazza returned once again to the spiderweb he'd drawn on the blackboard. Pausing dramatically, he adopted a quiet, confidential tone. "But, ladies and gentlemen," he said, "there is one thing that has not been talked about this whole trial. The whole focus of this trial has been on Lee Orsini. Lee Orsini is the hub of this incident. She's . . . the center of interest in this courtroom."

Whipping off his suit jacket, Piazza used it to scrub Orsini's name off the chalkboard. "I propose to you," he said more loudly, "that there was another name that should take some of your interest in this case, and, as Mr. Lessenberry did, I will wipe the board. And, ladies and gentlemen, that name is Alice McArthur."

The gallery burst into spontaneous cheering and applause.

The jury of eight men and four women stayed out for more than eight hours, fueling speculation of a mistrial. Mary Lee stayed in the courtroom, spending most of her time chatting animatedly with Dr. Wulz, Tiffany, and a small group of friends. Bill McArthur retired with a group of his own supporters to the coffee bar of the courthouse across the street. Chris Piazza joined them once or twice for a cup of coffee. He assured reporters that he'd expected the jury to deliberate for a long time. They had a great deal of complex evidence to sort through.

After taking a dinner break, the jury signaled that they'd reached a verdict at 9:20 P.M. Even before McArthur's party made its way across the street and back to the third-floor courtroom, the decision was being read.

"We the jury," said Foreman Tom Milton, "find Mary Lee Orsini guilty of capital murder and fix her sentence at a term of life imprisonment without parole in the Arkansas Department of Corrections."

Those sitting immediately behind the defense table saw Mary Lee's knees give away as if she'd been shot. Her lawyers held her upright. Lessenberry asked that the jury be polled. One by one, each juror affirmed the decision. Tiffany threw herself into the arms of her mother's sister, bawling like a calf. She clung to her aunt as TV cameramen did their best to capture every tear. A male relative begged fruitlessly for the photographers to leave her alone.

After being allowed a few moments alone with Dr. Wulz, Mary Lee was escorted out of the courtroom and into a PCSD van by Tommy Robinson and Larry Dill. They took her to the county jail to await transport to the penitentiary.

Lessenberry and Carpenter, complaining that they'd had insufficient time to prepare, promised an appeal. Brushing back a tear of his own, Bill McArthur expressed his satisfaction and refused comment about his own case. Chris Piazza, looking satisfied and almost boyish in victory, diplomatically thanked Dub Bentley for trusting a thirty-three-year-old assistant to handle so momentous a case. He emphasized to reporters that it had been the diligent work of Sergeant Al Dawson and the LRPD Homicide Division that was responsible for bringing Mary Lee Orsini to justice.

Sheriff Tommy, however, assured reporters later that he personally had solved the case. In keeping with the canons of journalistic objectivity, newspapers accorded equal weight to both claims.

4

At somewhere close to 3:00 A.M., Carol Griffee was awakened by a familiar voice on the phone. Having sat up for hours with Tommy and Larry, Orsini informed the groggy reporter, she'd finally decided to come clean. "She said she was guilty of conspiracy," Griffee said later. "*But* that there were other people involved who were equally guilty who were not convicted. Bill McArthur was one that she named, but there were others. I think she thought I would know who she was talking about."

Griffee did, in fact, have some ideas, all of which had been supplied to her by Sheriff Tommy. A shadowy figure known only as "Bill's nigger," Robinson insisted, had gotten into the McArthur house some time after the killers had fled—dragging Alice's body into the back of the closet and setting the bouquet of flowers at her feet.

Griffee had no idea what to think. Previously, she'd been led to believe that Alice's body had been found lying in the closet doorway with her feet sticking out into the room. Everything she'd written about the crime scene evidence had been based upon that presumption—and also the presence of flower petals in the hallway outside the bedroom door. Now the sheriff was telling her that neither of those things was true, but that an unknown black retainer of McArthur's—never again mentioned in connection with the case by Robinson or anybody else—had moved the body and cleaned up the flower petals.

Tommy's abrupt about-face worried the *Gazette* reporter. Orsini's new story she flat did not believe. She did, however, half-suspect that Mary Lee—whom she'd come to think of as a victim of multiple personality disorder—believed at least some of it. Even so, Griffee came to fear that somewhere beneath it all lay an even larger and more dangerous conspiracy than she'd previously imagined. The key word, she remained convinced, was "cocaine."

"What she said was that if she didn't play along—she told me this, okay?, I never bought it, but this is what she told me—if she didn't do what Bill wanted, that he would say that Tiffany shot Ron. And Lee would go to prison rather than let him do that.

"Bill had her hypnotized in Memphis, that she found the gun somewhere in the rafters, and that she gave the gun to Bill. And that from that point on, he was telling her that he, Bill, had figured out that Tiffany had done it. And he was going to use that gun as evidence to that effect. And if she, Lee, didn't do what Bill wanted her to do, that it was going to cost Tiffany.

"And she wasn't going to let that happen. She'd rather go to jail than let anything happen to Tiffany. She'd take the rap. This was the story that came out in the very rambling conversations where she would call me on the telephone."

Soon Griffee began hearing from Dr. Wulz as well, pushing the same story. Mary Lee's new version of Ron's death seemed to have resolved all of the veterinarian's doubts about her truthfulness. Griffee's talks with Orsini sometimes went on for hours. As near as the reporter could tell, Mary Lee was always alone. Normally she claimed to be calling from Dill's office in the CID, at other times on Tommy's personal phone. That much the *Gazette* reporter had no reason to doubt. Now a convicted murderer, Mary Lee had the run of the county jail.

. . .

On Friday, October 8, under a five-column front-page headline announcing Orsini's conviction, the *Gazette* published two large photographs side by side. One was of a weeping Mary Lee being escorted from the courtroom by Larry Dill. The other was a full-face closeup of Bill McArthur lighting a cigarette—his lips pulled tight and his eyes narrowly focused, making him look like the most cold-blooded customer west of the Mississippi. Traces of the tears of relief with which friends say he greeted news of Orsini's conviction are not apparent.

On Saturday, October 9, the front-page headline in the *Democrat* read:

"LEE" ORSINI AWAITS PRISON;

ROBINSON STALKS KINGPIN

In his Sunday column, John Robert Starr paused to consider the broader implications of the Alice McArthur trial. Chris Piazza's failure to ask Bill McArthur any tough questions struck the *Democrat* managing editor as highly suspicious, as did what he described as the almost incredible bungling of the LRPD. More to the point, however,

> I had lunch last Wednesday with some friends who are longtime observers of and participants in Arkansas politics. The discussion, quite naturally, turned to the political ramifications of the McArthur case.
>
> The consensus: If [Special Prosecutor Sonny] Dillahunty succeeds in convicting McArthur, both he and Robinson can write their own tickets in Arkansas politics for the next few years.

A few days later, Starr made it clear which ticket Tommy Robinson was inclined to write for himself. "The real battle," he opined,

> is between Sheriff Tommy Robinson and what he sees as a determined effort by the Pulaski County legal community to protect William C. McArthur at any cost. . . .
>
> Robinson calls his phantom opposition the Brotherhood of

Locomotive Engineers (no offense intended to the trainmen's union).

"They'll railroad the average citizen, but they'll go to any lengths to protect one of their own," Robinson said.

Robinson believes that the "establishment" is coming after him with everything they've got. . . .

Because she has been convicted, Mrs. Orsini is past the point where the state could make a deal for her testimony. Her sentence, set by a jury, cannot be reduced except by an act of clemency by a Governor.

The state has nothing to offer her, except . . .

Well, some wag suggested it, and I'll pass it on to you. Robinson could promise her clemency at some future date when he is elected governor.

The way *Democrat* reporters had it figured, the "wag" in question could only be Tommy himself.

Book IV

1

Like a man being swept away in a flood, Bill McArthur knew exactly what was happening to him. What he didn't know was how to save himself. No native Arkansan even halfway familiar with the state's history, much less one who'd lived through Orval Faubus's tumultuous six terms as governor, could fail to recognize that Sheriff Tommy had succeeded in raising an electronic lynch mob. Historically prone to outbursts of populist zeal, an aroused citizenry demanded justice. An anonymous woman on a radio call-in show in Little Rock spoke for thousands. "I wouldn't trust that Bill McArthur further than I could spit," she said. "And I ain't a spitter."

A small sampling of the daily media barrage in the weeks leading up to Bill McArthur's November 22 probable cause hearing suggests the near hysteria gripping the city and state. To those trying to make any sense of it, the press reports seemed almost slapstick. A few days after Orsini's conviction, Sheriff Tommy Robinson announced that he'd survived another assassination attempt by an unknown assailant who had taken potshots at him as he'd driven along the freeway after midnight. Once again, there were no witnesses and no physical evidence.

Next, Tommy announced that a death threat had been made against Mary Lee Orsini. According to a report on Channel 11, the sheriff had received an anonymous letter from an inmate at the Diagnostic Unit of the state penitentiary: the writer had overheard a plot being hatched between two assistant wardens and a man with a foreign accent to poison Orsini's food. Tommy had dutifully passed the letter on to Orsini's new attorney, whom she had hired at his urging. Tom Donovan, an obscure Yell County attorney, was to handle her appeal. Donovan stressed the importance of Mary Lee's remaining under the sheriff's vigilant protection in the Pulaski County Jail.

Meanwhile, Mary Lee continued to have the run of the joint. A prisoner who'd shared a cell with Orsini later told Dub Bentley that Mary Lee was never in it before midnight, and sometimes not even then. "One wonders," joked the prosecutor, "just what did their investigation consist of? There must have been a lot of foreplay." The same woman later swore that Orsini had offered her $5,000 cash to testify that she'd bought cocaine from McArthur.

PCSD deputies confided to former NLRPD Sergeant Buddy Miles, then a courthouse bailiff, that Mary Lee spent hours at a time alone and unsupervised in Robinson's office, working at the typewriter and chattering away on the phone. A *Gazette* reporter was interviewing Tommy one day in October when the sheriff dialed Larry Dill's number in the CID. Mary Lee answered the phone and informed him that Dill was not available.

A bit less than three weeks after her conviction, Orsini began telephoning jurors. According to Barry Haas, a thirty-four-year-old purchasing agent for the Southern Farmers' Association, Mary Lee wanted to talk about which jury members had shown the most skepticism about her guilt. She also wanted to know if Haas might have changed his mind had she testified.

Haas complained to the jury foreman, who took a letter to Judge Randall Williams. The judge ordered Robinson to monitor his prisoner more closely. Instead, the sheriff launched a public counteroffensive. On KARN radio, Robinson insisted that telephone logs showed that Orsini had not, in fact, made the call. "I smell a rat," Tommy said.

The sheriff alleged that the complaining juror was a golfing buddy of Chris Piazza's, and that the prosecutor had even bragged to him about having a close friend on the jury. (During voir dire, Haas had testified that he'd once played nine holes with Piazza as part of an impromptu foursome at a public course. Chris hadn't recognized him, and the defense did not object.) Accusing Piazza of willful misconduct, Robinson called Mary Lee's trial a "scam" and "a mockery of the criminal justice system." He gave a speech at Sylvan Hills High charging that she'd been framed.

Judge Williams had heard enough. After reading Tommy's accusations, he ordered Orsini removed from the county jail and taken to the state penitentiary. "Forthwith," he added, "means this afternoon." Addressing Robinson at the impromptu hearing, he reminded him that a gag order still applied. One violation and "someone is going to jail, and it won't be for two or three days."

Despite the judge's order, Mary Lee remained closeted with her attorney at an office at PCSD headquarters for several hours. Emerging that night, she faced the reporters and TV cameras and read a brief statement. "I have given Tom Donovan, my attorney, a sworn written statement concerning the death of Alice McArthur—who I did not have killed—to be opened in the event of my death. I directed my attorney to release the contents of this written statement in the event I should die."*

Two weeks later, on November 10, a near-jubilant Chris Piazza filed a pleading with Judge Williams. Tom Donovan had not filed a notice of appeal within the thirty days required by law. Donovan claimed the law was ambiguous regarding when the thirty days began to run. The thirty-day period was standard in all Arkansas felony cases. Orsini had forfeited her right to appeal in state courts. Piazza asked that Williams declare her sentence final.

After a brief hearing on Friday, November 12, the judge did so. Orsini might still file a federal writ of habeas corpus, but in the absence of a serious constitutional issue, she had little hope of success. In the hallway outside the courtroom, a melee erupted in full view of reporters and TV cameras as Tommy confronted Dub Bentley. Shouting and shaking his finger in the prosecutor's face, the sheriff told Dub he had him "under surveillance" and threatened to pick him up for questioning. Larry Dill added that he might haul Dub in personally, saying he wouldn't need anybody's help.

Bentley had no doubt that Tommy had been spying on him for months—if only for purposes of intimidation. PCSD patrol cars had shown up on his rural property on Stagecoach Road several times for no apparent reason. Just before Orsini's trial, one of the prosecutor's dogs had been shot. A receptionist on his staff had moved into a rented house down the road and found her telephone connected directly to Bentley's line. Dub wondered whether Tommy had some involvement

---

*Orsini's letter never saw the light of day, although Attorney Donovan eventually tried to broker Orsini's sale of it to a Little Rock TV station.

in these incidents too, but never found evidence linking Tommy to his problems.

A few days after Judge Williams's ruling, the sheriff announced that both Bentley and McArthur were prime suspects in Ron Orsini's murder. "We'll go to [Bentley's] office, and if he's not there," Tommy threatened beneath a five-column *Democrat* headline, "we'll find him wherever he is. Then we'll read him his rights." Two days later, the sheriff claimed he'd been misquoted.

•   •   •

As his November 22 court date approached, Bill McArthur felt paralyzed. David Hale, the municipal judge who would hear the case against him, was not the boldest jurist in town and seemed highly unlikely to throw himself in front of the Tommy Robinson steam-roller. No matter what kind of bullshit evidence Special Prosecutor Sonny Dillahunty put on, Bill believed that Hale would bind the case over to Circuit Court for trial.

A protégé of the late Senator John McClellan—the segregationist patriarch of the Arkansas Delta—Sonny Dillahunty had become a Republican during the Nixon administration's famous "Southern strategy." Having been appointed U.S. Attorney, Dillahunty subse-quently lost his job during the Carter administration. Like many lawyers in town, Bill had always had little respect for Dillahunty's legal acumen.

From the first, it appeared to McArthur's lawyers that Sonny Dil-lahunty had allied himself with Tommy 100 percent. On three sepa-rate occasions in September and October, Bill's attorney Jack Holt had written Dillahunty offering to bring his client to PCSD headquarters where the special prosecutor had set up shop. On the condition that Orsini give a sworn statement beforehand, McArthur agreed to answer any and all questions. They didn't expect to see Orsini's statement, merely to know that one existed. According to Holt, however, Dil-lahunty had never replied.

What little McArthur and Holt could gather about the much-touted investigation being conducted by Dillahunty puzzled them. The sher-iff's minions in the press continued to flail away at Bill's mythical $50,000 a month inheritance. Dillahunty, Dill, and the sheriff made a trip down to Golden Meadow, where they drank up a good deal of wine at Leonard Miller's restaurant on the bayou. Alice's brother tried to set them straight, and introduced them to the Louisiana attorney—then prosecuting attorney of St. Charles Parish—who had handled the original real estate transfer back in 1975, and who had also set up the McArthur children's trust. But PCSD files contain no record of the meeting, and Dillahunty failed to subpoena either man for the upcoming hearing.

Bill McArthur continued to reject the advice of friends to defend himself publicly. He intended to put on his defense only once—in a courtroom, not a press conference. And only *after* Orsini was locked into whatever story she told. That was not only his right, it had become a matter of survival.

2

Across the river in North Little Rock, meanwhile, Sergeant T. J. Farley had gone back to work on the Ron Orsini case with renewed vigor. Robinson and Dill's attempt to get him to arrest Tiffany had started him thinking. Mary Lee's power over her mother and daughter had been obvious all along. But if she were now willing to blame the kid, she must be confident that Tiffany couldn't return the favor. Back in 1981, Farley had looked into the possibility that Tiffany had been drugged unconscious. The family pharmacist assured him that Mary Lee had no access to sedatives strong enough to do the job. The grand jury had wondered too, and had sent Orsini to fetch the pharmacy records. It was on that unlucky day that her purse had vanished from her car. The pharmacist, since deceased, had then told the grand jury what he'd told Farley.

But what if the druggist had been mistaken? It seemed unlikely that he'd given Mary Lee his only copy of the records. Now, in October 1982, Farley got his hands on the originals, and what he found there jolted him. On September 18, 1980, Mary Lee Orsini had filled a prescription for fifteen 30-milligram capsules of Dalmane, a potent sedative. Written by a doctor other than the family's regular physician, the prescription had been refilled twice: on January 27, and then on March 3, 1981, a week before Ron's murder.

Two or three Dalmane capsules, he learned, would have rendered a horse unconscious, much less a 100-pound thirteen-year-old girl. Even more striking, the medication's side effects—dizziness, headaches, drowsiness, and confusion—were exactly the symptoms that Tiffany and Mary Lee had reported to the school nurse on March 12. Mary Lee might have been dosing the girl for days, experimenting to find out how much it took to put her out.

Farley should have found it eighteen months ago, but it was new evidence, and that was all Dub Bentley would need to reopen the case.

3

Under the Arkansas Criminal Code, a probable cause hearing only vaguely resembles a trial. Normally a formality, its purpose is to determine not guilt or innocence, but whether or not the prosecution has any case against a defendant sufficient to bring charges.

The stronger the evidence, therefore, the shorter the hearing. Most took less than half an hour. But Sonny Dillahunty had subpoenaed scores of witnesses, including several whose identity was unknown to McArthur and his lawyers. Unlike a grand jury proceeding, Bill had the right to cross-examine witnesses, and to present testimony of his own. But all kinds of evidence is admissible in front of a municipal judge that a trial jury might not get to hear—including the more exotic forms of hearsay in which Mary Lee specialized. Perhaps most important in the case of *State of Arkansas* vs. *William McArthur*, the Rules of Discovery did not apply. Apart from the transcripts of her jailhouse colloquies with Dill, made public during her own trial, until McArthur and his lawyers heard Orsini testify, they'd be flying blind.

And astonishingly enough, one witness Dillahunty had not called was Eugene "Yankee" Hall.

• • •

Things got under way at 8:30 A.M. on Monday, November 22, in the same third-floor courtroom at the UA-Little Rock School of Law where Orsini's trial had taken place six weeks earlier. The same TV camera crews, the same photographers, many of the same spectators, and almost all of the same newspaper reporters had returned for what they hoped would be an even more diverting spectacle.

Dillahunty called Dub Bentley as his first witness. The special prosecutor, whose slicked-down hair and dandified manner made him resemble a somewhat taller version of Senator John Tower of Texas, asked Bentley if he'd discussed the case with McArthur or his lawyers. Of course he had, Dub answered. McArthur had been a prosecution witness at Orsini's trial. Dillahunty seemed satisfied. On cross-examination by Jack Holt, Dub affirmed that he'd stepped aside only because of the allegations against his office.

"If it had been any other case," Holt asked, "is it fair to say that you would have nol-prossed it [i.e. dropped charges], absent accusations?"

"Without question."

Next Dillahunty presented several witnesses whose relationship to the case was not apparent. An LRPD officer testified to a burglary at McArthur's office more than a year ago in which several items—including a .38 revolver of a different make and model than the murder weapon—had been reported stolen. Buddy Miles read a list of handguns that had been removed from 7412 Pontiac on the morning of Ron Orsini's murder. Yankee's roommate testified about the 30.06 deer rifle found by LRPD detectives who searched his apartment on the day of his arrest. Dillahunty made no effort to link any of the weapons to the murder of Alice McArthur.

Things continued in the same bewildering fashion all morning. A waitress from Bob Troutt's place testified that she'd seen Bill McArthur talking to Mary Lee at the Kowboy Kountry Klub one night in 1981. In the version that had already appeared in the newspapers—courtesy of Troutt—McArthur had introduced Mary Lee as his wife. On cross-examination, however, it turned out that the waitress had merely assumed so.

"The biggest part of the people that sit in my section," she explained, "were usually husband and wife."

"So for that reason and that reason alone, you figured that this lady that you saw Bill McArthur with was Mrs. McArthur?"

"Yes."

"How many other couples would you say were at that table?"

"Probably, maybe eight couples."

"Did they all seem to know each other?"

They did. The incident had taken place on the same night Orsini had insinuated herself at the McArthurs' table, and Alice had snubbed her. Dillahunty had spent fifteen minutes establishing that McArthur and Orsini knew each other. Judge Hale seemed willing to allow the special prosecutor all the time in the world.

Dillahunty's fifth witness was an unfortunate Vietnam War veteran from Moro, Arkansas, a cottonpatch crossroads in the Mississippi River bottomlands of Lee County. Bobby Blair, an amputee McArthur had once represented in a lawsuit against the Veteran's Administration, remembered coming by the law office at 2020 Broadway one day in May and seeing a Cadillac parked across the street. Inside, he'd realized after seeing him on TV in July, was Larry Darnell McClendon.

Dillahunty produced a photo of McClendon's car, which Blair identified. The CB antenna on the trunk made him quite sure. The special
prosecutor exhibited a large-scale street map on which Blair indicated
where the automobile had been parked. He offered the witness a packet
of photographs, proving—if not beyond a doubt, since Blair explained
that McClendon's hair looked different and the distance left him uncertain—that he could identify a man whose image had appeared on
TV and on the front page of the newspaper numerous times in recent
months.

When Jack Holt, Bill's lawyer, questioned him, it emerged that
Blair had first voiced his suspicions to his psychiatrist. Under treatment
as a paranoid schizophrenic, he testified that the police followed him
everywhere, and that gunshots had been fired at his car, bullets whizzing in one open window and out another.

On Dillahunty's re-direct, his identification of McClendon faltered
even more. He began to tremble. "I've been over this with so many
people," he said, "that it's getting to where I'm not sure if the sun is
going to rise tomorrow."

Blair's time on the witness stand ended in pathos.

"You can't remember?" Holt asked him.

"No sir. I remember, but I just . . ."

The witness fell silent, staring blankly into space. "Let the record
reflect," Jack Holt said after a long moment, "he did not answer my
question."

. . .

After the lunch recess, Dillahunty presented several witnesses who'd
seen Yankee and McClendon together before Alice McArthur's murder. None had any evidence linking either man to McArthur. Then he
called the Reverend George Bynum, a self-anointed black preacher
who had lost a civil rights suit against two LRPD patrolmen for allegedly beating him during an investigation into the theft of two
chickens. Bill McArthur had represented the two police officers in
federal court.

Bynum testified that he'd been on his way to visit his attorney at 9:30
A.M. on July 1—the day before Alice McArthur's murder. Inside an
elevator in the Union National Bank Building downtown, he'd recognized Bill McArthur, Mary Lee Orsini, Larry Darnell McClendon,
and Yankee Hall. He said McArthur was carrying a leather briefcase
chained to his wrist.

Bill's law partner Jack Lassiter handled the cross-examination. It didn't take long. Bynum refused to identify an uncle and nephew he'd said had accompanied him to the bank. The lawsuit he'd come to discuss with his attorney, court documents proved, had actually been settled weeks earlier. Nicknamed "Chicken George," he was a familiar courthouse figure, having filed twenty-six auto insurance claims and lawsuits in a recent year.

Denying any grudge against McArthur, Bynum insisted that he'd seen Bill and the three killers in the Union National Bank. However, Bill had been involved in a hearing at the Saline County Courthouse in Benton, twenty-five miles away, on the morning of July 1.

. . .

By late afternoon, the special prosecutor had yet to present a single credible witness with evidence about the case. The significance of his calling Dr. Fahmy Malak, however, was lost on nobody. Born in Cairo, Egypt, and educated in London, the Arkansas medical examiner was widely regarded as a friend of law enforcement. Indeed, the general opinion among criminal defense lawyers was that Malak's autopsy findings tended to support what the police wanted to hear. Nobody accused Malak of dishonesty, just stubbornness. A stocky man with a clipped Arabic accent and an imperious air, Dr. Fahmy Malak had never made a mistake.

Contrary to what LRPD detectives, the coroner, and Malak's autopsy had concluded, Dillahunty hoped to suggest that Alice had been shot elsewhere and her body moved to the closet upstairs by her husband. What McArthur was supposed to have gained by this stratagem never was made clear.

The special prosecutor made no progress with the pathologist. Nowhere on the premises other than the bedroom closet, Malak pointed out, was there even a trace of the victim's blood. He demonstrated that the trajectory of the fatal bullet was identical with the one dug out of the wall. "Both of them traveled downwards in a forty-degree angle," he said. "So in my opinion, Mrs. McArthur died as a result of a single gunshot wound inside the closet, beneath the lower shelf. She had never been removed from there."

When Dillahunty sought to ridicule his contention that the victim had crouched beneath a shelf only thirty-nine inches from the floor, Malak twisted himself into the exact position in which Alice McArthur had been found. "From her neck to her buttocks," he demonstrated, "was 33 inches. So we can achieve a squatting position much less than 39 inches. This lady was in a defensive posture. . . . It was point blank."

Seated at the defense table, Bill McArthur flushed and averted his eyes. He took off his glasses and busied himself cleaning the lenses. Dillahunty asked Malak with heavy sarcasm to explain how Alice McArthur could have been found clutching a pen in her left hand.

"This is very simple to explain," Malak said. "In numerous occasions I did autopsies in cases [where] people shoot themselves and keep grasping the gun. . . . This is a post-mortem phenomenon known as cadaveric spasm."

With no positive evidence for Sheriff Tommy's scenario, Dillahunty did his best to muddy the water. Upon cross-examination, however, it emerged that Robinson and Dill had done a good deal more than that. Unhappy with the pathologist's ruling, they'd presented themselves at his home one Sunday night demanding that he change it. The discussion had grown heated.

"From what you tell me, Doctor," Holt said, "apparently the entire purpose of this trip . . . was to get you to do two things: to make a decision that you were wrong, in that Alice was holding that pen, that she should have dropped it; and number two, that there's no way she could be shot under that shelf. . . . They wanted to substitute their opinions for your opinions as the state medical examiner, isn't that true?"

"The answer is yes."

Dillahunty made no progress with Malak on re-cross either. As the first day of the McArthur probable cause hearing came to a close, it must have been clear to Sheriff Tommy that even bolder efforts would be necessary to secure McArthur's conviction.

• • •

First thing Tuesday morning, Sonny Dillahunty called Sally Pernell, and spent about half an hour putting the attractive, soft-spoken woman through her paces about the discovery of Alice McArthur's body. As he'd done in a previous interview with Pernell, Dillahunty avoided the question of the flowers. But on cross-examination, Jack Holt underlined the point.

"Did they even ask you whether or not there were any flowers in the closet?"

"I was never interviewed by anyone from the Sheriff's Department at all."

"Not at all. And yet you are the party that discovered Alice." Holt paused to let the irony sink in. "One other item that is of concern to me," he said. "I don't know whether you recall, but I do, reading an article which stated—and I believe it was in the *Gazette*—that 'There were feet sticking out of the closet.' Did you read that too?"

"Yes sir, I did."

The assertion had appeared in a front-page story implicitly questioning the truthfulness of McArthur's testimony at Orsini's trial.

"Is that a true statement?"

"No."

"It never has been a true statement?"

"No."

"Do you know how that even got reported?"

"I have never spoken to a reporter at all," Pernell said.

Next, Dillahunty spent the better part of an hour running an expert witness from Southwestern Bell through the same evidence from the traps on the Orsini and McArthur telephones that had already been explored at Mary Lee's trial. By mid-morning, it began to appear to McArthur's attorneys that Dillahunty's game plan was to go for sheer duration. Defense attorneys could normally rely upon impatient judges to speed things up, but Hale seemed willing to allow the special prosecutor infinite latitude.

Dillahunty was about ten minutes into questioning the proprietor of the Mason Jar—the dive where Yankee did a lot of his drinking—when Jack Holt finally objected. "Your Honor," he said, "there has been no connection or no tie-in to Bill McArthur on this matter. We will stipulate that this man knows Yankee Hall and he has seen Yankee Hall together with a black man that might be McClendon. We have been very lenient about this, but unless he can tie this to Bill McArthur, I want to interpose an objection."

Hale allowed Dillahunty to continue. But when he did, the special prosecutor got a nasty little surprise. To swallow Mary Lee's tale that McArthur had blackmailed her, it was necessary to believe that she and Yankee were mere acquaintances. Expecting him to affirm that he'd never seen Hall and Orsini together, Dillahunty was clearly taken aback when the bartender, Benny Edwards, answered that the couple had visited his apartment. To limit the damage, the prosecutor quickly sat down.

Holt pounced on it. "Did you know her to be one of his girlfriends at the time? I understood he had several."

"Right. Well, he had mentioned to me that he had dated her."

"So you just figured he was dating her and he brought her out for what? For you to look over? . . . Did you look her over?"

"Yeah, I did."

"Did you approve of what you saw?"

"I guess."

"All during that time, did you ever hear the name of Bill McArthur?"

No, Benny Edwards answered, he never had.

•   •   •

Late Tuesday morning, Dillahunty called Tiffany Orsini. For tactical reasons, it was imperative that the girl take the stand ahead of her mother.

Whether or not Tiffany was aware that her mother had accused her of Ron Orsini's murder, nobody seemed to know. Dillahunty appeared to have made it his business not to find out. In his pre-trial interview, the special prosecutor had avoided asking Tiffany about her stepfather's death.

Tiffany entered the courtroom in the company of Tom Donovan. Far from being fired for failure to file a timely appeal of Orsini's murder conviction, he had been retained to represent Tiffany too. It was unclear whether Donovan knew about the blackmail story. If he did, the attorney had an ethical problem of his own. Given the stakes, McArthur's lawyers could be expected to go for the jugular—if not in a probable cause hearing, then certainly during a murder trial. And when they did, whose interest would Donovan represent—Tiffany's or her mother's?

Under Dillahunty's careful guidance, Tiffany affirmed that Bill McArthur had called her mother several times on her own private line—listed under "T. R. Orsini" and never trapped. She said that Bill had visited her mother at home once or twice in the daytime. On several other occasions she'd been hustled off to spend the day at her grandmother's.

But the key to Dillahunty's case was to prove Orsini's contention that Bill had taken her to Memphis to be hypnotized.

"When your mother went to Memphis," Dillahunty asked, "do you know who she went with?"

"Mr. McArthur."

Bill Putman, who was assisting Jack Holt, objected. "Your Honor," he said, "I'm going to object unless a proper foundation is laid. If it is hearsay from her mother, it would be inadmissible."

"I asked her if she knew," Dillahunty responded.

"I understand," Putman said tartly. "I also have a statement that Mr. Dillahunty took from her, and I know how she knows."

A fifty-nine-year-old trial lawyer from the university town of Fayetteville, Putman had volunteered to defend McArthur free of charge. He and Bill's father were old friends from Bryan McArthur's railroad days.

Putman and Sonny Dillahunty had been friends at the U. of A. Law School back in the early fifties, but the longer he'd watched the special prosecutor in action, the more irritated he'd become. Known throughout the Ozarks for his flamboyant style of defense, Putman was also impatient with Jack Holt's more courtly style. As he saw it, Robinson and Dillahunty's prosecution of McArthur was pure demagoguery and needed to be confronted as vigorously as possible.

Dillahunty tried again. "Do you personally," he asked, "know this person she went with?"

"Yes, sir," Tiffany said. "She went with Mr. McArthur."

"Did she stay out of town all day, overnight, or come back the same day?"

"She came back the same night."

"Mr. Dillahunty," Judge Hale interjected, "unless you can show how she knew it, I'm going to strike it."

"How do you know?" the prosecutor asked.

"Well, because she told me."

Again Putman objected, and this time Hale agreed. Next the prosecutor hoped to get Tiffany to confirm Mary Lee's June 9 trip to Hot Springs. But the girl had forgotten. Dillahunty prompted her. "Do you recall giving me a statement about tennis shoes, borrowing yours?"

"Yes, sir. She went somewhere to a tennis tournament with Mr. McArthur."

Again Putman objected. Tiffany's knowledge, he knew from her pre-trial interview, was pure hearsay and Dillahunty knew it. Judge Hale, however, lost patience with the defense.

"Without a jury being here," he said, "I hope you understand I can distinguish between what is admissible and what is not." True enough. But the hearing record wouldn't, and unless he required Dillahunty to lay the proper foundation for his questions, the judge himself would only be guessing.

Putman decided to get the job done on cross-examination. "You say that you have seen Mr. McArthur at your house? . . . How many times?"

"I don't know."

"Well, can you give us a rough estimate? Are you talking about one time, or two or three times, or dozens of times?"

"I have only seen him over there a few times."

Putman produced a copy of a sworn statement Tiffany had given to Dillahunty and Robinson on October 29. "Did you tell the truth then?"

"Yes, sir." But she couldn't recall whether Dillahunty had asked her about McArthur's visiting her mother at 7412 Pontiac. "I don't remember exactly what all was asked me," she said.

"Let me ask you this," Putman pressed. "After asking you about Yankee Hall, did Mr. Dillahunty ask you this question: 'What about Mr. McArthur? How often have you seen him at your house?' Isn't it true that you answered, 'I haven't ever seen him over at my house because I was away at school most of the time?' "

Donovan whispered in her ear. "I'm not going to answer any more questions," she said stubbornly, "unless you give me a copy."

Putman handed her one. After glancing at it, Tiffany responded that she'd actually meant to answer an earlier question about seeing Yankee and McArthur together. Even for Mary Lee's daughter, it was nimble footwork for a fifteen-year-old.

Putman read the entire exchange for the record. According to the transcript, Dillahunty had clearly asked her if she'd ever seen Bill McArthur at her house, and she had replied that she never had. "Are you telling us that you were confused? . . . You were trying to say that you had never seen him over there when Yankee Hall was over there?"

That was precisely what Tiffany had been trying to say. "I remember seeing him after my father was killed quite a bit, because he was working on Mother's case—and there was other evidence that he'd been there when I wasn't there."

"You told Mr. Dillahunty that Mr. McArthur called on your telephone and talked to your mother. How many times?"

"I don't know. Just enough to get me angry."

"How many times did that take to get you angry, roughly?"

"From him, two or three."

Regarding the trip to Memphis, Putman finally asked, apart from what Mary Lee told her, "You have no personal knowledge of where she went or what she did or who she might have been with, is that correct?"

"Just what she told me."

"The same thing is true about the trip to Hot Springs, correct? All you know is what your mother told you?"

"I have no reason," Tiffany said defiantly, "to doubt what my mother told me."

•   •   •

Mary Lee Orsini took the witness stand immediately after the lunch recess. A stir of anticipation greeted her entry into the courtroom. Accompanied by Tom Donovan, Orsini wore her black hair swept up into a chignon, and a simple dark dress with a broad white sailor's collar. She answered Dillahunty's opening questions in a soft voice that could scarcely be heard at the defense table. The special prosecutor urged her to speak up.

"Mrs. Orsini," Dillahunty asked, "do you, of your own knowledge, know if there was an agreement between Bill McArthur and Yankee Hall to cause the murder of Alice McArthur?"

"I have personal knowledge that there was such an agreement."

"Mrs. Orsini, did you and Bill McArthur go to Memphis, Tennessee, to see a Dr. Foote, a hypnotist?"

"Yes, sir."

"What happened after you returned from that trip?"

"Bill climbed into my attic, found a gun, he wrapped it in a towel and took it with him, and I've never seen the gun since."

"He took the gun and you have not seen it since?"

"Yes, sir."

"I would like to show you one thing, Ma'am. Would you look at Exhibit Number 5? Can you tell me if that is your signature on that piece of paper?" He handed Orsini a copy of her Hot Springs motel receipt dated June 9.

Mary Lee read from a slip of paper in her hand. "At this time I respectfully decline to answer any further questions. I invoke the protection of the Fifth Amendment to the U.S. Constitution, which does not require me to testify."

"Would that be your answer if I asked you any further questions?"

"Yes, sir."

"I have no further questions," Dillahunty said. He sat down, his manner suggesting that he was not surprised.

A hubbub broke out among the spectators. At Jack Holt's request, the judge granted a fifteen-minute recess so that he might fetch some documents he'd left in his office. When the hearing resumed, Holt introduced himself to the witness.

"Mrs. Orsini, I'm Jack Holt, one of Bill McArthur's lawyers. I want to know what your personal knowledge is about Bill's participation in any conspiracy to kill his wife."

Orsini read her Fifth Amendment statement again.

"If the court please," Holt said, "I move to strike her testimony in this regard, in that it deprives the defendant the right of cross-examination."

"Your Honor," Dillahunty countered, "the witness answered the question that she does know that there was an agreement."

"This is in violation of the Sixth Amendment and the right of cross-examination, Your Honor."

"Anything she testifies to," Hale affirmed, "they have the right to cross-examine concerning it." No American judge could have ruled otherwise. The constitutional right to confront one's accuser is as fundamental to the Bill of Rights as the ban against self-incrimination.

Turning to Orsini, Holt asked his question again. Mary Lee once more read her statement verbatim.

"I move that it formally be stricken," Holt said. "Your Honor, it's not evidentiary in nature, or based on law."

"I don't think I have any choice," Hale said.

The spectators burst into an uproar. Without Orsini, Dillahunty had no case to present. The judge gaveled them into silence and threatened to clear the courtroom.

The farce continued for more than half an hour. Producing a large-scale blow-up of the transcript of Orsini's phone conversations with Larry Dill, Holt began to read aloud from the passages in which Mary Lee had laid Ron's murder off on Tiffany.

"Bill had her in that office," Holt read, "and he talked to her, and he talked to her. . . . He had me convinced that there was a very strong possibility that she could have done it."

Now the cat was out of the bag. Whatever Tiffany had known about her mother's accusing her of blowing her stepfather's brains out, it would be all over the TV and newspapers. Orsini had outsmarted herself again. The little smirk she'd been wearing vanished, but she continued to read the Fifth Amendment disclaimer from the paper in her hand.

Holt kept reading Orsini her own words. " 'You remember the trace metal tests where I had it just on the tip of my finger? That's because I picked the barrel of the gun up. See, I just barely picked the gun up.' What this means right here," Holt said, "is that you or someone close to you took your husband's life. You were there at the scene and picked up the murder weapon and got rid of it. That's what that means, doesn't it?"

Orsini invoked the Fifth again, but Holt bored in. "Have you claimed to many people," he asked, "that you have had a very close and deep, intimate affair with Jim Guy Tucker when, in fact, you don't even know the man and he doesn't know you? . . . Have you operated under alias names? . . . Have you told acquaintances that you've also had an intimate affair with Judge Tom Glaze, when in fact that is not true? . . . Have you not told your close friend Joyce Holt that Bill McArthur had nothing to do with Alice's death?"

After each question, Orsini read from the sheet of paper in her hand—thirty-four separate times in all.

"Did you have an agreement with Sheriff Robinson," Holt thundered, "that you would either receive a new trial or get commutation of your sentence if you would come here today and make your simple statement that you have a personal knowledge Bill McArthur was involved in his wife's death?"

Orsini read her prepared statement.

"Mrs. Orsini," Holt said, "I'm going to ask you whether or not you have had conversations with Sheriff Robinson and Deputy Dill concerning your testimony?"

He got no answer.

"Your Honor," Holt said, "I would like to state that this question has nothing that is self-incriminatory—the question as to whether she has conversed with these two people. I would like the Court to order her to answer, and if she refuses, then I ask the Court to place her in jail and keep her incarcerated until she answers the question."

"Mr. Holt," Mary Lee sassed, "I have a life sentence. I don't think you can get much further than that."

The judge reminded Holt that he had no power to compel testimony from a witness who took the Fifth. He would take under advisement the defense motion to strike Orsini's testimony. Her composure seem-

ingly restored by Holt's frustration, Mary Lee exited on Donovan's arm
like a successful leading lady.

Many judges would have dismissed the charges on the spot. Hale,
however, ordered the hearing to proceed. Nor had Dillahunty yet
touched bottom. Next he called Dr. William M. Foote, a "hypnotherapist" from Memphis. Foote testified that he'd attended Mississippi
State University and taken his doctorate from someplace called the
Bernheim Institute in Chicago.

"Do you recognize anyone in the courtroom that you've seen in
your office as Bill McArthur?" Dillahunty asked.

"Well, I wouldn't know what his name might be," Foote said hesitantly. "Now if you mean the man that came with Mary Orsini to see
me, he had a mustache. But he resembles that gentleman in the light
grey."

Foote indicated the clean-shaven McArthur.

"Doctor, did you have an occasion to see Mrs. Orsini and Mr.
McArthur at your office?"

"Yes I did. It was sometime in the spring or summer of 1981. I don't
recall the exact date. . . ." Foote began. A woman had called him and
made a Saturday appointment. "With hypnotherapy, I administer
treatment for weight loss, habit modification or self-confidence, various and sundry phobias, concentration, retaining memory. Or if a
person is an insomniac, or in cases of a person maybe misplacing
something such as papers, lost rings or whatever—because the sub-
conscious mind never forgets a thing."

"Now where would you have Mrs. Orsini, and where would Mr.
McArthur be during this procedure?"

Putman began to object, but Hale anticipated him.

"I understand that he does not know," the judge said. "It was some
gentleman that looks like him."

"Your Honor anticipated my objection precisely."

The hypnotist explained that he'd allowed the man accompanying
Mary Lee to sit in on the therapy session. "They were trying to locate
a pistol. . . ," he explained. "She said that she had come home and
found her husband dead on the bed, and figured it must have been a
suicide. But she thought that maybe there was something strange,
because they couldn't find a gun anywhere. And she said that she had
gone through somewhat of a state of shock, and couldn't remember
exactly what transpired immediately after that. So she wanted me to
hypnotize her and see if maybe she had possibly seen this pistol. And

during the hypnotic conduction, she did recall where she'd seen it. As I recall, it was in the attic, I believe under some asbestos or piling."

"Do you make any record when you are doing it, Doctor?"

"I usually do, yes."

But Foote could produce no record of the session, written or taped; he claimed that, in keeping with his standard practice, he'd turned these records over to Orsini. Aware that his witness had made less than a devastating impact, Dillahunty did his best to firm up Foote's identification of McArthur. The hypnotist reaffirmed that the man identifying himself as Orsini's lawyer had worn a mustache.

"Mr. Foote," McArthur's lawyer began with studied nonchalance, "I'm Bill Putman."

"I'm *Doctor* Foote, sir."

"I'm sorry, I did not mean to indicate any disrespect for your professional title." As Putman had hoped, the hypnotist had stepped right into the trap. "You said 'doctor,' " he continued. "What kind of doctor are you, an M.D.?"

"No, no, no. An M.D. knows nothing about hypnotherapy."

"Well, what kind of degree do you hold that gives you the right to call yourself a doctor?"

"Hypnotechnologist, a Doctor of Hypnotechnology."

Putman elicited from Foote a description of his two years of study at the Bernheim Institute. What, he wondered, were the requirements for admission?

"You should have at least two years of accredited college," Foote responded. He had attended Mississippi State, majoring in entomology.

"Entomology? The study of insects?"

"Right."

"That's quite a move, from insects to hypnosis."

"Yes, sir," Foote affirmed proudly. "It is."

Putman lured Foote into an elaborate description of his therapeutic powers—appetite control, memory enhancement, and the like. "Hypnotherapy," the witness said, "covers a wide field. . . . Most people's only knowledge of hypnosis is what they observe through the entertainment medium."

"You see it on TV?"

"It leaves a lot of misconceptions, yes sir."

"As all lawyers know," Putman conceded, "Perry Mason doesn't do it the way it's done in court." Having put his witness at ease, he asked in the same relaxed tone if there were anything really impressive Foote could do by hypnosis. "Something you think would be a real attention getter?"

The hypnotist, however, turned shy and needed to be coaxed. "Sir, I don't believe you're answering my question," Putman said. "My question is: Is there anything which you do or have done in the past as a hypnotherapist—or advertise yourself to the public as being able to do—which might be a little startling to ordinary uneducated people like myself?"

"Well, most things that are done through hypnotherapy are startling." Foote shifted nervously in his seat.

"What about breast enlargement in women, have you ever engaged in that?"

"Yes, I have."

"Through hypnosis?"

"Yes, sir."

"Have you been running an ad in the Yellow Pages of the telephone directory in Memphis advertising that women can come in to you, submit to your hypnotic therapy—if we want to call it that—and get their breasts enlarged?"

"I have done that before, yes sir. Shall I explain the procedure?"

"No, sir," Putman said with a perfect deadpan. He paused a beat. "I might want to catch you out of court."

Behind the glassed-in enclosure upstairs, the law students guffawed and stamped their feet. Foote's eyes began to dart from side to side as if he were seeking an avenue of escape. In quick order, Putman established that the Bernheim Institute of Hypnotechnology in Chicago apparently did not exist, that a second mail-order school in California where Foote claimed also to have done doctoral work had never heard of him, and that Foote had formerly performed in nightclubs under the stage name "Merrill the Master Hypnotist."

Clearly resentful of Putman's withering tone, Foote said that the first he'd heard of the Alice McArthur case had been eight days before the hearing, when Robinson, Dill, and Dillahunty had presented themselves at his office. On a second visit, they'd shown him a photo line-up. Among the four photographs had been one dark-haired, clean-shaven man and three newspaper shots of mustachioed blonds: Dill himself, former U.S. Open tennis champion Stan Smith, and Bill McArthur. Not surprisingly, Foote picked McArthur.

"Would it surprise you to know, Doctor," Putman asked, "that in the Spring and Summer of 1981, Bill McArthur did not wear a mustache?"

"No, sir. It wouldn't surprise me, because my memory is just like anyone else's. It's not infallible."

In the hallway during recess, Dillahunty was overheard complaining that Putman's recent handling of a case involving a hypnotist had given his old law school pal a big advantage. Not long afterward, what may have been the oddest day of testimony in the history of Little Rock Municipal Court came to a bewildering end.

• • •

By mutual agreement, the defense presented four witnesses the day before Thanksgiving. A prosecutor and a clerk placed McArthur in a Saline County courtroom at the time the Reverend "Chicken George" Bynum claimed to have seen him in a bank elevator with the three murderers. Two supervisors from the Levi Strauss plant where Larry Darnell McClendon worked affirmed that he was stitching blue jeans at that time.

Soon afterward, Judge Hale made an announcement that sent broadcast reporters scurrying for the telephones. Showing more backbone than many had expected, he granted Jack Holt's motion to throw out Mary Lee's testimony entirely. "The defense," he ruled, "was denied the right to cross-examine Mrs. Orsini on the subject matter which she testified to, and that testimony will be stricken, unless the witness subjects herself to cross-examination."

The defense called Leonard Miller. In no uncertain terms, Alice's brother insisted that McArthur had never stood to make a penny from her death—as he'd explained to Robinson and Dillahunty two weeks earlier. Nor, he said in answer to a question from Dillahunty, had he ever stated or implied that he believed Bill guilty.

Major Larry Dill, of course, had written a report dated July 3 describing Miller as having pounded his fist into a table and shouted, "That fucking Bill McArthur killed my sister." Sheriff Tommy had confided it to the press. In a later report describing the same incident, Dill would write that "it is believed" that Miller made the remark to a third party. Ignoring an FBI report to the contrary, Tommy had also told reporters that Miller was "connected" to the Mafia.

Holt had one more question to settle. "Let me ask you," Holt said, "in July 1981 when Bill was in your home, did he have a mustache or any semblance of a mustache?"

"No, sir."

"What about Thanksgiving?"

"That's when he started growing it," the witness recalled, "when he was down in Golden Meadow for Thanksgiving 1981."

4

Meanwhile, the climate inside Little Rock newsrooms had begun to change. On TV, things remained pretty much the same. The nightly exchange of insults and accusations between prosecutor Dub and Sheriff Tommy had descended to the level of sheer farce. During the weeks leading up to the probable cause hearing, however, a number of stories had appeared in both statewide newspapers alerting the skeptical minority to the possibility that what everybody and his Aunt Lurlene wanted to believe about the McArthur murder might not be so.

Although both papers hid the story on inside pages, reasonably accurate accounts of Alice's inheritance eventually appeared. The *Gazette*'s account of Tommy's speech at Sylvan Hills High charging that Orsini had been framed caused an awful lot of readers to wonder whether or not the sheriff was playing with a full deck.

But to say that anything resembling genuine accuracy was ever achieved would be a gross exaggeration. For that to have happened, reporters, columnists, and editors alike would have had to do what newspapers almost never do: not simply eat their words, but explain how they'd been taken, and assess their own role in fomenting hysteria. And that just wasn't in the cards. Newspaper war or not, for the time being, the *Gazette* and *Democrat* were in this one together.

Ironically, despite all the harm Carol Griffee's reporting had done, it took Orsini's answering the phone in Larry Dill's office to get the *Gazette* to question the reliability of Griffee's main source. *Gazette* editors were genuinely shocked to learn that a convicted murderess had the unsupervised run of the jail. And this time it wasn't Tommy's word against Dub Bentley's, it was Tommy's word against their own direct experience. They would continue to cover the sheriff's exploits, but he would never again be trusted by the newspaper's editors as a valid source.

Since Robinson had been Griffee's source for most of her McArthur case "scoops," she was suddenly out of luck. LRPD sources stonewalled her, as did the prosecutor's staff. Even Griffee herself no longer believed Orsini. Nobody at the *Gazette* remembered telling her she'd been pulled from the story; they just quit approving her ideas.

Editorially, Tommy Robinson and the *Gazette* were bitter enemies anyway. Lampooning Sheriff Tommy as "the unguided missile of Arkansas law enforcement," *Gazette* editorials treated the sheriff with bemused contempt. Brilliant editorial cartoonist George Fisher, regarded as a state treasure even by many who disliked his unabashed liberalism, delighted in portraying Tommy as a redneck buffoon leading an inept squad of "Keystone Kops" out of a silent movie—also as a Swami, investigating crimes with a crystal ball.

Several blocks south at the *Democrat*, in the meantime, different circumstances prevailed. Most reporters at the smaller paper had long ago concluded that Sheriff Tommy was playing managing editor John Robert Starr's ego like a bass fiddle. Like many another blood feud in Arkansas politics, Starr's grudge against the *Gazette* dated back to the Central High integration crisis of 1957. As a young AP reporter, Starr had been regarded as a sycophantic follower of Governor Orval Faubus. "Faubus's Boswell" [i.e. his personal publicist] they called him in the *Gazette* newsroom, and it stuck.

While the *Gazette* was winning two Pulitzer Prizes and surviving a segregationist boycott as a consequence of resisting Faubus's racial demagoguery, Starr was building a lifelong hatred. Winning the Little Rock "newspaper war" had become the managing editor's personal crusade—all the more because, under its publisher's orders, the *Gazette* refused in its news and editorial columns to acknowledge anything he or the *Democrat* said or did. But they couldn't ignore Sheriff Tommy, whose style made a perfect match for Starr's own brand of aggressive populism.

Griffee's disappearance left Robinson with just one newspaper source to manipulate. But a powerful source it was. By helping Tommy turn Bill McArthur into a symbol of corrupt privilege, the columnist could help his publisher win Arkansas's blue-collar readership—exactly where the *Gazette*, made soft by years of no real competition, was vulnerable.

5

The way McArthur's lawyers saw it, there wasn't but one reason for Dillahunty to call Susan Anders as a witness against their client, and that was to prejudice public opinion. Nothing the unhappy woman could say, they argued in briefs filed with Judge Hale over the holiday weekend, could be considered relevant to the sheriff's case. Bill's affair with Anders had come to a very public and embarrassing end six years earlier. Until she'd called him in a panic after his arrest, the two had not so much as spoken on the phone since 1976.

Jack Holt and Bill Putman had also filed briefs arguing that the press be barred from hearing oral arguments on the subject. Both the *Gazette* and the *Democrat* objected, and filed legal pleadings of their own. Judge Hale's first action on November 29 was to rule in favor of the newspapers. Reporters quickly crowded into the room.

McArthur's attorneys made one last try. Holt proposed to stipulate that a sworn statement Dillahunty had taken from Anders in October be entered into the record, and that the judge rule upon its relevance before allowing the special prosecutor to question her in open court.

"It still strikes at secrecy," Hale responded. "It would have to be agreed upon by the State."

"I wouldn't do that," Dillahunty said curtly.

Dressed as demurely as she knew how, Susan Anders reluctantly took the witness stand. Her ill-fated relationship with Bill McArthur, she said, had begun in 1975, when she'd visited his office and let him know she'd like to go out with him.

"When we speak of 'going out,' " Dillahunty asked, "what are we talking about in just plain common everyday ordinary language that folks understand?"

"Mr. Dillahunty," she said, "don't you know how that's done?" Having done her best to persuade him she knew nothing of value to his case, Anders resented being put on display.

"I think I do. But are we talking about sexual relations?"

Anders admitted that they were. Speaking in a barely audible whisper, she told the whole story. In her interview at Dillahunty's office, she described how she'd called Bill after his arrest and he'd urged her to simply tell the truth if questioned. "I don't think after what happened to him [in 1976] that he would even want to go out with anybody else," she'd said. "And Mr. McArthur is a nice man. He's a kind and gentle person. I don't think he could kill anybody. That's the way I feel about it."

But the special prosecutor never asked her that.

·   ·   ·

Her previous testimony stricken from the record, a completely different Mary Lee from the one who'd appeared six days earlier swept into the courtroom. On her first day of testimony, Orsini had dressed like a nun. This time, she'd decided upon a Scarlet Woman costume. She wore a bright red suit with an elaborately ruffled white blouse. Swept up into a modest bun for her first appearance, an elaborately curled mass of black hair now hung midway down her back. Tom Donovan stood attentively at her shoulder.

It seems unlikely that the special prosecutor was unaware that the testimony Orsini was about to give would contradict each of several previous statements she'd made under oath since March 12, 1981. He certainly should have known. If he did know, however, it is difficult to understand why he would call her as a witness.

Once again, Orsini quickly affirmed that she had personal knowledge of an arrangement between Yankee Hall and Bill McArthur to bring about Alice's death. Dillahunty sought no details. Instead, he questioned her about her July 2 visit to McArthur's office. The appointment, Mary Lee claimed, had been set up at McArthur's insistence to discuss her contacts with Art Baldwin regarding the Memphis gangster's interest in BJ's.

"Mr. McArthur started talking to me about the Art Baldwin call," Orsini said, "and I was telling him . . . that I'd been carrying a .38 in my purse. We were talking about the gun, and I was talking about how heavy it was, and I told him I was going to get someone to purchase me a .22. And he said he knew, that he'd been carrying a gun also. And he pulled a gun out."

The weapon McArthur showed her, Mary Lee said, was a revolver marked Exhibit 41—the same gun that LRPD detectives had found in a box hidden on a shelf in the closet where Alice's body had been found. What made her absolutely certain, she affirmed, was that her late husband had been a gun collector. She was familiar with handguns.

The implication was that McArthur had planted the gun at the crime scene to make it appear that Alice had fled into the closet to protect herself. As in an earlier scenario Tommy Robinson had provided to reporters, McArthur had also moved the flowers.

His task completed, Dillahunty quickly turned Mary Lee over to the defense. Holt tried to pick up where he'd left off before Thanksgiving. He handed Mary Lee a transcript of her September 1 phone conversation with Dill, and directed her to the passage where she'd discussed picking up a pistol from Ron Orsini's deathbed.

"I'm going to interpose an objection," Dillahunty said, "that this is collateral to the matter that has been brought out on direct. . . . He's talking about picking up a gun at another place. It has absolutely nothing to do with the issue before this court."

The judge sustained him. Of course, Orsini's conversations with Dill had everything to do with the issue, but Hale remained adamant. He would allow no questions about the Orsini murder.

Stymied, Holt asked Mary Lee to explain what she knew about the "arrangement" between Bill McArthur and Yankee Hall.

"Some time after the [car bombing]," Orsini answered, "I guess it was May 24th or 25th, Yankee Hall told me he had a contract."

"What brought about this conversation where Yankee Hall would tell you this?"

"He told me a lot of things he probably shouldn't have, and he was talking because he talked too much."

Frustrated, Holt took Orsini back to her first meeting with Hall. According to Mary Lee, Yankee approached her at a service station and offered to do body work on her car.

"While we're talking about body work, did y'all end up having an affair?"

"No, sir." In fact, Mary Lee insisted, while she did him a few personal favors, she didn't consider Yankee a friend. She'd never heard of Carl Ray Wilson (the man who'd sold Hall the Tovex explosive) until the sheriff told her. "From what I understand there was dynamite put in my car," she said. "But I did not know it was dynamite."

Thrown off balance by Orsini's brazenness, Holt got sucked into bickering. If Yankee wasn't her friend, why had she driven him to Mayflower and allowed him to charge a long-distance call to her phone?

"You are the one that is calling him my friend."

"Well you just got through saying your friends used you. Are you putting him in the category of a friend?"

"No," Mary Lee said acidly. "You're putting him there."

"Yankee was not a friend, and you had no close relationship with him, yet you're trying to tell the Court that this stranger . . . would sit down and tell you that he had a contract with Bill McArthur to take his wife's life?"

"Mr. Holt," Orsini said, "I could give you enough information that man has told me about half the people in this town. He has a habit of running his mouth off and bragging."

After Yankee revealed the murder plot to her, she'd done her best through Phoebe to warn Alice to change her habits. Mary Lee was eating the veteran defense lawyer alive. Frustrated by the judge's refusal to allow his opening gambit, Holt could not force her to contradict herself. Each time he tried, Dillahunty quickly objected and Judge Hale immediately sustained him.

"But not one time," Holt asked, "did you ever indicate to [Dill and Robinson] that there was a contract on Alice McArthur?"

"I came close to telling them, yes."

"You did not tell them, did you?"

"No, I didn't."

"Well, didn't you see fit to go see Bill McArthur and say, 'Shame on you, Bill?' "

"I did go to Bill." Though he was evasive at first, she stated, McArthur had eventually admitted to the plot. "Bill knew that he could trust me," she explained.

"Why did he know he could trust you?"

"Because of what he had over me."

"What did he have over you?"

Dillahunty jumped up to object. "It's collateral," he said.

"Your Honor," Holt responded, "it goes to the core of the matter. Can we order her to answer the question?"

"You may ask the question. But she may take the Fifth," the judge added helpfully.

"What did Bill McArthur have over you?" Holt repeated.

"I take the Fifth."

With Holt reduced to nitpicking, Orsini narrated a detailed account of how McArthur had supposedly brought $25,000 in a brown paper bag to the Hot Springs Holiday Inn on June 9. "He [told me] that he would give me something that I wanted from him if I would hand the money to Mr. Hall, and I refused to do it."

When she turned him down, McArthur, who was blackmailing her at the time, simply told her he'd make other arrangements, she said.

The sheer absurdity of this scenario reduced Holt to helpless sarcasm. "The day of Alice McArthur's death you were at Bill McArthur's office and y'all were comparing your pieces, your heaters, your guns?"

"What is a 'heater,' and a 'piece'?"

"Oh, you know that language. You've been around guns."

"I've never heard them called heaters and pieces."

"But you're . . . telling the judge that you were aware he [McArthur] was involved in a contract on his wife . . . and you were down at his office on July 2 and he was showing you his gun, and you said, 'Hey, I'll show you mine?' "

"We were talking about my purse," Orsini said. "Bill had picked my purse up, and it was heavy, and he says, 'Do you have your gun in your purse?' and I said, 'Yes.' And that's when he bought this one out and we were talking about it."

There was more. "I had been in his office maybe 10 or 15 minutes," Mary Lee said, "and one of his telephone lines rang and Bill grabbed it . . . and it was Alice. And he said that he was detained, but he was going to get away shortly. And then he says, 'OK, go ahead and get it.' And he hung up. And I asked him what was wrong, and he said the doorbell was ringing."

The purpose of Orsini's visit had been to discuss the phone calls she'd allegedly gotten from the shadowy "Art Baldwin." She now accused McArthur of setting them up. Sheriff Robinson, she explained, "had given him the information that Art Baldwin was going to try to buy the club . . . and only Bill knew that. I wouldn't have known the guy from Adam. [But] I don't think it was Art, because he was in the penitentiary."

"Why was he getting someone to call you?"

"So he could go back to the Sheriff, like he did, and tell him that he was getting these calls."

"[But] Bill wasn't getting the calls. You were getting the calls." Like everybody else in the courtroom, Holt was bewildered.

"I know, but Bill told them that a client of his was getting the calls. He refused to tell who the client was."

"Is this what the Sheriff tells you?"

"This is what he has told me, yes."

"That's all kind of crazy stuff, isn't it?"

"I don't think any of it makes any sense, Mr. Holt."

On that rare note of candor, the hearing recessed for lunch.

· · ·

Holt soldiered on during an interminable afternoon session. Why, of course, Orsini had lied to Joyce Holt and Larry Burge about McArthur's involvement. What else could she have done? Alternately waspish and condescending, she played the scene perfectly. Even Holt's trump card caused her no discomfort.

"Do you recall writing the script for [Larry Burge] to call in to the police department?" he challenged.

Orsini exchanged whispered confidences with her lawyer, Tom Donovan. "That wasn't a script," she announced. "It was notes taken from a telephone conversation."

"Where did you get the information?"

"Primarily," she said coolly, "from Bill McArthur."

In that case, the exasperated lawyer insisted, why had she gone out of her way to assure friends of Bill's innocence? After another whispered colloquy with Donovan, she addressed Holt as if he were a moron.

"Mr. Holt, I think if you knew about a murder, I don't think you would tell anyone, even your closest friend."

"Was it because Bill had this leverage over you?"

"That's right."

Approaching the bench, Holt moved that Orsini's mention of "leverage" opened the subject for cross-examination. Judge Hale agreed, but reminded Orsini that she retained the right to plead the Fifth Amendment, as she promptly did. Holt then asked that all testimony relating to McArthur's supposed blackmail be stricken, as he'd once again been denied the right to confront his accuser.

Dillahunty joined the argument, taking the position that since her earlier appearance at the hearing had been stricken from the record, Holt couldn't question Orsini about any aspect of it. Judge Hale agreed.

"Your Honor," Holt protested, "I can ask her whether or not she made that statement last Wednesday, whether it was out in the hall or on the street."

"You may ask her and I may sustain the objection of the state," Hale replied, "which I have." Once stricken from the record, Orsini's previous testimony had no legal existence.

Under normal circumstances, Holt would have been well advised to throw in his cards and prepare for trial. But the purpose of cross-examining Orsini was twofold: To find out as much as they could about what fantasies she'd concocted for Sheriff Tommy, and to commit her to the record. The defense attorney came at her from a different angle.

"You are telling us that you've stayed quiet, that you've gone through a trial in which you did not testify, you were convicted of a conspiracy you had nothing to do with, yet up until today, you've made no statement implicating Bill McArthur? . . . Did he still have leverage over you then?"

"It's not funny, Mr. Holt."

"No, none of this hearing is funny. . . . He had leverage on you last week when you sat up here?"

"Yes."

"Then tell us why he doesn't have the same leverage over you right now."

"He does," she responded. "But I've gotten some protection for my daughter and my mother now . . . I've asked the Sheriff to make sure that my mother and daughter can call him when they need to. Right after my trial my daughter got a telephone call that said she'd be killed if I testified against Bill McArthur."

No matter how Holt came after her, she had an answer. Every single thing she knew about Alice's murder she claimed to have learned from either Yankee or Bill McArthur. Her performance was a masterpiece of psychopathic cunning from beginning to end. Like virtually every aspect of the convoluted saga she'd narrated since March 12, 1981, there were no witnesses to any of the evidence she gave against McArthur except herself.

Mary Lee hadn't stayed in school long enough to take a philosophy course. But every psychopath knows one elementary rule of logic: it's impossible to prove a negative. Nobody could prove that she *hadn't* overheard Bill McArthur tell Alice to answer the doorbell, nor that he *hadn't* called her on Tiffany's phone to tell her to pretend that a black man with a box of flowers was ringing her doorbell. Nobody could prove that Bill *hadn't* dictated the script she'd given to Larry Burge. It was her word against his.

Even in their present frustration, McArthur's lawyers knew that when the inevitable murder trial came, it would be her word against a lot of others. But would a jury decide to believe her anyway? Another thing every psychopath understands is that human beings tend to believe what they want to believe almost no matter what.

With that in mind, Holt wanted one last particular on the record. "Was [Bill] having an affair with you," he asked, "where he wanted her out of the way so y'all could get married?"

"No."

"So we get back to the basic premise that as far as you know the only reason he wanted her killed is that she was going to leave him and take the kids, and he couldn't bear that?"

"Well," Mary Lee answered, "he went into some detail about some affairs that he had had in the past. That she caught him at it, and she had never let him get over it."

Holt had flat run out of questions. As McArthur and his lawyers left the courtroom at the end of an exhausting fourth day of testimony, Bill Putman took McArthur aside for a moment. "When we go to trial," the Fayetteville lawyer said, "let me take her."

"She's all yours," Bill promised.

. . .

Knowing the case file better than anybody in the courtroom, Chris Piazza and Dub Bentley knew that for all her cunning, Mary Lee had perjured herself several times. On three previous occasions under oath, she'd denied any knowledge of the Ron Orsini murder weapon.

Dillahunty's examination of Mary Lee, moreover, troubled both men. Instead of questioning Mary Lee in detail, the special prosecutor had chosen to take a seat and let Holt bring out most of her testimony on cross. When Dillahunty failed to ask Orsini about her prior inconsistent statements, Piazza had scribbled a note about the conflicting evidence and given it to the defense.

The gesture hadn't escaped Dillahunty's notice. He made a grandstand play Tuesday morning, filing a complaint with Judge Hale, who jumped down Piazza's throat.

"It's been obvious from the beginning," Hale said loudly enough for the reporters to hear, "that you've been consulting with the defense in this case. . . . If it happens again, you're going to jail."

"Your Honor," Piazza protested, "it is obvious that Mrs. Orsini's testimony is inconsistent with the facts."

The judge repeated his warning, and Piazza bit his tongue. As Bentley and he saw it, it was their right and duty to keep both sides informed of the factual record. But it was also Hale's courtroom.

. . .

Dillahunty had worked his way around to the official PCSD side of his case. He called Major Larry Dill, who affirmed seeing flower petals in the foyer. Except to the press, carefully coached by Sheriff Tommy, the phantom petals had no meaning as evidence.

McArthur's lawyers, however, did want to make a point of Dill and Robinson's extensive contacts with Mary Lee prior to the bombing and the murder. Under vigorous cross-examination by Jack Holt, Dill admitted several meetings with Orsini at PCSD headquarters. He and Tommy had visited 7412 Pontiac once, and so had Captain Bobby

Woodward. Dill had spoken with Orsini numerous times on the phone, but never with McArthur.

Holt and Dill went back and forth for the better part of an hour. Tempers grew short, particularly after Holt began to press the glowering deputy about allowing Orsini to read Yankee's confession.

" 'Lee was advised of her rights. . .,' " Holt read aloud from Dill's August 30 report. " 'She commented that Yankee had been truthful in his deposition, except it was before 9 P.M. when they went to do the bombing. Lee also said he forgot to tell you about the rifle and the plan to shoot Alice at the tennis center.' Those are the only corrections she made in the entire 60 pages?"

"In that particular interview it was, yes sir."

"Did you hear that Monday in court she had changed every bit of it and said none of it was true?"

"No. I'm not aware of her testimony in court. I can only tell you what she had told me."

Why, Holt demanded, had the PCSD not arrested Orsini for murdering Ron Orsini—or, at the very least, for perjury—on the basis of her admission that she'd handled the revolver? Because, Dill returned angrily, she was already under arrest. Even being confronted with his own written words failed to faze the sheriff's right-hand man. Holt challenged him to square his August 30 report with Orsini's new story that Yankee's confession was all lies.

"She maintained all along that he was not completely truthful in his deposition," Dill said.

"Why didn't you put it in your report?"

"I did. In my way, Mr. Holt, that's exactly what it says."

· · ·

Sheriff Tommy was the kind of man who could swagger sitting down. He entered the courtroom waving and smiling to supporters. From the outset it was clear that he regarded his time on the witness stand as a chance to make a speech.

"Will you tell the court," Dillahunty asked, "the circumstances that led up to the arrest [of Bill McArthur], sir?"

Radiating confidence, the sheriff launched into a stemwinder. "I'll have to go back and put it into perspective," he announced, and spoke for more than five minutes. He said that in talking to Orsini and McArthur separately, he found them very protective of each other, making him very suspicious. He launched into a description of his efforts to fight organized crime.

Bill Putman objected that everything Robinson had said amounted to hearsay and conclusions, not evidence, but Judge Hale overruled him.

Next Tommy described how he had run a "scam" on Bill McArthur, warning him about a dangerous mobster named Art Baldwin. "Lee Orsini came in. Bill McArthur never came in. She contacted my office and told me Art Baldwin had contacted her because he thought that she was part owner in BJ's Star-Studded Honky Tonk. Art Baldwin," the sheriff concluded triumphantly, "today is in the Federal Penitentiary in Tallahassee, Florida. Bill McArthur took it hook, line and sinker."

The sheriff's story depended entirely upon his own say-so. Not even Dill had been made privy to the secret. But again, the defense couldn't prove a negative—particularly not against the word of the charismatic lawman.

Tommy jumped ahead to his feud with the prosecutor. "Each time we went in there to discuss Bill McArthur," he said, "all they would do was debate us. They didn't want to hear about any evidence about William C. McArthur."

Putman objected more vigorously. This time Hale sustained him.

"Then I started trying to set up a session in which they would take a deposition from Yankee Hall," Robinson said. "Even though I knew that he was not going to tell the complete truth."

Putman cut him off again. "Every time I make an objection and the court rules," he said, "the witness gives a speech."

As Putman hoped, the sheriff began to smolder. Dillahunty came to his rescue. "You finally did get the deposition. What was your next step, sir?"

Sheriff Tommy had then gone to the McArthur home, analyzed the crime scene two months after the fact, developed his list of sixteen questions and determined he had probable cause to arrest McArthur.

"He refused to give you any answers?" Dillahunty asked.

"That's correct."

When Bill Putman introduced himself to the sheriff prior to beginning his cross-examination, Tommy's eyes narrowed. "I know who you are," he all but hissed. "I'm very much aware of you."

Unknown to the defense lawyer, Robinson had been whispering to reporters that Putman was a well-known "mouthpiece" for organized crime. Putman wasted no time getting down to cases. Yankee's confession, he asked, was a lengthy statement, was it not?

"Not as long as I wanted it to be," Tommy answered. Against his wishes, a plea bargain had been struck between Yankee and the prosecutor. That was a lie. Robinson had been urging Dub Bentley to cut a deal with Yankee from the moment of his arrest. Chris Piazza, Robinson added, had insisted that the tape recorder be shut off for large parts of Yankee's statement—another falsehood. Two separate recordings show no interruptions. Putman let it go. He had a particular goal in mind. He asked Tommy the purpose of the Art Baldwin "scam."

"I wanted to prove," Robinson said, "that he and Lee Orsini were dealing directly with each other."

"So all this," Putman asked, "is part of the brilliant deductive process that you went through to conclude that Lee Orsini and Bill McArthur were in this together?"

"That was only one part of it."

The sheriff appeared to be enjoying the battle of wits. Then Putman made his move.

"Sheriff, if you read the newspaper, you know that Lee Orsini got on the witness stand in here and said that what Yankee Hall said was not true. All of the time, she was not involved, except to the degree that she was coerced and blackmailed. . . . That is certainly not part of the investigation that you conducted and the conclusions that you reached?"

"Now repeat that question," Tommy said warily.

"I say, her testimony is not in accord with the conclusions that you reached by your process of deduction?"

"No, it's substantially the same."

"Are you telling the court," Putman asked, "that your investigation indicated to you that Lee Orsini was not involved in efforts to kill Alice McArthur by placing a dynamite bomb—or causing one to be placed—underneath her car on the 21st of May?"

"I'm certainly not saying that."

"Your investigation indicated that she was criminally involved?"

"That is correct."

"Well, why have you told the press then and announced for the world to read that the State had no case against Lee Orsini?"

"At the time she was arrested they had no probable cause."

The sheriff had accused his star witness of perjury as well as murder. Putman was only getting started. "You knew before the time that Bill

McArthur was arrested that Lee Orsini was criminally involved in the case herself because she had told you so?"

"That's correct."

"Did you testify at her trial?"

"They would not call me as a witness," Robinson said firmly. "I was subpoenaed, but I did not testify. I was never called." Chris Piazza, he insisted, had refused to allow him to testify in Orsini's trial. Was it really possible that Robinson didn't remember testifying in the most highly publicized murder trial in Arkansas history? He was sitting in the very same chair.

Bill Putman attempted to draw the sheriff out about what kinds of things Piazza had supposedly wanted kept out of Yankee's statement. "Let's get back to this business of Art Baldwin," he suggested. "You assumed because Lee Orsini called you and said that she had contact with a person that identified himself as Art Baldwin, that information came from Mr. McArthur?"

"It either had to come from Mr. McArthur or an FBI agent," Tommy said. "And I don't think the FBI agent called."

"Did you ever come into possession of information that she, in fact, learned about Art Baldwin from some other source?"

Tommy denied it. Flourishing a copy of Hall's confession, Putman read aloud from page 45, in which the Sheriff himself had asked Yankee if he'd ever heard the name "Art Baldwin" and Yankee answered that he had. LRPD Officer Mike Willingham had warned him that Baldwin might be in town trying to move in on some clubs. Yankee had passed the information along to some of his bartender pals and to Mary Lee Orsini.

"It would appear," Putman concluded, "that your remarkable powers of retention are not quite as infallible as you would like for us to believe, isn't that right, Sheriff?" For all his sarcasm, he'd let Tommy off easy. Immediately following the exchange he'd read aloud, Robinson had laid out the entire Art Baldwin "scam" for Yankee's edification—only to have the prisoner sympathize that it had blown up in his face.

"I'm not Jesus Christ," Tommy said, "but I have a good memory and a fairly good I.Q."

"Have you offered [Orsini] any kind of a reward," Putman asked, "or promised . . . to get her a new trial in exchange for her testifying the way you want her to testify?"

"No. As a matter of fact, she's a suspect in another crime, along with

Bill McArthur and Dub Bentley. So I'm not making deals. She's ultimately going to have some real serious problems with me."

"You say Dub Bentley is a suspect in a crime," Putman said incredulously, "and Bill McArthur is a suspect in a crime, and Lee Orsini is a suspect in another crime?"

Robinson narrowed his eyes like Clint Eastwood. "That's right," he said evenly, "the Ron Orsini homicide."

"Just to relieve my mind, Sheriff," Putman taunted, "am I a suspect in any crime you have in your portfolio today?"

"I had rather not answer that question. Not in anything to do with the Ron Orsini or the McArthur case."

"Do you think you've got probable cause to arrest me now?"

"No."

"Isn't it true," Putman charged, "that your sole purpose in arresting Bill McArthur was for the purpose of gaining headlines [and] promoting yourself politically?"

"No. I already have enough publicity," Tommy smirked. "I have 100 percent name recognition. Why do I need more?"

"I don't know," Putman said. "You seem to enjoy it. It's like money. Some people can't get enough."

Dillahunty objected to Putman's baiting his witness, and Hale sustained him. Putman signaled that he was through. Seemingly unabashed, Tommy swaggered out of the courtroom.

Before the judge could adjourn for the day, however, Dillahunty appeared to think he'd spotted an opening. He asked for Chris Piazza to be called to the stand.

"Mr. Piazza," the special prosecutor said stiffly, "at the last recess were you not around the corner huddled with Mr. Holt, conferring with him about the witness that was on the stand?"

"Mr. Holt came up to me and said, 'Did not Sheriff Robinson testify for you at Orsini's trial?' And I said, 'Yes, he did.' "

Putman could hardly believe his ears. "Mr. Piazza," he asked, "are you telling the court that the sheriff did, in fact, testify in the Orsini murder trial?"

"Yes, sir. He did."

Possibly fearing further damage, Dillahunty abruptly rested. Putman's cross-examination of the sheriff had been devastating to the special prosecutor's case. Not only had he forced Tommy to admit that his star witness had perjured herself, he'd caught Tommy in a couple of humdingers of his own. A judge with an ounce of political courage would have pitched Sheriff Tommy and his merry men out the court-room door. But as McArthur and his lawyers had known going in, Judge David Hale hardly fit that description.

Dillahunty must have suspected it, too. Otherwise, it was hard to imagine how the special prosecutor could have laid down his hand without calling Yankee Hall to the witness stand. Dillahunty had boasted to the press that when McArthur's attorneys heard Yankee, it would give them a heart attack. But as Hale gaveled the fifth day of testimony to a weary close, it had become clear that if they wanted to risk a trip to the cardiac unit, the defense would have to call Yankee themselves.

• • •

The hearing reopened on Wednesday, December 1, in Room 206 of the Pulaski County Courthouse. Putman moved again to strike the testimony of Mary Lee Orsini on the grounds that her refusal to answer questions about the so-called leverage McArthur had over her deprived him of his Sixth Amendment right to cross-examine hostile witnesses.

Judge Hale refused. Orsini's testimony would stand. For the record, Putman made a ritual motion for dismissal, and Hale denied it.

The defense called Yankee Hall. Dressed in the same slacks and polyester sport shirt he'd worn to testify against Orsini, Hall affected the world-weary air of one who'd spent much of his adult life answering questions under oath. Guided by Putman, he told the story of his involvement with Orsini. For the first time since his arrest, he showed regret. "She brought it about," he said, "but I don't think she talked me into it. I'm 43 years old, I can't blame her for what I've done."

Putman walked Yankee step by step through the now-familiar maze. To reporters awaiting bombshells, the testimony seemed like old hat. To McArthur's attorneys, however, it was crucial to get Yankee on the record in as much detail as possible. Nobody could be absolutely certain he would never recant. It had also occurred to them that he might die in custody. Stranger things had happened.

Orsini, Hall testified, had planned all along to pin the blame on Bob Troutt. As Sheriff Tommy's number one all-purpose suspect, he made a natural fall guy. "She indicated after the bombing that the police's first thought was that Troutt . . . had it placed, and she was sure that, when the shooting was over, they would think the same thing."

Toward the end of Yankee's second hour on the witness stand, Bill

Putman got down to the nitty-gritty. "You never, in fact, met and conspired with Mr. McArthur to enter into a contract to take his wife's life at all, did you?"

"Not personally, no."

"You never had any contact with him at all?"

"No. I've never had any contact with him at all."

"Everything you know about Bill McArthur's involvement, as far as you know, came from the mouth of Lee Orsini, right?"

"Yes."

"And you've subsequently found that this woman is not an entirely truthful woman."

"That's right."

Putman turned the witness over to Dillahunty, who grilled Yankee about his previous convictions, presumably in the interest of establishing that a confessed murderer was not an entirely reliable character. But if he had any further surprises, he failed to produce them.

When he was through, Jack Holt stood and said, "If it please the court we have some 20 other people subpoenaed . . . but we do not see any need or necessity of putting them on the stand, or Mr. McArthur. Therefore we will submit no further evidence and stand on the record."

Judge Hale began to shake his head. "Gentlemen," he said, "I don't have any choice. I just don't have any other choice."

Holt asked to make a brief speech for the record. He repeated the defense's Sixth Amendment argument, and argued that Arkansas law required independent evidence besides the testimony of a co-conspirator. "I submit to the Court," he argued, "that there is not one scintilla of evidence . . . to show a conspiracy, which I say has been rebutted and is non-existent. . . . And I would like to say this in closing: I don't see how the Court, I don't see how the press, I don't see how the public can accept and tolerate and utilize her statement to further the prosecutorial abuse of going forward to a trial . . . after she testified that she had nothing to do with the conspiracy.

"I submit to this Court that it would be a serious injustice for this case to be moved forward."

Sonny Dillahunty promised to be brief. "Lee Orsini, yes, she is a convicted criminal," he said. "So is Yankee Hall a convicted criminal. He's involved in the conspiracy, Lee Orsini is involved in the conspiracy and Bill McArthur is involved in the conspiracy. It would be equally an injustice to let one walk while the others are charged—and two now stand convicted. . . . You don't show conspiracies," he argued. "They are not performed out in the middle of War Memorial Stadium with the lights on. They are done in the closet, behind the door, in the alleys. They are secret. That's the reason why they are conspiracies."

The judge had listened to six days of testimony and decided to kick the problem upstairs. But whatever happened to Bill McArthur and his family, he wanted everybody to understand, there would be no blood on the hands of Judge David Hale.

"I do not feel like the State has a very good case. I have serious doubts about it. But under the circumstances, I have no option. I have to send it to Circuit Court. . . . Mr. Prosecutor, I think you need to look seriously into the credibility of much of your evidence. . . . We are talking about a man's life, and it may already be ruined—whether he's guilty or innocent."

•   •   •

Sheriff Tommy was already ranting in front of the TV cameras. Judge Hale "had no right to comment on the evidence. If there was no evidence, then he shouldn't have bound it over." As for Dub Bentley, the sheriff would see to it that Bill McArthur stood trial for murder. Otherwise he would have Bentley removed from office and see to it that a prosecutor with some guts took his place.

The prosecutor had a tough decision to make. Bentley could step aside and allow the public the show trial it demanded, or he could stand on principle and commit political suicide. "We are waiting, Dub, patiently," taunted John Robert Starr in his *Democrat* column. "The morning line is eight to five that you can't do it." Anybody who knew the methodical prosecuting attorney knew that it was not the kind of decision Dub would make overnight.

Damn near everybody else in Arkansas, meanwhile, was having the time of their lives.

Chapter 2

1

On December 14, exactly two weeks after the McArthur probable cause hearing, the trial of alleged triggerman Larry Darnell McClendon took place in Circuit Court. In the interim, despite a constant din from Sheriff Tommy and his allies in the press, Dub Bentley hadn't budged. The prosecutor made it clear that he'd decide how to handle the charges against Bill McArthur when he got damned good and ready.

Several times since his July 6 arrest, Chris Piazza had offered McClendon the same deal Yankee had taken—a life sentence in return for his testimony. But the ex-convict had clung to his right to remain silent like a tick to a hound's ear. Bentley instructed Piazza to seek the death penalty. Nobody could say Dub had gone soft on the triggerman to keep his mouth shut. Picking a "death qualified" jury took two days: six men and six women—one of the women black.

As expected, McClendon's lawyers pounded away at Yankee's credibility. Public Defender Bill Simpson told the jury that Yankee had fingered his client only after he was "caught red handed . . . [and] found himself facing the electric chair." Even some of the investigators suspected that Hall's whole purpose in bringing McClendon into the plot was to have a black man to shove out front in case things went wrong. Did he actually expect the jury to believe, McClendon's lawyer challenged, that the defendant "trusted you so much you didn't have to give him a nickel down?"

"That's what I said," Yankee answered. "I didn't say it was a shrewd business deal. But that was the deal."

In a move that infuriated both Piazza and Bentley, Sheriff Tommy testified for the defense. Robinson told the jury that scientific calculations and a diligent search had led him to conclude that Yankee couldn't possibly have thrown the murder weapon into the Arkansas River as he'd sworn in his confession. Had he done so, Tommy and his team of divers would have found it. Asked whether he would trust Hall's testimony under oath, the sheriff replied enigmatically, "In some matters yes, and in some matters no."

Silent to the end, McClendon declined to testify. With the accused killer's mother and a group of about twenty relatives and friends keeping a vigil in the courtroom, the jury stayed out almost eight hours, deadlocked 11–1 for conviction. The lone black juror held out for acquittal. Agreeing at last upon a compromise, they found McClendon innocent of capital murder, but guilty of a reduced charge of first-degree murder. They fixed his sentence at twenty years.

As the sentence was read, McClendon closed his eyes and shook his head slowly from side to side. Moments later he broke into the relieved smile of a man who had gambled with his life and won. He shook hands with his three male lawyers and gave the one woman on the defense team a big hug. Then he crossed the courtroom and shook hands with a flustered Dub Bentley. "Merry Christmas," he said. He repeated the wish to reporters. "What about McArthur?" spectators shouted as bailiffs handcuffed McClendon and led him from the courtroom.

2

The longer Dub Bentley postponed his decision, the more vigorously Tommy Robinson pressed his campaign against McArthur. Hardly pausing for Christmas, the sheriff issued almost daily threats and ultimatums. Dub was so dumb, he announced on a call-in radio show one night, it took him an hour and a half to watch "60 Minutes."

Meanwhile, judges like David Hale weren't the only public officials hunting cover. To the dismay of Sergeant Farley, NLRPD Chief Bubba Younts abruptly switched sides. After a meeting to which Farley was conspicuously not invited, Younts appeared on TV standing side by side with Robinson to join the attack upon the prosecutor. Tommy's complaint was that Bentley wouldn't allow him access to the 1981 grand jury transcripts he needed to solve the Ron Orsini case.

According to Farley, Younts ordered him to cease cooperation with
Bentley's office and assist the sheriff. The NLRPD detective felt
trapped. To his way of thinking, the order was improper. By law, the
prosecutor was the chief law enforcement officer in the district. Younts
could fire him, but Dub Bentley could send him to jail. He made
confidential arrangements to meet the prosecutor one night during the
third week in January. With paranoia running rampant, both men
brought tape recorders.

Despite lingering hard feelings over the 1981 grand jury, they came
to a quick understanding. Bentley had no objection to any investigator's reading the grand jury transcripts in his office. He'd offered them
to Robinson and Dill on that basis. But he refused to let them out of
his sight. When he'd entrusted his confidential investigative notes to
Dillahunty, he'd ended up being handed them on the witness stand
with Mary Lee's handwriting all over them.

"You know Lee as well as I do, maybe better," Bentley told Farley.
"If Lee gets access to testimony and other statements, she's the world's
greatest fabricator. She can tailor her testimony, based upon her knowledge and the testimony of other people. . . . I think it'd be a terrible
mistake for her to get it. I'm not saying Larry [Dill] would give it to her.
But based upon past experience, dammit, he's given her everything
else!"

Farley agreed. The detective also had good news, two bits of new
evidence on the Orsini murder he thought were significant. The first,
T.J. had dug up immediately after Mary Lee's conviction: the pharmacy records showing that Mary Lee had filled three prescriptions for
a potent sleeping pill just before Ron's death—a medication whose side
effects were exactly those Tiffany had complained of to the school
nurse.

The second plum had dropped into Farley's lap only days earlier.
Ever since the Orsini homicide, rumors had circulated around Indian
Hills that a friend of Tiffany's had visited that night. Her name was
supposed to be Amy, but Farley hadn't found her. Then he'd noticed
a newspaper photo of the cheerleaders at Tiffany's school. Out of
habit, he scanned their names. Finding an Amber, he dialed her
parents' number and the girl answered. Identifying himself, he asked
to speak with her mother or father. "She says, 'Oh, you want to talk to
me about the night I was over at Ron Orsini's house the night he was
killed.' The feeling that went through my body," Farley said, "was like
getting hit by lightning. I just sat there and said, 'Yeah. I sure do.' "

Nothing the girl had seen turned the case upside down. But Mary Lee and Tiffany had denied having visitors on March 11. Her memory also conflicted with their story—none too consistent to begin with—in several particulars. According to Amber, Tiffany had also been telling friends something else during the weeks before her stepfather's murder. Something Tiffany and her mother had specifically, vehemently, and repeatedly denied to NLRPD detectives: that Mary Lee was fed up with Ron Orsini and intended to seek a divorce.

The girl's own account wasn't entirely consistent. She'd recalled walking home from school with Tiffany, but Tiffany's dizzy spells had kept her home that day. But it was new evidence, all Bentley needed to bring the Ron Orsini case out of legal limbo and into Circuit Court.

3

Bentley's meeting with Sergeant Farley helped stiffen the prosecutor's spine. If anything, his painstaking review of the McArthur case had aroused even further his suspicion that Tommy Robinson himself had something to hide. Like everybody on the LRPD side, Bentley had never understood how Tommy's troops—called six minutes later by McArthur—could have beaten the police to 24 Inverness Circle, much less why they showed up in battalion force at a crime scene inside city limits.

Furthermore, now that Yankee, Orsini, and McClendon had all been sentenced, LRPD detectives felt free to press upon Bentley things he *hadn't* known about the chaotic events of July 2—specifically the PCSD deputies' forcible ejection from the closet where Alice McArthur's body was found, and the enigmatic remark about looking for the flowers.

The prosecutor could think of no reason why the LRPD officers would lie. It made no difference to them which deputy had moved the flowers. Bentley flirted with the idea of calling a grand jury to investigate Sheriff Tommy's actions. As Dub saw it, they'd have plenty to look into. Take the "hit list" containing the names of Holly Troutt, Alice McArthur, and Mary Lee Orsini that had been tipped to several police agencies on July 2. Two things seemed likely: that Orsini had concocted it, and that she'd done so for Tommy. The names wouldn't have made sense to anybody else. Yet Tommy claimed he hadn't gotten the tip, and accused other agencies of leaving him out of the loop.

The prosecutor listened over and over again to the taped exchange between the PCSD radio dispatcher and an anonymous deputy on the afternoon of Alice McArthur's murder. During the McClendon trial, a Robinson henchman had testified that the tapes had been accidentally destroyed. But Chris Piazza had later retrieved them from the PCSD radio room. At least one exchange seemed to hint that something was supposed to go down at the McArthur home. "Well, do you think that *we* shot one or that *they* shot?" an unidentified deputy asked. "Who shot who?"

While Dub had no proof that Tommy's boys had bungled a stakeout at 24 Inverness Circle on the fatal afternoon, the rumor persisted in law enforcement circles. Where Captain Bobby Woodward was involved, other cops suspected the worst.

Was it even possible that Orsini was holding something over Robinson's head? From Yankee's arrest onward, it seemed the sheriff had acted consistently to protect her. Even her conviction had done nothing to slow him down. Never had Dub witnessed any prisoner given the favors the PCSD had allowed Orsini. Just how cunningly Orsini had manipulated the situation Bentley had learned from a young woman who'd shared a cell with Mary Lee during the McArthur probable cause hearing.

Brought to the prosecutor by her own lawyer—no friend of McArthur's—Pamela Sue Goodrich had been incarcerated in the Pulaski County Jail on hot check charges when Orsini arrived from the state prison to testify against Bill McArthur. Rarely in her cell, Mary Lee spent most of her time on the phone—arousing resentment among the other prisoners. But sure enough, Mary Lee had quickly established a friendship with Goodrich and begun pumping her for information.

Oddly, Orsini had let her hair down about Yankee Hall. "First she said that she wasn't involved in any violence. She didn't know that much about him. What he did was his business. And it was kind of weird, one of the girls after seeing Mr. Hall on TV said that he wasn't bad looking or something. This is embarrassing. She told one of the girls, she says, 'No, he's not bad looking. He's better in bed.' "

Another time, Orsini confided to the girls exactly the opposite—that Yankee was a dud in the sack. "Then she turned around," Goodrich continued, "and she told me how upset she was about Yankee getting life because they had been involved. And she said there wasn't nothing she could do to help him because it would mess her up with her boyfriend Charles. That was all she had going for her right now. I don't know who Charles is. And then she changed back from one subject to another. She skips a lot when she talks. She doesn't bother to think."

Soon Orsini persuaded the woman that she was well acquainted with Goodrich's ex-husband, who had a record of drug dealing. She'd described the man's car, the tattoo on his arm, and other particulars. Bentley was well aware of Orsini's ability to ferret out useful information, particularly given the run of Robinson's and Dill's offices.

"She wanted me to testify," Goodrich said, "that my ex-husband sold Bill McArthur cocaine. . . . She said that she had never had anything to do with drugs until she met Mr. McArthur and she met [my ex-husband] Robert."

"And did she offer you anything to testify that way?"

"$5,000. We got to talking about [my case], and my two kids and everything. And she said, 'Well, $5,000 would help you a whole lot, wouldn't it?' I said, 'Sure.' And she goes, 'I think I can arrange for $5,000 if you could handle this for me.' And then I got a message one night to call Charles with a phone number. One of the matrons gave me a piece of paper. . . . [But] I always thought Lee was kind of unbalanced or something. So I really didn't pay that much attention to it."

"Did she indicate that she had any reason for doing what she had done in the case?"

"She said that Mrs. McArthur—Alice, her name was—stood between any relationship she could have had with Bill. . . . First she said that Bill—Mr. McArthur—was a spiteful-type person that played people, you know. Like toyed with her affections or something like that, and then he just dropped her. Like he wanted an investment for this club, and then he just dropped her. She felt as long as Mrs. McArthur was there, you know, they didn't have any kind of relationship going between her and Bill. She had a lot of words for Mrs. McArthur."

"She was in love with him?" Dub asked.

"Yeah."

"And he didn't respond? Do you think that was what it was?"

"That's the impression I got," Goodrich said. "She said that she couldn't cope with no more rejection."

.   .   .

Dub was so frustrated with Tommy's refusal to recognize that there was no credible evidence against McArthur that he toyed with the idea of trying to put Sheriff Robinson in jail. Under Arkansas law, false arrest and malicious prosecution were both felonies. But Bentley knew Tommy would never be convicted and couldn't bring himself to start a course of action that could only worsen the bitter feuding among police agencies in his district. The price in public cynicism would be far too high.

Nor, however, could the prosecutor justify putting Bill McArthur through a murder trial simply to clear the air. As Dub saw it, he had only one honorable choice. On the afternoon of Monday, January 24, he summoned the press to the courthouse to witness his political suicide.

Handing out copies of a ten-page letter he had written to Circuit Judge John Langston, Dub announced that he would not file charges against McArthur. "To base the prosecution of a man for allegedly conspiring to kill his wife," Bentley had written, "solely on the un-supported assertion of a woman who has already been convicted by a jury of causing the death of the wife, especially when she denies any part in the conspiracy, is ludicrous. It becomes even more absurd when viewed in light of the complete lack of credibility of this person."

He invited Judge Langston to review the transcript of McArthur's probable cause hearing. Should the judge have any doubts, Bentley would step aside and "acquiesce to a special prosecutor." But no matter what the judge decided, Dub made clear, he would file first-degree murder charges against Mary Lee Orsini for the March 11, 1981, slaying of her husband Ron.

Bentley's announcement drew five-column front-page headlines in both Little Rock newspapers. Predictably, Robinson pitched a fit. Scurrying around town like an apprentice evangelist, the sheriff made live appearances on KARN radio and two TV news shows, denouncing the prosecutor and claiming to have discovered shocking new evidence of corruption that very day.

McArthur himself was comparatively restrained. Appearing willingly on live TV for the first time since Alice's murder, Bill spoke bitterly of the sheriff's role. "He's made a mockery of my wife's death," he said. "He's made a circus of it. He wants to claim all the credit for those that have been convicted, when my observation has been that he has done everything he can to foul the cases up to where no conviction could be had. His actions have been reprehensible."

Under Arkansas law, however, an elected prosecutor's power to determine whether or not to press criminal charges was virtually absolute. Robinson could rant, rave, and run for governor. But legally speaking, Bill's terrible ordeal appeared to be over.

Fat chance.

4

While Bentley had dallied, Sheriff Tommy had stolen his thunder. By mid-January 1983, Robinson had begun to lean on Circuit Judge John Langston to convene a grand jury. He argued that only a full-scale investigation directed by a special prosecutor, preferably Dillahunty, could penetrate the maze of corruption.

Legally, the sheriff was on shaky ground. Langston did have the authority to convene a grand jury. But the law regarding special prosecutors couldn't have been more specific. In order to safeguard judicial neutrality, only two circumstances allowed a judge to replace an elected prosecutor with a substitute of his own choosing. One was for the prosecutor to disqualify himself. The other was upon the presentation of evidence implicating him in a crime.

Politics prevailed. On January 26, two days after Bentley announced his decision to drop charges against McArthur, Judge Langston announced that he would call a grand jury to conduct yet another investigation. Allegations in the case, the judge wrote in a high-minded letter to Sheriff Tommy which he also released to the press, had "left a stain upon the judicial system and law enforcement in general. Of greater importance, the tragic death of Mrs. Alice McArthur is yet unresolved. I feel that the only way it can ever fully be resolved . . . is through the empaneling of a Grand Jury composed of impartial citizens."

Shoving Bentley aside required some fancy footwork. Langston revealed that the sheriff had written him a letter accusing the prosecutor of hindering the apprehension of Ron Orsini's killer. The judge hadn't found Tommy's charges "sufficient for the disqualification of Mr. Bentley because they are mere allegations, and sufficient proof . . . has never been given to this court."

Even so, what the judge called the "appearance of impropriety" dictated that he appoint not a special prosecutor, but a "special counsel" to the grand jury. Langston promised to pick a suitable lawyer— one completely uninvolved with the case—within a week. But should the grand jury decide to indict Bill McArthur, the case would once again belong to the elected prosecutor, Dub Bentley.

This dizzying paradox seemed to satisfy almost everybody. The Arkansas Trial Lawyers' Association emitted a few tentative squawks that Langston's action had no basis in law. But the important thing was that the circus was not leaving town. With any luck at all, Arkansans might still get to witness the show trial they demanded.

Chapter 3

1

Robinson's satisfied mood lasted only a few days. By the weekend, the sheriff and his sidekick John Robert Starr had embarked on what would turn out to be perhaps the most bizarre episode in the entire saga. On Sunday, January 30, virtually every man and boy in Arkansas, and upwards of half the women, saw Sheriff Tommy once again slap the cuffs on Bill McArthur on statewide TV.

Thousands watching the Super Bowl on NBC-TV witnessed the handsome attorney being led into the courthouse dressed in a one-piece orange prisoner's uniform. Timed perfectly to coincide with the halftime show of the game between the Miami Dolphins and Washington Redskins, McArthur's second arrest shocked the state. As he'd done exactly five months earlier, the sheriff acted without a warrant. Once again, McArthur was charged with conspiracy to commit capital felony murder. This time, the intended victim was none other than Sheriff Tommy himself.

Accompanied throughout by the *Democrat* editor, Robinson bragged that he'd worked around the clock to put together an airtight case. The sheriff told a dramatic tale. Allegedly frantic over the upcoming grand jury investigation, McArthur had lost his cool. He'd contracted with two "hit men" in the Hot Spring County town of Malvern to pay $500,000 to blow Tommy away.

The would-be assassins, a pair of lank, stringy-haired country boys named Marty Freeman and Michael Swayze, had given videotaped confessions. This time around, Robinson boasted on TV, McArthur's courthouse connections could do nothing to save him. This time, Tommy had him dead to rights.

According to a breathless account by John Robert Starr, Sheriff Tommy had received an alarming call. Pausing only long enough to fetch the *Democrat* editor, he and Dill raced forty-seven miles to Malvern.

One Marty Freeman, it seemed, had presented himself to Sheriff Doyle Cook claiming that a drinking buddy had tried to hire him to assassinate Tommy Robinson. With the help of local authorities, Tommy arrested both men and brought them to Little Rock. At first Swayze swore the whole thing was a drunken prank, but somewhere along the road Tommy and Larry persuaded him to come clean. According to Starr's account, Swayze's story was as follows:

> About six weeks ago, he was approached at the Play Pen, a Little Rock night spot, by . . . McArthur and another man who introduced himself only as Ted. They wanted to know if he would like to make some quick, easy money. Swayze said he was interested and told the men that he hung out at The Pantry in Malvern.
>
> The next contact, Swayze said, was "about dinner time" [i.e., noon] on the preceding Thursday. He saw McArthur drive past The Pantry in a big car. He got into his truck, he said, and the car followed him out a rural road to a place called the "Pits."
>
> There, Swayze said, a nervous McArthur told him that Robinson had "stirred up a hornets' nest" by getting the conspiracy to murder charge against him referred to a grand jury. Swayze said McArthur wanted Robinson done away with before the grand jury met and that he would pay $500,000 and provide two sawed-off shotguns with pistol grips for the job. . . .
>
> Swayze confirmed that McArthur had promised to kill "me and my family" if he messed up the job.

Back in Little Rock, Tommy put a wire on Swayze and had him phone McArthur. Calling himself "Mike from Malvern," Swayze mentioned their supposed meeting and asked Bill if he still wanted Tommy rubbed out. Accustomed to crank calls, McArthur told him he was crazy, hung up, and reported the incident to the LRPD. Once again Tommy was red hot to bust Bill McArthur; once again his only evidence consisted of the uncorroborated testimony of a co-conspirator. He summoned Dub Bentley to PCSD headquarters around midnight Saturday. Even with the sheriff's videotaped confessions, Dub found his case unconvincing. Swayze struck him as a drunken fool. Even if McArthur had any reason to have Robinson killed, he thought it absurd to imagine that he would solicit a total stranger in front of a bar. And for $500,000, Bill could hire the KGB. Tommy had folks around Arkansas so riled up that they'd begun to see McArthur's face in the moon. He refused to issue a warrant, saying that if any charges were to be filed, they should be filed in Hot Spring County.

By Sunday afternoon, Robinson had also been turned down by the prosecutor in Hot Spring County, who said that any charges should be filed in Pulaski County. To nobody's surprise, he decided to act anyway. This time, he promised a statewide TV audience that this time McArthur had met a cop who was too tough to handle.

• • •

For a day or so, the sheriff was riding high. Even McArthur's being set free on a $50,000 personal recognizance bond served his purposes. "Oh what swift justice one can get if he knows somebody," the sheriff told Starr. "Here goes the dual standard again." Actually, weekend bond hearings were common in Pulaski County courts.

The hearing had given the *Democrat* editor another chance to display his partisanship. Summoned from painting a trellis at his home on Stagecoach Road, Dub Bentley told Judge John Langston that he'd advised the sheriff that he saw no evidence to indicate an act of conspiracy in Pulaski County.

Robinson went wild. Instead of gaveling Tommy into silence, the judge instructed him to play his videotapes. Robinson proceeded to take over the hearing. The sheriff paraded back and forth in front of the bench giving his version of the facts and arguing points of law as if he, not Dub, were the prosecutor. The judge brushed the humiliated prosecutor's objections aside.

McArthur and his attorney watched Swayze's videotaped confession with growing incredulity. While Robinson would later assure reporters that Bill had refused to answer questions, McArthur said he'd never been asked any. Jack Holt himself testified that Bill couldn't possibly have met Swayze in Malvern at noon Thursday. Between 12:25 and

1:00 P.M. that afternoon, McArthur had met with him at the court-house.

Bill himself testified that he could produce a score of witnesses who could confirm his whereabouts all day Thursday. As for Marty Freeman and Michael Swayze, he'd never laid eyes on either one—neither in Malvern nor anywhere else.

· · ·

After several friends signed $50,000 property bonds on his behalf, Langston set McArthur free without dismissing the charges. Robinson was outraged. "The state today represented the defense," he insisted to reporters. Starr wrote a vitriolic attack on the prosecutor in his *Democrat* column:

> Before a packed courtroom Bentley did everything he could judiciously do to keep the facts from coming out. Langston was having none of that. . . .
>
> Robinson was magnificent. While Bentley was arguing that the crime could not be prosecuted in Pulaski County because the alleged plot was hatched in Hot Spring County, Robinson quoted by number the statute which permits prosecution of such a crime in any county in which any part of it occurred.
>
> Not only did Bentley argue for dismissal of the case on jurisdictional grounds, he failed to conduct any meaningful cross-examination of defense witnesses, including McArthur. There were holes in defense testimony that any lawyer who was trying could have run a truck through.
>
> It was in summary a great day for Tommy Robinson and perhaps the worst day in a series of disastrous days for the prosecutor who has lost the will to prosecute.

By Monday, however, the sheriff's airtight case had already sprung a leak. Despite five-column headlines trumpeting the dramatic arrest, both newspapers quoted several individuals who'd seen Bill at the courthouse on Thursday. Circuit Judge Lowber Hendricks informed the *Gazette* that McArthur had been defending a client in his court that morning until 11:50 A.M. Reporters had seen him in the courthouse coffee shop afterward. The deputy prosecutor in the same case joked that Bill would have needed a Lear jet to reach Malvern by noon.

Alert to the possibility that Sheriff Tommy had finally gone too far, Little Rock TV stations gave prominent play to McArthur's Monday press conference. Near tears, Bill defended himself at length for the first time since Alice's murder. "Under the circumstances," he said, "I think it would take an absolute idiot to do the things that were testified to yesterday. I'm not some madman running around in the streets contacting total strangers to do illegal acts for me." The only threat he posed to the sheriff, McArthur said, was to expose him as a fraud.

By Tuesday, February 1, the leak in Robinson's latest airtight case had grown alarmingly. A front-page report by the *Gazette's* George Bentley and C. S. Heinbockel told the story:

JUDGES REPORT THEY SAW MCARTHUR; SHERIFF ISN'T FAZED

A lineup of judges and others said Monday that they could account for William C. McArthur's whereabouts around the time Thursday that Sheriff Tommy Robinson charges that McArthur was in Malvern hatching a plot to have the Sheriff killed for $500,000.

But that did not seem to faze Robinson. "I'm not concerned about his alibis," the Sheriff said.

The Sheriff added that he didn't even ask McArthur . . . about what he might have been doing Thursday before arresting him Sunday afternoon on the charge of soliciting capital murder.

"He was going to be arrested no matter what he said," Robinson said. . . .

However, judges, deputy prosecutors, lawyers, court employees and news reporters have said that McArthur was in the Pulaski County courthouse from 9 a.m. to about 1 p.m. Thursday— with McArthur handling a trial until a little before noon in front of Circuit Judge Lowber Hendricks.

During the noon hour McArthur visited with or was seen at the courthouse by Chancellor Lee A. Munson, four newspaper reporters, a policeman, one of McArthur's attorneys, Jack Holt, Jr. and other lawyers.

Holt said McArthur then went to the Black-Eyed Pea Restaurant on Rebsamen Park Road for lunch. Arkansas Court of Ap-

peals Judge Tom Glaze said he saw McArthur there at 1 p.m.
Then Circuit Judge John Langston said McArthur visited with
him at around 3 p.m.

McArthur said he then was at his law office, where he had
several appointments.

USES "BIOLOGICAL TIME"

Robinson's explanation on the time of the meeting was that
Swayze wasn't wearing a watch. "He goes by biological time—
when he gets hungry," Robinson said.

Robinson said he made the 47 mile trip to Malvern Saturday
in 21.5 minutes, but he wouldn't say how fast he was driving.

With everybody in Arkansas hanging on each twist and turn in the
melodrama, the sheriff's claim to have set an overland speed record to
Hot Spring County provoked general hilarity. At last the McArthur
saga found the comic relief it had lacked. Even people who had no
trouble at all swallowing any of Tommy's tall tales of conspiracy and
corruption choked on that one. At noon on a weekday, stock car
champion Richard Petty would be hard-pressed to make it from downtown to Little Rock city limits in 21.5 minutes. Temporarily, at least,
the sheriff became a figure of fun.

Everybody was laughing but John Robert Starr. A Little Rock
woman who had calculated that the sheriff's patrol car would have to
have hurtled through three counties at an average speed of more than
130 mph appeared at the courthouse to file a citizen's complaint
against Tommy for reckless driving. "Put me down as a witness," the
Democrat editor harumphed. "I was in the car."*

Politically speaking, however, the sheriff's blunder was far from
decisive. His most fervid supporters could be counted upon to remain
undaunted by minor inconsistencies. But things got even worse for
Tommy on Wednesday. No sooner had Michael Swayze met with an
attorney from the public defender's staff than the supposed "hit man"
recanted his confession—every word of it. The whole thing had been
a figment of his drunken imagination.

At a bond hearing in municipal court, Swayze broke into tears on

---

*Starr's subsequent written account of his weekend at the sheriff's side neglected to
mention the record-setting trip. After he and Tommy fell out years later, Starr wrote
a column citing the incident as proof that the man was a habitual liar.

the witness stand. His voice quavering and his hands shaking, the twenty-six-year-old unemployed truck driver came across as anything but a cold-blooded killer. "All they had to do was ask me," Swayze said to the TV cameras Judge David Hale had permitted into the courtroom, "and I would have told them it was a joke. We were settin' up there. We'd been drinkin'. That's all there is to it. It was a stupid, lousy joke. That's all it was."

"Have you ever seen Bill McArthur?" Dub Bentley asked.

"On the news. I did not meet him at the Playpen. Everybody wants to hear the truth. Here it is: I did not meet him at the Playpen. I did not meet him in Malvern. I tried to tell Tommy Robinson it was a joke on the way up here. And they didn't want to hear that. They said, 'We might even let you escape on the way up here.' I been down there in that hole since Saturday.

"I might be guilty of one thing," Swayze concluded, "guilty of lying on them tapes, because I was scared."

Municipal Judge David Hale, however, hadn't gotten any more decisive since the probable cause hearing. He denied a joint motion by Jack Holt, Jr., and Dub Bentley to dismiss. Ordering Swayze and Freeman held without bond, the judge also removed the prosecutor from the case and appointed Sonny Dillahunty to carry the ball. Bentley objected strenuously. Without the elected prosecutor's voluntarily stepping aside, Hale had neither constitutional nor statutory authority to force him. He simply took it.

Adopting his sternest demeanor, Hale also warned that a gag order he'd issued earlier still applied. Comments to the media, the judge warned, would result in somebody's going to jail.

· · ·

Little Rock Municipal Court, however, was not where Bill McArthur planned to make his stand. Within hours of the farcical proceeding before Judge Hale, McArthur had taken the offensive. He filed a lawsuit for false arrest and malicious prosecution against Robinson and Dill in Federal District Court. Federal judges didn't have to answer to the Arkansas electorate, and none had ever been known to cower before John Robert Starr. Based upon his many columns railing against them, it seemed to be one of the *Democrat* editor's main disappointments in life.

Bill had been contemplating the action every since his August 30 arrest. Grieving or not, it wasn't in his nature to take the sheriff's attacks lying down. But he'd meant to postpone the counterattack until the melodrama played itself out in Arkansas courts. The Swayze affair had changed all that. Whether or not Robinson had orchestrated the whole thing—as Bill first suspected—the sheriff was truly out of control. Judges were rolling over like bowling pins.

Two of Little Rock's most formidable legal talents stepped forward to volunteer their services free of charge. One was William R. Wilson, a flamboyant and politically savvy native of the town of Waldron, located on the edge of the Ouachita National Forest. As the president of the Arkansas Bar Association, Wilson's stepping forward sent a strong message to lawyers around the state. Appointed chairman of the State Police Commission by Governor Bill Clinton during Robinson's stormy tenure there, Wilson had nothing but contempt for Tommy.

Spoiling for a fight, Wilson took the unusual step of writing to McArthur's parents and children—something he'd never done for a client—saying he was certain of Bill's innocence and apologizing for not speaking out earlier. "I am persuaded beyond peradventure," he wrote, "that he is a victim of this madman we have elected Sheriff."

Also stepping forward was Phil Kaplan, one of the state's best-known civil rights advocates. A Harvard graduate and native of Massachusetts, Kaplan had come to Arkansas directly out of the University of Michigan Law School. Since becoming a founding partner in Arkansas' first racially integrated law firm, he'd helped win one battle after another against the state's whites-only establishment.

Kaplan had found particularly offensive Robinson and Dill's boast that they'd arrested McArthur for refusing to answer questions—a bare-faced violation of his rights that troubled all too few Arkansans. Even so, until the Swayze episode Kaplan had felt that Bill was perfectly capable of looking out for himself.

Neither Wilson nor Kaplan were particularly friends of McArthur's, but their coming forward touched him deeply. And it also meant that Tommy Robinson was in for one hell of a fight. Some law school friends of McArthur's began a fund to help pay his expenses, and several other attorneys volunteered to help any way they could. Drafted by Kaplan, the stringently worded complaint alleged that Robinson's warrantless arrests of McArthur had been made in bad faith on the basis of "incredible and insubstantial information," violating his rights under the Fifth, Sixth, and Fourteenth amendments.

Either because they'd had professional dealings with Tommy during his brief career as a U.S. Marshal, or with one or another of the attorneys, every federal judge in Little Rock recused. A judge would have to be appointed to hear the case by the 8th Circuit Court of Appeals in St. Louis.

•   •   •

Seemingly unhinged by the day's developments, Sheriff Tommy summoned the press to PCSD headquarters Wednesday night, announcing that he planned to defy Judge Hale's gag order. There he put on an astonishing performance even by his own standards. Shouting at the top of his lungs much of the time, Robinson cried that "there was a fix put on today and there's no guarantee there won't be a fix put on tomorrow!"

Wall-eyed and gesturing wildly, Sheriff Tommy appeared visibly drunk to members of a Channel 7 camera crew. Other reporters feared that the sheriff had finally gone over the edge. The *Democrat*'s Cary Bradburn suspected that Tommy was suffering a manic episode and might require hospitalization.

Amidst all the hubbub, John Robert Starr's apparent confidence remained unshaken. In his Thursday column, the *Democrat* editor speculated that among other possibilities, the Swayze affair "is a set-up by McArthur, designed to cause the Sheriff to make an invalid arrest which would, when it came down, further damage Robinson's credibility"—a scheme requiring Tommy's full cooperation, as Starr neglected to point out.

In what would become his and Sheriff Tommy's dominant theme in coming weeks, however, Starr advanced a theory that might well have been borrowed intact from an episode of *Columbo*. McArthur, he wrote,

> said he is not stupid enough to have [attempted the assassination scheme]. Nobody believes McArthur is stupid. But a brilliant person might conclude that the best way to engineer a murder plot would be to make it appear on the surface so ridiculous that no one would believe a brilliant man concocted it.

The follies continued in municipal court on Thursday. In response to separate motions from McArthur's attorneys, the public defender, and the prosecutor, Judge Hale held a contempt hearing involving

Robinson and Dill. Feelings ran high as Jack Holt, Jr., urged the judge to prove to Robinson that he was not above the law. Pounding a lectern, Bill Wilson delivered a blunt attack upon the sheriff in open court.

The sheriff, he declared, constituted "the gravest threat to our society in current times. . . . I'm scared of this man. Not of the verbal abuse. I'm scared of this man who's armed with a badge and a gun. Send a message to this man," Wilson urged the judge.

Hale solemnly examined videotapes of Tommy's defiant press conference before finding yet another escape route. Holding the sheriff and Dill guilty of contempt, he affixed no penalty. "I know this is emotional," he sympathized, "you've had your life threatened." Then he denied a motion to dismiss charges against McArthur and bound the case over to Circuit Court—once again kicking it upstairs.

His role pre-empted, Sonny Dillahunty made a superfluous motion to withdraw, commenting that Dub Bentley's handling of the Swayze affair had constituted a "mockery of justice." Bentley, who'd filed a motion in Circuit Court to have Dillahunty's appointment voided, cried foul. Hale ordered Dillahunty's remarks stricken from the record, but not, of course, from the newspapers and TV. THE SEASON'S TOP DUO—J.R. AND THE DILLY, read the headline over John Robert Starr's column.

Later that afternoon, Bentley filed a libel suit against Starr and the *Democrat*. The prosecutor's action alleged that two columns accusing him of a cover-up in the Swayze case were both false and malicious. Knowing that as a public figure Dub had virtually no chance of winning a judgment against the newspaper, Starr reacted jubilantly.

• • •

For all the excitement, the Swayze affair quickly vanished from public scrutiny. As with the Alice McArthur case, no sooner had Judge Hale bound the case over to Circuit Court than it reverted into Dub Bentley's hands, and there was nothing Hale or the sheriff could do about it. While the prosecutor debated filing perjury charges against Swayze—less to punish him than to expose Sheriff Tommy's bullying tactics—he eventually decided that the drunken fool had been punished enough, and set him free.

On February 15, after the media hubbub had subsided somewhat, Circuit Judge Floyd Lofton quietly dismissed the charges against Bill

McArthur on the same procedural grounds that Dub had warned Robinson about in the first place. Without commenting upon the substance of the evidence, Lofton ruled that if any crime had been committed, it had taken place in Malvern, not Little Rock.

Nothing prevented Robinson from taking his evidence before a Hot Spring County grand jury as the prosecutor there had invited him to do. But what with his busy schedule of TV appearances, the sheriff never got around to it.

2

To the great majority in the Arkansas press, the sheer absurdity of the Swayze affair confirmed all their suspicions about Sheriff Tommy. If still unwilling to confront the media's own role in turning the McArthur murder into the crime of the century, editorial writers across the state condemned Robinson. The most pungent appeared in the *Warren Eagle-Democrat.* "You read it in this column 60 days ago. We now repeat it," the southeast Arkansas newspaper warned its readers.

> Tommy Robinson is the most dangerous man in Arkansas today. He combines all of the rabble-rousing skills of a Huey Long. He appeals to the mass mind of Arkansas voters much in the same way the slick country boy from Huntsville, Orval Faubus, appealed to them a quarter of a century ago.
>
> Robinson will run, either for governor or for Congress. If it's in 1984, it'll be for Congress. If it's in 1986, it'll be for governor.
>
> May the Almighty save the people in Arkansas . . . mainly from themselves and their fascination with characters like the current occupant of the Sheriff's office in Pulaski County.

But editorial writers were preaching to the choir; at best their efforts reached the literate minority. Of more significance to a politician like Robinson was an extraordinary piece of TV journalism broadcast on Channel 7—a six-minute video history of Robinson's wildest stunts as sheriff. (Local stories normally ran thirty seconds.) "Throughout his career in law enforcement," reporter Bob Steele read over a freeze frame of the wild-eyed sheriff jabbing his finger into the air, "Tommy Robinson has masterfully rallied public opinion to support his self-proclaimed image as a super-cop. Tonight to many, he appears to be something less."

But among his core constituency in the blue-collar neighborhoods and the country towns, the Swayze affair damaged Tommy hardly at all. Nobody in Arkansas, moreover, heard the voice of the people more clearly than John Robert Starr. Seizing the chance to identify himself and his newspaper with the sheriff's heroic quest for justice, the *Democrat* editor threw himself into the fray with renewed vigor. Day after day, Starr praised Tommy and attacked his enemies with every weapon at his disposal. He wrote about almost nothing else. From a psychological perspective alone, it was a hypnotic performance. And the *Arkansas Democrat* was selling like crazy.

Chapter 4

1

Almost unnoticed amid the hysteria surrounding the Swayze affair, on February 2 Judge Langston announced the appointment of a relatively little known lawyer named Darrell Brown to be "special counsel" to the McArthur grand jury. Politically, Brown was an inspired choice. Despite being a native Arkansan, the thirty-five-year-old attorney could hardly be described as a member of the Little Rock establishment. Few black lawyers could. Since graduating from the UA-Fayetteville Law School in 1972, he'd spent most of his career as a U.S. Magistrate in the Canal Zone. He had no ties with anybody involved in the McArthur case.

In keeping with his policy of pacifying the sheriff, Judge Langston set up a meeting between Brown and Robinson. Moving cautiously, Brown also took it upon himself to visit with Dub Bentley. He paid a call upon Bill Wilson as well. Although he reacted frostily to Wilson's warning that the county might stiff him—as no legal mechanism existed to pay his fee—Brown satisfied himself that McArthur's lawyers had no objection to his taking the job. If possible, he wanted to avoid getting caught in a political crossfire.

After several conversations with the sheriff, Brown passed muster. According to Tommy, he'd investigated Brown's background and pronounced him clean. "We talked," Brown explained later, "and I said, 'Now, Tommy, if you have something that you think needs to be said, just say it now, because once I get involved as Special Prosecutor I'm going to be preoccupied with doing my job.' I did not want to get into any mud-slinging contest. Tommy assured me that there would be no problems."

Possibly the sheriff mistook Brown's caution as an indication that he could be bullied. If so, he was making a serious mistake. A native of Horatio, in the piney woods of southwest Arkansas, Brown had a lifelong habit of asserting himself in ticklish situations. The son of a pulpwood worker and a schoolteacher, Brown had walked on as a non-scholarship defensive back at the University of Arkansas—the first black player ever to wear a Razorback jersey. Welcomed by most of the other players but shunned by the coaches, Brown stuck it out until he wrecked his knee in a scrimmage and gave up athletics to concentrate on his dream of becoming a lawyer.

The McArthur case had the capacity to make Brown's reputation overnight. But before agreeing to the job, he researched the history of grand juries in Arkansas. What he learned convinced him that in order to arrive at a just verdict and make it stick, he would have to take the institution back to its roots. "I decided," Brown emphasized, "that I did not want to take on the traditional prosecuting role—that being that the prosecutor walks into the grand jury room and simply presents his file and says, 'I can get a conviction,' and walks away with an indictment. Historically, the grand jury evolved as an instrument to stand between the King and the people. I wanted to put everything before those sixteen people, and let them make a decision. I wanted them to understand that 'I don't care what you do. If it's Bill McArthur, by God, it's Bill McArthur. If it's Tommy Robinson, it's Tommy Robinson.' "

And that, in turn, was the kind of grand jury everybody told Darrell Brown that they wanted. Even Sheriff Tommy.

• • •

McArthur's lawyers reserved judgment. They liked what they'd heard of Brown, but noble words came easy. And Judge Langston's consulting Robinson over the selection wasn't the only sign that he was bending over backward not to offend the sheriff. They were particularly dismayed by the judge's treatment of a series of defense motions. In a brusque letter dated February 15, Langston denied them all. He would not direct the grand jury to hear McArthur's testimony, and refused to order Orsini held somewhere other than Sheriff Tommy's jail. He thought it unnecessary to sequester the jurors, or to instruct them to ignore what they read in newspapers or saw on TV.

Bill Wilson was outraged. He objected bitterly to the judge's taking action without a hearing, and he objected to the *form* of the denial as well. A formal court order, which Wilson believed almost mandatory in a case of this magnitude, would become a permanent part of the record in the event of an appeal. Langston's letter would not.

But rather than taking the judge head-on by filing a motion to include his letter in the record—which Langston could also deny— McArthur and his lawyers decided to back off. Jack Holt wrote Darrell Brown promising full cooperation. Bill himself could not help but recall the words of his mentor, the late Judge Bill Kirby. "The two most perilous times in our lives," Kirby had said, "are when the grand jury is in session or the Arkansas legislature comes to town." It was a bit less than two years since he had quoted them to Mary Lee Orsini.

•   •   •

The McArthur grand jury convened on February 17, 1983. To avoid the turmoil in the courthouse, the panel had been assigned a room overlooking the Arkansas River in a county office building at the foot of the Main Street Bridge. In the two weeks since accepting the prosecutor's job, Darrell Brown had become obsessed with the McArthur case. Reluctant to hand over his case files, Sheriff Tommy had ordered Dill to prepare a written summary. The document turned out to be one of the oddest Brown had ever read. Running to more than sixty pages, Dill's summary never stated exactly how and why McArthur allegedly conspired to murder his wife.

Almost everywhere Brown knocked, the report gave off a hollow sound. Dill presented hearsay and double hearsay as if it were direct evidence. Second- and third-hand information from people who knew nothing other than what Mary Lee told them was treated like holy writ. Even when—like Joyce Holt—they'd ceased to believe it themselves. Dill made factual assertions that could not be supported by the file, and others that contradicted it. Any skepticism he may have felt about Orsini's story, he'd managed to restrain.

The deeper Brown dug, moreover, the clearer it became that everybody involved had too much at stake to sit quietly and allow the grand jury investigation to take its course. Sheriff Tommy in particular had taken to calling Brown or dropping by his office to harangue him almost daily. Sometimes Tommy wanted to talk about the evidence, and sometimes he wanted to talk about how much the McArthur case meant to his political future.

Trusting nobody, Brown decided to take steps to protect himself. Even before testimony began, he sent a confidential letter to the commander of the Arkansas State Police. Because of the sensitivity of the grand jury probe, Brown explained,

> and the possibility of jury tampering, bribery, undue influence, coercion, entrapment, and other improprieties, I would request that you provide me with any recording or electronic devices and other equipment that would have the capability of detecting or otherwise accomplishing these ends. . . . I reiterate that your cooperation is of utmost importance.

Colonel Tommy Goodwin was happy to comply. Within twenty-four hours, troopers had hard-wired Brown's office with a hidden videotape recorder and a backup audio system as well. The special prosecutor himself controlled the apparatus with a switch under the desk. He told nobody, not even Judge Langston. Anybody who wanted to tamper with Darrell Brown's grand jury would end up reliving the experience on TV.

• • •

Sheriff Tommy began his testimony on February 17 by flattering Brown fulsomely. The special prosecutor, he assured the jurors, was absolutely top-notch. Before entrusting Darrell with the dramatic evidence he was about to present, he had checked his background carefully. "He came out with a Tommy Robinson clearance from A to Z," the sheriff assured them, "which is pretty good."

The McArthur case, Tommy announced, had occupied at least 85 percent of his waking hours since the fateful afternoon of July 2. The evidence he had assembled was of almost dizzying complexity. But if the jurors would bear with him, Tommy would make it all come clear. Unlike some people he could name, Robinson dealt in facts. "Not theories, not assumptions," he said, "but facts . . . I'm not going to deal in theories, even though everyone else does."

That much said, the sheriff embarked upon a rambling, two-hour soliloquy that left the jurors shaking their heads in confusion. "Mary

Lee Orsini," Tommy assured them, "is more gullible than any person I ever met in my life. You could sell her swampland and she would buy it. I don't know what she's going to say. She may walk in here and say, 'They're all crazy, I'm innocent.' "

Paradoxically, Orsini was also the world's biggest liar. "She told so many lies," he said, "I got tired of looking at the woman. Everything she told us that we checked out was basically a lie." But no Indian Hills housewife, the sheriff reasoned, could possibly invent the stories Orsini was telling. "I suspicioned," Tommy testified, "that Bill McArthur was looking for an excuse for the bombing." So Robinson had come up with the Art Baldwin "scam" to test his theory that McArthur was calling the shots. And sure enough, Baldwin's name "came back full circle on the day of Lee Orsini's arrest." (In previous testimony, Tommy's gambit had paid off three weeks earlier, before Alice's death.)

Pieced together from Robinson's hours of disjointed, repetitious testimony, the story went more or less as follows: "Objectively, based on the evidence that we have at this time," Tommy explained "I could just about unequivocally tell you that Ron Orsini committed suicide. They got in over their heads in debt."

The larger truth that Robinson claimed to have corroborated, though, was essentially the Tiffany–shot–Ron scenario with a twist—the twist being that the child too was innocent. The cunning Bill McArthur, however, had convinced the distraught mother otherwise. Too excited to keep his seat, Tommy paced back and forth in front of the sixteen jurors gesturing excitedly. "Lee Orsini will tell you," he promised, "that what Bill McArthur had on her [was that] he'd convinced her that Tiffany had done it. And she told me, 'Charge me before you charge my daughter. I'll serve the rest of my life in the penitentiary for my daughter.' "

McArthur's friends, Robinson warned, might try to portray the marriage as a happy one. Bill had bought them all off with profits from cocaine trafficking. His motive was crystal clear: trapped in a loveless, adulterous marriage, with his law practice floundering, Bill wanted to get his hands on his wife's $50,000 a month oil inheritance. McArthur was the King of Sleaze.

2

Over at the *Democrat*, meanwhile, John Robert Starr was stalking the biggest scoop of his career. An unimpeachable source had told him that the cunning Dub Bentley had pulled a legal technicality. Come hell or high water—and no matter what the grand jury decided—unless McArthur went to trial within ten days, he would walk. The "speedy trial rule" in the Arkansas Criminal Code was due to expire on February 26.

Summoned from his courthouse beat, reporter Cary Bradburn says he told Starr his source was mistaken. Since McArthur was out on bond, the state had eighteen months to try him, giving the speedy trial clock another year to run. But Starr insisted, so Bradburn went to the library and Xeroxed the law. Then he interviewed two Circuit Court judges who assured him that the notion was ridiculous: next he went to see Dub Bentley. Indeed, if the charges were nol-prossed [dropped] as Dub had recommended, McArthur would remain vulnerable for the rest of his life.

Confident he'd laid the rumor to rest, Bradburn says he told Starr that there was no story. But the managing editor refused to be persuaded. On Sunday, February 20, the story appeared smack in the middle of the *Democrat* front page under Starr's own byline:

MCARTHUR CASE: "SPEEDY TRIAL" RULE MAY BAR PROSECUTION ON CONSPIRACY CHARGE

Unless William C. McArthur is brought to trial for conspiracy to commit murder this week, the speedy trial provision of the U.S. Constitution will bar his prosecution on that charge, sources in the Pulaski County criminal justice system have told the *Arkansas Democrat*.

The sources said that the rules under which Pulaski County courts operate call for dismissal of charges against a defendant if he had not been tried within 180 days of his arrest. McArthur was arrested last Aug. 30. His 180 day period runs through Feb. 26.

Prosecutor Wilbur C. Bentley, who had declined to prosecute McArthur on the conspiracy charge, confirmed that in his opinion, the "speedy trial" clock is still running in McArthur's case.

Bentley said he had not given any thought to the rule. "There's nothing underhanded going on," Bentley said. "No attempt is being made to try to defeat justice."

Bradburn was horrified. His interview with the prosecutor had been written up in such a way that Bentley seemed to be endorsing what he'd explicitly denied. The young reporter feared for his job. But by

Monday, the *Democrat* had gotten so many calls from lawyers and judges that Starr was forced to write a front-page retraction. In a remarkable column, Starr took full responsibility. "The information my sources gave me was correct," he manfully admitted.

> I mistranslated it. . . . [My] source told me the rule required trial within 18 months of the arrest, or charges must be dismissed. . . . Without any help from anybody, I translated 18 months into 180 days. I owe a world of thanks to Sheriff Tommy Robinson, who caught the mistake and told me about it in time for me to write the correction for Monday's paper.

Who Starr's source could have been in the unlikely event that it *wasn't* Tommy remained almost as great a mystery as where he got his calendars. The *Democrat* editor never would tell.

3

Mary Lee followed Sheriff Tommy to the witness stand on the afternoon of February 17. She spent most of her first afternoon maneuvering for position. Before agreeing to testify, she demanded immunity from prosecution. A contempt citation, she made clear, meant nothing to a woman serving a life sentence. To the dismay of Dub Bentley, who feared it could contaminate the upcoming Ron Orsini trial, the grand jury gave it to her. Along with immunity, Orsini got anonymity too. No transcript of her testimony has ever emerged.

By all accounts, however, she gave a command performance. Weeping at times, laughing bitterly at others, Orsini held the jurors spellbound. Even as a convicted murderess, Mary Lee had lost none of her uncanny ability to persuade total strangers of the most amazing things in the world. Like many of those she'd chosen as bit players in the melodrama that had swirled around her for two years, some of the jurors could not help but be swayed. "We had a couple," commented a juror named Mark Taylor, "who had seen too many episodes of *Perry Mason.*"

Eight months of innuendo, speculation, gossip, and character assassination had done their job. Any doubts jurors may have had about Tommy Robinson were more than balanced by mistrust of criminal defense lawyers in general—and "debonair, nightclub-owning" spec-

imens named Bill McArthur in particular. If there was an early bias,
it ran in favor of indictment.

If nothing else, Mary Lee's testimony convinced Darrell Brown that
he had some more homework to do. On Friday, February 18, the
special prosecutor met at his office in the Union National Bank Building with Dub Bentley and Sergeant T. J. Farley. They spent five hours
walking Brown through Farley's investigative file. Dub stressed that if
Mary Lee was now trying to persuade the grand jury that her husband
had killed himself—having guessed as much from Sheriff Tommy's
late-night phone calls—it was at least the fifth story she'd told. The
prosecutor ticked them off on his fingers. First she'd blamed her
brother, Dub said, then drug dealers, next NLRPD Chief Bill Younts,
and eventually her own child. And she'd begun spinning fantasies and
telling lies, he emphasized, long before she'd hired McArthur.

It was all news to Darrell Brown. Despite having ridiculed the
NLRPD investigation to the grand jury, Sheriff Tommy had never laid
eyes on Farley's case file. Neither had Dill. It hadn't been included in
the evidence they'd turned over to the McArthur grand jury. Nor had
the 1981 grand jury transcript. Fearful that Tommy would slip it to
Orsini's lawyers, Dub had refused to let him read it anywhere but the
courthouse. The sheriff hadn't bothered. Trusting Brown to keep it to
himself, Dub handed it over. The special prosecutor had another long
weekend ahead of him.

On Tuesday, February 22, Orsini took the witness stand for several
more hours. Much of her testimony concerned a new series of allegations she had come up with since the probable cause hearing. According to Dill's summary, Bill had not only blackmailed his client
into a murder conspiracy, but also

> discussed the possibility of her picking up cocaine for him and
> finding someone who could cut and distribute it. . . . Orsini
> stated the roles in the narcotic traffic would be as follows: (1) Bill
> McArthur would finance it and has all the connections; (2) that
> she would transport the narcotics from out of state to McArthur's
> connections; (3) Yankee Hall would be the man to assist in
> cutting the cocaine and distributing to various dealers. . . . Mary
> Lee Orsini stated McArthur made arrangements for her to meet
> Yankee Hall and this is when she became acquainted with him.

Over the weekend, meanwhile, Sheriff Tommy had made yet another stunning breakthrough. Bearing remarkable resemblance to the

Swayze affair, it happened like this: A sometime confidential informant of the PCSD phoned from the North Little Rock city jail. Locked
up for DWI, a young woman from England, Arkansas, offered to make
Tommy a deal. If he'd spring her from the hoosegow, she'd swap him
information that would help him convict Bob Troutt and Bill
McArthur.

Robinson jumped at the chance. Released to his custody, Elaine
Willett told the sheriff exactly the kind of story he'd long wanted to
hear. Most of it turned out to have been gathered in barrooms like the
Mason Jar. Supposedly, a liquor store owner named Jim Bullard had
revealed to her that a friend of his—a convicted arsonist named Herbie
Wright—had helped Troutt set fire to his own nightclub for the purpose of insurance fraud.

But that was not all Willett told the eager sheriff. Bullard, she
claimed, had also admitted that the selfsame Herbie Wright had built
and tested the bomb that exploded under Alice McArthur's car. The
liquor store owner had supposedly accompanied Wright to a wooded
area out in the country to test the device.

Willett's story couldn't have suited Tommy's needs better if he'd
invented it himself. At best, every bit of her videotaped statement was
the rankest kind of hearsay—and self-serving to boot. Ample evidence
existed to contradict it. As a part of his guilty plea, Yankee had described the precise manufacture of the bomb to ATF agents. Not only
had the description squared with evidence ATF had gathered about the
purchase of the batteries and switches, but he'd directed them to a spot
on a dirt road out Highway 10 where he himself had detonated a
blasting cap. Agent Spurgeon had found the site and collected the
physical evidence.

On June 29, 1982, moreover—three days before Alice McArthur's
death— the selfsame Herbie Wright had tipped an LRPD detective
that Yankee had been asking around for dynamite. Wright's tip had led
to the ATF agent's walking into 24 Inverness Circle on the night of
July 2 carrying a mug shot of the murderer.

Nevertheless, Tommy wasted no time. He quickly rounded up the
liquor store owner, sweated a statement out of him, and arrested
Wright. He phoned both Darrell Brown and the jury foreman with the
good news. Not only would the two men's testimony falsify Yankee's
confession—proving that the dapper little junkie had been lying to
protect McArthur all along—but Elaine Willett herself could give
evidence that would prove a conspiracy to murder Alice and use her
money to finance a criminal empire.

No sooner had Orsini finished testifying than Tommy showed the grand jury a videotape of his newest informant. He announced his intention to place the pert "mystery witness" under armed guard. According to Tommy, McArthur was so fearful of what Willett knew that she too had gotten telephoned death threats. Strangers had supposedly been prowling around her home town of England, and an attempt had been made to burn down her house.

Warning that he'd be dead within a week if word of what he was about to show them leaked, the sheriff produced a hand-lettered, posterboard chart purporting to reveal the hidden structure of organized crime in Arkansas. Listed were the names of some of the best-known men in the state—multi-millionaire businessmen, prominent state senators, and Arkansas Supreme Court justices. Name brands, every one, including some whose names would be familiar to readers of the *Wall Street Journal*. Dub Bentley occupied a niche, a *consigliere* of sorts. So did Bill McArthur. As usual, the only authority Robinson provided for the information was himself.

Tommy's "Organized Crime Flow Chart," as it became known, may have temporarily awed the more gullible members of the panel. But the sheriff's show-and-tell project also made others wonder if the fabled lawman hadn't been letting his imagination work overtime. In retrospect, however, it may have represented Robinson's highest point of credibility with the grand jury.

The day after Mary Lee finished testifying, Sheriff Tommy herded three witnesses before the panel: Jim Bullard, Herbie Wright, and Yankee Hall. Once safely behind closed doors, however, the liquor store owner recanted. Michael Swayze's confession had stood for four days; Bullard's lasted fewer than twenty-four hours. Tommy and Dill, he testified, had all but tortured him into a bogus statement.

Where Elaine Willett had come up with her story, Bullard said, he had no idea. Until the day before PCSD deputies had called him in for questioning, he'd been hospitalized with a bleeding ulcer caused by chronic alcoholism. Kept in intensive care for several days, he'd checked himself out against medical advice as soon as he could walk. He needed to take doses of Tagamet every four hours to prevent his ulcer from erupting.

Brought to PCSD headquarters shortly before 6:00 P.M., he'd told Robinson and Dill that whoever they'd talked to was pulling their leg. He knew nothing. He also asked to be allowed to telephone his lawyer and send for his medication. Tommy refused and ordered him locked up. Hours passed. Deputies ignored Bullard's pleas that he was in terrible pain. Around midnight, the sheriff and Dill returned. By then, Bullard was in agony.

Tommy insisted that Bullard and Herbie Wright—a lifelong friend—had set fire to Troutt's club and made a car bomb for Yankee Hall. "I kept telling them we didn't and that I would take a lie detector test," Bullard testified, "but they weren't interested in that." The sheriff, he said, made it clear that Bullard wouldn't be allowed to leave until he confessed.

Having vomited blood and fearful he would die, Bullard caved in. "I told the Sheriff Herbie Wright had told me Yankee wanted him to make a bomb," he testified. "That's what the Sheriff wanted me to tell him and that's what I told him. It's not true."

Darrell Brown pressed Bullard very hard. Helping a friend blow up stumps, he emphasized, was not a crime. But telling conflicting stories under oath could lead to a perjury indictment. Offered a chance to recant, Bullard stuck to his story. He was even willing to submit to a lie detector to prove that Tommy had coerced him to implicate his friend. *

Herbie Wright took a similar line. Nicknamed "the Torch," for a 1977 arson conviction, Wright had also done time for bookmaking. He wouldn't have made the most persuasive witness in the world except for one thing: he had federal agents to back him up.

Yankee confirmed both men's testimony. As he'd previously sworn to ATF, he'd built the car bomb himself. He'd gotten the Tovex explosive and blasting caps from Carl Ray Wilson, the batteries from a supermarket in Indian Hills, and the rest of what he needed from Ron Orsini's shop in the garage at 7412 Pontiac. Besides helping Yankee identify Alice's car and scout the neighborhood, Mary Lee had actually disguised herself in a blond wig, a pillow, and a maternity dress to buy some parts he'd needed. Herbie Wright had nothing to do with the crime.

• • •

Darrell Brown never would discuss the testimony of individual witnesses. But the treatment allegedly given Bullard, whose physician also testified, sickened him. Equally upsetting was the sheriff's reaction to

---

* In fact, Bullard was later charged with perjury based on the conflict between his confession to Tommy and his testimony to the grand jury. He died before the charges against him were resolved.

the February 23 testimony. Tommy made no attempt to conceal his fury
over the collapse of yet another flawless scenario. But how had he
known what the witnesses said? Grand jury proceedings were supposed
to be secret. Aware of Robinson's history of allegedly spying on political
opponents, Brown suspected the sheriff of electronic eavesdropping.

The special prosecutor had the grand jury room swept for bugs, but
none were found. Could Tommy have a spy on the jury? Suspicion
eventually focused upon two unmarked PCSD patrol cars parked across
the river in the lee of the Main Street bridge. An operative with a
parabolic microphone trained upon a window could have picked up
every word spoken inside the grand jury room. But again, no evidence
was found.

After Brown and the jury foreman met to discuss the situation with
Judge Langston, the special prosecutor went public. Without naming
anybody, he issued a stern warning that electronic surveillance of the
grand jury violated state and federal law. Reporters reduced to camping
out in the hallway hoping to identify witnesses were happy to oblige
him with headlines.

Brown knew that his vagueness would only fuel public speculation
about organized crime. But as far as he was concerned, the public
could imagine anything it wanted; it usually did. The idea was to back
Tommy off without open confrontation. Subtlety, however, rarely had
any impact on Sheriff Robinson. As long as the grand jury met at the
Wallace Building, the two PCSD patrol cars remained in place. The
special prosecutor himself began to live with the suspicion that he was
under constant surveillance.

"It never got to the point where I was paranoid," Brown said later.
"But there was no doubt in my mind that I was not walking down the
street alone." He began to get hang-up calls at odd hours, even on
out-of-town business trips when he'd taken precautions to keep his
whereabouts confidential. If he hadn't known better, he could easily
have imagined himself back in Manuel Noriega's Panama City.

·   ·   ·

Several weeks would pass before Tommy's "mystery witness" put in
her final appearance before the grand jury. In the interim, the downtown Executive Inn had run up more than $4,000 in charges for
Elaine Willett and several deputies assigned to prevent her from coming to harm. The bar tab alone came to more than $700. Deputies

spent several hundred dollars feeding round steak to the departmental German shepherd.

Somewhat leery of Willett after the collapse of her first exercise in double hearsay, the grand jury hardly knew what to make of Part Two—an elaborate tale in which two ex-clients of McArthur's had supposedly approached her to front for him in running a combination nightclub/whorehouse/cocaine distributorship on I-40 near the Lonoke County line.

Willett also claimed to have held the McArthur murder weapon in her hot little hands—although she couldn't recall whether it was a revolver or an automatic—and to have driven to Fort Smith with one of the ex-clients to retrieve $50,000 cash from a safe deposit box to pay off Yankee Hall. Willett hadn't actually *seen* any money. She'd gone to get her hair done while her companion went to the bank. But she had no doubt it was there.

Before she finished testifying, Sheriff Tommy's $4,000 mystery witness admitted to the grand jury that she hadn't actually met Bill McArthur either. Not in person anyway. She hadn't even talked to the man on the telephone. But she sure had heard an awful lot about him, and she *had* seen him on TV.

Not surprisingly, perhaps, Elaine Willett's great ambition in life was to become a deputy sheriff.

Chapter 5

1

Witness after witness, day after day, Sheriff Robinson's case against Bill McArthur fell apart in front of the grand jury's eyes. True to his original intention, Darrell Brown kept his own growing skepticism to himself. For the most part, he restricted himself to educating the jurors about what constituted admissible evidence and what did not. It didn't take a legal genius. "I guess you could characterize most of the testimony," he said, "by saying it *started* as hearsay."

Rather than basing their decision upon what Mary Lee Orsini told them somebody told her, the jurors decided to find out for themselves. For the first couple of weeks, the evidence became progressively more confusing. Yankee Hall told the grand jury the same thing he'd told Dub Bentley: If he were going to lie to save anybody, he'd save himself, not McArthur. With seven sober months since his arrest to think it over, Yankee had pretty much decided that his early belief in Bill's involvement was part of the same con job Orsini had done on him in the first place.

Having nothing more to lose, Hall let it all hang out. He told them how Mary Lee had revealed the Tiffany–shot–Ron scenario to him during the probable cause hearing. He warned them against her duplicity. Had the car bomb killed Alice McArthur as planned on May 21, Hall realized, he would have been dead meat. It would have been goodbye Yankee, hello front-page news. Standing over his body like the heroine of a thousand action/adventure movies, Orsini would have been free to plan her next move.

As for the July 2 murder, Hall had come to believe that the LRPD had saved his life. "If Tommy had found me before the LRPD found me," he said, "I'd have been dead, man. They wasn't fixing to bring me and Larry in alive. Look at the way they went to Larry's house. They didn't go up there to ask him no questions. They went in there with sawed-off shotguns. They were looking for me at the same time. But I was up at the Mason Jar, having no idea what was coming."

In a later interview, Hall made no secret of his belief that Orsini had hoaxed Tommy every bit as much as she'd suckered him—and that if McArthur hadn't set the flower bouquet down at his dead wife's feet, then somebody from the PCSD surely had.

· · ·

The grand jury had been in session for almost four weeks before it called Bill McArthur. Emotionally, McArthur was a wreck. The effort of keeping his rage and sorrow bottled up inside had begun to tell. Battling depression, McArthur found it almost impossible to concentrate on serious work. He'd begun to drink more than he should.

McArthur began the first of his three days of testimony on Thursday, March 10—almost two years to the day after the murder of Ron Orsini. Sitting erect in a straight-backed wooden chair with the sixteen jurors surrounding him at a U-shaped table, he found the experience harrowing, but oddly cathartic. At first Darrell Brown asked all the questions, but others eventually joined in too. The questioning went on for several hours each day.

"I think the thing that surprised me most," Bill said later, "was that there were no unfair questions asked me. Difficult questions, yes. And they knew they were difficult, but we did it anyway. Certain things I have trouble talking about even now—my relationship with Alice, the feelings I had that day when I got home, my dealings with the children then and afterward. Then on the third day we went out to my house and they looked at that."

Despite a concerted effort by the grand jury to keep its plan a secret, reporters and photographers were waiting outside 24 Inverness Circle when they arrived. The sheriff, they said, had notified them. The house had stood empty for several months after Alice's murder while Bill and the children lived with his parents. But after Christmas he had yielded to Robyn and Chuck's wish to return to their own neighborhood and friends.

Two years earlier, McArthur had stood watch as another grand jury solemnly inspected the Orsini home in Indian Hills. Now the shoe was on the other foot—exactly as Mary Lee had doubtless intended. Part of him burned with resentment at having to guide sixteen strangers through the most private parts of his home. But the lawyer in him understood that the jurors needed to satisfy their curiosity about the crime scene in order to resolve the sheriff's accusations in their minds. He came away impressed with the grand jury's seriousness.

"There were no wild or wildly accusatory-type things," Bill said, later. "They had a pretty good grasp of what was going on, it seemed to me. Because their questions were pertinent, they were to the point, they didn't go off on any wild tangents or anything. They were very businesslike. They were truly inquiring about what had *happened*, and not on a witch hunt.

"I didn't think that they'd made up their minds. But I felt considerably better, because they obviously were looking into the thing. They'd called a lot of people that we would have called as defense witnesses—especially as to Orsini's lies. How she used people, and had different sets of friends and was a different person to those groups. At least I felt that this was not some bogus deal. At least they were going for the truth."

Which was really all McArthur had a right to ask.

2

Dub Bentley, meanwhile, continued to press forward on the Ron Orsini case. In a stormy hearing on March 14—the same day the grand jury explored the crime scene in Pleasant Valley—the prosecutor persuaded Judge Langston to set a July 1983 trial date.

To nobody's surprise, Sheriff Tommy appeared on Mary Lee's behalf. His testimony took an odd twist even for Tommy. Weeks before, the sheriff had assured the grand jury that Ron Orsini had committed suicide. No doubt about it. Nobody in Circuit Court that day knew that, however. So Tommy was on safe ground in testifying that he considered Dub Bentley a suspect for the felony of hindering apprehension of Ron's killer!

Obviously, both things could not be true. What Robinson expected the grand jury to make of his testimony when they read the newspapers is anybody's guess. Counting on grand jury secrecy, the sheriff appeared to be improvising as he went along.

3

Despite Sheriff Robinson's public bravado, the longer the grand jury met, the more anxious he got. And the more anxious Tommy got, the more pressure the grand jury began to feel. Jurors who lived outside city limits began to notice PCSD patrol cars parked outside their houses at odd hours. While a second sweep of the grand jury chamber just before McArthur's appearance turned up no evidence of bugging, Darrell Brown remained convinced that Tommy had daily access to the testimony. The special prosecutor also became aware that somebody had been inside his office during the night. The anonymous threats and hang-up calls continued. Brown had no evidence to link Tommy to these incidents, but he had his suspicions.

Just to be on the safe side, Darrell and the jury foreman took to lugging heavy boxes of evidentiary files everywhere they went. In late March, the special prosecutor managed to borrow an interior room at the federal courthouse for a couple of weeks. Security improved immediately. Not a day passed, however, but that Tommy didn't phone the special prosecutor at least once or twice. The sheriff's visits to Brown's office also became more frequent. While Tommy did most of the talking, Dill invariably came along. Exactly as he'd done with Dub Bentley, Tommy alternately blustered and cajoled.

As he babbled on, Tommy eventually crossed the line. He confided to Brown that there was more at stake in his crusade to convict McArthur than vindicating the system. The sheriff also had his political future to think about. If the special prosecutor played his cards right, Tommy would take him along for the ride.

"Tommy Robinson made a number of statements to me, two . . . I remember very vividly," Brown would one day swear under oath. "Tommy Robinson said to me that 'Darrell, we have to get an indictment. My political career depends upon it.' He made a second statement to me which basically was that 'we have to get an indictment. And if we get an indictment, we can write our tickets anywhere we want to go.'"

According to Brown, there was no mistaking the sheriff's meaning. He repeated it several times in different ways. If Brown got Sheriff Tommy the indictment, Governor Tommy would see to it he prospered. "Yeah, it was clumsy," Darrell said later. "But I was supposed to be a dumb black. I was going to dance to the tune and do whatever he wanted me to do. . . . But I was not going to be that little puppet."

Tommy had misjudged his man in more ways than one. Brown was tougher than he realized. Controlled by a hidden switch under the special prosecutor's desk, the video camera installed by the state police rolled silently onward—recording the histrionic sheriff's every word.

Also his actions. On one occasion, Brown said, he left Robinson and Dill alone in his office while he went to do an errand. No sooner had the special prosecutor closed the door behind him than Robinson and Dill jumped to their feet and began rifling his desk and peering into confidential files. And those were TV performances Tommy couldn't afford to have *anybody* see.

.   .   .

By the time Detective Al Dawson's turn came to testify in late March, the grand jury was getting restless. Sheriff Tommy's credibility was shot. There had been far too many discrepancies between his and Dill's version of the evidence and the testimony jurors heard. Every "mistake" the PCSD made ran in the same direction: to protect Mary Lee and convict Bill McArthur.

That was where Al Dawson came in. The curly-haired, laconic young LRPD detective had spent eight months beating his head against the same wall. Although unknown to the general public, Dawson was probably more responsible than anybody else for nailing down the case that had sent Yankee, McClendon, and Orsini to the penitentiary.

The jurors were relieved to find themselves dealing with an honest-to-God professional who knew the difference between suspicion and evidence, and called them the way he saw them. The detective's down-home twang and caustic wit combined to make him a forceful witness. Had Bill and Mary Lee been lovers? "Well, if *that* was against the law," Dawson would say, "the prisons would be bigger than the graveyards." But even if McArthur had been fool enough to bed down with a murder suspect, that didn't mean he wanted his wife killed. It wasn't a short jump from adultery to murder; it was the longest jump in the world.

Then Dawson would add that no matter what just about every woman under every beauty shop hair dryer in every country town in Arkansas suspected, there wasn't a scrap of evidence that McArthur had laid a hand on Orsini. For what it was worth—absolutely nothing in Dawson's opinion—even *she* denied it.

Dawson's testimony was like a revelation. The LRPD detective not only carried his huge investigative file into the grand jury, but he knew what was in it and where to put his hands on it. "Dawson gave us an excellent account of why things were the way they were," said Foreman Stan Brown, a junior high civics teacher and football coach from Jacksonville. (No kin to Darrell.)

Not only had Dawson confirmed McArthur's whereabouts on June 9, 1982, but LRPD detectives had interviewed the desk clerk, the maids, and any and everybody else at the Holiday Inn who might have seen the attorney had he somehow contrived to appear simultaneously in two places ninety miles apart. They'd drawn a complete blank. Phoebe had produced a letter from the mother of Bill's client—postmarked a couple of days later—thanking him for visiting with her son.

The conclusion was inescapable. The crucial meeting described by Orsini in which Bill supposedly showed up in Hot Springs carrying champagne, a .38 revolver, and $25,000 cash in a brown paper bag had simply never happened. Having played a hunch that McArthur was attending the state Bar convention, Mary Lee had simply invented the story. Exactly, jurors decided, as she made up about 99 percent of what she said.

"Tommy didn't have nothing," said Juror Moody Bird, a mechanic from Sherwood. "It was unbelievable. All he could do was ad-lib a bunch of stuff that didn't have nothing to do with anything. After a while, everybody could see right through him. It just made you halfway sick. Every last one of [his stories] went straight back to Mary Lee Orsini. There wasn't a bit of it was true. . . . I don't think Tommy believed it himself. It was about one thing: publicity. He just went publicity crazy."

.   .   .

Al Dawson suspected that there was more to Robinson's behavior than mere self-aggrandizement. After all, it was Robinson and Dill who seemed to have been meeting with Orsini almost daily during the weeks between the car bombing and Alice's murder. Not Bill McArthur. It was the PCSD to whom Mary Lee had run with her invisible hit men and make-believe tape recordings. Not the LRPD. The three-woman "hit list" of Alice, Mary Lee, and Bob Troutt's ex-wife that somehow reached every law enforcement agency in Little Rock *except* the PCSD would have made sense only to somebody who had bought into Orsini's mad stories and Tommy's exaggerated rumors of organized crime infiltrating the city's night spots.

At the grand jury's request, Dawson spent most of March 22 at Little Rock TV stations reviewing unedited videotapes of the activity outside the McArthur home on the fateful afternoon, seeking concrete evidence of Captain Bobby Woodward's presence. Unfortunately, the videotapes turned out to be of little use. What it all came down to was LRPD Patrolmen McNeely and Edgar's word against Dill and Woodward's. Other PCSD deputies experienced failures of memory.

The grand jury subpoenaed the audio logs of PCSD radio and phone traffic on July 2, 1982. On the morning they planned to play them, a bomb threat emptied the chambers. When Stan Brown and Mark Taylor returned to the room to fetch the tapes, they found sheriff's deputies there—searching for a bomb, they claimed.

Using audio equipment borrowed from the LRPD, the grand jury listened to the cryptic conversation recorded within minutes of the discovery of Alice's body between the PCSD radio dispatcher and an unidentified deputy:

> *Deputy*: Well, do you think that *We* shot one or that *They*
>   shot? Who shot who?
> *Dispatcher*: I have no idea. . . .

On the same tape, they heard Tommy Robinson tell LRPD Assistant Chief Doc Hale, "We've been working on a couple of deals for about the last two days. . . . We've got some things going that ya'll don't know about. . . . It would be in the best interest of your department and mine . . . to work together, because ya'll have got some information. We've got a hell of a lot that we've been working our ass off on for about . . . Around the clock for about three days."

Many of the jurors came to agree with LRPD Detective Dawson's conclusion: "I honestly believe, and I always will," Dawson said later, "that it was a set-up deal from the git-go. I think that Lee Orsini had peddled information to Tommy, got scared off, something went wrong and she felt like she was going to get caught. . . .

"The only thing is, they [the PCSD] didn't figure on the car trouble and figure Yankee and McClendon would be almost an hour late. They set out there and set out there, and then they pulled out. They went over to Rodney Parham [Road] to use the phone. That's the reason why when our backup people got there, there was five county cars out there and they'd already been through the house from top to bottom. But we looked at the situation real hard, and we couldn't prove it." And Tommy and Dill continued to deny it.

.   .   .

By the time Sergeant T. J. Farley made his second appearance before the grand jury on April 11, any thought of indicting Bill McArthur had long ago been put aside. The question was whether or not they would indict Robinson, Dill, and Woodward, and for what.

Since his first appearance, limited to outlining his case against Mary Lee for killing Ron Orsini, Farley had been taken off the hook. Having defied Chief Bubba Younts's instructions to stiff Dub Bentley and cooperate with Tommy, Farley had feared that his career with the NLRPD was finished. But for reasons having nothing to do with the Orsini case, Younts had been abruptly fired by the Civil Service Commission. The new chief had shown enough faith in Farley to transfer him from Homicide to Internal Affairs—the most sensitive job in any police agency.

If the grand jury wanted to hear what T.J. knew about the McArthur case, he was only too happy to oblige. Maybe a little bit too happy, as things turned out. He told them how he'd warned Dill about Yankee Hall three days after the car bombing. He also shared with them some new evidence in the Orsini case. A North Little Rock florist had told him that Dr. Wulz had been in her shop buying flowers for Ron Orsini twenty minutes before Mary Lee called the NLRPD on March 12.*

Unaware that the sheriff had assured the grand jury that Ron Orsini had killed himself, Farley testified about Tommy's attempt to get him to arrest Tiffany for the slaying. That episode had taken place in September 1982, roughly one week before Mary Lee went on trial for Alice McArthur's death.

He told them why the Tiffany–shot–Ron scenario made no sense— including Buddy Miles's search of the attic where McArthur supposedly dug up the murder weapon. "I didn't want to arrest Tiffany,"

---

*Within weeks of Farley's testimony, the florist would discover that she'd made a terrible mistake. Her written records indicated that Wulz had bought the flowers a day later than she'd thought. But the woman had also volunteered the same erroneous information to PCSD deputies a month before contacting Farley. Tommy had kept it under his hat.

Farley said, "because everything I could see at the crime scene, Tiffany didn't do it. And then I've been displeased about Robinson getting up—saying right in public—that Lee Orsini didn't do it and all this other good jazz. I know in my heart and soul—and I've got the facts to prove it—that she did."

Chapter 6

1

The grand jury began its deliberations on April 20, 1983. Over ten weeks, the jurors had heard close to ninety witnesses. The outcome had long been a foregone conclusion. "Looking at all the evidence," Darrell Brown had privately concluded, "Bill McArthur should never have been arrested. Talked to? No doubt. Interrogated? You've got to do that. But there was nothing close to probable cause to arrest him."

The vote against indictment was 16–0. What remained to be seen was whether or not the jurors had the staying power to pursue an investigation of the PCSD role in the murder of Alice McArthur.

• • • • •

For McArthur himself, the suspense finally ended shortly before 4:00 P.M. on April 28. Judge Langston read the two-sentence order with all the animation of a traffic judge dismissing an overdue parking ticket. The moment was electric all the same. When he heard the verdict, Bill bowed his head and began to cry. A broad grin spread across Jack Holt's face as McArthur's mother, father, and brother rushed tearfully to embrace him. Phoebe too cried and hugged her boss.

Later that night in a live interview on Channel 7, the only Little Rock station McArthur thought had treated him fairly, Bill stressed that while he felt like a victim, the real victim was Alice. He'd long ago concluded that aspects of his wife's murder might always remain a mystery to him. As for his own reputation, he'd let that take care of itself. McArthur said that his real worry was the damage done to his children.

Did he intend to pursue his false arrest lawsuit against Sheriff Tommy Robinson?

"Absolutely," he said.

• • •

For reasons nobody could ever satisfactorily explain, the grand jury chose to accompany its verdict with three cryptic paragraphs that mystified everybody. Part of the statement read:

> The Grand Jury reports that the investigation of the Alice McArthur homicide by the duly impaneled special Grand Jury has been frustrated and unduly prolonged as a result of the inefficiency demonstrated by the police department in its investigation of the crime scene. And further that the conduct of the prosecuting attorney's office should be the subject of further investigation.
>
> This report is not intended to suggest or imply that any evidence was brought before the Grand Jury or that any evidence exists or existed implicating William C. McArthur. . . . Additional reports will follow.

Contacted by reporters, neither Dub Bentley nor LRPD Chief Sonny Simpson had any clear notion of how to answer the implied criticism. "I have no earthly idea of what they [the jurors] have reference to," the prosecutor told the *Gazette*. "I don't agree with their assessment of the LRPD investigation, but . . . there's no way I can defend myself against the implications of the statement because I'm at a complete loss as to what they meant."

Chief Simpson could only speculate that what the grand jury had in mind was the crucial half hour it had taken LRPD patrolmen to secure the crime scene. Simpson explained that the presence of high-ranking sheriff's deputies had confused his officers. Once the LRPD officers had contacted headquarters, the sheriff's men had been ordered to vacate the premises.

In fact, the LRPD chief was correct. Still undecided how vigorously to pursue its investigation of PCSD wrongdoing, the grand jury hesitated to arouse Sheriff Tommy's ire. Some jurors had also come to believe that if Dub Bentley had charged Mary Lee with Ron Orsini's murder back in 1981, none of the subsequent tragedies would have happened.

But they didn't say so, and putting things in code only strengthened Tommy's hand. Promising a full report to follow, the grand jury continued to call witnesses from the PCSD and elsewhere.

The sheriff took the offensive. The special prosecutor, Tommy said, had betrayed him. "Darrell Brown," he claimed, "led us down the primrose path." Right up until the eleventh hour, Tommy insisted, Brown had assured him that Bill McArthur would be indicted.

Sure enough, the special prosecutor soon began to look like a candidate for a niche on Tommy's "Organized Crime Flow Chart." He informed Democrat reporters that Darrell Brown had associations with known gamblers and ties to organized crime.

With several jurors standing by in his office—Stan Brown, Mark Taylor, and Moody Bird among them—the special prosecutor telephoned the sheriff and confronted him about the allegations. Had they not agreed to avoid mudslinging? When Robinson began to bluster, Darrell punched the button on his speakerphone that made the conversation audible to everybody in the room. He didn't bother to inform Tommy. Gradually, the sheriff calmed down.

In the morning, they were all surprised to read an account of the same conversation in the Democrat. Darrell Brown, Tommy claimed, had threatened him. But the two-fisted sheriff had refused to back down. As far as everybody else who heard the exchange was concerned, Robinson's version was sheer fabrication.

But when push came to shove, the grand jury backed off. After almost three months of service at $15 per day, the majority felt they'd done enough. Some were frightened, and they were all eager to get back to their jobs and families. Even those most inclined to push for an investigation of the PCSD had grown cynical and doubted their ability to find the truth.

Darrell Brown was reluctant to push the jury. "I've asked myself a lot of times," he admitted later, " 'Why didn't we go another couple of weeks and resolve this mess?' I was ready to go. . . . But it might have taken a lot longer than two weeks. And it wouldn't have been fair to the grand jury to have been as incensed as they were, to expect them to be objective and patient enough to listen to a lot of other evidence."

On Friday, May 13, the grand jury delivered its final report. Like the enigmatic April 28 statement, this report also needed deciphering. Perhaps more fearful of Robinson than anybody cared to admit, the grand jury made a point of criticizing both the LRPD and the PCSD. The headline in Saturday's *Gazette* more or less typified the befuddled press reaction:

JURY REPORT CRITICIZES LR CHIEF, LAW AGENCIES
SAYS FEUDING MAY HAVE HURT MRS. MCARTHUR.

Commending LRPD detectives for solving the crime, and hardly mentioning Sheriff Tommy by name, the jurors zeroed in on Chief Simpson for "not taking steps that could have prevented tampering with the crime scene by the Sheriff's office after Mrs. McArthur's body had been found in an upstairs bedroom."

In effect, the grand jury chastised Simpson for failing to control Tommy Robinson's deputies. But the irony was lost on the Little Rock press. Given months of feverish speculation based upon inaccurate information about the crime scene supplied by Robinson, by any reasonable news judgment standards the revelation that Tommy's boys had tampered with the evidence should have been a bombshell. Instead, it got buried. To the Little Rock media, the McArthur case was history.

2

Once the grand jury put itself out of business, Mike Mahone's investigation fell into limbo. But not before the former state police detective hired by Darrell Brown to assist the grand jury had unearthed a few fascinating tidbits. Several witnesses had heard Tommy Robinson threaten to destroy Bill McArthur years earlier, after the attorney's successful representation of two Jacksonville policemen Tommy had tried to fire.

Mahone also found a friend of Susan Anders from whom a PCSD deputy had twice tried to buy copies of the recordings Anders had made of her phone conversations with Bill—the same tapes that had provoked Alice McArthur to confront her husband's former lover. Tommy, the deputy told her, had put him up to it. The first attempt had come in 1977, the second after Alice's murder.

The most tantalizing evidence Mahone found, however, came from the bar manager at the Camelot Hotel across the street from the courthouse. Back during the McArthur probable cause hearing in November 1982, Connie Anderson said, the sheriff and a group of revelers had retired to the bar every night—drinking heavily and carrying on.

One night, Anderson said in a sworn statement, it had gotten late. The group had been drinking for hours. Sheriff Tommy himself had already gone, and there were no other customers in the bar. Among the half dozen or so men she identified were Major Larry Dill, Special Prosecutor Sonny Dillahunty, and Mary Lee Orsini's attorney Tom Donovan. She'd recognized them all from TV, and recalled the incident partly because Dill had paid the $155 bar tab with a PCSD credit card and left no tip.

"Every time I would come to the table," she said, "they would quit talking. [But] this particular time when I came to the table they kind of got used to my presence and just kept talking."

One particular deputy, whose name she never learned, seemed to be the butt of everybody's jokes. "I had been following the McArthur case, as everyone had, and reading about it in the paper every day," she explained. "And the one thing that seemed unresolved was how the flowers got moved. So when they started talking about the flowers, I picked up on it immediately, and that is why I remember the statement."

"And that statement one more time to the best of your recollection [was]?"

" 'If it hadn't been for you moving the flowers,' " Anderson replied, " 'we wouldn't be in this mess anyway.' "

3

Regardless of what happened to its report, the grand jury verdict had turned everything upside down. Now Tommy Robinson was the defendant. And so was Larry Dill. For public consumption, Tommy was breathing smoke and fire. Bill McArthur would rue the day he ever thought of filing suit. On cross-examination in federal court, McArthur would be exposed as the criminal he was; even if the attorney dropped his lawsuit, Tommy vowed to file a countersuit.

Behind the scenes, meanwhile, Robinson's lawyers were doing all they could to limit discovery. On May 25, Phil Kaplan sat down with Darrell Brown to work out the conditions under which the special prosecutor would give a deposition. It was a potentially tricky business. Due to laws safeguarding grand jury secrecy, Brown couldn't talk about the actual testimony, nor about the jury's deliberations.

Anything that had taken place outside the grand jury chambers, however, was potentially fair game. And while the press and public may have ignored the grand jury's written report, Kaplan certainly hadn't. Allegations that deputies had tampered with the crime scene and phrases like "bizarre allegations of Pulaski Sheriff's Office conduct" had jumped out at him like neon signs.

Kaplan had some reason to expect Darrell Brown to trust him. They had several mutual friends. Even so, Darrell's eagerness to cooperate took him by surprise. Already angry, Brown had been infuriated by Tommy's charges of corruption and cover-up. If the sheriff thought he was going to do him the way he'd done Dub Bentley, he'd picked the wrong man.

Brown told Kaplan that he was almost certain that Tommy had spied on the grand jury with a parabolic microphone, and that he believed the sheriff to be a manipulator who would do almost anything to protect Mary Lee Orsini. Indeed, Darrell suspected that Mary Lee's seemingly self-destructive actions—hiring two hit men she had no means of paying, making repeated calls on July 2 to a phone she *knew* to be trapped, and the faked tape with Larry Burge that she'd placed into Tommy's hands—all indicated a degree of collusion with the PCSD.

Kaplan couldn't help but be excited. Theories, however, came cheap. Persuasive evidence was something else. But Brown had some of that too. He told Kaplan about the "Organized Crime Flow Chart," listing some of the state's most prominent politicians and businessmen as cocaine dealers. Kaplan was astonished. If publicized, the chart might sink Tommy politically.

Darrell also confided that Tommy had made explicit statements that his political future depended upon getting an indictment. Also that he'd made it equally clear that Brown could write his own ticket if he delivered. Unknown to Robinson, audio and videotapes of those meetings existed.

The tapes, however, Brown would surrender only if compelled to by a judge. Ostensibly he feared being sued. But it didn't take much imagination to realize that once the sheriff learned of their existence, they would become Darrell Brown's personal insurance policy too.

Kaplan realized that the tapes could turn out to be the proverbial smoking gun. Even the glib sheriff would have a hard time persuading a jury that he'd acted in good faith. "The electronic recordings," he wrote in a notarized file memo, "concern the matters which go directly to the heart of the issues in *McArthur* vs. *Robinson*."

The McArthur team had to have them.

· · ·

Alerted by Kaplan's motion to compel Brown to turn them over, Robinson's lawyers fought to keep the documents and tapes secret. But the roof fell in on July 22. In a Memorandum Opinion, Federal Judge H. Franklin Waters of Fayetteville ruled that Robinson would have to turn over his complete files to McArthur's attorneys—including Dill's summary. Grand jury testimony was confidential. But Darrell Brown would be required to produce any notes or recordings he had made of his dealings with Robinson and Dill *outside* the grand jury's hearing.

McArthur's lawyers quickly made plans to take a deposition from Brown at a Little Rock recording studio in early September. *McArthur* vs. *Robinson* was scheduled for trial at the federal courthouse in November. With any luck, the "Tommy and Larry Show" would be broadcast statewide.

Robinson continued to bluster. According to the *Democrat,* Tommy had opened an investigation into what the newspaper called "possible Arkansas State Police involvement in improper video-taping." Darrell Brown, he announced darkly, had "lured me and Major Larry Dill into his office to try to make us make certain statements about the [McArthur] case." An anonymous woman dropped off copies of Dill's summary at the *Democrat* and all three Little Rock TV stations. Tommy professed outrage. He made plans to read the entire investigative file aloud on KARN radio, but backed off after Judge Waters refused to censor the broadcast in advance, but granted a motion allowing McArthur to add libel and slander to the lawsuit.

Unknown to his worshipful supporters, however, Tommy had run his last bluff. With Darrell Brown's deposition scheduled to take place on September 7, the sheriff's "Organized Crime Flow Chart" would soon fall into enemy hands. So would the videotapes of Tommy rifling through the special prosecutor's desk, and offering Brown a guaranteed future if he got an indictment.

On September 2, Tommy's attorneys threw in their cards. After bargaining with Bill Wilson, they agreed to settle the lawsuit on terms highly favorable to McArthur. According to one source the deal was as follows: If Bill agreed to drop his suit for false arrest, libel, and slander, Sheriff Tommy would pay McArthur between $90,000 and $100,000. In addition, Robinson would shut his mouth. He would never again, in public or private, accuse McArthur of murder. Should Tommy do so, Bill could keep the money and reopen the case at any time. While the sheriff would never admit to any wrongdoing, McArthur's friends viewed the settlement as a complete vindication.

In an era of multi-million-dollar jury awards, the money didn't seem like much. But Bill Wilson argued strongly in favor of settlement. No matter how strong the evidence, the veteran trial lawyer argued, there was a good chance that Sheriff Tommy would succeed in confusing a trial jury exactly as he'd done in the Beaumont-Growcock false arrest suit—where the evidence couldn't have been clearer, and yet the jury had found a way to fudge the issue.

With his political survival at stake, Sheriff Tommy could be counted upon to fight dirty. The trial would be long, ugly, emotionally draining, and fearfully expensive. The more desperate Tommy got, the more recklessly he would counterattack, with unforseeable consequences for Bill and his family.

Phil Kaplan disagreed. He acknowledged that a favorable settlement was almost always preferable to a long trial. Nor did he disagree with Wilson's analysis of the dangers involved. But he also thought that the evidence against the sheriff was so stark and dramatic that even Tommy wouldn't be able to persuade a jury of twelve citizens that he had acted in good faith. Phil also believed that Bill *needed* to defeat Robinson publicly to restore not only his reputation but his self-respect. Some cases needed to go to trial, Kaplan believed, and *McArthur* vs. *Robinson* was one of them. He also wanted a piece of Tommy himself. So badly he could taste it.

As a native Arkansan, Wilson may have felt even more strongly about the baleful effect of a demagogue like Tommy on his home state. But he felt so strongly about Bill's need to put the whole tearful saga behind him that he tracked him down at a jury trial in Danville—more than one hundred miles from Little Rock—to urge him to settle.

For McArthur, the money never mattered. Most of it went toward paying his expenses. He saw the arguments on both sides, and felt almost equally drawn in two directions. Bill wanted revenge against Robinson in the worst way. But taking the settlement offered an end to almost a year and a half of public and private torture—for himself, Robyn and Chuck, his mother, father, and brother. Also for Phoebe and Sally Pernell and other dear friends inextricably caught in the same web. It meant peace and quiet, and the return to something like normal life for them all. It meant that Alice could finally rest in peace.

He took the settlement.

• • •

The announcement on September 2 caught the Little Rock media completely by surprise. Both newspapers acted as if the Razorback football season had suddenly been canceled. Judging by the petulant tone of their accounts of the settlement, the terms of which were not revealed, reporters had been spoiling for a fight. A *Gazette* reporter reminded the sheriff that he'd vowed to file a countersuit of his own. At first he denied it. But when reporters insisted, Two-gun Tommy turned to mush. "My attorneys," he said, "represent another entity besides me and notwithstanding any of my personal opinions, there are some variables beyond my control that I have nothing to do with."

Beyond that, Tommy had—as they say—no further comment.

Chapter 7

1

Going into Mary Lee's October 1983 trial for her husband's murder, neither the Orsini family nor the prosecution had any idea which story the defense planned to tell. Would she claim that Ron committed suicide? Try to pin the crime on her brother? Tell the jury about her husband's odd behavior and the mysterious bags of cash in his closet? Invoke drug dealers, hit men, and crooked cops? Or would she go with the Tiffany–did–it version she'd come up with after Alice McArthur's murder?

Taking no chances, Dub Bentley prepared for them all. If Mary Lee dared testify, old "Double Bubble"—as she and John Robert Starr were so fond of calling him—would grind her to fine particles. Back in the spotlight after nearly a year in prison, Mary Lee appeared to have regained her old verve. No longer the painted woman in a tight red dress, she'd undergone another metamorphosis. Neatly turned out in a skirt, blouse, and tailored jacket, she smiled brilliantly for photographers. She had even taken an active role in cross-examining prospective jurors during the voir dire. She had asked an accountant on the panel whether she realized that many women were hopelessly bad at balancing their checkbooks. The juror said she did.

"Are you a light or a heavy sleeper?" Mary Lee asked.

"I am usually a heavy sleeper."

"What about your husband?"

"He is a light sleeper."

"Of the following," Orsini continued, "which do you think is the strongest love: a man for his wife, a woman for her husband, or a mother for her child?"

"They usually all divide up equally."

"Do you believe that an innocent person can be convicted?"

"Yes."

. . .

Then, on the afternoon before actual testimony was set to begin, the circus came back to town. Based upon an invalid warrant from a Little Rock municipal judge, Sheriff Tommy arrested lead prosecution witness Sergeant T. J. Farley on five counts of perjury. Also Larry Burge. Supposedly, both men had lied to the McArthur grand jury. According to Orsini's attorneys, Robinson had gotten copies of the transcripts by threatening to arrest the lawyers—Tom Donovan among them—unless they turned them over.

But the sheriff had finally pushed Dub Bentley too far. Without the prosecutor's endorsement, a municipal judge had no authority to issue a felony warrant. Judge Alan Dishongh had acted solely on the basis of affidavits sworn by Robinson and Dill. After a meeting with Farley convinced Dub that the NLRPD detective could prove that the charges were bogus, the prosecutor acted forcefully at last. He ordered the sheriff and his chief deputy arrested on felony perjury charges. The county coroner did the honors. Robinson and Dill were fingerprinted, booked, and released on their own recognizance.

The Little Rock media went crazy. Once again, Tommy and Dub exchanged insults and threats on TV, radio, and the front pages of both statewide newspapers. Mary Lee must have been ecstatic. Things had gotten far more complicated than she had ever planned. But now it was her and the charismatic sheriff against the world. Or so she must have imagined.

Without Orsini's help, Robinson's case against Sergeant Farley showed little imaginative flair. Three of the five perjury counts boiled down to what Farley had told Dill, or Dill had told Farley, about the Orsini and McArthur murders—a swearing contest between two cops. But Farley also had witnesses. Three NLRPD officers had accompanied him to PCSD headquarters in September 1982. What with "Say" McIntosh hanging from a cross, Sheriff Tommy gunning a chain saw, and TV cameras everywhere, it wasn't a day they would easily forget.

Unknown to Robinson, Farley also had a tape recording of the North Little Rock florist who had mistakenly put Dr. Wulz in her shop buying flowers for the widow Orsini a half hour before NLRPD officers arrived at 7412 Pontiac on the day of the murder.*

Wasting no time, Farley hired Phil Kaplan—the same trial lawyer who'd volunteered his services to Bill McArthur. They made plans to file a false arrest suit in federal court. But finding an Arkansas judge with the courage to rule against Sheriff Tommy would prove more difficult. Acting with no statutory or constitutional authority, Judge Dishongh refused to dismiss charges against Farley. He then disqualified Chris Piazza, appointed a special prosecutor, and announced plans to hold a probable cause hearing. Kaplan immediately filed a civil suit in Chancery Court to prevent the illegal hearing from taking place.

•   •   •

The Orsini trial went forward despite the hubbub outside the courtroom. After Judge John Langston polled the jurors, Dub Bentley reluctantly withdrew his motion for a mistrial. He couldn't help but be a mite apprehensive about his star witness. Orsini's lawyers had made no secret of their intention to make Farley's credibility the basic issue in her defense. If the volatile detective blew his stack in the courtroom, all bets could be off.

Anybody who knew T.J. could sense the strain he was under. Not the mellowest cop in the world to begin with, Farley bristled at every slight. He still suspected that Orsini had tried to hire somebody to kill him in 1981. Now, as he saw it, Tommy Robinson and a team of jackleg lawyers were trying to help her destroy his career.

Farley took the witness stand on the afternoon of Wednesday, October 26. Guided by Bentley's methodical questioning, Farley described his and Sergeant Buddy Miles's crime scene investigation. Despite searching every nook and cranny of the Orsini home for several hours, he told the jury, they'd found no sign of the murder weapon, nor genuine evidence of forced entry. The prosecutor finished his direct examination just before 5:00 P.M. and Judge Langston adjourned for the day.

Somewhat to Bentley's surprise and relief, defense lawyer Harold

---

*Farley had already recanted the accusation during a preliminary hearing in Orsini's trial, and newspapers had covered it.

Craig told the judge he had no intention of bringing Sheriff Tommy's sideshow into the courtroom. Now all Farley had to do was get through the probable cause hearing in municipal court before returning to face cross-examination. The NLRPD detective had a long, sleepless night.

Sitting with Phil Kaplan in municipal court the next morning, Farley figured he was a goner. Judge Dishongh's handpicked special prosecutor had just gotten started when a clatter arose in the hallway. An assistant of Kaplan's, her high heels echoing loudly on the tile floor, swept dramatically into the courtroom.

"You talk about a grade-B movie," Farley said later. "[Kaplan's assistant] came up behind him and handed him a document, and Dishongh says, 'Well, Mr. Kaplan, I guess I might as well go ahead and take a recess. I've got a funny feeling you'd like to make a motion.' "

Indeed he did. The document was a writ from Chancery Judge Lee Munson ordering Dishongh to shut down the hearing at once. Until the higher court ruled on Kaplan's civil suit challenging the special prosecutor, the proceedings against Farley must stop. Confining himself to a few bitter remarks, Dishongh did as he was told.*

Farley and Kaplan hurried across Broadway to the courthouse. In chambers, Kaplan asked Judge Langston to recess the Orsini trial overnight to give his client time to compose himself. The tumult had left Farley feeling dizzy and sick to his stomach. Orsini's attorneys protested. Not to be able to cross-examine the witness as soon after his direct testimony as possible, they argued, would damage their case. The judge agreed. He declared a two-hour recess to let Farley settle down. Then he would have to face the cross-examination that could make or break the case he'd been working on for two and a half years.

Farley took the witness stand at 1:30 P.M. Defense attorney Harold Craig did the questioning. From previous encounters, the two men had no fondness for each other. A bearded, heavyset man wearing thick eyeglasses, Craig was known for his relentless style. He adopted a barbed, withering tone, attempting to portray Farley as rash, reckless, and obsessed with Orsini.

Craig returned to the same themes repeatedly. Ron's pillow, for

---

*Munson then transferred Farley's suit to the 1st Circuit. Within two days, Judge Lowber Hendricks had written a sharply worded order putting Dishongh firmly in his place: "No law . . . affords *any* power to *any* court to prosecute cases. Thus, the decision to prosecute or not prosecute is solely within the province and discretion of the prosecuting attorney. . . . Moreover, there is no provision in the law for a municipal judge to appoint a special prosecutor in a felony case."

example. The detective's written report had indicated that the .38 slug found under the body had passed through the pillow. Coroner Dr. L. Gordon Holt's report concluded that it hadn't. Could Farley account for the discrepancy? He could not.

As the afternoon wore on, the tension in the courtroom grew almost palpable. Tight-lipped and pale, Farley was seething. His tone approaching mockery, Craig hammered away. Another object of contention was the door between the laundry room and the garage. How could Farley be sure that the gouges by the doorknob were fresh? Did the detective know what factors caused bare wood to weather? Had Farley ever been a carpenter? Did he have any scientific expertise? Then how could he say with any certainty that the marks hadn't been there for a long time?

By the time the defense attorney got around to the "hit man" theory, it was late afternoon and tempers were getting frayed. Tipped by Farley's testimony to the McArthur grand jury, Orsini's attorneys had dug up a report he'd given the state police in August 1981. At the time, Farley had suspected that Gary Glidewell—the private eye working for Mary Lee—had a contract on his life. He'd even sent his wife to Florida for a week and helped two troopers stake out his house. Nothing had happened.

Craig, however, acted as if Farley's report to the state police hinted at secrets the prosecution wanted to hide.

"In your conversation with Sergeant Eddins on August 18, 1981, did you mention to him a suspect vehicle in the Ron Orsini case?"

"Possible suspect vehicle."

"OK, possible suspect vehicle," Craig agreed. "Was it described as a black Trans-Am with wide tires and a little loud, with two white males—one middle 30s and one over 40, one a heavy-set big man with close-cropped hair, curly and wavy, salt and pepper. The other one smaller with brown hair?"

"But it was not in connection with Ron Orsini's murder."

"Not at all?"

"That wasn't the reason I turned it over to them."

Farley thought Craig was deliberately trying to confuse the issue, and it made him furious. Cindy Kinsolving, the ten-year-old who lived on the opposite side of Pontiac Drive, had described a car with big tires to the 1981 grand jury—but only *after* the intervention of a private detective. When Farley had first interviewed her, she'd described a dark mid-size like Mary Lee's Caprice.

"Did you have a suspect vehicle in the Ron Orsini case? Perhaps the car was loud. It had larger tires on the rear?"

"The way you're saying it, it's going back to the Orsini . . ."

"Officer Farley," Craig interrupted, "just please . . ."

"I'm just trying to answer the question."

Recognizing that Farley was near the edge, the prosecutor objected to Craig's badgering his witness. The judge ordered Craig to let him answer. Everybody began shouting all at once.

"The reason I passed that . . . over to [state police investigator] Bill Eddins," Farley blurted out, "is because I thought I was going to get killed!"

A furious row erupted in front of the bench. Craig accused the prosecution of deliberately trying to prejudice the jury.

"This is inadmissible. Mr. Farley knows it's inadmissible. Mr. Bentley knows this is inadmissible. . . He's trying to put in this crap about Lee hiring somebody to kill him."

"Mr. Craig, you opened it up about a suspect and a black Trans-Am," the judge scolded. "The Sergeant is evidently trying to explain but you keep cutting him off—that it was generally involved with Orsini but that it was not a vehicle that was suspected in the Ron Orsini murder. If you bring up an answer, you're going to have to live with it."

Sensing the explosive potential, Judge Langston recessed for the day and ordered the courtroom cleared. No sooner had the jury been escorted outside than Farley lost it. Tears of anger and frustration in his eyes, he lunged from the witness stand. "You son of a bitch!" he shouted. Dub Bentley and two bailiffs held him back while Craig retreated into the judge's chambers.

Half pushed and dragged down the hall into the prosecutor's office, Farley flew into a rage—kicking chairs, flinging ashtrays and law books across the room. Nobody tried to interfere. As long as the jury was out of sight, Dub would have let T.J. tear the courthouse down brick by brick if it made him feel better.

．　．　．

First thing Thursday morning, the defense moved for a mistrial. Judge Langston denied it. Craig's withering cross-examination proceeded into a second day. Calmed by Wednesday's outburst, Farley refused to be provoked. No matter how many times the defense attorney wanted to talk about the skewer or the pillow, the detective was willing to accommodate him. Dub had persuaded him that Craig's nitpicking was doing Mary Lee more harm than good. The defense attorney never knew when to stop. At times his persistence became almost comical.

"Officer Farley," he asked about an hour into the detective's third day on the stand, "you've seen the bullet that was recovered at the scene, have you not?"

"Yes, sir."

"Is that the bullet that killed Ron Orsini?"

Farley gave him a deadpan look. "I can only make an assumption," he said. "It was found next to his body and he had a hole through his head."

After another pass or two at the pillow, the defense finally let Farley step down. Leaving the courtroom, Farley felt pretty good about his three days on the witness stand. Win or lose, he'd done his duty.

And he was through with Mary Lee Orsini forever.

2

Meanwhile, Mary Lee's last hero had gone AWOL. For all his public bravado, Sheriff Tommy seemed to be running scared. Arresting T. J. Farley and Larry Burge would turn out to be his last move on her behalf. Shaken by the prosecutor's aggressive response, the last place Robinson wanted to see Dub was inside a courtroom. Playing dueling sound bites on the evening news was more his style.

Prating to the McArthur grand jury about Ron Orsini's "suicide" had been one thing; defending his testimony under cross-examination by Bentley quite another. Robinson had contradicted himself numerous times to the grand jury alone. With one perjury charge already hanging over his head, Tommy didn't dare go further. Harold Craig despised Robinson anyway, and believed that calling him would have been a disaster.

Just to make sure, Tommy took a vacation. According to a front-page story in the October 31 Democrat:

Pulaski County Sheriff Tommy Robinson was listed in satisfactory condition Sunday afternoon following his admission into Jacksonville's Rebsamen Memorial Hospital, apparently because of high blood pressure and chest pain.

Robinson said he became acutely ill and felt as if he were about to pass out on the way home from his office in Little Rock. He drove to the hospital emergency room and was admitted by Dr. Joe Daugherty of Jacksonville.

"We're having to get him evaluated for a few symptoms that I feel are the result of seven-day work weeks for the past two or three years," Daugherty said. The sheriff was tested for symptoms of high blood pressure and chest pains.

Tommy remained at the hospital under medication for several days. It would later be announced that the tests had proved negative, and that the sheriff merely needed rest. When he and Dill showed up in Circuit Court on November 3 to plead innocent to perjury charges, he appeared pale and somber, and had little to say to reporters. He remained in seclusion for several more days.

Years later, Tommy would embroider the story, claiming that he'd been hospitalized due to exposure after falling into ice-encrusted water on a duck-hunting expedition. An avid outdoorsman, Robinson often made a point of being photographed in his duck-hunting camouflage—far too virile to have suffered what otherwise might have been interpreted as an anxiety attack or an old-fashioned nervous breakdown.

In reality, the 1983 Arkansas duck season would not begin until three weeks later. Afternoon temperatures on the day Tommy checked himself into the hospital reached 75 degrees. Even if he was poaching, hypothermia seems unlikely.

One way or another, Tommy was out of the picture. Mary Lee and the sheriff never laid eyes on one another again.

3

Deprived of the opportunity to create a spectacle, Orsini had no choice but to follow the advice of her lawyers. Her best chance to avoid a second murder conviction was to stay off the witness stand and allow them to present her as an innocent victim of circumstance.

Just before his closing argument on Wednesday, November 9, 1983, Dub Bentley got cold feet. What if the jury decided that Tiffany had lied about sleeping soundly all night? Or what if they suspected that Mary Lee had let an accomplice into the house? He asked Judge Langston to include in his jury instructions the standard paragraph relating to criminal conspiracies: "In this case the State does not contend that Mary Lee Orsini acted alone in the commission of the offense of Murder First Degree. A person is criminally responsible for the conduct of another person when he is an accomplice in the commission of an offense."

Orsini's lawyers were livid. No evidence, they argued bitterly, had been presented to prove a conspiracy. The judge sided with the prosecution; he read out the instructions Dub had requested.

● ● ●

The jury retired to its deliberations at 3:38 P.M. While everybody else in the stuffy courtroom hunkered down in nervous anticipation of a long siege, Mary Lee flitted about like a sorority girl during sophomore rush. Wearing a simple plaid shirtwaist dress, her hair pulled back under a modest beret, she laughed and joked with her lawyers, and paid animated visits to Tiffany, Dr. Wulz, and her family.

To Dub Bentley's astonishment, she even directed a few lighthearted quips his way. After this was all settled, she told the prosecutor, they'd have to get together one day to talk about old times. "If you'll bring your four-wheeler," she said, referring to a broken hand Dub had suffered in a recent accident, "I'll bring my broom."

Sitting mutely clutching her husband's hand in the very back row, Linda House could hardly contain her loathing. "Here's a woman that's already been convicted of one murder and is being tried for another," she explained much later. "Just laughing, cutting up and having a big time. People say, 'Oh, I hate him.' Or, 'I hate you.' They don't *know* what the word 'hate' means."

The jury returned at 5:45 P.M. It had taken them two hours to find Mary Lee guilty. They sentenced her to life without parole.

"I didn't do it," Mary Lee sobbed. "My God, I didn't do it." She fell weeping into Tiffany's arms. As bailiffs pried them apart and led Mary Lee wailing from the courtroom, her mother began to curse the prosecutor.

"You dirty bastard," Mrs. Hatcher shouted.

Tiffany flung herself at Linda House. Bailiffs held her off. "You bitch," she shrieked. "I hope you're satisfied."

Tiffany continued to screech as Dub escorted Linda and Buddy through the judge's chambers to safety.

Epilogue

1

Six days after Orsini's conviction, a team of NLRPD detectives walked into J.R.'s Gold & Silver Exchange on McArthur Drive carrying a search warrant. They arrested the owner, a thirty-one-year-old Lebanese named Issah Zacariah, and seized a cache of electronic equipment, guns, jewelry, and bags of silver and gold ingots. The serial numbers on many items confiscated matched those on a list of items reported stolen in a recent wave of burglaries all over Pulaski County. Locked inside a safe in the back room NLRPD detectives also found a .38 caliber Miroku Colt revolver—a Japanese-made weapon fitting the specifications of the gun that had killed Ron Orsini.

One week later, Captain Bobby Woodward of the PCSD was formally charged with conspiracy to commit theft and burglary. The arrest of the second highest-ranking officer in Sheriff Tommy's CID, Prosecutor Dub Bentley explained to reporters, had resulted from a joint investigation into a corrupt "sting" operation by the NLRPD and the state police. The prosecutor did not, however, see fit to mention the .38 revolver.

On the surface, Woodward's "sting" looked like a typical PCSD rogue operation. Secretly set up inside North Little Rock city limits, its theoretical purpose was to catch burglars trying to "fence" stolen property. But no arrests had been made. Woodward and Zacariah had only one crooked customer, a drug addict and convicted thief named Jerry P. Norman. At their urging, Norman had committed a string of burglaries during October and November, exchanging the booty for cash.

The silverware and jewelry Woodward had melted down and cast into ingots; guns he'd kept for himself. Electronic gear and appliances he and Zacariah had either resold or thrown into a creek.

Jerry Norman didn't realize it, but he had one special qualification to be Woodward's partner in crime: he had once been represented by Bill McArthur. Always a soft touch for a client trying to go straight, Bill had even paid him to do some housepainting for Alice. He had trusted Norman never to steal from him, and having him around the house at odd hours during the day had made Alice feel safer.

After a while, Norman said he got suspicious of Bobby Woodward's motives. The PCSD deputy began suggesting targets for him to burglarize, which he ignored. Eventually, Norman claimed, Woodward proposed an armed robbery. He supposedly knew a time and place when the county tax collector would be carrying a large sum of cash. Woodward even offered to furnish a gun—a Miroku Colt .38 revolver. Norman refused. He was a thief, not a stick-up man. He'd never used a gun.

Then, on the night of November 9, Norman got caught red-handed by a homeowner who walked in on him. He fled, only to find LRPD detectives waiting for him at his girlfriend's apartment. Almost relieved, Norman came clean at once—confessing to twenty-three burglaries over five weeks and revealing Woodward and Zacariah's role. He took them on a guided tour of the homes he had robbed. After LRPD detectives had cleared their books, they took Norman to NLRPD headquarters.

Requesting assistance from the state police, NLRPD brass and the prosecutor's office did their best to keep the case from being contaminated by politics. Jerry Norman was offered no deals in exchange for his testimony and passed a state police polygraph exam. He eventually received a twenty-year sentence. Investigators compiled an itemized list of goods reported stolen by Norman's victims. The raid on the pawnshop caught Woodward and Zacariah flat-footed. State police even found an eyewitness who had seen Woodward melting down the jewelry.

When he heard the news, Sheriff Tommy bellowed and roared and told reporters that Woodward was a victim of a political conspiracy. He went on TV with a private lie detector exam Woodward had supposedly passed. Woodward himself claimed that Dub Bentley had him framed to prevent him from linking large-scale drug dealing to the McArthur case.

The first thing Sergeant T. J. Farley heard about the "sting" investigation was when a detective from the NLRPD burglary squad walked into Internal Affairs on the day of Woodward's arrest. The detective laid the Miroku Colt .38 on Farley's desk and ran down Jerry Norman's story to him. Of all the many guns in Captain Bobby Woodward's possession, why would he keep this particular revolver in the pawnshop safe?

Farley and another NLRPD detective wasted no time putting the gun in front of a ballistics expert at the State Crime Lab. What the expert told them after a brief look through his microscope took their breath away. "He took a look at it," Farley said, "and this was late in the afternoon, 'This is the gun. However, I'm an old man, my eyes are tired. Let me look at it in the morning.' Next day he came on back and said, 'I've looked at it, and off the record, it is the gun. On the record, the ballistics have been minutely changed. You can either use steel-jacketed bullets or fire about five hundred rounds with soft lead bullets and lead it up.' But the bottom line was that he couldn't testify."

The stakes were potentially huge. If it did turn out to be the Ron Orsini murder weapon, where had Captain Bobby Woodward gotten it? And when? Nobody believed that Bill McArthur had taken Mary Lee to a Memphis hypnotist. Could she have play-acted that script with somebody else? Farley could think of possibilities from among her playmates.

Or what if the PCSD had tried to put the squeeze on Orsini all the way back in June 1982—between the car bombing and Alice's murder—and she'd tried to hand them Yankee, McClendon, and McArthur instead? That would certainly explain some of the deputies' actions. The harder they looked at it, the more they wondered whether the real purpose of Captain Bobby Woodward's phony "sting" had been to put the Miroku Colt into the hands of a client of McArthur's. And if Woodward hadn't gotten greedy, who could say that it might not have worked?

Just for good measure, NLRPD detectives got permission to send the Miroku Colt to the FBI Crime Lab in Washington. After a couple of weeks they got the same ambiguous result. The gun was probably the Orsini murder weapon, but experts could argue about it.

Just for the hell of it, Farley drove down to the penitentiary. To his amazement, Orsini acted glad to see him. She even surprised him by telling him the truth about a few things. He asked her if somebody other than Bill McArthur had blackmailed her into having Alice killed. "She told me Robinson, Woodward, and Dill," Farley said with a bitter laugh. "Another thing she told me is that she'd told so many lies nobody would believe her if she told the truth."

Farley certainly didn't. It took him a long time to accept it, but his investigation had reached a last dead end. Eventually, he returned the .38 Miroku Colt to the property room, where it remains.

Ironically, the best evidence supporting the conspiracy theory of the busted "sting" may have come from Sheriff Tommy himself. Testifying for the defense at Woodward's trial for conspiracy to commit burglary and theft in September 1984, the sheriff maintained his complete innocence. Sweating profusely, he became highly agitated under crossexamination. Tommy charged that Dub Bentley—who was not in the courtroom—was conspiring against him and the PCSD.

The whole purpose of Woodward's "sting," the sheriff said, had been to investigate Jerry Norman, whom he identified as a close friend of Bill McArthur's and a major drug dealer. He did not explain why a major drug dealer needed to pull twenty-three nickel and dime burglaries to support his habit. "I thought he was the key to the McArthur homicide," he said. But Tommy offered no proof, and the jury convicted Woodward, sentencing him to three years and a $10,000 fine.

Announcing his disappointment that a policeman had broken the law, Tommy fired Woodward the following day.

• • •

Having publicly vowed to fight Sergeant T. J. Farley's false arrest suit to the bitter end, and to expose the NLRPD detective as "a liar and a damn nut," Tommy quietly settled out of court for $25,000.

2

On June 17, 1985, the Arkansas Supreme Court unanimously overturned the murder conviction of Mary Lee Orsini for the death of her husband Ron. With Chief Justice Jack Holt, Jr., having recused, the sharply worded opinion was written by Special Chief Justice Alston Jennings, Jr., a prominent Little Rock attorney appointed to hear the case.

The court ruled that the state had presented no real evidence that more than one person had participated in the crime, and that Judge John Langston's jury instructions had therefore unfairly allowed Dub Bentley to have it both ways. "The instructions permitted the State," Jennings wrote, "to maintain simultaneously that [Mary Lee] killed her husband because no one else could have done it and that if someone else killed him, she must have participated in the crime."

The Supreme Court refused, however, to rule that Orsini could not be retried if Prosecuting Attorney Chris Piazza chose to do so. The 1981 grand jury's failure to indict Mary Lee, it held, was not binding upon an elected prosecutor. Nor would the court dismiss the charge for lack of evidence. "It is sufficient to advise," the justices concluded, "that we cannot say that there was no substantial evidence to support the jury's verdict."

Having declined to run for another term as prosecutor and badly beaten in a race for the Arkansas Supreme Court, Dub Bentley still believed he and the trial judge had been correct all along.

Four days later, Piazza announced that after consulting with Ron Orsini's sister and mother, he had decided not to give Mary Lee the satisfaction of another trial.

"We concur," Piazza said, "that it would not be healthy for Pulaski County to have Mrs. Orsini in jail here again. She has an uncanny ability and knack for creating turmoil. It's better to leave her where she can't have this forum at public expense. She could use a trial to promote her own fantasies and beliefs. Why give her that opportunity?"

Linda House didn't really agree with Piazza at all. She had merely given up. The fact that Mary Lee had escaped punishment for her brother's murder would always leave a hollow place in her heart. But she had fought as long and hard as she could.

3

On July 28, 1989, third-term U.S. Congressman Tommy Robinson of the 2nd District of Arkansas stood in the press room at the White House shoulder to shoulder with President George Bush to announce that he had become a Republican—the first incumbent congressman in Arkansas history to switch political parties.

Handsomely groomed in a blue business suit and striped red, white, and blue necktie, Robinson beamed as the President praised him as "a man who stands by the faith of his principles and has helped keep America free . . . a man of exceptional character. Tommy Robinson is a man of the people, a man who believes in straight talk, hard work and getting the job done."

Following Bush to the rostrum, Tommy pronounced hard times for the Democrats of Arkansas. "The hard fact," he said, "is that there is, and will be, no room for conservative Southern Democrats in today's national Democratic Party." Ever the populist, Robinson observed that his parents had brought him up in "the tradition of Harry Truman, lunch bucket Democrats and patriotism without apology. But today—to best serve the people of Arkansas and to stay true to the values of my family and an ever-increasing number of Arkansans—I can no longer be a member of the Democratic Party."

Back home in Little Rock, Democrats were not too sorry to see him go. Pointing out that Tommy had only a year earlier cast his delegate vote at the 1988 Democratic National Convention for the Reverend Jesse Jackson—a gesture of contempt at the time—Governor Bill Clinton questioned whether or not Tommy had any real political principles. Robinson had switched parties, Clinton maintained, only because polls showed him running third in a primary race for the Democratic gubernatorial nomination. Other Democrats called upon Robinson to resign and run for re-election as a Republican. Tommy paid them no mind.

In 1990, Robinson came home to run against his old friend, patron, duck-hunting and business partner Sheffield Nelson for the Republican gubernatorial nomination. The primary campaign was marked by extraordinary personal bitterness. Robinson charged that Nelson and Tommy's own lifelong friend and bankroller Jerry Jones, owner of the Dallas Cowboys, had conspired to get rich in a fraudulent $150 million natural gas swindle.

Backing Nelson, the *Democrat* printed congressional medical records showing that Tommy had admitted to his doctor that he drank a pint of bourbon a day, and relied upon Halcion to get to sleep during periods of stress—a medication suspected of inducing agitation and paranoia in some patients.

In May 1990, ex-Sheriff Tommy got the political shock of his life. In a characteristically sparse turnout—roughly 86,000 Republicans voted in Arkansas' Republican primary, compared to more than 500,000 Democrats—Robinson lost to Nelson by a bit more than 8,000 votes. While Tommy narrowly lost the traditionally Republican counties around Fort Smith, he lost Pulaski County almost two to one. Many of the wealthier and better-educated precincts in Little Rock voted against Robinson more than four to one.

During the House banking scandal of 1992, it was revealed that Tommy was the number one rubber check artist in the Congress—

having written 996 overdrafts against his account. Following the nomination of Governor Bill Clinton to the presidency, Tommy announced his reconversion to the Democratic Party.

Widely regarded as politically defunct, Robinson claims to have found contentment as a farmer. He grows soybeans, winter wheat, and rice on an 800-acre spread in Monroe County in the Delta between Little Rock and Memphis, purchased with the aid of $1.3 million in loans made by a Missouri bank during Tommy's time in Congress— paying an exorbitant price for land local farmers say is nothing but sand and clay. Absent an invisible financial angel, people are skeptical about his prospects.

4

On Friday, October 18, 1991, the Gannett Corporation, having purchased the *Gazette* from its owners in 1986, declared surrender in the Little Rock newspaper war. Having reportedly lost over $20 million a year in a five-year circulation and advertising battle, Gannett sold the newspaper's assets to Walter Hussman, owner of Wehco Media and publisher of the *Democrat*, for $69 million.

On Saturday morning—coincidentally the day of the last Arkansas-Texas football game, the Razorbacks having left the Southwest in favor of the Southeastern Conference—the *Gazette* failed to appear for the first time since 1819. In its place Arkansas would be offered a hybrid publication to be known as the *Arkansas Democrat-Gazette*, but staffed largely by writers and editors from the winning side.

John Robert Starr had won the Little Rock newspaper war.

5

Having exhausted her appeals, Mary Lee Orsini is serving life without parole at the Women's Unit of the Arkansas Department of Corrections. While she's gained a fair amount of weight, the personality that Yankee Hall described as "cheerful" and "bubbly" remains unaffected. She thrives on what little attention she gets from the outside world, although her pale blue eyes grow cold and stony whenever a visitor questions her truthfulness.

During the prison's annual Christmas celebration for inmates' families, Mary Lee takes part in a living nativity scene. Wearing a white sheet, gold wings, and a cardboard halo dipped in glitter, she impersonates an angel.

6

Bill McArthur has rebuilt his law practice. He lives with his children on a quiet country road west of Little Rock on ten acres of land, with a creek, a fishing pond, a bunch of dogs, and several horses.

Acknowledgments

This book could never have been written without the help and co-operation of many individuals. I owe the profoundest gratitude to those for whom being interviewed involved confiding to a near stranger some of the most intimate and painful moments of their lives, particularly Linda House and Bill McArthur. No question was too hard or too embarrassing; they tried to answer them all. Sergeant T. J. Farley of the North Little Rock Police Department gave me many hours of his time. Also at the NLRPD, Sergeant Buddy Miles, Sergeant Bill Mallett, and Lieutenant Jim McFarlane.

At Central Heating & Air Conditioning, Pete Zinn, Vern Copeland, and Evelyn Daley. Also Betty Tucker at Metropolitan National Bank. Ron Orsini's ex-wife, Linda Davis, provided valuable insight into his character, as did Buddy House and the Reverend James Keith. Several sources helped immensely with the North Little Rock part of the story, especially Joyce Holt, Diane Kinsolving, Mary Jane Murphree, Gary Glidewell, Ivan Duda, Bernice Orsini, Larry Burge, Dr. C. H. Wulz, and E. Grainger Williams.

At the Little Rock Police Department, the late Chief Jess "Doc" Hale helped open many doors, among them John Terry's. Also at the LRPD, Captain Bobby Thomas, Lieutenant Fred Hensley, and Sergeant Al Dawson. Former prosecutor Wilbur C. "Dub" Bentley opened up his files and his prodigious memory. Also former prosecutor Chris Piazza (now a judge), Lloyd Haynes, Judy Kaye Mason, Jim

Perry, and Chris Palmer. At the Bureau of Alcohol, Tobacco and Firearms, Special Agents Bill Buford and John Spurgeon; Colonel Tommy Goodwin of the Arkansas State Police, Sergeant Bill Eddins, Brad Bennett, Mike Mahone, and Jerry Reinold. David White of the Arkansas Department of Corrections helped set up interviews with Yankee Hall and Mary Lee Orsini. The late Bob Sarver taught me about prisons and prisoners. Tommy F. Robinson and Major Larry Dill gave me several hours of their time.

Among lawyers directly or indirectly involved with the cases, Chief Justice Jack Holt of the Arkansas Supreme Court, Associate Justice Tom Glaze, Judge Judith Rogers, Esther White, Tom Carpenter, Judge Jack Lessenberry, Harold Craig, Tom Donovan, Howard Koopman, Bob Roddy, Joe Purvis, Bill Wilson, and Steve Engstrom. Phil Kaplan guided the way to a treasure trove of files, depositions, and transcripts. Darrell Brown proved hard to schedule, but easy to interview. Arkansas Governor Jim Guy Tucker and former Governor Frank White showed patience and forbearance.

Among Alice McArthur's friends, Anita Prather and Judy Harris opened their hearts to an inquisitive stranger, as did Billie and Bryan McArthur. Phoebe Pinkston helped immensely in a million big and little ways. Also Jim Lester in Eureka Springs and Bob Troutt in Hot Springs. McArthur grand jury foreman Stan Brown provided invaluable assistance, as did Moody Bird and other jurors who wished to remain anonymous.

Among Little Rock journalists, Jim Pitcock and his staff at KATV, Channel 7, went out of their way to assist me. Also Bill Rogers, Bob Steele, and Steve Barnes at KARK, Channel 4; Amy Oliver at AETN; and Pat Lynch at KARN radio. At the late and bitterly lamented *Arkansas Gazette*, Ernie Dumas, Bob McCord, Max Brantley, and George Fisher. Also Carol Griffee, Cary Bradburn, John Brummett, Karen Knutson, Mike Gauldin, Steve Buel, Steve Keesee, Mara Leveritt, and David Gottschalk of the *Arkansas Democrat-Gazette*. Jay Friedlander at the UA-Little Rock Journalism Department and Bob Douglas at UA-Fayetteville gave me good advice. The Media Center at UALR gave me much help, as did the tireless souls in the reference department at the Little Rock Public Library. Debbie Wilson and her assistant, Brenda Naylor, helped me find photographs. Laurie McFarland printed the manuscript.

My agent, Esther Newberg, always pretended to believe my vows to deliver this book, and gave me the kind of hard-nosed practical advice

I didn't always want to hear. Alice Mayhew at Simon & Schuster proved to be the kind of rigorous, tough-minded editor who theoretically doesn't exist in New York anymore. George Hodgman did much to lighten my burden, and Ursula Obst's suggestions were right on the money, as were those of Marcia Peterson and Leslie Jones. My friends and colleagues Tina Jordan and Betsy Pochoda at *Entertainment Weekly* made every allowance possible at times when I suspect it inconvenienced them far more than they let on.

Any number of friends, neighbors, and assorted fishing, tennis, and beagling pals suffered mostly in silence while I beat them about the ears with what threatened at times to become an obsession. They know who they are.

My wife, Diane, and my sons, Gavin and Douglas, kept me going through what was a very hard time for our family. Doug's stubborn optimism, Gavin's amazing courage, and Diane's stubborn, amazing love sustained me.

About the Author

Gene Lyons is a former associate editor of *Newsweek* and a winner of the National Magazine Award for his reporting in *Texas Monthly*. His book *The Higher Illiteracy* was published in 1988 by the University of Arkansas Press. A book reviewer for *Entertainment Weekly*, he lives in Little Rock.